The
Psych
101
Series

James C. Kaufman, PhD, Series Editor

Neag School of Education
University of Connecticut

James C. Kaufman, PhD, is a professor of educational psychology at the Neag School of Education at the University of Connecticut. An internationally recognized leader in the field of creativity, he is the author/editor of more than 35 books, including the *Cambridge Handbook of Creativity* (2010) and *Teaching for Creativity in the Common Core Classroom* (2014), and more than 250 papers. Dr. Kaufman was a cofounding editor of both *Psychology of Aesthetics, Creativity, and the Arts* and *Psychology of Popular Media Culture*; he currently edits the *International Journal of Creativity and Problem Solving*. He has won the Torrance Award from the National Association for Gifted Children, the Berlyne and Farnsworth Awards from the American Psychological Association (APA), and Mensa's research award. A former president of APA's Division 10, Dr. Kaufman is a popular media expert on creativity. He has appeared on CNN, on NPR, at the 92nd Street Y, and in *Redesign My Brain*, and narrated the comic book documentary *Independents*. He is also a playwright/lyricist whose musical *Discovering Magenta* made its New York City debut in 2015.

Creativity 101

Second Edition

James C. Kaufman, PhD

SPRINGER PUBLISHING COMPANY

NEW YORK

Springer Publishing Company, LLC
11 West 42nd Street
New York, NY 10036
www.springerpub.com

Acquisitions Editor: Nancy S. Hale
Composition: S4Carlisle Publishing Services

ISBN: 978-0-8261-2952-9
e-book ISBN: 978-0-8261-2953-6

16 17 18 19 20 / 5 4 3 2 1

The author and the publisher of this Work have made every effort to use sources believed to be reliable to provide information that is accurate and compatible with the standards generally accepted at the time of publication. The author and publisher shall not be liable for any special, consequential, or exemplary damages resulting, in whole or in part, from the readers' use of, or reliance on, the information contained in this book. The publisher has no responsibility for the persistence or accuracy of URLs for external or third-party Internet websites referred to in this publication and does not guarantee that any content on such websites is, or will remain, accurate or appropriate.

Library of Congress Cataloging-in-Publication Data

Names: Kaufman, James C., author.
Title: Creativity 101/James C. Kaufman, PhD.
Description: Second edition.|New York: Springer Publishing Company, [2016]
  | Includes bibliographical references and index.
Identifiers: LCCN 2015051152 | ISBN 9780826129529
Subjects: LCSH: Creative ability.
Classification: LCC BF408 .K364 2016 | DDC 153.3/5--dc23 LC record available at
http://lccn.loc.gov/2015051152

Printed in the United States of America by Gasch Printing.

I dedicate this edition, like the first edition,
to my mentor and advisor,
Dr. Robert J. Sternberg,
who has continued to be a source
of advice, inspiration, and perspective,
even when he doesn't have to do so anymore.

Contents

CONTENTS

Acknowledgments

This book is a revision of the first edition. Much has happened (in the field and in my life) since the book first came out in 2009. I would like to start by acknowledging the many people at Springer who have made this book and the 101 Series a reality. Phil Laughlin, now at MIT Press, first signed the book and came up with the concept. Jennifer Perillo, now at Columbia University Press, also helped in the development of the series, and Nancy S. Hale is now the editor in charge. Many thanks to them, Rose Mary Piscitelli, and everyone else at Springer.

Many, many people helped with the first edition, and I thank them all. Writing this second edition has felt more like writing a new work than a revision; some sections are intact, but much has been a completely new journey. About two-thirds through the process, my hard drive crashed. It was lost, and I'd managed not to back up anything for the eight previous months. Thankfully, I'd e-mailed the book to someone the day before—but all of my new references were lost. I debated pioneering a new, reference-less approach to the material, but instead found two graduate students who helped make this new edition possible by compiling all of the references—a very special thank you to Cody Hatcher and Xiaochen Liu. My past and present UConn PhD students (Paul J. Barnett, Sarah R. Luria, and Lamies Nazzal) have also given helpful feedback and insight.

I reached out to several friends during the writing of the first edition, and I decided to double down for this edition. I sent sentences, paragraphs, sections, and the entire dang manuscript to many world-class experts in all aspects of creativity. Many thanks to Roger Beaty, Ron Beghetto, David Cropley, Dan Fasko, Marie Forgeard,

ACKNOWLEDGMENTS

Thalia Goldstein, Richard Hass, Catrinel Haught, Beth Hennessey, Alan Kaufman, Nadeen Kaufman, Yoed Kenett, Alex McKay, Jonathan Plucker, Jean Pretz, Mark Runco, Dean Keith Simonton, Robert Sternberg, Christa Taylor, Thomas Ward, and Dasha Zabelina for offering advice, answering questions, correcting mistakes, and bringing new work to my attention. Extra-special thanks to Matthijs Baas, Mathias Benedek, Bonnie Cramond, Colin DeYoung, Jessica Hoffman, Roni Reiter-Palmon, Judith Schlesinger, and Oshin Vartanian for detailed and incisive critiques and discussions in their areas of expertise above and beyond the call of duty. Finally, I was lucky enough to have a few trusted friends and gifted scholars collate the entire book word for word, offering commentary, advice, and suggestions, and even catching stupid typos. Eternal gratitude to John Baer, Vlad Glăveanu, Maciej Karwowski, Scott Barry Kaufman, and Zorana Ivcevic Pringle.

In between the first edition and the second edition, I moved across the country to the University of Connecticut. Many thanks to Program Coordinator Catherine Little, Department Head Del Siegle, and Vice Provost Sally Reis and Joseph Renzulli. My dear friend Jonathan Plucker (now at Johns Hopkins) helped bring me out to UConn. I now have the pleasure of working with a team of great students and faculty, including my trusted collaborator and friend Ron Beghetto.

As I finished this new edition, I also saw my musical, *Discovering Magenta*, finally make its New York City debut after so many years; revisiting my own creativity with my composer Michael Bitterman, director Valeria Cossu, and the cast and crew has been a profound and terrifying experience. After more than a decade, I am once again working on new plays.

In a recent column for the *Chronicle*, my once-and-always advisor Robert Sternberg urged academics to pay heed to family. Although I crank out a lot, I've generally been able to keep my evenings and weekends free to spend with my family and friends because I like them. I am lucky to have so many dear friends in the creativity community (John, Ron, Zorana, Scott, Jonathan, Roni, etc.), and moving back East has meant getting to see my dear friends Dave Hecht and Nate Stone and their families. My sister Jennie Kaufman Singer and her family have been a wonderful source of strength and friendship, as have my late brother's family. My grown nieces Nicole Hendrix Herman and Kate Singleton, both creators themselves, are two of my best friends. My parents, Alan and Nadeen, are often the first people to read my work and discuss my ideas; they have been loving pillars of support through my entire life (even as I sometimes argue that IQ tests are bad for not including creativity). The center of my life—my rock, my soul, my world—is always Allison. And my hope for the future rests in the two sweetest and funniest boys I know, Jacob and Asher.

Introduction

was asked during an interview about my intended audience for the first edition of *Creativity 101*. Squelching my initial response ("anyone who has $25"), I thought about it and realized that I didn't know. Mostly I wrote the book I wanted to write (and read). It was never intended to be a vast brick of a book that had every bit of information about creativity, nor was it designed to be a breezy, citation-less chat. In revising the book, I've revisited lots of feedback, especially the anonymous kind—from letters from college students to Amazon reviews to publisher-solicited professional responses—as well as discussions with trusted colleagues.

When I first started writing *Creativity 101*, I was ready to defend the study of creativity from those who would diminish it. The original book started with a story about a time I was interviewed by a journalist who asked me, "Engineers give us better machines. Doctors find cures. What does studying creativity do? Does it make better art? Is the goal ... to destroy the artist—and perhaps art itself—through a process of reductive demystification?" Aside from being an interesting break from the usual questions (such as "Are all creative people crazy?"), this discussion made me think carefully about why studying creativity is important.

I thought (and still think) that the study of creativity *does* give us better art, and far from destroying the artist, I think it can improve an artist's life. Or a scientist's life or a businessperson's life; creativity affects a lot of different people. Studying creativity and learning more about it also help make the case that creativity is important. This statement—"creativity is important"—is not, however, a given assumption. On one hand, it is hard to imagine a teacher or a boss saying that he or she *didn't* want a creative student or employee. People who value creativity may point to its role in inventions, in culture, in progress—in short, to most things that define our civilization. Yet if creativity is so essential, why is it so absent from most educational or business assessments? Why are there so many negative associations and perceptions and myths about creativity?

In the years that have followed since I wrote the first edition, I feel like creativity needs a little less defending. It's one of the official 21st-century skills. There have been multiple new journals created, dozens and dozens of new books, and countless new papers. Yet, conversely, creativity is not always helped by those who beat its drum. As creativity becomes a buzzword, it brings new people to the table—people who are usually not academics. In some ways, this development is wonderful—it can be a sad (and common) thing when academics only talk in academese to other academics (academic academic academic). But oftentimes, experts in one topic (such as business or education) will assume they are experts in other areas (such as creativity). Such an overestimation of his ability led Nobel Prize winner/transistor inventor William Shockley to loudly spout off about intelligence, race, and eugenics (and publicly donate sperm to the Repository for Germinal Choice, or at least publicly announce his plan to do so); he is but one of many presumably bright people who seem to specialize in saying stupid things about an important topic. Without going into details (it takes at least two drinks), some "creativity" experts are as knowledgeable about the topic as I am about cheese. I mean, I like cheese and I eat a lot of cheese. I am vaguely aware that cheese is something that happens when milk gets angry. But I know enough to not tell people which cheese to buy or suggest new methods for curdling milk. Yet these books (on creativity, not cheese) nonetheless flood the market and make it hard to figure out the truth. As a researcher, I can usually tell the difference between science, pop psychology, psychobabble, and pseudoscience, but I'm not sure I could if I wasn't enmeshed in the field. Creativity is certainly not unique in attracting so many nonexpert experts (I imagine the folks who study nutrition or climate change have it much worse), but it's more than just a nuisance. Thanks to the "University of Google," it's much easier to find wrong information on creativity than ever before. As a result, a certain Ouroboros (snake eating it-self) effect has happened in that creativity still isn't accepted by the scientific establishment. When I spoke to an officer at a major grant-ing agency this past year, she strongly urged me not to use the word "creativity" in my application because the committee would think it was soft and fluffy. Perhaps we haven't come quite so far.

Avitia and Plucker (2014) did an overview of books about creativity that could potentially serve as textbooks (including the first edition of this book). They highlighted 13 themes of these books: theories/definitions, domain specificity/generality, types of creativity (levels of c), measurement/assessment, cognition and development, neuropsychology, mental health, personality, motivation, case studies/biographies, role of groups/organizational creativity, education, and enhancement/efficacy. Each book profiled had its strengths and weaknesses in terms of coverage. This overview made me really think about what should be included in the revision. Some topics on their list were things I already covered extensively. Other topics (case studies/biographies) I see as a little less central to how I see the field of creativity. There are also topics I acknowledge as being important, but I also recognize my own limitations. For example, although I briefly cover the neuropsychology topic in this book, it's a little out of my knowledge base (which didn't keep me from co-editing a book on this topic that has a lot of information; see Vartanian, Bristol, & Kaufman, 2013).

Their themes inspired me to more directly highlight topics such as measurement/assessment and to cover in more detail such themes as role of groups/organizational creativity and enhancement/efficacy. That said, I have my own biases and specialties. My background is in psychology (specifically cognitive psychology), and I tend to take an individual-differences approach.

A brief note about all of the Kaufmans in this book—I do cite my own work quite a bit (I'm human), so J. C. means it's me. Then you have A. S. Kaufman and N. L. Kaufman, who are my parents, Alan and Nadeen. A. B. Kaufman is my wife Allison. S. B. Kaufman is my dear friend Scott Barry (no relation). And Kaufmann and Kaufmann are my friends Geir and Astrid. I have trouble sorting it all out myself.

In any case, this revision is my attempt to continue to add my voice to the mix. It's definitely not an encyclopedia (nor was it ever intended to be). It's not a layperson book (too many citations, which apparently are very distracting to some readers). It's not a textbook (too much opinion). It's . . . Creativity 101: The Sequel (This time . . . It's professional).

REFERENCES

Avitia, M. J., & Plucker, J. A. (2014). Teaching the foundations of the field: A content analysis of potential creativity texts. *Psychology of Aesthetics, Creativity, and the Arts, 8*, 378–382.
Vartanian, O., Bristol, A. S., & Kaufman, J. C. (2013). *Neuroscience of creativity.* Cambridge, MA: MIT Press.

The Basics

I

What Is Creativity?

What is creativity, anyway? Are you creative? Is your kid creative? Or your parrot? How about Bill Gates or J. K. Rowling or Lady Gaga? Kim Kardashian or Paris Hilton? Or the CEO of Nike or the starting second baseman for the Minnesota Twins or the advertising copywriter who wrote, "That's a spicy meatball!"?

Is Bobbie Gentry, who wrote and sang "Ode to Billy Joe" in 1967, creative? Would it change your answer if you realize she hasn't been active as a singer or songwriter for the last three decades? Would it matter if she had died (she hasn't)? What about J. D. Salinger, who stopped writing publicly in 1965, yet seems to have continued writing until his death in 2010? A recent biography (Shields & Salerno, 2013) indicates that there may be a stream of new Salinger books available with his passing. How will your view of Salinger's creativity change if these books are published? Each new book may be a new masterpiece— or they may detail the further adventures of Holden Caulfield, teenage crime-fighter. How did your mental summary of Harper Lee's creativity change with the publication of *Go Set a Watchman*?

How about Vivian Maier, a nanny who took amazing street photographs? She was completely unknown when she died in 2009 (indeed, many of her pictures were never developed). A few years before her death, the owner of her storage unit auctioned off a large box of her photos and negatives due to nonpayment; John Maloof purchased them and subsequently recognized her talent. Her work has since spawned posthumous galleries, books, and a documentary (Bailey, 2013).

Or what do we do with Elisha Gray? The engineer worked on an early prototype of the telephone, and many historians claim that Alexander Graham Bell barely beat him to the patent office; others even claim that Bell stole his designs (Evenson, 2001). Gray's certainly creative (he patented 70 other things and is called the father of the music synthesizer)—but is he a creative genius? Or would that only be true if he was clearly the creator of the telephone? Is Alexander Graham Bell a creative genius?

Think about a beautiful abstract painting. Is that creative? What if you knew that the artist literally threw the paint onto the canvas randomly, never even looking at the final product—would it still be creative? What if it was painted by a 3-year-old? Or a chimp? Or a computer?

Is everyone creative? Or is that like giving participation ribbons to everyone who enters the country fair pie-eating competition, even the guy who ate a little crust and then fell asleep? If we're all creative, then maybe none of us is creative, to paraphrase *The Incredibles*.

DEFINING CREATIVITY

The easiest way to figure out some of these questions is to start with a definition. A lot of articles about creativity say that there's no universally agreed-upon definition, and I suppose in a very technical sense that might be true, just as there's no universally agreed-upon definition for literature, love, pizza, or turtles; there's always someone who will argue that turtles are actually winged insects from the Lepidoptera family and that we've been mislabeling butterflies. But we really do have a pretty consistent definition for creativity, and those who claim otherwise have not delved deeply in the literature (Cropley, 2015).

Most creativity researchers consistently focus on two key determinants, and these core concepts have stayed consistent for more than 6 decades (Barron, 1955; Guilford, 1950; Stein, 1953). First, creativity must represent something different, new, or innovative. If I ask you to sing me a creative song and you sing "Happy Birthday," it's not something original (and you might get sued because, shockingly, it's still under debatable copyright protection). If you mumble "La, la, la," then it's likely not terribly new, either. But being blazingly different is usually not enough. Someone like John Zorn, an avant-garde composer, might create a symphony called *Kristallnacht* that has long stretches of no sound but breaking glass and have the piece accepted as a brilliant work of art (albeit one with a warning label that cautions that repeated listening may cause permanent hearing loss). If I ask you to sing a creative song and you respond by breaking my windows, you don't get to come over to my house again.

It isn't enough to just be different—creativity must also be appropriate to the task at hand. A creative response is useful and relevant. I say I'm hungry and you prepare a bowl of steamed bolts. It's unusual—it may be the first time I will have been served such a dish—but it's not useful. I will still be hungry if I eat the whole bowl, and I will likely have intense intestinal discomfort to go with it.

The need for task appropriateness is harder to intuitively grasp and, indeed, it may be less important than originality. One study found that ratings of originality were more predictive of (independent) creativity ratings than those for task appropriateness, with the latter ratings most important to distinguish highly original ideas (Diedrich, Benedek, Jauk, & Neubauer, 2015). That said, both "new" and "appropriate" are absolutely necessary; neither is sufficient by itself.

In other words, creativity is an all-or-nothing multiplicative game. Simonton (2012) frames it as Creativity = Originality × Appropriateness. If there is zero originality or zero appropriateness, then you have zero creativity (if you have the capacity to successfully multiply by zero and get a positive number, then we should talk; I see a bright future on late-night talk shows).

Again, to clarify—you could have the MOST ORIGINAL IDEA EVER (one that involves dancing calamari, three-piece suits on albino badgers, and the New York Philharmonic putting their socks on their feet and singing the entire score of *The Marriage of Figaro* a cappella). But if it is not appropriate to the task at hand—if it is not useful or relevant but simply original to the point that we worry about schizophrenic tendencies—then you WOULD NOT BE CREATIVE.

There have been several suggestions of a third component. Sternberg and colleagues (Sternberg, 1999; Sternberg, Kaufman, & Pretz, 2002) argued that in addition to something being original and appropriate, it should also be of high quality. Relatedly, Hennessey and Amabile (2010) defined creativity as being a "novel product, idea, or problem solution that is of value to the individual and/or the larger social group" (p. 572). It is reasonable to assume that something of value is also task appropriate.

Another recurring suggested third component is the idea of creativity being something unplanned and surprising. Boden (2004), for example, argued that creativity was novel, valuable, and surprising, and Simonton (2012) included new, useful, and nonobvious as criteria. Both Amabile (1996) and Perkins (2000) pointed out that creativity is less algorithmic/planned and more heuristic/unplanned; there should be an "Aha!" moment. As Simonton (2012) pointed out, these are all consistent with the idea of surprise.

Kharkhurin's Four-Criterion Construct of Creativity (2014) attempts to integrate both Western and Eastern conceptions of creativity. In addition to the basic two constructs (which he calls novelty and utility), Kharkhurin proposes the more Eastern-related ideas of aesthetics (providing an essence or truth) and authenticity (reflecting one's values and beliefs) as being part of the creativity equation.

Even as additional parts are discussed and proposed, the core pillars of new and appropriate remain the most often recited. Yet what does it mean to be new? Does something have to be a completely brand-new idea? How about a company that makes a generic version of a popular painkiller—is the company creative? What do you do about a case like George Harrison's song "My Sweet Lord," which was later ruled to be partially (if subconsciously) plagiarized from the Chiffons hit "He's So Fine"? Or a child's story that takes plot details from a summer blockbuster? Does *West Side Story* get dinged for being an update of *Romeo and Juliet* (those musical theater

6

buffs in the crowd can substitute, respectively, *Your Own Thing* and *Twelfth Night* and feel superior to the riff raff who don't understand)?

Even the question of what constitutes "appropriate" is under question. I am reminded of a story from one of my former students (and frequent current collaborators), Melanie. She was talking about an event at her daughter's school, at which the children drew a picture of what they wanted to be when they grew up—doctors, lawyers, princesses, and cowboys. When it was one little boy's turn, he said, "When I grow up, I want to be a tuna fish sandwich." Is this creative? Again, it's certainly different—most children do not aspire to be sandwiches—but it doesn't seem to meet the "appropriate" condition. Yet this example calls into question where to draw the line. What about the child who wants to be a princess? That's at least possible (there are some unmarried princes lingering around somewhere), so it seems to be appropriate (if not terribly original). When does a child's aspiration cross the line from appropriate and therefore potentially creative to inappropriate? What if a child wants to sniff armpits for a living? I mean, it's *possible*, isn't it?

There tend to not be recurring themes in nonfiction books; there are no Billy Pilgrim time jumps or gigantic billboards of eyeglasses to deconstruct. But there are questions that will pop up several times, such as: *Who gets to decide what's creative?* The answer to that question can lead to a series of even deeper questions. My friend and colleague Vlad Petre Glăveanu likes to ask *How is a thing creative?* I am often drawn to the question of *Who is creative?* Think about how you would respond to these questions.

There are some questions that have been answered with a reasonable consensus, but many more that are answered with more questions. Resist the temptation to think, "Ah, see, there is no way of studying creativity after all—they don't agree!" Science doesn't work that way, particularly as told in the popular press. We are drawn to stories more than facts, which is why it is rare for a scientist deep in the trenches of active research to cross over with a bestseller. I try to find some stories in the facts, but I'm not going to willfully ignore or misinterpret results to tell a prettier story (I could easily ignore or misinterpret out of blissful stupidity, of course). Despite such inconsistencies or disagreeing studies, we have a pretty decent understanding of what's creative.

A LITTLE HISTORY

The history of creativity research within the field of psychology has two "eras" so far—before 1950 and after 1950. Before 1950, there was little serious research being conducted on creativity. Prominent thinkers have always thought about creativity. Plato argued that creativity (such as a poet's work) involved dictating whatever the Muse chanced to speak (Rothenberg & Hausman, 1976). Freud wrote an essay titled "Creative Writers and Day-Dreaming," in which he wrote about the "strange being," the creative writer (1908/1959). Einstein frequently discussed imagination and creativity; he was once quoted as saying that "imagination is more important than knowledge" (Calaprice, 2000). Educational reformer John Dewey (1934) wrote an essay on "art as experience." Similarly, Vygotsky and Carl Jung wrote well-known essays on the topic. But none of these people primarily studied creativity.

Most of the early researchers who may have discussed or studied creativity actually focused on something else. Many were interested in genius or intelligence, such as Alfred Binet, Catherine Cox, William James, or Charles Spearman (Becker, 1995). Others interested in questions of creativity were modern-day Renaissance types who are now long forgotten to even the ardent student of the field. W. S. Jevons taught logic and economy but dabbled in multiple fields (Mosselmans & White, 2001). George Bethune was a preacher, wrote popular hymns, studied fly-fishing, and was active in Democratic politics (Stedman, 1900/2001). William Hazlitt was an aspiring painter who befriended many notable creators before frequently angering them with his political or literary commentaries (Wu, 2008). As one psychologist wrote at the time: "It would seem futile to speak of a literature on the process of creative thinking" (Hutchinson, 1931, p. 392).

There were still isolated studies and papers of note. Chassell (1916) adapted or created 12 different measures of originality. Some of these tests tapped into problem solving and others reflected high-level intellectual ability. However, some of these tests are remarkably similar to the same assessments used nearly 100 years later. In Chassell's Novel Situation tests, she asked college students six different questions, such as "If all water, because of some change in

8

its chemical constitution, should contract instead of expand upon freezing, what would be the effect upon animal life, including man?" The responses were then graded for originality. Chassell's work predates by many decades the work of later pioneers—yet virtually no one cites or acknowledges her work.

Some of the other early work is less impressive. Witty and Lehman (1929) argue that creative geniuses, particularly creative writers, suffer from "nervous instability." They also provide no evidence or data to support their ideas (which, indeed, would be a harbinger of research to come). Hutton and Bassett (1948), meanwhile, helpfully point out that lobotomized patients tended to be less creative.

Everything changed at the 1950 convention of the American Psychological Association. In his presidential address, Joy P. Guilford called for psychologists to increase their focus on creativity. He argued that creativity was an important topic and was not being studied or researched at the level it warranted. Before Guilford, less than 0.2% of all entries of Psychological Abstracts concentrated on creativity (Guilford, 1950). He helped move the field forward.

It is not true to say that Guilford single-handedly brought creativity from the realm of esoterica to prominence. On the other hand, it can often feel this way. What Guilford did was to both galvanize the field and make it acceptable to study creativity. Many of the ideas and studies that were published in the decade that followed his speech are still widely cited and respected. In contrast, there are only a handful of papers that are still commonly used from the decade before his seminal address.

Guilford's own work in creativity emphasized the cognitive processes. Another legendary champion of creativity was E. Paul Torrance, who built off some of Guilford's concepts and developed the Torrance Tests of Creative Thinking (which are still the most popular measures). A third pioneer was Frank Barron, whose work with the Institute for Personality Assessment and Research (IPAR) at the University of California, Berkeley (with Donald MacKinnon) helped spearhead a multidecade effort to interview and study eminent creators (such as musicians, writers, and scientists). In a different vein, Alex Osborn was an advertising executive whose work in applied creativity has been extremely influential. He created brainstorming, among many contributions.

RELATED CONCEPTS

Academic scholarship has a tendency to pigeonhole, categorize, and develop hierarchies, and creativity is no different. Much of this book is based on psychology research. Part of this emphasis is because that's my own training and background; another reason is that it mirrors the field's prominence in the actual research. The main two other disciplines I will draw from are education and business; with psychology, these three fields have produced the most doctoral dissertations about creativity (Kahl, da Fonseca, & Witte, 2009; Wehner, Csikszentmihalyi, & Magyari-Beck, 1999). Just as there are numerous approaches to the study of creativity, there are also many keywords from different fields (see Glăveanu, Tanggaard, & Wegener, 2016, for a larger array of terms).

The word *innovation* is sometimes used interchangeably with creativity, but usually conveys a greater emphasis on application and is more associated with the worlds of business, management, engineering, and industrial/organizational psychology. One distinction between creativity and innovation that has been proposed is that creativity is thinking of new ideas and deciding on which ones are best, whereas innovation also entails implementing these ideas (West, 2002; West, Hirst, Richter, & Shipton, 2004). According to this approach, it's creativity if I think of a terrific idea for a new game (such as "Angry Berts," in which tiny Berts are cannonballed into an array of Ernies, à la Angry Birds). It's innovation if I actually make the game. Going even further on the applied spectrum is the concept of *entrepreneurship*, which emphasizes actually creating new sustainable businesses or organizations (Low & MacMillan, 1988). Creativity is traditionally seen as a key component of this process (Zampetakis, 2008).

Imagination is also sometimes used as a synonym for creativity, but there is less an emphasis on a final product. Imagination can be only in your head—it can be sheer fantasy with little basis in reality—or it can emerge in *play* (Singer & Singer, 1990). With imagination, the "appropriate" component of the creativity definition does not play a key role. Imaginative play in children—often seen as an important precursor to creativity—is a more technical way of describing what happens when kids pretend and make-believe (Russ, 2013; Russ & Fiorelli, 2010). Imaginative play is related to a young child's creativity,

10

particularly when an imaginary friend is involved (Mottweiler & Taylor, 2014). Sometimes an outgrowth of imaginative play can be *improvisation*, in which the audience gets to see the actual creative process (Sawyer, 2011). Improvisation often occurs in groups, such as a comedy troupe or a jazz ensemble; training children with improvisation techniques can increase their creativity (Sowden, Clements, Redlich, & Lewis, 2015). Another adult manifestation of play is *creative leisure*, a growing field (Hegarty, 2009; Hegarty & Plucker, 2012).

Aesthetics is the study of the arts. As Tinio (2013) argues, creativity is interested in how people create art (or science or business or something else), whereas aesthetics is more focused in how people perceive, view, and interpret art. When they did a special exhibit of Magritte's work at the Metropolitan Museum of Art many years ago, I was entranced; my wife was creeped out and wanted to leave. Some people think Banksy is brilliant; others think he's a vandal. Barnett Newman painted huge canvases with large swathes of bright colors and was hailed by some as a genius. Others may be reminded of the emperor's new clothes (a museum-goer with a knife actually attacked one of Newman's paintings). The play *Art*, by Yasmin Reza (1996), shows how the purchase of an enormous white canvas nearly destroys a close friendship.

Genius is the study of highly eminent individuals. Dean Keith Simonton has done an astounding array of both theoretical and empirical work on genius (a great place to start is another book in the 101 series: *Genius 101*; Simonton, 2009). As Simonton (2009) outlines, genius usually refers to people who are either extremely smart or are high achievers. These can include accomplishments that are creative, require leadership, or represent outstanding performance. Tied to the concept of genius is the idea of *expertise*, which traditionally comes after approximately 10 years of active study and practice (Bloom, 1985; Ericsson, 2014; Hayes, 1989; Simonton, 2014). I'll discuss creative expertise in more detail in a few more chapters.

LOOKING AHEAD

Many theories of creativity often incorporate these concepts. In the next chapter, I review some of the major theories in the field.

REFERENCES

Amabile, T. M. (1996). *Creativity in context: Update to "The Social Psychology of Creativity."* Boulder, CO: Westview Press.

Bailey, H. (2013). Finding Vivian Maier: A new doc tries to unearth clues about the life of a mysterious street photographer. *Yahoo News.* Retrieved from http://news.yahoo.com/vivian-maier-street-photography-194916112 .html

Barron, F. (1955). The disposition toward originality. *Journal of Abnormal and Social Psychology, 51,* 478–485.

Becker, M. (1995). Nineteenth-century foundations of creativity research. *Creativity Research Journal, 8,* 219–229.

Bloom, B. S. (Ed.). (1985). *Developing talent in young people.* New York, NY: Ballantine Books.

Boden, M. A. (2004). *The creative mind: Myths and mechanisms.* London, England: Routledge.

Calaprice, A. (2000). *The expanded quotable Einstein.* Princeton, NJ: Princeton University Press.

Chassell, L. M. (1916). Test for originality. *Journal of Educational Psychology, 7,* 317–328.

Cropley, D. H. (2015). Teaching engineers to think creatively. In R. Wegerif, L. Li, & J. C. Kaufman (Eds.), *The Routledge international handbook of research on teaching thinking* (pp. 402–410). London, England: Routledge.

Dewey, J. (1934). *Art as experience.* New York, NY: Minton, Balch.

Diedrich, J., Benedek, M., Jauk, E., & Neubauer, A. C. (2015). Are creative ideas novel and useful? *Psychology of Aesthetics, Creativity, and the Arts, 9,* 35–40.

Ericsson, K. A. (2014). Creative genius: A view from the expert-performance approach. In D. K. Simonton (Ed.), *The Wiley handbook of genius* (pp. 321–349). Oxford, England: Wiley.

Evenson, A. E. (2001). *The telephone patent conspiracy of 1876: The Elisha Gray-Alexander Bell controversy and its many players.* Jefferson, NC: McFarland.

Freud, S. (1959). Creative writers and day-dreaming. In J. Strachey (Ed.), *The standard edition of the complete psychological works of Sigmund Freud* (Vol. 9, pp. 141–154). London, England: The Hogarth Press. (Original work published 1908)

Glăveanu, V. P., Tanggaard, L., & Wegener, C. (Eds.). (2016). *Creativity: A new vocabulary.* London, England: Palgrave.

Guilford, J. P. (1950). Creativity. *American Psychologist, 5,* 444–454.

Hayes, J. R. (1989). Cognitive processes in creativity. In J. A. Glover, R. R. Ronning, & C. R. Reynolds (Eds.), *Handbook of creativity* (pp. 135–145). New York, NY: Plenum Press.

Hegarty, C. B. (2009). The value and meaning of creative leisure. *Psychology of Aesthetics, Creativity, and the Arts, 3,* 10–13.

Hegarty, C. B., & Plucker, J. A. (2012). Self-expression in creative leisure. *International Journal of Creativity & Problem Solving, 22,* 63–78.

Hennessey, B. A., & Amabile, T. M. (2010). Creativity. *Annual Review of Psychology, 61,* 569–598.

Hutchinson, E. D. (1931). Materials for study of creative thinking. *Psychological Bulletin, 28,* 392.

Hutton, E. L., & Bassett, M. (1948). The effect of leucotomy on creative personality. *Journal of Mental Science, 94,* 332–350.

Kahl, C. H., da Fonseca, L. H., & Witte, E. H. (2009). Revisiting creativity research: An investigation of contemporary approaches. *Creativity Research Journal, 21,* 1–5.

Kharkhurin, A. V. (2014). Creativity4in1: Four-Criterion Construct of Creativity. *Creativity Research Journal, 26,* 338–352.

Low, M. B., & MacMillan, I. C. (1988). Entrepreneurship: Past research and future challenges. *Journal of Management, 14,* 139–161.

Mosselmans, B., & White, M. V. (2001). Introduction. In *Economic writings of W. S. Jevons* (pp. v–xxv). London, England: Palgrave/MacMillan.

Mottweiler, C., & Taylor, M. (2014). Elaborated role play and creativity in preschool age children. *Psychology of Aesthetics, Creativity, and the Arts, 8,* 277–286.

Perkins, D. (2000). *The Eureka effect: The art and logic of breakthrough thinking.* New York, NY: W. W. Norton.

Reza, Y. (1996). *Art* (Christopher Hampton, Trans.). London, England: Faber and Faber.

Rothenberg, A., & Hausman, C. R. (Eds.). (1976). *The creativity question.* Durham, NC: Duke University Press.

Russ, S. W. (2013). *Pretend play in childhood: Foundation of adult creativity.* Washington, DC: American Psychological Association.

Russ, S. W., & Fiorelli, J. A. (2010). Developmental approaches to creativity. In J. C. Kaufman & R. J. Sternberg (Eds.), *Cambridge handbook of creativity* (pp. 233–249). New York, NY: Cambridge University Press.

Sawyer, R. K. (2011). *Structure and improvisation in creative teaching.* New York, NY: Cambridge University Press.

Shields, D., & Salerno, S. (2013). *Salinger.* New York, NY: Simon & Schuster.

Simonton, D. K. (2009). *Genius 101.* New York, NY: Springer Publishing Company.

Simonton, D. K. (2012). Taking the US Patent Office creativity criteria seriously: A quantitative three-criterion definition and its implications. *Creativity Research Journal, 24,* 97–106.

Simonton, D. K. (2014). Creative performance, expertise acquisition, individual differences, and developmental antecedents: An integrative research agenda. *Intelligence, 45,* 66–73.

Singer, D. G., & Singer, J. L. (1990). *The house of make-believe: Children's play and the developing imagination.* Cambridge, MA: Harvard University Press.

Sowden, P. T., Clements, L., Redlich, C., & Lewis, C. (2015). Improvisation facilitates divergent thinking and creativity: Realizing a benefit of primary school arts education. *Psychology of Aesthetics, Creativity, and the Arts, 9,* 128–138.

Stedman, E. C. (Ed.). (2001). *An American anthology, 1787–1900.* Boston, MA: Houghton Mifflin. (Original work published 1900) Retrieved from http://www.bartleby.com/248

Stein, M. (1953). Creativity and culture. *Journal of Psychology, 36,* 311–322.

Sternberg, R. J. (1999). A propulsion model of types of creative contributions. *Review of General Psychology, 3,* 83–100.

Sternberg, R. J., Kaufman, J. C., & Pretz, J. E. (2002). *The creativity conundrum.* Philadelphia, PA: Psychology Press.

Tinio, P. L. (2013). From artistic creation to aesthetic reception: The mirror model of art. *Psychology of Aesthetics, Creativity, and the Arts, 7,* 265–275.

Wehner, L., Csikszentmihalyi, M., & Magyari-Beck, I. (1991). Current approaches used in studying creativity: An exploratory investigation. *Creativity Research Journal, 4,* 261–271.

West, M. A. (2002). Sparkling fountains or stagnant ponds: An integrative model of creativity and innovation implementation in work groups. *Applied Psychology, 51,* 355–387.

West, M. A., Hirst, G., Richter, A., & Shipton, H. (2004). Twelve steps to heaven: Successfully managing change through developing innovative teams. *European Journal of Work and Organizational Psychology, 13,* 269–299.

Witty, P. A., & Lehman, H. C. (1929). Nervous instability and genius: Poetry and fiction. *Journal of Abnormal and Social Psychology, 24,* 77–90.

Wu, D. (2008). *William Hazlitt: The first modern man.* New York, NY: Oxford University Press.

Zampetakis, L. A. (2008). The role of creativity and proactivity on perceived entrepreneurial desirability. *Thinking Skills and Creativity, 3,* 154–162.

Theories of Creativity

I f there is but one conclusion that we can make about creativity researchers, it is that we like letters. One letter we particularly like is "P." It stands for many wonderful things—popcorn, Pinocchio, psychology, Pablo Picasso, plays, Padres, pleasure principle, playwrights, Parker Posey, and potato pancakes. Within creativity, however, there are four P's that are used to help shape how we conceptualize this broad concept.

Indeed, consider: When I talk about creativity, am I talking about a beautiful piece of art or an ingenious computer program? How about the sensation of the "a-ha" process when I suddenly understand what I need to do next? Maybe, instead, I'm talking about how a creative person behaves. Or maybe it's the synergy that happens when many different people share and exchange ideas together. Throwing all of these things together and labeling them as "creativity" is not much different than using the word "love" to mean your feelings for your mom, your best friend, your significant other, and spicy calamari. It may be technically correct, but it's not terribly useful.

THE FOUR P'S

Here is where the four P's come in (like the four horsemen of the apocalypse, but with less pestilence):

Person: Who is creative?

Process: How are we creative?

Product: What is creative?

Press (or Place): Where are we creative?

These distinctions have been around for many years (Rhodes, 1962). They are not necessarily the only four possible ways of approaching creativity (Kozbelt, Beghetto, & Runco, 2010). Simonton (1990) proposed "persuasion," with the logic that creative people impact the way others think, and Runco (2003) argued that "potential" should be one of the P's. D. H. Cropley (2015) offers a different fifth P with "phases," which refers to the steps needed to be creative (which I will discuss later). Sawyer and DeZutter (2009) argue for the idea of distributed creativity, which considers creativity to be a collaboration between multiple persons and the environment (or press).

More recently, Glăveanu (2013) proposed an adapted version of the four P's called the five A's. Taking a sociocultural perspective, he places particular emphasis on the context of creativity. The person becomes the actor and includes how someone interacts within the societal environment. Process and product become action and artifact, and press is split into two dimensions. First is audience, which encompasses both those people who might initially respond to a creative work (from the person's mother to a collaborator) and the eventual (possible) larger audience, whether listeners at a concert or scientists reading a journal. Second is the idea of affordances, possibilities for action allowed by the things needed to create (which could be anything from a pen to a computer to vials filled with sulfuric acid). Indeed, the ability to recognize how to best utilize the affordances around you can be seen as one of the essences of creativity (Glăveanu, 2012b). Glăveanu sees the creative action, limited or nurtured by the affordances, as occurring between the actor, audience, and artifact. More than just a change of terminologies, the five A's are more rooted in the cultural context than the four P's and reflect a more dynamic and interactive conception of creativity.

The four P's will resurface many times throughout the book, often implicitly. In later chapters, when I'm talking about different lines of creativity research, try to think about which P is the most relevant. A nice definition of creativity that integrates both the new and appropriate concepts with the four P's is proposed by Plucker, Beghetto, and Dow (2004): "Creativity is the interaction among aptitude, process, and environment by which an individual or group produces a perceptible product that is both novel and useful as defined within a social context" (p. 90). In other words, creativity is the how (ability and process) and the where and when (environment) made by the who (individual or group) making the what (a specific product both new and useful).

THE FOUR C'S

Another way of conceptualizing how to approach creativity is the idea of C's. A core distinction is made between little-c and Big-C. Big-C is the big-time, genius-level creativity. Big-C is Mozart, Jane Austen, Louis Armstrong, and Einstein. Big-C is the kind of creativity that will last for generations; it may be remembered, used, or enjoyed a hundred years from now (or more). In contrast, little-c is everyday creativity. Nearly all of us can be creative at this level, whether we're making birdhouses or cooking interesting meals or telling bedtime stories. Although these ideas have been present in the creativity literature for some time, Csikszentmihalyi (1998) may have been the first to articulate this distinction (Simonton, 2013). These certainly aren't the only terms; Boden (2004) framed the question as P-creativity (psychological, or little-c) and H-creativity (historic, or Big-C). Glăveanu (2009) employed the terms He-paradigm (for genius), I-paradigm (for everyday creativity), and added we-paradigm (for group creativity).

Beghetto and Kaufman (2007) argued that little-c is too broad of a construct. Everyone who isn't a Charles Dickens or Maya Angelou is lumped as a little-c writer. Yet where do you place a high school student falling in love with words? The everyday creativity that students experience as they discover a new concept or make a new metaphor is given short shrift in the world of little-c. A fourth-grade student doing a beginning scientific experiment (perhaps creating a volcano) is placed in the same category as a noted microbiologist. It's all considered "little-c." Beghetto and Kaufman proposed a third category, mini-c.

Remember that creativity is traditionally defined as being something new and appropriate. The key is, to whom? For little-c, the answer might be that the average person might think it is new and appropriate. In mini-c, the initial spark of creativity doesn't have to be held up to the same standards that we use for typical everyday creativity. An idea or product doesn't need to be new and appropriate in the opinion of another person, necessarily; it just needs to be new and appropriate to the creator at the time. The standards are different from little-c. With mini-c, the emphasis is on the personal meaning that the creative idea or product has to the individual.

Kaufman and Beghetto (2009) further argue for a fourth category, Pro-c. They point out that there is not an appropriate category for individuals who are professional creators, but have not reached highly eminent status. For example, the little-c category is useful for the everyday creativity of the home cook who can creatively combine ingredients to develop unique and tasty meals. The Big-C category is appropriate for chefs who have revolutionized the profession (e.g., James Beard, Marie-Antoine Carême, or Ruth Graves Wakefield). Yet what about the professional chef who makes a living developing creative entrées (clearly surpassing the creativity of the innovative home cook) but has not yet attained (or may never attain) Big-C status? In this case, the "new and appropriate" may mean what professionals in the field think.

Kaufman and Beghetto (2009) therefore propose the Four C Model as representing a developmental trajectory of creativity in a person's life. Early in life, a typical creator might be beginning to play with her creativity and exploring mini-c as she discovers new things. Most people will first experience mini-c early in life. Mini-c can be encouraged by teachers, parents, and mentors to nurture creativity. There are several discussions of the best way to foster a creativity-nurturing environment. Harrington, Block, and Block (1987), for example, show that rearing practices based on Carl Rogers's work (such as encouraging curiosity and exploration, letting children make decisions, and respecting children's opinions) lead to increased later creative potential. Yi, Plucker, and Guo (2015) found that social modeling (exposing children to an example of high creativity) led to increased creative performance. Mini-c isn't just restricted to children, though. A person can continue to get mini-c inspirations and ideas across his or her lifetime as different domains and possible areas for creativity are explored (Beghetto & Kaufman, 2009).

After repeated attempts and encouragements, the creator might then reach the realm of little-c. Some people may happily remain at the little-c level for their entire lives; others may advance in some areas and remain at the little-c in other areas (e.g., an accomplished author who has advanced to the Pro-c level of writing, publishing many novels, may enjoy the little-c level of landscaping his garden or cooking gourmet meals). As part of this process of enjoying creativity in everyday life, the creator may stumble upon the domain for which he or she feels an initial pull of passion. With years of acquired expertise (and, perhaps, advanced schooling), the creator may move onto the stage of Pro-c. Although she will still have mini-c insights, the creator has now achieved professional-level status and is capable of working on problems, projects, and ideas that affect the field as a whole.

An interesting aside is that an implication of the model is that a Pro-c creator should be able to make money with his or her creativity. Getting paid is not a requirement, and it is quite possible that some people can make substantial money at the little-c level and others may be Pro-c quality but not be able to make a living. What are the ethical implications, then, of people who use modern technology to obtain the creative work of others without paying for it? Many of my students, who are now a generation or more younger than me, fully admit that they illegally download most of their movies or music or books. What happens if a Pro-c musician doesn't make enough money from her work because of this general trend and thus is unable to pursue her career? The basic question is nothing new—certainly studios and executives have been ripping off artists for decades. Yet there will definitely be consequences of the concept of liking something enough to pay money for it gradually shifting toward liking something but not expecting to pay for it. Further, if you're reading this book as an illegal download, all will be forgiven if you mail me a couple of bucks.

Back to the Four C Model, a creator may continue to produce original and task-appropriate work at the Pro-c level throughout her entire life, with specific peaks occurring at different ages based on the domain (e.g., Simonton, 1997). After many years have come and gone, the creator may achieve a lasting Big-C contribution to a field (e.g., the Nobel Prize) or the creator may have passed away, and history will make the final judgment as to whether she has entered the pantheon of Big-C or has been long forgotten. Is it possible to reach Big-C without going through Pro-c (go directly to jail, do not pass Go)? I would argue that even if someone might reach Big-C without ever being recognized as Pro-c, his or her work would still be at the Pro-c level while alive. In other words, those few people (such as Emily Dickinson, Franz Kafka, or John Kennedy Toole) who were barely considered little-c in their lifetime were actually misjudged by their contemporaries and were producing high-level work without reaping the benefits. Such creators are rare exceptions; most Big-C creators are recognized in their own lifetimes, as I will soon discuss. In addition, perhaps going against our instinctual beliefs, quality *is* related to quantity. Simonton found that for both composers (1977) and psychologists (1985), the most productive creators were also the ones who did the best work.

Mini-c might be singing in the shower. Little-c might be filming yourself singing, uploading it to YouTube, and having other people listen to your song and enjoy it. At the Pro-c level, your songs might hit iTunes and people around the world choose to pay and download them. Big-C could extend to being inducted into the Songwriters or Rock and Roll Hall of Fame.

For the rest of the chapter, I'll be reviewing other theories of creativity. I've broken them down into two broad lines, How We Create and What We Create. Other questions, such as Why We Create or Who Creates, are covered later in the book under motivation and personality.

HOW WE CREATE

One of the early theories of creativity was by Wallas (1926), who proposed a model of the cognitive creative process (you can call it "creative problem solving," if you want). His model was partially based on the ideas of physicist Hermann von Helmholtz. According to his five-stage model, you first use preparation to begin work on a problem. Next, there is incubation, in which you may work on other things while your mind thinks about the problem. In intimation, you realize you are about to have a breakthrough (this phase is sometimes dropped from the model), and then you actually have the insight in the illumination phase. Finally, with verification, you actually test, develop, and use your ideas.

Other researchers have expanded and developed this line of thought. Michael Mumford and his colleagues (Blair & Mumford, 2007; Mumford, Mobley, Uhlman, Reiter-Palmon, & Doares, 1991) have argued for an eight-part model consisting of problem construction, information encoding, category selection, category combination and reorganization, idea generation, idea evaluation, implementation planning, and solution monitoring. Basadur, Runco, and Vega (2000) offer a simplified model centered around finding good problems, solving these problems, and then implementing these solutions. Sawyer (2012) presents a beautiful compilation of the many different creative process models. I will only go into detail for a few key components.

The first step, problem construction, is often overlooked and undervalued; Reiter-Palmon and Robinson (2009) offer a review of the importance of this component of creative problem solving. It consists of figuring out exactly what problem you are trying to solve. It may also often involve figuring out which constraints you are facing (Stokes, 2014). Let's say that you are a bit of a slob and you are tired of people coming into your apartment and telling you how messy you are. You would proceed quite differently if you decide that the problem is "I need to be neater" as opposed to "My friends are all insensitive jerks." Sometimes finding the problem is easy; the automatic bagel slicer was likely invented after someone kept getting cut while trying to separate bagels. But if you realize that you're having trouble paying all of your bills, for example, the actual problem could range from "I'm not making enough money" to "I'm spending too much on nonessential items" to "I'm paying too much on rent" to "I need to cook more and eat out less often."

This process is often automatic—we may instinctively gravitate toward framing a problem in a particular way without even realizing we are doing so (Mumford, Reiter-Palmon, & Redmond, 1994). Yet, conversely, more creative people will actively engage in this stage—problem construction is less likely to be an automatic response (Getzels, 1979; Getzels & Csikszentmihalyi, 1976). Experts in different fields, such as art (Rostan, 1994), creative writing (Hayes & Flower, 1986), and political science (Voss, Wolfe, Lawrence, & Engle, 1991), spend more time on constructing the problem than do novices. For example, Csikszentmihalyi and Getzels (1971) studied artists and observed their behavior while completing a drawing (with the same 27 potential objects as models). Examples of problem construction included time spent with the objects—picking them up, feeling their texture, rearranging them into different shapes, looking at them from different angles, and so on.

Reiter-Palmon and colleagues discovered that the ability to construct a problem was related to the solution's eventual originality and quality (Reiter-Palmon, Mumford, O'Connor Boes, & Runco, 1997; Reiter-Palmon, Mumford, & Threlfall, 1998). If you're given a new problem to solve at work or a new class assignment, do you immediately dive in or do you stop, think, plan, and develop a strategy? You can guess what the experts do. Even if this approach isn't your default style, you can change. If people are trained on problem construction or given instructions to spend more time on this part of the process, the resulting solution is more creative (Scott, Leritz, & Mumford, 2004).

Idea generation and idea exploration are in many ways the foundation of creativity. Guilford (1950, 1967) placed creativity into a larger framework of intelligence in his Structure of Intellect model. He attempted to organize all of human cognition along three dimensions. The first dimension was called "operations," and simply meant the mental gymnastics needed for any kind of task. The second dimension, "content," referred to the general subject area. The third dimension, "product," represented the actual products that might result from different kinds of thinking in different kinds of subject matters. With five operations, four contents, and six products, Guilford's (1967) model had 120 different possible mental abilities. Indeed, one later (and less-used) expansion of the model included 180 different abilities (Guilford, 1988). Perhaps true creativity could be figuring out a way to accurately measure a person's entire range of all 180 different abilities without having this person try to escape after the first 20 hours of testing.

One of Guilford's operations (or thought processes) was divergent thinking—the ability to generate many different solutions to an open-ended problem. This concept is one of the cornerstones of creativity measurement, and its operationalization is discussed in great detail later in the book. Guilford also included convergent thinking as part of his model, namely, the ability to select the best solution out of many potential ideas. This dimension is often overlooked; indeed, when you think of a creative person, do *you* think of someone pondering and selecting the best alternative? Yet there is no doubting the importance of this component. "Creativity is allowing yourself to make mistakes," *Dilbert* cartoonist Scott Adams once said. "Art is knowing which ones to keep" (Adams, 1996, p. 324).

Arthur Cropley (2006) argues that the field's preoccupation with divergent thinking may allow "quasicreativity" to be included as actual creativity. Such quasicreative works may not have a basis in reality (such as basic daydreaming) and do not meet the "task-appropriate" component of the creativity definition. The field's focus on divergent thinking, A. J. Cropley (2006) argues, may come from our wish for "effortless creativity"—to have brilliance erupt from our heads like Athena bursting from Zeus, ready with sword and shield. Much less sexy is the idea of "effortful creativity," which requires task appropriateness, as well as knowledge, expertise, and even making creativity a habitual routine (Glăveanu, 2012a). Indeed, in the pages to come, I visit the idea of radical versus incremental creators and innovators versus adaptors—in general, the ones who do the shockingly original work get more credit, even though we need both kinds of creators for society to advance.

Another Guilford (1967) concept is convergent thinking, which is when we explore and analyze the potential new solutions. It tends to be an unrecognized and understudied topic. Without this ability, a creative person risks losing opportunities, pursuing red herrings, and general stagnation. There are certain actors, for example, who keep choosing wrong projects (think of Nicolas Cage), and others who tend to pick exciting and challenging films (such as Leonardo DiCaprio). Or imagine someone working in an ad agency. You may first think about the importance of divergent thinking—coming up with many different ideas for promotions or commercials. Being able to use convergent thinking to say no to 98% of the initial suggestions is just as important; do a quick Google search on "worst commercials ever" to see the results of bad ideas being implemented.

One prominent theory that expands on these concepts is the Geneplore (Generate-Explore) model, which is based on the idea of creative cognition. The Geneplore model has two phases: generative and explorative. In the generative phase, someone constructs a pre-inventive structure, or a mental representation of a possible creative solution (Finke, Ward, & Smith, 1992). For example, Elias Howe was working on his invention of the modern sewing machine. He couldn't quite get the needle correctly designed. Howe had an odd dream in which he was chased by savages who threw spears at him. The spears had a circle loop at the end—and Howe realized that adding the circle (or an "eye") to the end of the needle was the solution he needed (Hartmann, 2000). The image of a spear with a circle at the end—the image that preceded Howe's insight—would be an example of one of these preinventive structures. They don't need to be as dramatic or sudden as Howe's story. Indeed, the generation of pre-inventive structures is only one part of the creative process according to the Geneplore model. The thinker must then explore these different preinventive structures within the constraints of the final goal. There may be several cycles before a creative work is produced.

Using a comparable generate-explore framework, the Blind Variation and Selective Retention (BVSR) theory takes a macro approach. Originally proposed by Campbell (1960) and further pursued, expanded, and championed by Simonton (1999, 2011), this theory argues that ideas are generated blindly—unplanned and without a real inclination about their possible success. Ideas are then selectively retained as we progress over time (presumably, the best ones). BVSR is controversial and often debated (e.g., Dasgupta, 2011), in part because of a Darwinian thrust of the model that has been underemphasized by more recent development (Simonton, 2011).

The same broad concepts of BVSR have been applied to many different fields, such as cultural evolution. Think about memes, for example. There is the original term, which means a specific cultural unit that passes from person to person. More commonly, people think of a funny picture or brief video that is passed around social media sites with different captions or uses (such as Scumbag Steve, Overly Attached Girlfriend, Good Guy Greg, or Ridiculously Photogenic Guy). What makes a meme catch fire? The answer would make someone a billionaire; everyone in marketing has at one time been told by an older boss to make something go viral, as if it were that easy. There are thousands of aspiring memes cranked out every day all around the world (blind variation), but only a tiny percentage will make it out of a small circle of friends. An infinitesimally small percentage of those will travel around the web and become famous (selective retention).

Many of the other stages of the creative problem-solving process are of greater importance to the concept of innovation. Guilford (1967) also included an Evaluation operation, in which you would decide if your solution met the criterion for being successful. Mumford et al. (1991) include implementation planning (how to make it work) and solution monitoring (does it work?) as the last two phases. D. H. Cropley's four-stage model (2015) starts with the traditional trio of problem recognition, idea generation, and idea evaluation, and then ends with solution validation. Clearly, the last phase involves making sure your creative idea works in the real world—and it is a poorly studied phase outside of organizational psychology.

Componential Models

Other theories of the creative process focus on which elements are needed for creativity to take place. For example, Amabile (1983a, 1983b, 1996) proposed the componential model of creativity. She argued that three sets of variables are needed for creativity to occur: domain-relevant skills, creativity-relevant skills, and task motivation. Domain-relevant skills include knowledge, technical skills, and specialized talent. If you're going to be a creative mathematician, you probably need to know your basic algebra and geometry. Creativity-relevant skills are personal factors that are associated with creativity. One example is tolerance for ambiguity—can you handle not knowing how a project might turn out, or not knowing your plans for a weekend? This ability is linked with being creative (Zenasni, Besançon, & Lubart, 2008). Other creativity-relevant skills include self-discipline and being willing to take sensible risks (Amabile, 1983b). Finally, Amabile singles out your motivation toward the task at hand. As is discussed later, people who are driven more by enjoyment, passion, or the desire for challenge tend to be more creative than people motivated by money, praise, or grades.

Piirto proposes the Piirto Pyramid (1998, 2004, 2014). At the bottom is genetics, and additional qualities build off of the base of genetics as the pyramid grows higher: personality attributes, minimum intellectual competence, and specific-domain talent forming the upper part of the pyramid. Above the pyramid, influencing one's creativity, is the environment, which is represented by five suns—of chance, home, school, community/culture, and gender. She has also analyzed creativity for broad themes (Piirto, 2010) and identified Seven I's: Inspiration, Imagery, Imagination, Intuition, Insight, Incubation, and Improvisation.

Motivation also plays a role in Sternberg and Lubart's (1995) Investment Theory of creativity, in which they argue that the key to being creative is to buy low and sell high in ideas. In this model, a creator is like a successful Wall Street broker. A good investor knows which stocks are performing poorly but hold great long-term promise. Similarly, a creator can sense a topic or medium or idea that is not currently "hot" but has potential. The creator invests in these ideas, makes them her own, and then convinces the world that they matter. A talented investor also knows when to sell, and so does a smart creator. Just as others jump on the bandwagon, the creator is likely to move on to other ideas. Television offers a marvelous microcosm of this phenomenon. When *Lost* premiered, it seemed like a long-shot. The show was a serial narrative, which meant that if viewers missed even one episode, they would be confused. *Lost* was steeped in mythology and filled with obscure literary and philosophical references; it did not seem a good bet to be a blockbuster. *Lost* was built on ideas that were "cold." In fact, the pilot episode exceeded costs and before it aired, the executive who shepherded it through the development process was fired (Craig, 2005). In the years that have followed, there have been dozens of attempts to replicate *Lost*'s success with similar shows—and most have failed miserably. The true creators are the ones who start fads, not the ones who follow them. Sternberg and Lubart argue that the successful creative investor needs the right kind of motivation, intelligence, knowledge, personality, environment, and thinking style.

Hunter, Cushenbery, and Friedrich (2012) offer a model designed for human resource professionals. They outline four factors as contributing to creative potential in the KSAO model. Unlike Amabile and Sternberg and Lubart, they distinguish between

26

knowledge and skills, equally valuing domain-specific expertise and a broad knowledge base (the "K") as well as domain-specific skills and creative processing skills (the "S"). Domain-specific expertise might be having years of experience programming computers, whereas the skills might involve specific software tools. The third component is Abilities (the "A"), which encompasses intelligence, divergent thinking, and the ability to make remote associations and analogies. The "O" is the broad category of "Other," which would include personality and motivation. The KSAO components first contribute to a person's creative potential; they then interact with contextual moderators of the environment and eventually result in innovative outcomes. These moderators might include the organizational climate, strong leadership and teams, and the availability of rewards, recognition, and resources (Hunter et al., 2012).

Karwowski and Jankowska (in press), building off of earlier work in Polish by Karwowski, propose a Typological Model of Creativity, which can be particularly well applied to the classroom. Their three core components that intersect are creative abilities, independence, and openness. They present these components as overlapping circles. Those people high in all three abilities have what is called Complex Creativity (and they are rare; a classroom of 30 may have three or four such students). People high in creative abilities and independence have Rebellious Creativity, those high in openness and independence have Self-Actualizing Creativity, and those higher in openness and creative abilities have Subordinate Creativity. I find the concept of Subordinate Creativity particularly interesting; its mere existence feels counterintuitive, yet I often think that when companies say they want creative workers, they actually are thinking of this type of creativity.

WHAT WE CREATE

We are a society that likes measuring things. One of the biggest reasons why I've become less of a baseball fan since the whole steroid debacle isn't self-righteousness (my guess is that if there was a drug that would double your publication output, most academics would be first in line as guinea pigs) but rather frustration that the data have become meaningless. My father and I wrote a book on the worst baseball pitchers of all time (A. S. Kaufman & Kaufman, 1995) that used a lot of statistical analysis to identify the very worst, and we always assumed we'd revise it. But when there's a confounding variable (i.e., steroids) tossed in the mix, it makes the measurement issue a bit muddled.

Of course, few measurement-related issues are more muddled than creativity, which I explore in some detail in chapters to come. Before we can begin to think about how to measure something, we have to have some idea about what exactly it is. In baseball, a single is a single and a home run is a home run. It gets complicated when we look at interactions (such as trying to figure out how a player in Boston in the 1920s would perform in San Diego in the 1990s). Creativity is all about interactions.

How the Field and Domain React

For example, consider one popular theory of creative products, Csikszentmihalyi's (1996, 1999) Systems Model. Creativity, according to this model, is an interaction between the domain, the field, and the person. A domain is a preexisting area of expertise. It could be as broad as mathematics or science; it could be as specific as game theory or particle physics. Creativity occurs when a domain is changed in some way.

The field is defined as consisting of the "gatekeepers"—teachers, editors, critics, and so on. The field can be thought of as the people whom you need to impress if you want to be successful. The field interacts directly with the domain; the field shapes a domain (e.g., the editors of psychology journals help determine how the domain of psychology is advanced) and the domain shapes the field (e.g., it may be hard for someone trained as a psychologist to be hired by an education department, even if she can make tremendous contributions to the department, because some consider the domain of education to be restricted to people with specific training and hands-on experience in education).

The third component is the person—the one who creates an idea or theory or piece of art. The success of such a creative product will likely depend on the interaction between the field (the gatekeepers) and the person. If a person creates a product that is uninteresting or offensive, the field will be unlikely to appreciate the product. A field can be a positive source of inspiration as well; a person may be mentored or advised by a more senior creator, or she may adapt and expand past work. Finally, the domain defines the space in which a person creates. A creative person designing a product within the domain of skyscraper building is not likely to use balsa wood and glue as a medium because skyscrapers *require* a certain level of strength and building finesse.

An interesting addition to Csikszentmihalyi's theory is Gangadharbatla's (2010) addendum about the role of technology. He argues that technology serves, in essence, as a fourth component. It impacts the field, quickens the roles of the gatekeepers, and changes how people are creative.

Certainly, technology has changed things. In the past, for example, the gatekeepers dominated the movie and music industries. It was virtually impossible for a young artist to rise through the ranks without the blessing of a studio or a label. Now, singers are discovered on YouTube and can sell their own music on iTunes. A performer can use social media to build a following; actor/comedian Kevin Hart is a prime example. He utilizes Twitter to connect with his fans and build a following. One movie executive was quoted as saying, "Kevin has the ability to market a project to his audience more effectively than a studio can" (Stewart, 2014).

In Csikszentmihalyi's theory, the domain, field, and person work interactively. So let's examine Bach's work. Let's say that while he was alive, the field did not believe his later work was creative in the domain of music. If this tidbit is true (and it apparently was), then according to Csikszentmihalyi, *Bach's work was not creative at that time*. It is only later, when our more modern critics, professors, and musicians recognized his talent, that his work could be called creative.

This theory should drive fear into the heart of the most successful creators. James Patterson? John Grisham? Sure, your books sell now, but how about in 50 years? Michael Bay? Brett Ratner? Let's see what film classes say in the next century. And, conversely, this theory may bring hope to people who fancy themselves as undiscovered geniuses. "Perhaps," a languishing poet might say, "my work will be found 200 years from now, and people then will realize I was misunderstood and unappreciated."

Yet it is interesting to note that the work of Dean Keith Simonton has discounted the myth of the unappreciated genius. He studied 496 operas and compared how they were initially received versus how often they are performed today. What he found was that, in general, operas that opened to good reviews and solid runs are the operas that are most commonly performed today (Simonton, 1998; also see Eysenck, 1995). Indeed, if you think of the most popular writers of the 19th century, you come up with writers like Mark Twain and Charles Dickens—who were much more akin to the Jon Stewart and Stephen King of their time. Even more recently, the musicals of Harold Rome were considered the "highbrow" theater of the 1950s, whereas Rodgers and Hammerstein were seen more as populist tripe. Yet can you name a Harold Rome musical today? If you can, I'm impressed (and a little scared). If you can't, think of *Pins and Needles, Fanny,* and *I Can Get It for You Wholesale,* which introduced the world to Barbra Streisand.

Another area of research that discounts the neglected-genius idea is Simonton's work on career trajectories. Simonton has conducted extensive research on the relationship between age and achievement (see Simonton, 1997, 2012, for a review). He has found that most successful people begin producing in their 20s, peak in their 40s, and then gradually decline. Some fields peak particularly young; theoretical physicists and poets, for example, tend to make a major contribution by their mid- to late 20s, or not at all (Simonton, 1994). Kozbelt and Durmysheva (2007) looked at life-span creativity in Japanese printmakers from the 18th century and found similar patterns and peaks.

The earlier a creator begins her or his career, the more works she or he produces; however, there is no relationship between how old someone is when she starts and how old she is when she produces her best work (Simonton, 1997, 2007). A later career start is associated with being older at the time of the individual's last major contribution. Simonton (1989) analyzed the last works of composers and found that they tended to be less original and shorter than other pieces, but scored higher in popularity and aesthetic significance. I discuss life-span trajectories of the average person later in the book, in Chapter 7.

An alternate perspective was proposed by Galenson (2005), who argued that different types of creators peak at different ages.

He constructs two life cycles: early conceptual creators (finders), who burst onto the scene with a splash of greatness, as compared with later-peaking experimental creators (seekers), who made contributions based on a vast body of work. Galenson argues that it is the type of approach that results in early or late peaks, not the domain. Simonton (2007) specifically addressed this question empirically and found that the question of domain (poetry vs. fiction) was equally important to predicting when a writer peaked (see also Kaufman & Gentile, 2002).

How the Field and Domain Are Changed

Another theory, the propulsion theory of creative contributions, examines how a product changes the field and domain (Sternberg, 1999; Sternberg & Kaufman, 2012; Sternberg, Kaufman, & Pretz, 2001, 2002, 2003). This theory describes eight different ways that someone can make a creative contribution, and categorizes these contributions based on their relationship to the domain. The first four contributions all represent achievements that stay within the framework of an existing paradigm.

Perhaps the most basic type of contribution that someone can make is *replication*. Replication tries to keep things status quo—to reproduce past work. Think of a romance novel that is mighty similar to earlier ones, with slightly different characters and settings. Or remember—if you dare—*Saw 3D: The Final Chapter*.

But there shouldn't be a negative connotation. Perhaps, instead, think of the people who spend Sunday afternoons in a museum, trying to copy a famous painting. Are they creative? Absolutely. Even if these painters are not necessarily trying to advance the artistic domain, they help create that nice ambience that make museums fun on the weekends. In science, a replication study is one that shows an earlier experiment can be reproduced. Given the many cases of scientific fraud, flukes, and human error that can occur (check out the terrific website Retraction Watch to see the underbelly of science), these replications are important, needed work. It's not glamorous work, and a career spent only conducting these types of studies will likely not get tenure. But as Makel and Plucker (2014a, 2014b) note, creativity is not just originality. Replication studies are a creative contribution, and the fervent push for novelty at the expense of grounded, careful work can lead to false starts and wasted resources.

31

The second type of contribution, *redefinition,* takes a new look at the domain. A redefinitive contribution doesn't necessarily try to push forward, but rather tries to present a different perspective. Think of the videos on YouTube that recut a movie's trailer such that it seems to be something completely different, such as making *The Shining* seem like a sweet family comedy. Indeed, a good director often uses redefinition when working in the theater—he or she may take a famous play and then put a new "spin" on it so that an audience may see something new. A good businessman may be able to see a new use for a product that hasn't sold well. A classic example is Art Fry of 3M, who found a new use for an adhesive that wasn't strong enough to sell as a glue—so he invented Post-It notes.

A third contribution, and perhaps the type of contribution that achieves the most immediate success, is called *forward incrementation.* This type of contribution pushes forward the domain just a little. Maybe the creator makes a slight change in what already exists. These additions usually are not groundbreaking—it takes the domain in the same direction it was heading. Think of really good genre writers. Many solid successes have introduced some twists. Jeffrey Deaver's hero, Lincoln Rhyme, is a quadriplegic, and Faye Kellerman's cop converts to Orthodox Judaism. Other thrillers place their lead detectives in less conventional locations (such as Laura Lippman's love for Baltimore) or give them more unusual jobs (such as Lee Child's military policeman–turned-wanderer Jack Reacher). There are a few who are psychologists, such as Jonathan Kellerman's Alex Delaware, and I can verify that we psychologists do indeed spend most of our time helping the police understand the underlying motivations of serial killers. My favorite is Harlan Coben's unlikely hero Myron Bolitar, a sports agent who teams up with his financial planner Win to solve crimes, sing musical theater songs, and generally kick butt.

The final contribution that stays within the existing definitions of a domain is *advance forward incrementation.* This contribution pushes the domain ahead two steps instead of one—and the creator often suffers for it. This type of creative product includes people who were a little before their time. Think of the musicals of Stephen Sondheim, such as *Anyone Can Whistle, Follies, Pacific Overtures,* or *Merrily We Roll Along.* Several of his shows have become mainstream due to movie adaptations, such as *Sweeney Todd* or *Into the Woods,* but both the obscure and the popular are considered brilliant by true theater buffs. Sondheim's musicals represent an enormous leap forward from earlier theatrical shows. His intricate lyrics and complex music are still following in the path of previous creators (such as Cole Porter or Kurt Weill). One big push forward about his work can be found in his serious, dark subject matters. He writes about a murderous barber and his (human) meat-pie-making partner, a secret society that lives in department stores, Japanese imperialism, Georges Seurat paintings come to life, presidential assassins, and a partially deformed Italian woman's romantic obsession. One of Sondheim's shows reminds us that art is not easy; indeed, *Sondheim's* art isn't easy—and is an advance forward incrementation.

The final four types of creative contributions represent attempts to reject and replace the current paradigm. *Redirection* represents an attempt to redirect the domain to head in a new direction. The toy company Mattel, for example, helped redirect the domain of toy selling in the 1950s. Up until this time, toy manufacturers targeted wholesale suppliers and toy stores for their products. If companies decided to stock the toy, then it sold; if not, it didn't. Sometimes, manufacturers might try to target parents. But Mattel spent its last financial resources to purchase commercial time on the Mickey Mouse television show and reach the children directly. This decision changed the ways that toys were advertised (to many a parent's chagrin). Children all across America demanded Mattel's Burp Gun, and millions were sold (Stern & Schoenhaus, 1990).

If most of these contribution types represent "forward" thinking, *reconstruction/redirection* looks backward. This contribution is an attempt to move the field back to where it once was (a reconstruction of the past) so that it may move forward from this point—in a different direction. Most retro art movements are broad examples of this category; a favorite specific one is when *Mad Magazine* "rewrote" old Dave Berg observational humor ("The Lighter Side of. . ." comics). What if, they asked, Dave Berg were still alive and writing his old strip? They used his old artwork and rewrote the punchlines, incorporating modern issues and a slightly darker sense of humor ("The Darker Side of the Lighter Side," 2008).

Perhaps the most radical of all of the creative contributions is *reinitiation*. In reinitiation, the creator tries to move the field to a new (as-yet-unreached) starting point and then progress from there.

Reinitiation is Lavoisier inventing a revolutionary new chemistry. It is Ian Finlay's poetry, which uses visual props such as wildflowers, stone, sundials, and glass combining with the words of the poetry to result in the overall creation of a certain emotion or feeling (Parker & Kermode, 1996). One of my standard examples is Marcel Duchamp entering a urinal into a 1917 art exhibit and calling it "Fountain"—yet in recent years there has been some debate over when he actually stole this concept from someone else, namely, Baroness Elsa von Freytag-Loringhoven (Frizzell, 2014).

Finally, the last contribution is *integration* (sometimes called *synthesis*), in which two diverse domains are merged to create a new idea. Two of the most popular science fiction creations represent similar integrations of different fields. Gene Roddenberry's *Star Trek* and George Lucas's *Star Wars* both were able to integrate the fields of science fiction and westerns. *Star Trek* was a television show that was based on a similar concept as the western show *Wagon Train*—sturdy and resilient men and women prevailing over an assortment of different types of people. *Star Trek* used human and Vulcan characters, and had them triumph over a variety of different alien species (Panati, 1991). In a similar vein, George Lucas used a famous western plot in a science fiction setting. The basic story of *Star Wars* closely mirrors the plot of the John Wayne classic *The Searchers*; again, however, the setting of the Old West is replaced by outer space. *Star Wars* also integrates the field of Japanese Samurai movies; the plot of *Star Wars: A New Hope* is reminiscent of *Kakushi Toride no San Akunin*. The character of Obi-Wan Kenobi can be seen to represent a Samurai warrior, and the two robots, R2-D2 and C-3PO, resemble the two crooks who were hired to help rescue a princess in the original Japanese movie.

Another theory that examines the nature of the creative contribution with an industrial/organizational spin is a more straightforward dichotomy. Gilson and Madjar (2011) propose radical versus incremental creativity. Radical creativity is a notable shift from past work (akin to reinitiation or perhaps advance forward incrementation), and incremental creativity is a modification of existing work (analogous to forward incrementation or even replication). Radical creativity has been shown to be linked to risk taking and career commitment (Madjar, Greenberg, & Chen, 2011), and higher creative self-efficacy (Jaussi & Randel, 2014). Company identification (i.e., taking your job's values and beliefs as part of your own personality identity) and, interestingly, having more creative coworkers predicted incremental creativity. Unsurprisingly, conformity predicted noncreative work. Gilson, Lim, D'Innocenzo, and Moye (2012) argue that the radical–incremental distinction needs to be considered when managing creative employees.

The radical–incremental distinction is comparable to Kirton's (1976) distinction between adaptors and innovators. He argues that people solve problems in one of two ways. Either they adapt by using preexisting resources to arrive at a solution (the adaptors) or they think of new possibilities (the innovators). Another relevant model is Boden's (2004) combinational, exploratory, and transformational creativity. Combinational creativity is putting together existing ideas in a new way; certainly this type would include synthesis, but also likely a number of other categories. Exploratory is being creative within a particular style or genre; it could range from replication to forward incrementation. Transformational creativity is defined as changing a core concept such that the impossible can happen. Most akin to reinitiation, these types of discoveries are often groundbreaking.

The Nature of the Product

Creativity is filled with assumptions, some true and some not so true. One of the often unspoken assumptions is that creativity is another word for "the arts." Most research that doesn't explicitly look at creativity in a particular domain (such as math or science) uses the arts as a default proxy, such as visual art or writing. Some studies that look at creative or noncreative majors use "the arts" as a substitute for "creative." But, of course, you can be creative in *anything*.

Cropley and Cropley (A. J. Cropley & Cropley, 2009; D. H. Cropley & Cropley, 2008, 2010) argue for a distinction between functional and aesthetic creativity. Returning to the dual "new" and "task-appropriate" requirements for creativity, we find that most artistic work has a wide latitude for what might be considered "task appropriate." Yes, there are very specific guidelines for writing a haiku or painting a picture in the pointillist style, but most visual art, creative writing, or performance contributions have a certain amount of freedom. When you think of modern, free-form dance, it is unlikely that the words "rigid" or "proscribed" pop to mind.

In contrast, the Cropleys argue that creative work that has a useful social purpose requires a stronger emphasis on the task-appropriate component. An architect may design the most beautiful bridge in the entire world, but if it collapses, it is not task appropriate and therefore not a creative bridge. If a traffic light fails, people can die. There was that one incident with an umbrella designed by Christo that impaled a woman, but, in general, art can fail and people don't die. For example, I was excited to see the movie *World War Z* after adoring the book. Yet as my wife and I stared at each other in mute disgust as the credits rolled, all of our internal organs still worked just fine—the movie didn't destroy our spleens with its suckitude. Thus, the Cropleys propose a distinction between functional creativity, which requires effectiveness in order to not be a hazard to society, and aesthetic creativity, which can be ineffective and merely annoying.

They propose a hierarchical organization of products based on the criteria that are met. They start with the criteria of novelty and effectiveness and then add two more: elegance and genesis. Elegant solutions are often simple and seem obvious, yet have a certain beauty to them (D. H. Cropley, 2015; Kay, 2013). Genesis refers to the degree to which a solution is universal (whether the insights might be applied to other domains).

The Cropleys propose five types of products. Routine products are effective, but nothing else (comparable to replicative works). Original products are novel and effective (traditionally creative). Elegant products add the quality of elegance, and truly innovative products include all four attributes. In contrast, they argue, aesthetic products do not need to be effective, must be novel, and can go either way with the other two criteria. They include some of the components of the propulsion model in an expanded list of novelty attributes (A. J. Cropley & Cropley, 2009; D. H. Cropley, 2015; D. H. Cropley & Kaufman, 2012).

LOOKING AHEAD

We will encounter many other theories of creativity within these pages as we discuss core research topics in the field. One last theoretical aspect of creativity, which I have given its own chapter, revolves around the structure of creativity: Is creativity one thing? Is it many things? Or something in between?

REFERENCES

Adams, S. (1996). *The Dilbert principle.* New York, NY: HarperBusiness.

Amabile, T. M. (1983a). *The social psychology of creativity.* New York, NY: Springer-Verlag.

Amabile, T. M. (1983b). The social psychology of creativity: A componential conceptualization. *Journal of Personality and Social Psychology, 45,* 357–376.

Amabile, T. M. (1996). *Creativity in context: Update to "The Social Psychology of Creativity."* Boulder, CO: Westview Press.

Basadur, M. S., Runco, M. A., & Vega, L. A. (2000). Understanding how creative thinking skills, attitudes and behaviors work together: A causal process model. *Journal of Creative Behavior, 34,* 77–100.

Beghetto, R. A., & Kaufman, J. C. (2007). Toward a broader conception of creativity: A case for "mini-c" creativity. *Psychology of Aesthetics, Creativity, and the Arts, 1,* 73–79.

Beghetto, R. A., & Kaufman, J. C. (2009). Intellectual estuaries: Connecting learning and creativity in programs of advanced academics. *Journal of Advanced Academics, 20,* 296–324.

Blair, C. S., & Mumford, M. D. (2007). Errors in idea evaluation: Preference for the unoriginal? *Journal of Creative Behavior, 41,* 197–222.

Boden, M. A. (2004). *The creative mind: Myths and mechanisms.* Hove, England: Psychology Press.

Campbell, D. T. (1960). Blind variation and selective retentions in creative thought as in other knowledge processes. *Psychological Review, 67,* 380.

Craig, O. (2005). The man who discovered "Lost"—and found himself out of a job. *The Telegraph.* Retrieved from http://www.telegraph.co.uk/news/worldnews/northamerica/usa/1496199/The-man-who-discovered-Lost-and-found-himself-out-of-a-job.html

Cropley, A. J. (2006). In praise of convergent thinking. *Creativity Research Journal, 18,* 391–404.

Cropley, A. J., & Cropley, D. (2009). *Fostering creativity: A diagnostic approach for higher education and organizations.* Cresskill, NJ: Hampton Press.

Cropley, D. H. (2015). *Creativity in engineering: Novel solutions to complex problems.* San Diego, CA: Academic Press.

Cropley, D. H., & Cropley, A. J. (2008). Elements of a universal aesthetic of creativity. *Psychology of Aesthetics, Creativity, and the Arts, 2,* 155–161.

Cropley, D. H., & Cropley, A. J. (2010). Functional creativity: Products and the generation of effective novelty. In J. C. Kaufman & R. J. Sternberg (Eds.), *Cambridge handbook of creativity* (pp. 301–320). New York, NY: Cambridge University Press.

Cropley, D. H., & Kaufman, J. C. (2012). Measuring functional creativity: Empirical validation of the Creative Solution Diagnosis Scale (CSDS). *Journal of Creative Behavior, 46,* 119–137.

Csikszentmihalyi, M. (1996). *Creativity: Flow and the psychology of discovery and invention.* New York, NY: HarperCollins.

Csikszentmihalyi, M. (1998). Reflections on the field. *Roeper Review, 21,* 80–81.

Csikszentmihalyi, M. (1999). Implications of a systems perspective for the study of creativity. In R. J. Sternberg (Ed.), *Handbook of creativity* (pp. 313–335). Cambridge, England: Cambridge University Press.

Csikszentmihalyi, M., & Getzels, J. W. (1971). Discovery-oriented behavior and the originality of creative products: A study with artists. *Journal of Personality and Social Psychology, 19,* 47–52.

Dasgupta, S. (2011). Contesting (Simonton's) blind variation, selective retention theory of creativity. *Creativity Research Journal, 23,* 166–182.

Eysenck, H. J. (1995). *Genius: The natural history of creativity.* Cambridge, England: Cambridge University Press.

Finke, R. A., Ward, T. B., & Smith, S. M. (1992). *Creative cognition: Theory, research, and applications.* Cambridge, MA: MIT Press.

Frizzell, N. (2014). Duchamp and the pissoir-taking sexual politics of the art world. *The Guardian.* Retrieved from http://www.theguardian.com/commentisfree/2014/nov/07/duchamp-elsa-freytag-loringhoven-urinal-sexual-politics-art

Galenson, D. W. (2005). *Old masters and young geniuses: The two life cycles of artistic creativity.* Princeton, NJ: Princeton University Press.

Gangadharbatla, H. (2010). Technology component: A modified systems approach to creative thought. *Creativity Research Journal, 22,* 219–227.

Getzels, J. W. (1979). Problem finding: A theoretical note. *Cognitive Science, 3,* 167–172.

Getzels, J. W., & Csikszentmihalyi, M. (1976). *The creative vision.* New York, NY: Wiley.

Gilson, L. L., Lim, H. S., D'Innocenzo, L., & Moye, N. (2012). One size does not fit all: Managing radical and incremental creativity. *Journal of Creative Behavior, 46,* 168–191.

Gilson, L. L., & Madjar, N. (2011). Radical and incremental creativity: Antecedents and processes. *The Psychology of Aesthetics, Creativity, and the Arts, 5,* 21–28.

Glăveanu, V. P. (2009). The cultural genesis of creativity: An emerging paradigm. *Revista de Psihologie şcolară, 2,* 50–63.

Glăveanu, V. P. (2012a). Habitual creativity: Revising habit, reconceptualizing creativity. *Review of General Psychology, 16,* 78–92.

Glăveanu, V. P. (2012b). What can be done with an egg? Creativity, material objects, and the theory of affordances. *Journal of Creative Behavior, 46,* 192–208.

Glăveanu, V. P. (2013). Rewriting the language of creativity: The five A's framework. *Review of General Psychology, 17,* 69–81.

Guilford, J. P. (1950). Creativity. *American Psychologist, 5,* 444–454.

Guilford, J. P. (1967). *The nature of human intelligence.* New York, NY: McGraw-Hill.

Guilford, J. P. (1988). Some changes in the Structure-of-Intellect Model. *Educational and Psychological Measurement, 48,* 1–4.

Harrington, D. M., Block, J. H., & Block, J. (1987). Testing aspects of Carl Rogers' theory of creative environments: Child-rearing antecedents of creative potential in young adolescents. *Journal of Personality and Social Psychology, 52,* 851–860.

Hartmann, E. (2000). *Dreams and nightmares: The origin and meaning of dreams.* Reading, MA: Perseus.

Hayes, J. R., & Flower, L. S. (1986). Writing research and the writer. *American Psychologist, 41,* 1106–1113.

Hunter, S. T., Cushenbery, L., & Freidrich, T. M. (2012). Hiring an innovative workforce: A necessary yet uniquely challenging endeavor. *Human Resource Management Review, 22,* 303–322.

Jaussi, K. S., & Randel, A. E. (2014). Where to look? Creative self-efficacy, knowledge retrieval, and incremental and radical creativity. *Creativity Research Journal, 26,* 400–410.

Karwowski, M., & Jankowska, D. M. (in press). Four faces of creativity at school. In R. A. Beghetto & J. C. Kaufman (Eds.), *Nurturing creativity in the classroom* (2nd ed.). New York, NY: Cambridge University Press.

Kaufman, A. S., & Kaufman, J. C. (1995). *The worst baseball pitchers of all time.* New York, NY: Citadel Press.

Kaufman, J. C., & Beghetto, R. A. (2009). Beyond big and little: The Four C Model of Creativity. *Review of General Psychology, 13,* 1–12.

Kaufman, J. C., & Gentile, C. A. (2002). The will, the wit, the judgment: The importance of an early start in productive and successful creative writing. *High Ability Studies, 13,* 115–123.

Kay, S. I. (2013). Designing elegant problems for creative thinking. In F. Reisman (Ed.), *Creativity: Process, product, personality, environment & technology* (pp. 28–36). Cambridge, UK: Knowledge, Innovation & Enterprise.

Kirton, M. (1976). Adaptors and innovators: A description and measure. *Journal of Applied Psychology, 61,* 622–629.

Kozbelt, A., Beghetto, R. A., & Runco, M. A. (2010). Theories of creativity. In J. C. Kaufman & R. J. Sternberg (Eds.), *Cambridge handbook of creativity* (pp. 20–47). New York, NY: Cambridge University Press.

Kozbelt, A., & Durmysheva, Y. (2007). Lifespan creativity in a non-Western artistic tradition: A study of Japanese ukiyo-e printmakers. *International Journal of Aging and Human Development, 65*, 23–51.

Madjar, N., Greenberg, E., & Chen, Z. (2011). Factors for radical creativity, incremental creativity, and routine, noncreative performance. *Journal of Applied Psychology, 96*, 730–743.

Makel, M. C., & Plucker, J. A. (2014a). Creativity is more than novelty: Reconsidering replication as a creative act. *Psychology of Aesthetics, Creativity, and the Arts, 8*, 27–29.

Makel, M. C., & Plucker, J. A. (2014b). Facts are more important than novelty: Replication in the education sciences. *Educational Researcher, 43*, 304–316.

Mumford, M. D., Mobley, M. I., Uhlman, C. E., Reiter-Palmon, R., & Doares, L. M. (1991). Process analytic models of creative capacities. *Creativity Research Journal, 4*, 91–122.

Mumford, M. D., Reiter-Palmon, R., & Redmond, M. R. (1994). Problem construction and cognition: Applying problem representations in ill-defined domains. In M. A. Runco (Ed.), *Problem finding, problem solving, and creativity* (pp. 3–39). Westport, CT: Ablex Publishing.

Panati, C. (1991). Panati's parade of fads, follies, and manias. New York, NY: Harper's.

Parker, P., & Kermode, F. (Eds.). (1996). *A reader's guide to twentieth-century writers.* New York, NY: Oxford University Press.

Piirto, J. (1998). *Understanding those who create* (2nd ed.). Scottsdale, AZ: Gifted Psychology Press.

Piirto, J. (2004). *Understanding creativity.* Scottsdale, AZ: Great Potential Press.

Piirto, J. (2010). The five core attitudes, seven I's, and general concepts of the creative process. In R. A. Beghetto & J. C. Kaufman (Eds.), *Nurturing creativity in the classroom* (pp. 142–171). New York, NY: Cambridge University Press.

Piirto, J. (2014). *Organic creativity in the classroom: Teaching to intuition in academics and the arts.* Waco, TX: Prufrock Press.

Plucker, J. A., Beghetto, R. A., & Dow, G. (2004). Why isn't creativity more important to educational psychologists? Potential, pitfalls, and future directions in creativity research. *Educational Psychologist, 39*, 83–96.

Reiter-Palmon, R., Mumford, M. D., O'Connor Boes, J., & Runco, M. A. (1997). Problem construction and creativity: The role of ability, cue consistency and active processing. *Creativity Research Journal, 10*, 9–23.

Reiter-Palmon, R., Mumford, M. D., & Threlfall, K. V. (1998). Solving every-day problems creatively: The role of problem construction and person-ality type. *Creativity Research Journal, 11,* 187–197.

Reiter-Palmon, R., & Robinson, E. J. (2009). Problem identification and con-struction: What do we know, what is the future? *Psychology of Aesthetics, Creativity, and the Arts, 3,* 43–47.

Rhodes, M. (1962). An analysis of creativity. *Phi Delta Kappan, 42,* 305–311.

Rostan, S. M. (1994). Problem finding, problem solving, and cognitive con-trols: An empirical investigation of critically acclaimed productivity. *Cre-ativity Research Journal, 7,* 97–110.

Runco, M. A. (2003). Creativity, cognition, and their education implications. In J. C. Houtz (Ed.), *The educational psychology of creativity* (pp. 25–56). Cresskill, NJ: Hampton Press.

Sawyer, R. K. (2012). *Explaining creativity: The science of human innovation* (2nd ed.). New York, NY: Oxford University Press.

Sawyer, R. K., & DeZutter, S. (2009). Distributed creativity: How collective creations emerge from collaboration. *Psychology of Aesthetics, Creativity, and the Arts, 3,* 81–92.

Scott, G., Leritz, L., & Mumford, M. D. (2004). The effectiveness of creativity training: A quantitative review. *Creativity Research Journal, 16,* 361–388.

Simonton, D. K. (1977). Creative productivity, age, and stress: A biographical time-series analysis of 10 classical composers. *Journal of Personality and Social Psychology, 35,* 791–804.

Simonton, D. K. (1985). Quality, quantity, and age: The careers of 10 distin-guished psychologists. *International Journal of Aging and Human Develop-ment, 21,* 241–254.

Simonton, D. K. (1989). The swan-song phenomenon: Last-works effects for 172 classical composers. *Psychology and Aging, 4,* 42–47.

Simonton, D. K. (1990). *Psychology, science, and history: An introduction to his-toriometry.* New Haven, CT: Yale University Press.

Simonton, D. K. (1994). *Greatness: Who makes history and why.* New York, NY: Guilford Press.

Simonton, D. K. (1997). Creative productivity: A predictive and explanatory model of career trajectories and landmarks. *Psychological Review, 104,* 66–89.

Simonton, D. K. (1998). Fickle fashion versus immortal fame: Transhistorical assessments of creative products in the opera house. *Journal of Personality and Social Psychology, 75,* 198–210.

Simonton, D. K. (2007). Creative life cycles in literature: Poets versus nov-elists or conceptualists versus experimentalists? *Psychology of Aesthetics, Creativity, and the Arts, 1,* 133–139.

Simonton, D. K. (2011). Creativity and discovery as blind variation and selective retention: Multiple-variant definitions and blind-sighted integration. *Psychology of Aesthetics, Creativity, and the Arts, 5*, 222–228.

Simonton, D. K. (2012). Creative productivity and aging: An age decrement – or not? In S. K. Whitbourne & M. Sliwinski (Eds.), *The Wiley-Blackwell handbook of adult development and aging* (pp. 477–496). New York, NY: Wiley-Blackwell.

Simonton, D. K. (2013). What is a creative idea? Little-c versus Big-C creativity. In K. Thomas & J. Chan (Eds.), *Handbook of research on creativity* (pp. 69–83). Cheltenham, England: Edward Elgar Publishing.

Stern, S. L., & Schoenhaus, T. (1990). *Toyland: The high-stakes game of the toy industry.* New York, NY: Contemporary.

Sternberg, R. J. (1999). A propulsion model of types of creative contributions. *Review of General Psychology, 3*, 83–100.

Sternberg, R. J., & Kaufman, J. C. (2012). When your race is almost run, but you feel you're not yet done: Application of the Propulsion Theory of Creative Contributions to late-career challenges. *Journal of Creative Behavior, 46*, 66–76.

Sternberg, R. J., Kaufman, J. C., & Pretz, J. E. (2001). The propulsion model of creative contributions applied to the arts and letters. *Journal of Creative Behavior, 35*, 75–101.

Sternberg, R. J., Kaufman, J. C., & Pretz, J. E. (2002). *The creativity conundrum.* Philadelphia, PA: Psychology Press.

Sternberg, R. J., Kaufman, J. C., & Pretz, J. E. (2003). A propulsion model of creative leadership. *Leadership Quarterly, 14*, 455–473.

Sternberg, R. J., & Lubart, T. I. (1995). *Defying the crowd.* New York, NY: Free Press.

Stewart, A. (2014, March 6). How did Kevin Hart get so damn hot? *Variety.* Retrieved from http://variety.com/2014/film/news/how-did-kevin-hart-get-so-damn-hot-1201125964

Stokes, P. D. (2014). Thinking inside the tool box: Creativity, constraints, and the colossal portraits of Chuck Close. *Journal of Creative Behavior, 48*, 276–289.

The darker side of the lighter side. (2008, March). *Mad Magazine, 487*, 16–17.

Voss, J. F., Wolfe, C. R., Lawrence, J. A., & Engle, R. A. (1991). From representation to decision: An analysis of problem solving in international relations. In R. J. Sternberg & P. A. Frensch (Eds.), *Complex problem solving: Principles and mechanisms* (pp. 199–158). Hillsdale, NJ: Erlbaum.

Wallas, G. (1926). *The art of thought.* New York, NY: Harcourt, Brace, & World.

Yi, X., Plucker, J. A., & Guo, J. (2015). Modeling influences on divergent thinking and artistic creativity. *Thinking Skills and Creativity, 16*, 62–68.

Zenasni, F., Besançon, M., & Lubart, T. (2008). Creativity and tolerance of ambiguity: An empirical study. *Journal of Creative Behavior, 42*, 61–73.

The Structure
of Creativity

uring the last 4 months of 1987, the world lost a
number of renowned creative people. One such loss
was Bob Fosse, director and choreographer extraor-
dinaire noted for his openly sexualized dances in
which even the slightest movement—a turn of a knee, a tilt of a
head, a roll of a hip—had meaning (Gottfried, 1990). Other people
who passed away during this period include James Baldwin, the
well-known civil rights activist and author; Joseph Campbell, perhaps the world's foremost expert on mythology; famed violinist
Jascha Heifetz (who happened to be my fourth cousin); Henry Ford
II, who took over as CEO of the Ford Motor Company and helmed
its expansion; and Nobel Prize–winning Walter Brattain, who built
the first transistor. Of course, the list could go on: Jacqueline du
Pre, Alf Landon, Woody Herman, Dan Rowan, Jean Anouilh, Harold Washington, and many others.

The Fosse "style" has been assumed into modern theatrical
dance so much that it is becoming a cliché. Fosse worked his way up

through vaudeville, into choreographing musicals, and then taking on director roles, as well. He became one of the few show people to be as much of a star if not more so than the actors on stage. Indeed, many casual theatergoers are aware of the name "Bob Fosse" and may know a little bit about him. Conversely, *Pippin* (which he directed and choreographed) was a smash on Broadway; can anyone but an ardent fan identify John Rubinstein as the original titular character?

Yet what if Fosse had decided, early in his life, to pursue writing or activism like James Baldwin? Would we still be reading his stories (perhaps about his unhappy home life or successive series of girlfriends)? Or what if Fosse became fascinated by mythology, instead? Or what if he decided to pursue cars, transistors, or politics? Might there be a "Fosse Motor Company"? Meanwhile, let's ponder the reverse—might Walter Brattain be remembered as a Broadway hoofer if that was how his muse appeared? Could Henry Ford II have left the family business and devoted his life to playing the violin?

The answer to these questions lies in the nature of creativity. If creativity is truly and completely "general," or if it is one single thing, then the answer would be yes. A Fosse would be a "Fosse" no matter what domain he chose. A Jascha Heifetz or a James Baldwin or a Joseph Campbell would show his creativity in any variety of domains. If, on the other hand, creativity were "domain specific," then such a transition would not be as easy. Someone with an aptitude for poetry might not necessarily be able to use this creativity to compose music or solve mathematical problems.

There is an intense debate over the question of domain specificity or generality within the intelligence field, although it's not called that. Some researchers argue passionately for a general factor of intelligence, g, in which there is one factor that is largely responsible for academic and job performance (among many other things). Other researchers argue just as passionately against g, offering instead theories of multiple intelligences or theories that paint a broader and more complex picture of intellectual abilities. The debates can sometimes have a nasty edge to them—g advocates can point to an astounding array of data in their favor that they accuse the anti-g crowd of ignoring; the anti-g contingent can point to an unpleasant connection between the g theory and racist ideas and implications.

Is there a c, analogous to intelligence's g, that transcends domains and enhances the creativity of a person across many different areas?

44

This question has fueled numerous debates in the literature (Baer, 1998, 2015; J. C. Kaufman & Baer, 2005; Plucker, 1998; Sternberg, Grigorenko, & Singer, 2004), although I believe the general consensus is converging to be somewhere in the middle—namely, that there are both domain-specific and domain-general aspects of creativity.

BIG-C AND DOMAIN SPECIFICITY

One way of thinking about the question of creativity and domains is to ponder the lack of renaissance men and women—people who are truly creative in multiple arenas. It is important to note that both a domain-general and domain-specific point of view would allow for polymaths—a domain-generalist would say that these polymaths are using the same creative processes to paint and sculpt and be an accountant, whereas a domain-specificist would argue that they use different processes. From the domain-specific perspective, the tiny handful of people who have reached Big-C in multiple areas are like pigs who can ride bicycles and recite the alphabet—remarkable, but not proof of any underlying mechanism.

It is easier to find polymaths at lower ends of the Four Cs. For one thing, as I've mentioned, it takes time to reach basic proficiency in a domain, let alone creative genius. Most people simply won't be allotted enough years to live in order to pursue elite greatness—let alone mere talent—across many fields (Plucker & Beghetto, 2004). As much as one might love to see how Martin Scorsese might approach architecture, or how Bill Gates might tackle interpretative dance, it's not going to happen anytime soon. The handful of renaissance people who are accomplished at Big-C creativity in multiple areas stand out: Leonardo Da Vinci, Benjamin Franklin, Paul Robeson, Johann Wolfgang von Goethe, and Bertrand Russell. Or consider those who have won Nobel Prizes in two different categories, such as Marie Curie (Physics and Chemistry) and Linus Pauling (Chemistry and Peace). However, there are not many of them. Miss Piggy may sing (in *Muppets Take Manhattan*) about wanting to be a neurosurgeon, movie star, scuba diver, singer, airplane pilot, model, and veterinarian (in addition to having Kermit's children), but she may be overreaching a bit.

There are certainly many people who have achieved the Pro-c level of creative achievement in two domains. William Carlos Williams and Anton Chekhov, for example, are two famed writers who were also medical doctors (Piirto, 1998); the deeper question remains, however, of whether they were *creative* medical doctors. Accomplishment is not always the same thing as creativity. Their success in their chosen fields may be argued as an indicator of creativity, but not as proof.

It is easy to identify others who are successful in multiple fields, and it can be fun identifying people with seemingly discrepant interests. Byron "Whizzer" White was but one of many athletes to become notable in another field (although the only one to become a Supreme Court justice). John Glenn, like many others, became a successful politician after a top-notch career in another area (in his case, being an astronaut). Vladimir Nabokov was a well-known entomologist whose collection of caterpillar genitalia is still exhibited in the Harvard Museum of Natural History—but is likely better known for writing such novels as *Lolita* (Powell, 2001).

Among people still active, Brian May is the founding guitarist of the classic 1970s band Queen—and he has a PhD in astrophysics and has written about the history of the universe (May, Moore, & Lintott, 2008). Danica McKellar, who grew up on television as *The Wonder Years'* Winnie, went on to co-discover an original mathematical theorem. Mayim Bialik (*Big Bang Theory*) has a PhD in neuroscience. Many genre writers have expertise in another area, whether it's forensic anthropology (Kathy Reichs), psychology (Jonathan Kellerman, Stephen White), law (Linda Fairstein, John Grisham, Scott Turow), medicine (Robin Cook, Tess Gerritsen), secret service (John le Carré), politics (Ken Follett), graphic design (Alex Kava), or field ecology (Nevada Barr).

One reason to be a little wary of polymaths who are best known for one domain is that people may get opportunities in a second or third domain solely because of their success in a first domain. Does anyone remember the 1985 Chicago Bears' hit song "Super Bowl Shuffle?" It's not as if these guys went on to great operatic careers (or, in most cases, even continued on in great football careers). Shaquille O'Neal didn't get his acting and singing breaks because of his inherent charm or smooth vocalizations—he was just famous. Where do we even start with the Kardashians?

46

It is important to reiterate, however, that domain specificity does not say that people are only allowed to be creative in one domain; it instead suggests that the underlying components of creativity are different from one domain to another. In other words, were the elements that enabled Danica McKellar to be successful in acting and math the same? Or is she creative in both acting and math in much the same way that someone might be able to run a mile in 4 minutes and learn French (both great abilities, but quite unrelated)?

LITTLE-C AND DOMAIN SPECIFICITY

Everything we've talked about so far is Big-C (or Pro-c). How about us everyday schnooks? Does the evidence lean more toward domain specificity or generality? The first thing to consider is that the answer depends on the methods used to ask the question (Plucker, 2004). Usually, if a study focused on the creative product, then creativity often appears domain specific. John Baer has conducted much of the recent research that argues for domain specificity. In several different studies (e.g., Baer, 1991, 1993, 1994), he tested students ranging from second graders to college students. He had these students produce creative work through writing poetry, writing short stories, telling stories out loud, creating mathematical equations, creating mathematical word problems, and making a collage. Baer consistently found low and usually nonsignificant correlations between creative ability in these different areas. In other words, a student who wrote a creative poem was *not* more likely to also tell a creative story or write a creative mathematical equation (a creative algebraic equation might use numbers in a playful or unusual way). If you remove variations due to IQ, the small correlations get even smaller.

In contrast, more psychometric assessments typically focus on the creative *person* (e.g., Plucker & Makel, 2010; Plucker & Renzulli, 1999). Scores are often grouped together as representing one central construct. Many of these studies rely on people describing or answering questions about their own creativity (e.g., Hocevar, 1976; Plucker, 1999). There is a question as to how much insight someone might have into herself or himself—can you accurately describe

47

how creative you are (or how charming, or how funny)? Some people can, some people can't (and I will go into more detail on this topic later).

In addition, people are influenced by what they may implicitly think about creativity. There are certain characteristics or behaviors that you might associate with being creative in general—perhaps taking risks, or liking to try new things. But there are also certain things that you may associate with being creative in a certain area. Your image of a creative scientist may be of Albert Einstein thinking deep thoughts or of a mad Dr. Frankenstein cackling in his lab. But it is certainly different from your image of a creative poet.

Regardless, when researchers use products to measure creativity (and we will discuss the details of this technique in the following chapter), they tend to find domain-specific results. When researchers use either self-assessments or tests rooted in how people think creatively, they find that creativity is domain general (Plucker, 1998, 1999, 2004). One model I've co-developed has examined this question and tried to integrate both perspectives.

THE AMUSEMENT PARK THEORY

John Baer and I developed the Amusement Park Theoretical (APT) model of creativity to integrate generalist and domain-specific views of creativity. We are not the first to try to synthesize these ideas. Others, for example, have proposed a "hybrid" view in which creativity is primarily general but appears domain specific in "real-world" performance (Plucker & Beghetto, 2004). According to this theory, the level of specificity changes according to social context, and matures as a person advances from childhood into adulthood.

The APT model uses the metaphor of an amusement park to explore the nature of creativity (J. Baer & Kaufman, 2005; J. C. Kaufman & Baer, 2004, 2005, 2006). We start with the initial requirements. What do you need to go to an amusement park? First, you need the time off to go. Amusement parks usually take up an entire day; trying to cram everything into one or two hours would just be silly. If you don't have a day to take off, you probably won't be going to an amusement park. But having the time is just the beginning. You

48

need money to get in. You need a way of getting to the amusement park. You need the basic desire to go—if, like me, you are terrified of roller coasters, then you likely won't be going to a Six Flags (or one of those anonymous hard-core roller coaster palaces on the sides of the freeway), even if given 2 weeks off work and a few thousand bucks.

Initial Requirements

Initial requirements are things that are necessary, but not by themselves sufficient, for any type of creative production. They include such things as intelligence, motivation, and suitable environments. Each of these factors is a prerequisite to creative achievement in any domain, and if someone lacks the requisite level of any of these initial requirements, then creative performance is at best unlikely. Higher levels of these initial requirements, in combination with other more domain-specific factors, predict higher levels of creative performance in general. It must be noted that although all of these initial requirements are necessary for creativity in any domain, the specific degrees of intelligence, motivation, and suitable environments needed to succeed in different areas of creative endeavors vary (just as the height requirements found at different rides may vary depending on the nature of the ride).

As an example of this, intelligence is an important contributor to creative performance in all domains, but it is much more highly correlated with creativity in certain domains than others. Picturing a less intelligent creative dancer or woodworker, for example, may be easier to do than picturing a less intelligent creative physicist. But some degree of intelligence is needed for creativity activity; there's a reason why rocks don't compose sonatas (other than the fact that they don't have opposable thumbs). Think about children engaged in imaginative play. Usually, play is not particularly related to IQ (Moran, Sawyers, Fu, & Milgram, 1984)—but in children with learning disabilities, there is a relationship between play behavior and IQ (Feagans & Short, 1986). Even when intelligence is not important, a certain level may be needed.

Similarly, when I talk about motivation, I'm not being specific about what things motivate people or what techniques they may use to motivate themselves. I'm simply referring to the motivation to get up off the couch and do something. If someone is not motivated to do something—anything—for any reason, then that person isn't going to be creative. Someone who lies on the couch all day and doesn't have the motivation to do anything will not be creative. A writer who never translates his or her ideas into words at the keyboard is not going to be a creative writer (or any type of writer).

Finally, environments are important in both the past and present tenses. A person who grows up in a culture or in a family in which creative thoughts or actions are not encouraged (or are even punished) will have a harder time being creative. A person living or working in an environment that is supportive of original thought is more likely to be creative than a person in an environment that discourages such thought. Being creative is a different thing to a woman living in Saudi Arabia or Pakistan as compared with a woman living in England or Portugal. And no matter what the country, a child growing up in an abusive household may have a more difficult time expressing novel ideas than may a child growing up in a nurturing family (although, conversely, such difficult experiences may nurture creativity, as I discuss in Chapter 10).

As with motivation, I mean environment here in a general way. There are also certainly specific environmental influences to be found at other levels of the model, such as a family that invites study or inquiry in one area (e.g., music) but not in another (e.g., engineering), or an environment that contains the tools and materials necessary to encourage one kind of creativity but not another—if you grow up with an abundance of sports equipment but no musical instruments, then your environment is more conducive to athletic creativity than to musical creativity.

General Thematic Areas (Broad Domains)

Once you have decided to go to an amusement park, you must decide what kind of park you wish to visit. Maybe you are in the mood to go to a water park and splash around. Or perhaps you are feeling more daring (or you don't like the way you look in a swimsuit), and you want to enjoy extreme roller coasters or those rides that plunge you into free fall. Maybe you want to see animals or fish, or you want to visit a theme park centered on a cartoon character.

Just as all of these different places fall into a larger category called "amusement parks," so can many different types of creativity fall into larger categories that we called general thematic areas, or broad domains. How many general thematic areas are there? One? Twenty? Two hundred? This broader question has been one that has confounded us since ancient times. In Greek mythology, there are nine muses—goddesses who helped inspire those mortals who would attempt to be creative in the arts or sciences. They were the daughters of Zeus and Mnemosyne (who lives on when we try to remember the order of the planets and use a mnemonic).

Consider the muses and what they represented (D'Aulaire & D'Aulaire, 1992): Calliope (epic poetry), Euterpe (lyric poetry/music), Erato (love poetry), Polymnia (sacred poetry), Clio (history), Melpomene (tragedy), Thalia (comedy/pastoral poetry), Terpsichore (choral song/dance), and Urania (astronomy/astrology). These nine muses could easily be rearranged as nine broad domains. Clearly, our values and conceptions of creativity have changed from the times of Greek mythology—one senses a preponderance of poetry muses. But even all those years ago, the choice of muses showed certain awareness about creativity. If you were creative and looking to be inspired, you might need different stimuli depending on your area of creativity. An alternate interpretation, of course, is that these nine goddesses simply preferred these particular nine areas, and no mortals were brave enough to suggest that they become more creatively diversified. If there's one thing that mythology has taught us, it's that you don't try to argue with an angry goddess (also, if a god with winged heels gives you a shield and sword, he probably wants something from you).

In more modern days, the debate continues. For example, Hirschfeld and Gelman (1994) propose eight domains of mind (cognitive neuroscience, cultural anthropology, biological anthropology, developmental psychology, education, linguistics, philosophy, and psycholinguistics), whereas Feist (2004) proposes seven (art, biology, linguistics, math, music, physics, and psychology).

Gardner (1999), famously, has proposed eight intelligences; although they are usually interpreted as aspects of intellectual ability, they serve just as well as areas of creative achievement (e.g., Gardner, 1993). His eight areas are interpersonal (i.e., dealing with other people), intrapersonal (dealing with yourself, so to speak), spatial, naturalistic, language, logical-mathematical, bodily-kinesthetic (which could be dancing or playing baseball, for example), and musical. Gardner (2006) has also debated adding existential intelligence.

51

Holland's (1959, 1997) theory of vocational choice (or interests) could also serve as a model of general thematic areas. His RIASEC model stands for Realistic, Investigative, Artistic, Social, Enterprising, and Conventional. Holland, Johnston, Hughey, and Asama (1991) hypothesized that the interests most related to creativity would be as follows (in descending order): artistic, investigative, social, enterprising, realistic, and conventional. Indeed, artistic interests have been found to correlate with self-reported creative behaviors (Kelly & Kneipp, 2009) and creative thinking styles (Zhang & Fan, 2007).

Moving beyond interests, academic majors could also serve as a proxy for general thematic areas. The typical divide is between the arts and science, which has been called the two cultures (Snow, 1959). For example, in one study, arts students claimed more creative achievements and had higher self-reported creativity than did science students . . . yet there were no measured differences on actual creativity measures (Furnham, Batey, Booth, Patel, & Lozinskaya, 2011). In a second study by Furnham et al. (2011), they separated science into natural sciences and social sciences, to come up with the same basic results—arts students thought they were more creative, but there was no evidence to back up these beliefs. J. C. Kaufman, Pumaccahua, and Holt (2013) looked at a wide spectrum of majors and found that both arts and science majors rated themselves higher on creativity than did other majors (i.e., criminal justice and health sciences), but only the science majors scored higher on measured creativity. Conversely, Silvia et al. (2008) compared arts majors and "conventional" majors (i.e., not the arts) and found that arts majors scored higher on measured creativity.

Within creativity research, many studies have categorized creative domains. Sometimes these may seem a little repetitive or confusing; if you're having trouble figuring out what's what amid all of the domain structures, it's okay to skim for a few pages.

One key work is that of Carson, Peterson, and Higgins (2005), who devised the Creativity Achievement Questionnaire (CAQ) to assess 10 domains. They broke the domains down into two larger factors: the Arts (Drama, Writing, Humor, Music, Visual Arts, and Dance) and Science (Invention, Science, and Culinary). The tenth domain, Architecture, did not load on a factor.

In another investigation, Ivcevic and Mayer (2009) used open-ended questionnaires and group discussions to devise a large set of behavioral items and found three main factors. The first one was called the creative lifestyle and consisted of crafts, self-expressive creativity, interpersonal creativity, sophisticated media use, visual arts, and writing; creative lifestyle thus describes everyday creativity, and it involves areas laypeople associate with creativity (e.g., arts and crafts, writing), as well as intellectual and artistic interests (e.g., sophisticated media use). The second factor was dubbed performance arts, and encompassed music, theater, and dance. The third factor, intellectual creativity, consisted of creativity in technology, science, and academic pursuits. In a separate paper, Ivcevic and Mayer (2006) used these same creative activities scales to derive five "types": Conventional, Everyday Creative Individuals, Artists, Scholars, and Renaissance Individuals.

In the first of many studies on this topic, J. C. Kaufman and Baer (2004) asked novices to rate their creativity in nine areas: science, interpersonal relationships, writing, art, interpersonal communication, solving personal problems, mathematics, crafts, and bodily/physical movement. They next did a factor analysis of their responses (for people who don't know, a factor analysis is a spiffy way of interpreting many different variables and condensing them into fewer variables; I could go into more detail, but I prefer the Sidney Harris cartoon that uses the explanation of "and then a miracle happens").

They found three factors from these nine domains: Creativity in Empathy/Communication (creativity in the areas of interpersonal relationships, communication, solving personal problems, and writing), "Hands-On" Creativity (art, crafts, and bodily/physical creativity), and Math/Science Creativity (creativity in math or science). Interestingly, these are pretty close to three factors found in the area of student motivation—writing, art, and problem solving (Ruscio, Whitney, & Amabile, 1998). Rawlings and Locarnini (2007) replicated the factor structure, and found that professional artists scored higher on the "Hands-On" factor and professional scientists scored higher on the Math/Science factor. Silvia, Nusbaum, Berg, Martin, and O'Conner (2009) found that being open to new experiences was related to all factors except Math/Science; in addition, Math/Science and Empathy/Communication were negatively related to neuroticism. Empathy/Communication was also positively correlated with being conscientious. Similarly, Silvia and Kimbrel (2010) found that people high in Empathy/Communication were lower in social anxiety. Silvia and Nusbaum (2012) found that arts majors were more likely than nonarts majors to rate themselves low on the Math/Science factor and high on the "Hands-On" factor. A study of Turkish undergraduates found a mostly similar factor structure (Oral, Kaufman, & Agars, 2007).

J. C. Kaufman and colleagues (J. C. Kaufman, 2006; J. C. Kaufman, Cole, & Baer, 2009) expanded on this work and collected over 3,500 self-ratings across 56 domains. J. C. Kaufman, Cole, et al. (2009) found seven factors, which they dubbed Artistic-Verbal, Artistic-Visual, Entrepreneur, Interpersonal, Math/Science, Performance, and Problem-Solving. These seven factors were found as second-order factors. In other words, there was a larger, general creativity factor (c, perhaps analogous to g), but the subfactors best explained the data.

Some domains were strongly related to the larger c factor, such as Performance and Artistic/Visual, whereas others (such as Math/Science) were less related. One possible reason is that mathematics and science may not fall into people's conceptions of creativity (J. C. Kaufman & Baer, 2004). The average person may not consider such areas as math or science as representing their mental images of what it means to be creative. This idea is consistent with Paulos's (1988) idea of innumeracy, the inability to accurately use numbers and chance. "Romantic misconceptions about the nature of mathematics," Paulos wrote, "lead to an intellectual environment hospitable to and even encouraging of poor mathematical education and psychological distaste for the subject and lie at the base of much innumeracy" (1988, p. 120). Perhaps we should not be surprised to find that a society that does not value mathematical ability also does not associate creativity with mathematics.

It would be interesting to see if this same pattern was found in Asian populations; although Western perceptions of creativity typically revolve around the arts (e.g., Sternberg, 1985), studies of Eastern perceptions do not show this same connection (Rudowicz & Yue, 2000; Yue & Rudowicz, 2002). Similarly, the idea of humor being related to creativity (especially interpersonal creativity) is found in Western cultures (Sternberg, 1985) but less so in the East (Rudowicz & Hui, 1997; although see Tang, Baer, & Kaufman, 2015). Tan and Qu (2012) used the same 56 domains with Malaysian undergraduates and found only five factors; the two Artistic components were combined together, and Entrepreneur was spread across other factors. A shorter, revised questionnaire was then created with 21 items and found to have four factors: (a) Math/Science (algebra, chemistry, computer science, biology, logic, mechanical), (b) Drama (acting, literature, blogging, singing, dancing, writing), (c) Interaction (leadership, money, playing with children, selling, problem solving, teaching), and (d) Visual Arts (crafts, decorating, painting) (J. C. Kaufman, Waterstreet, et al., 2009; Silvia, Wigert, Reiter-Palmon, & Kaufman, 2012). This shorter version was then tested on a Chinese sample (Werner, Tang, Kruse, Kaufman, & Spörrle, 2014). Three of the four factors held (Math/Science, Visual Arts, and Interaction), with Drama being split into Verbal Arts and Performance Arts.

J. C. Kaufman (2012) did yet another darn study on this topic to develop yet another iteration of the instrument, settling on the Kaufman Domains of Creativity Scale (K-DOCS), which resulted in five dimensions: Everyday, Scholarly, Performance, Math/Science, and Artistic creativity. These mirror Kerr and McKay's (2013; see also Kerr & Vuyk, 2013) five creative profiles of gifted adolescents: verbal/linguistic creativity, mathematical/scientific inventiveness, interpersonal/emotional creativity, musical and dance creativity, and spatial/visual creativity.

It is also important to note that factor analysis is not the only approach to winnow down the number of general thematic areas. Silvia, Kaufman, and Pretz (2009) applied latent class analysis to large samples of both creative accomplishments and creative self-ratings (if factor analysis intimidates you, then latent class analysis will follow you home and beat you up). In essence, latent class analysis determines whether you can divide up a group of people into subgroups or types. When Silvia et al. analyzed people's reports of creative accomplishments, they found one big subgroup of people who did not list any notable creative achievements. There were smaller subgroups that indicated specific creative proficiency in visual and performing arts.

Regardless of what the general thematic areas actually are, what do they mean for the APT model? Let's assume that you have enough brains and motivation and are in a suitable environment—the general thematic areas are the next step. Regardless of the number of general thematic areas of creativity, each of them requires different skills and traits. For example, there might be a certain profile of abilities and preferences that you might associate with someone interested in the performance general thematic area. Some might be abilities (such as a sense of pitch), and some might be more related to personality (probably more extraverted, because it's hard to perform with stage fright). Someone more inclined to be creative in the mathematical/ scientific general thematic area might have a completely different profile. For example, Jeon, Moon, and French (2011) examined artistic and mathematical creativity. Domain-related knowledge was more predictive of higher creativity in math than in art, whereas higher divergent thinking scores were more predictive of higher creativity in art than in math. Another study had both experts and novices in two areas (visual art and computer programming) solve problems within their domains and talk out loud about their thought processes. Visual artists used more emotion-related words than did computer programmers, regardless of expertise status (Kozbelt, Dexter, Dolese, Meredith, & Ostrofsky, 2014).

Park, Lubinski, and Benbow (2007) conducted an interesting study that examined intellectual patterns of ability and eventual creativity in different domains. Using math and verbal SAT scores given to people at age 13, they then tracked these same people's accomplishments 25 years later. Unsurprisingly, early prowess was associated with eventual success. However, a person's specific strengths (in this case, math vs. verbal) predicted patents (math) and literary publications (verbal). Although the authors offered this study as evidence of a link between IQ and creativity (which it certainly provides), I also see evidence of the separation of different creativity domains. It would be fascinating to see how a more diverse battery of tests might predict even more specific creative works (such as our seven general thematic areas). Similarly, Wai, Lubinski, and Benbow (2005) found in the same population that math and verbal SAT scores predicted success by occupation—math SAT scores predicted success in science-related fields, and verbal SAT scores predicted success in humanities-related fields. A recent study by S. B. Kaufman et al. (2015) did find cognitive differences by domain; general cognitive ability was a stronger predictor of creative achievement in the sciences than in the arts.

There are similar results with personality and creativity across general thematic areas; I discuss these later when I talk about personality. But let's get back to the Amusement Park Theory.

APT: Domains

We've now spent considerable time discussing how many general thematic areas exist, but this question is only one piece of the puzzle. Indeed, once you have decided on a type of amusement park to visit, there are still many more decisions left. Even within one genre, there are many different parks to choose from. If you want roller coasters, do you choose Six Flags or Disneyland? If you've decided on an animal theme, do you pick the San Diego Zoo, Sea World, or the Wild Animal Park?

Similarly, within each of the general thematic areas are several more narrowly defined creativity domains. For example, the painting/crafts general thematic area might include drawing, painting, woodworking, pottery, sewing, scrapbooking, making collages, and many other things. And each of these domains may have a unique profile of related strengths and weaknesses.

Let's compare, for example, a creative poet and a creative journalist. Both would fall in the general thematic area of verbal creativity or language or scholarship. Indeed, there will likely be many similarities between the two writers. Both will have good vocabularies and a love (or at least tolerance) of the written word. Despite their similarities, creative writers and journalists have different goals. Boswell (1989) argued that "the beat journalist's ultimate goal isn't a dramatic or poetic effect, much as any writer lusts after such moments of luck . . . 'That's right' is what we're after, more than 'That's beautiful'" (p. xii).

Journalists and creative writers work often under radically different conditions and with varying expectations—a top-notch journalist may have to crack out a piece in 10 minutes to make a deadline, whereas an equally respected novelist may be allowed 10 years to perfect a book. Creative writers such as novelists, poets, and, to a lesser extent, playwrights may be introverted or avoid social encounters; their success or failure depends on a product that may be created with little outside input. Journalists, in contrast, must thrive on such interactions, as much of their work typically involves gathering information and opinions from other people.

Indeed, journalists and poets show many individual differences. For example, journalists and other nonfiction writers outlive poets by approximately 6 years, although this is only at the most eminent level (J. C. Kaufman, 2003). Many other differences are less readily apparent—journalists, for example, have been found to have different thinking styles than poets (J. C. Kaufman, 2002a, 2002b).

If motivation is important as a general construct at the level of initial requirements, the type of motivation is more important at the level of domain. Perhaps the poet does his or her most creative writing when motivated by a desire to create a beautiful poem, whereas the journalist may put forward his or her best and most creative work under a deadline (or perhaps when angling for a front-page story). One's motivation to write may be quite strong for one kind of writing but at the same time weak for another.

Knowledge plays a large role at the domain level. Let's explore domains in the sciences. Chemistry and physics and biology and geology may all fall under the same area and may all involve a certain type of analytic and precise thought. However, the knowledge bases for these four natural science subjects are strikingly different, with only modest overlap, as are the knowledge bases that are foundational for work in the social sciences, such as the differences between psychology and political science.

Some personality traits may also be particularly useful in some domains, which I discuss in the chapter on personality (Chapter 5). Environment and opportunity are also components here. As an example, some creative acts require a particular kind of nurturing background. A child who wants to play the violin (or take up horseback riding) may be out of luck if his or her family cannot afford lessons. If that child's sibling has an interest in poetry—which requires less of a financial investment to get started—then poverty may be less of an obstacle for him or her. And if one is working for Exxon, the working environment may be more conducive to creativity in the domain of geology than in the domain of pure math.

APT: Microdomains

Imagine that you have gone to a zoo, such as the world-famous Wild Animal Park. All the activities at the Wild Animal Park involve animals, but they still vary greatly. Maybe you want to spend time feeding leaves to long-necked giraffes. Maybe you want to look at the lions stretching and majestically sunning themselves. Or else you might not feel like walking around, so you take the WGASA monorail and see the animal preserve from the comfort of a slow-moving train.

Similarly, there are many commonalities among all the tasks that are part of a domain. Yet there are still big differences in what one needs to know, and what one needs to know how to do, in order to be creative when undertaking different tasks in that domain. It's rather like the transition from undergraduate to graduate education. As an example, everyone in a graduate program in psychology may be preparing for a career as a psychologist, but future clinical psychologists, social psychologists, and cognitive psychologists likely take few of the same courses. Similarly, studying fruit flies intensively for 5 years may help one develop creative theories in one of biology's microdomains but be of little use in another, and practicing on a 12-string guitar may help one perform creatively in some microdomains of the music world but not others.

The nature of what creativity is can vary by microdomains under the same domain. Keinänen, Sheridan, and Gardner (2016; Keinänen & Gardner, 2004) argue for the twin concepts of axis and focus, two ways of looking at creativity in its many forms. Axis consists of vertical and horizontal orientations, which focus on the constraints in the task. Vertical orientations have restrictive constraints; think about being creative in programming computer code or singing an opera aria. There are specific ways of how something is done, and the creativity comes in the slight variations. Horizontal orientations have few constraints; think of a slapstick comedian or an abstract painter. When I cook, I cook in a particularly horizontal way. Granted, I'm using the word "cooking" quite loosely (it mostly consists of making instant mashed potatoes, much to my wife's dismay). But I toss in everything—meat powder seasoning, sliced almonds, cinnamon, grated cheese, hot sauce, and so on (often in the same dish). In contrast, really good sushi is made in a vertical way. There are specific rules for how sushi is made and presented, and the creativity in cooking comes from how the chef can work within those rules.

Focus has modular tasks and broad situations. Modular tasks are specialized (think mechanical engineering), whereas broad situations are more general (think advertising). Three of my favorite courses that I taught at my former university, the California State University at San Bernardino, were Critical Thinking, Psychology and the Movies, and Intelligence and Creativity. Critical thinking is a broad topic—the course ended up covering whatever I wanted it to, so I ended up minimizing topics like Venn diagrams and maximizing topics like what you should do if you need help in the middle of a crowded street. Psychology and the Movies was a more modular class. The topics ranged quite a bit, but they all had something to do with movies, and they all began with me screening a movie. The topics might vary from "how people with mental illness are portrayed" to "examples of creativity in film," but the class dealt with movies in some way. Intelligence and Creativity was even more modular. The class covered (not surprisingly) intelligence and creativity. What I talked about was limited to (also not surprisingly) intelligence and creativity.

Keinänen et al. (2016) use the examples of dance and law, and I'll paraphrase their law example. A small-town lawyer is an example of a vertical axis and a broad focus. Most of the law that goes on in a small town is typically pretty traditional—most small-town lawyers will not rewrite the law books, making it in the vertical axis. Yet the focus is broad; a lawyer who only specializes in hostile corporate takeovers, for example, would not survive long in this situation. A good small-town lawyer will be able to do many different things. Trust and estate law is also vertical (again, there are many specific restraints in place for how things can be done), yet with a modular focus (i.e., specialized). Mergers and acquisitions law, meanwhile, shares a modular focus with trust and estate law, but has a horizontal axis. There are much fewer constraints on what a mergers and acquisitions lawyer can do, and something new and different is more likely to be rewarded. Also in the horizontal axis but with a broad focus is cyberspace law—something that is almost completely new (hence, horizontal) but spread across many different areas, from copyright infringement to slander (hence, broad).

APT: Strange Bedfellows

No theory can explain everything, and there are still a lot of weird connections that go on. On one hand, the nested hierarchy of microdomains grouped within domains grouped within general thematic areas feels nice and tidy. On the other hand, there are all sorts of things that are left unexplained. Just as there are important similarities among the differently themed roller coasters located in different theme parks, there may occasionally be connections among domains and microdomains in different general thematic areas that will surprise us. In studies with elementary and middle school children, for example, Baer (1993) found relatively small and generally statistically nonsignificant correlations among the creativity ratings given to different kinds of creative products (including poems, collages, mathematical word problems, equations, and stories), but there was a surprisingly consistent (but as yet unexplained) correlation between creativity in writing poetry and creativity in producing interesting mathematical word problems. These two tasks would seem to be comparatively unrelated—they come from different general thematic areas—yet there has to be some kind of link somewhere.

In addition, there will also always be strange bedfellows that make sense only upon closer examination. Someone may decide to pick an amusement park based only on how good the popcorn is at the food court. Someone else may only go to cheap amusement parks (Big Dave's Generic Roadside Attraction). In a similar way, microdomains or domains may be selected for reasons that are less obvious. Jane may be a multitalented renaissance woman, but she may be motivated to do things that will impress Cassandra—and only do things that will impress Cassandra. So Jane may learn how to be a creative chef and cook her delicious meals, and she may become a creative poet and deliver sonnets about Cassandra's beauty, and she may become a creative animal trainer and teach a flock of seagulls to spell out "Cassandra" in the sky, and she may become a creative web programmer and build a great website at www.Cassandrawillyoupleasegowithmethanksabunc hbyeJane.com. Yet if you only looked at the microdomains that Jane pursued, the resulting data would look like gobbledygook (unless, of course, Cassandra had a whole host of similarly single-minded suitors).

LOOKING AHEAD

The APT Model is not the only or best such model that integrates domain-specific and domain-general perspectives (remember the hybrid model discussed earlier; Plucker & Beghetto, 2004). More recently, domains in creativity have been explored as part of the individual-versus-environment perspective (Glăveanu et al., 2013). The question of creative domains needs to be addressed, however, in any major conceptualization or assessment. As we will see when we explore the question of creativity measurement, older assessments tend to assume that creativity is domain general. There is a preponderance of evidence for some amount of domain specificity in creativity. Few researchers, even those who may lean toward the general side of the spectrum, would agree with the domain-general leanings of divergent thinking tests. I believe that these tests' reliance on this singular concept is one reason that other creativity assessments (such as the Consensual Assessment Technique, as I will discuss) have continued to gain favor.

REFERENCES

Baer, J. (1991). Generality of creativity across performance domains. *Creativity Research Journal, 4*, 23–39.

Baer, J. (1993). *Creativity and divergent thinking: A task-specific approach.* Hillsdale, NJ: Erlbaum.

Baer, J. (1994). Divergent thinking is not a general trait: A multi-domain training experiment. *Creativity Research Journal, 7*, 35–46.

Baer, J. (1998). The case for domain specificity in creativity. *Creativity Research Journal, 11*, 173–177.

Baer, J. (2015). *Domain specificity of creativity.* San Diego, CA: Academic Press.

Baer, J., & Kaufman, J. C. (2005). Bridging generality and specificity: The Amusement Park Theoretical (APT) model of creativity. *Roeper Review, 27*, 158–163.

Boswell, T. (1989). *The heart of the order.* New York, NY: Doubleday.

Carson, S. H., Peterson, J. B., & Higgins, D. M. (2005). Reliability, validity and factor structure of the Creative Achievement Questionnaire. *Creativity Research Journal, 17*, 37–50.

D'Aulaire, I., & D'Aulaire, E. P. (1992). *D'Aulaires book of Greek myths* (reprint ed.). New York, NY: Delacorte.

Feagans, L., & Short, E. J. (1986). Referential communication and reading performance in learning disabled children over a 3-year period. *Developmental Psychology, 22*, 177–183.

Feist, G. J. (2004). The evolved fluid specificity of human creative talent. In R. J. Sternberg, E. L. Grigorenko, & J. L. Singer (Eds.), *Creativity: From potential to realization* (pp. 57–82). Washington, DC: American Psychological Association.

Furnham, A., Batey, M., Booth, T. W., Patel, V., & Lozinskaya, D. (2011). Individual difference predictors of creativity in art and science students. *Thinking Skills and Creativity, 6*, 114–121.

Gardner, H. (1993). *Creating minds.* New York, NY: Basic Books.

Gardner, H. (1999). *Intelligence reframed: Multiple intelligences for the 21st century.* New York, NY: Basic Books.

Gardner, H. (2006). *Five minds for the future.* Cambridge, MA: Harvard Business School Press.

Glăveanu, V., Lubart, T., Bonnardel, N., Botella, M., de Biaisi, P. M., Desainte-Catherine, M., . . . Zenasni, F. (2013). Creativity as action: Findings from five creative domains. *Frontiers in Psychology, 4,* 176.

Gottfried, M. (1990). *All his jazz.* New York, NY: Bantam.

Hirschfeld, L. A., & Gelman, S. A. (1994). *Mapping the mind: Domain specificity in cognition and culture.* New York, NY: Cambridge University Press.

Hocevar, D. (1976). Dimensionality of creativity. *Psychological Reports, 39,* 869–870.

Holland, J. L. (1959). A theory of vocational choice. *Journal of Counseling Psychology, 6,* 35–45.

Holland, J. L. (1997). *Making vocational choices: A theory of vocational personalities and work environments* (3rd ed.). Odessa, FL: Psychological Assessment Resources.

Holland, J. L., Johnston, J. A., Hughey, K. F., & Asama, N. F. (1991). Some explorations of a theory of careers: VII. A replication and some possible extensions. *Journal of Career Development, 18,* 91–100.

Ivcevic, Z., & Mayer, J. D. (2006). Creative types and personality. *Imagination, Cognition, and Personality, 26,* 65–86.

Ivcevic, Z., & Mayer, J. D. (2009). Mapping dimensions of creativity in the life-space. *Creativity Research Journal, 21,* 152–165.

Jeon, K. N., Moon, S. M., & French, B. (2011). Differential effects of divergent thinking, domain knowledge, and interest on creative performance in art and math. *Creativity Research Journal, 23,* 60–71.

Kaufman, J. C. (2002a). Dissecting the golden goose: Components of studying creative writers. *Creativity Research Journal, 14,* 27–40.

Kaufman, J. C. (2002b). Narrative and paradigmatic thinking styles in creative writing and journalism students. *Journal of Creative Behavior, 36,* 201–220.

Kaufman, J. C. (2003). The cost of the muse: Poets die young. *Death Studies, 27,* 813–822.

Kaufman, J. C. (2006). Self-reported differences in creativity by gender and ethnicity. *Journal of Applied Cognitive Psychology, 20,* 1065–1082.

Kaufman, J. C. (2012). Counting the muses: Development of the Kaufman Domains of Creativity Scale (K-DOCS). *Psychology of Aesthetics, Creativity, and the Arts, 6,* 298–308.

Kaufman, J. C., & Baer, J. (2004). Sure, I'm creative—but not in mathematics!: Self reported creativity in diverse domains. *Empirical Studies of the Arts, 22,* 143–155.

Kaufman, J. C., & Baer, J. (2005). The Amusement Park Theory of creativity. In J. C. Kaufman & J. Baer (Eds.), *Creativity across domains* (pp. 321–328). Mahwah, NJ: Erlbaum.

Kaufman, J. C., & Baer, J. (2006). Intelligent testing with Torrance. *Creativity Research Journal, 18,* 99–102.

Kaufman, J. C., Cole, J. C., & Baer, J. (2009). The construct of creativity: A structural model for self-reported creativity ratings. *Journal of Creative Behavior, 43,* 119–134.

Kaufman, J. C., Pumaccahua, T. T., & Holt, R. E. (2013). Personality and creativity in realistic, investigative, artistic, social, and enterprising college majors. *Personality and Individual Differences, 54,* 913–917.

Kaufman, J. C., Waterstreet, M. A., Ailabouni, H. S., Whitcomb, H. J., Roe, A. K., & Riggs, M. (2009). Personality and self-perceptions of creativity across domains. *Imagination, Cognition, and Personality, 29,* 193–209.

Kaufman, S. B., Quilty, L.C., Grazioplene, R. G., Hirsh, J. B., Gray, J. R., Peterson, J. B., & DeYoung, C. G. (2015). Openness to experience and intellect differentially predict creative achievement in the arts and sciences. *Journal of Personality.* Advance online publication. doi:10.1111/jopy.12156

Keinänen, M., & Gardner, H. (2004). Vertical and horizontal mentoring for creativity. In R. J. Sternberg, E. L. Grigorenko, & J. L. Singer (Eds.), *Creativity: From potential to realization* (pp. 169–193). Washington, DC: American Psychological Association.

Keinänen, M., Sheridan, K., & Gardner, H. (2016). Opening up creativity: The lenses of axis and focus. In J. C. Kaufman & J. Baer (Eds.), *Creativity and reason in cognitive development* (2nd ed., pp. 261–281). New York, NY: Cambridge University Press.

Kelly, K. E., & Kneipp, L. B. (2009). You do what you are: The relationship between the Scale of Creative Attributes and Behavior and vocational interests. *Journal of Instructional Psychology, 36,* 79–83.

Kerr, B., & McKay, R. (2013). Searching for tomorrow's innovators: Profiling creative adolescents. *Creativity Research Journal, 25,* 21–32.

Kerr, B., & Vuyk, M. A. (2013). Career development for creatively gifted students: What parents, teachers, and counselors need to know. In K. H. Kim, J. C. Kaufman, J. Baer, & B. Sriraman (Eds.), *Creatively gifted students are not like other gifted students: Research, theory, and practice* (pp. 137–151). Rotterdam, Netherlands: Sense Publishers.

Kozbelt, A., Dexter, S., Dolese, M., Meredith, D., & Ostrofsky, J. (2014). Regressive imagery in creative problem solving: Comparing verbal protocols of expert and novice visual artists and computer programmers. *Journal of Creative Behavior.* Advance online publication. doi:10.1002/jocb.64

May, B., Moore, P., & Lintott, C. (2008, April 10). *Bang!: The complete history of the universe.* Baltimore, MD: Johns Hopkins University Press.

Moran, J. D., Sawyers, J. K., Fu, V. R., & Milgram, R. M. (1984). Predicting imaginative play in preschool children. *Gifted Child Quarterly, 28,* 92–94.

Oral, G., Kaufman, J. C., & Agars, M. D. (2007). Examining creativity in Turkey: Do Western findings apply? *High Ability Studies, 18*, 235–246.

Park, G., Lubinski, D., & Benbow, C. P. (2007). Contrasting intellectual patterns predict creativity in the arts and sciences: Tracking intellectually precocious youth over 25 years. *Psychological Science, 18*, 948–952.

Paulos, J. A. (1988). *Innumeracy.* New York, NY: Vintage.

Piirto, J. (1998). *Understanding those who create* (2nd ed.). Scottsdale, AZ: Gifted Psychology Press.

Plucker, J. A. (1998). Beware of simple conclusions: The case for the content generality of creativity. *Creativity Research Journal, 11*, 179–182.

Plucker, J. A. (1999). Reanalyses of student responses to creativity checklists: Evidence of content generality. *Journal of Creative Behavior, 33*, 126–137.

Plucker, J. A. (2004). Generalization of creativity across domains: Examination of the method effect hypothesis. *Journal of Creative Behavior, 38*, 1–12.

Plucker, J. A., & Beghetto, R. A. (2004). Why creativity is domain general, why it looks domain specific, and why the distinction does not matter. In R. J. Sternberg, E. L. Grigorenko, & J. L. Singer (Eds.), *Creativity: From potential to realization* (pp. 153–168). Washington, DC: American Psychological Association.

Plucker, J. A., & Makel, M. C. (2010). Assessment of creativity. In J. C. Kaufman & R. J. Sternberg (Eds.), *The Cambridge handbook of creativity* (pp. 48–73). New York, NY: Cambridge University Press.

Plucker, J. A., & Renzulli, J. S. (1999). Psychometric approaches to the study of human creativity. In R. J. Sternberg (Ed.), *Handbook of creativity* (pp. 35–61). New York, NY: Cambridge University Press.

Powell, A. (2001). Warm, fuzzy, weird, funny: The Museum(s) of Natural History spin some tall tales. *Harvard Gazette.* Retrieved from http://www .hno.harvard.edu/gazette/2001/07.19/14-talltales.html

Rawlings, D., & Locarnini, A. (2007). Dimensional schizotypy, autism, and unusual word associations in artists and scientists. *Journal of Research in Personality, 42*, 465–471.

Rudowicz, E. & Hui, A. (1997). The creative personality: Hong Kong perspective. *Journal of Social Behavior & Personality, 12*, 139–157.

Rudowicz, E., & Yue, X. (2000). Concepts of creativity: Similarities and differences among Mainland, Hong Kong and Taiwanese Chinese. *Journal of Creative Behavior, 34*, 175–192.

Ruscio, J., Whitney, D. M., & Amabile, T. M. (1998). Looking inside the fishbowl of creativity: Verbal and behavioral predictors of creative performance. *Creativity Research Journal, 11*, 243–263.

Silvia, P. J., Kaufman, J. C., & Pretz, J. E. (2009). Is creativity domain-specific? Latent class models of creative accomplishments and creative self-descriptions. *Psychology of Aesthetics, Creativity, and the Arts, 3*, 139–148.

Silvia, P. J., & Kimbrel, N. A. (2010). A dimensional analysis of creativity and mental illness: Do anxiety and depression symptoms predict creative cognition, creative accomplishments, and creative self-concepts? *Psychology of Aesthetics, Creativity, and the Arts, 4*, 2–10.

Silvia, P. J., & Nusbaum, E. C. (2012). What's your major? College majors as markers of creativity. *International Journal of Creativity & Problem Solving, 22*, 31–44.

Silvia, P. J., Nusbaum, E. C., Berg, C., Martin, C., & O'Connor, A. (2009). Openness to experience, plasticity, and creativity: Exploring lower-order, higher-order, and interactive effects. *Journal of Research in Personality, 43*, 1087–1090.

Silvia, P. J., Wigert, B., Reiter-Palmon, R., & Kaufman, J. C. (2012). Assessing creativity with self-report scales: A review and empirical evaluation. *Psychology of Aesthetics, Creativity, and the Arts, 6*, 19–34.

Silvia, P. J., Winterstein, B. P., Willse, J. T., Barona, C. M., Cram, J. T., Hess, K. I., . . . Richard, C. A. (2008). Assessing creativity with divergent thinking tasks: Exploring the reliability and validity of new subjective scoring methods. *Psychology of Aesthetics, Creativity, and the Arts, 2*, 68–85.

Snow, C. P. (1959). *The two cultures.* New York, NY: Cambridge University Press.

Sternberg, R. J. (1985). Implicit theories of intelligence, creativity, and wisdom. *Journal of Personality and Social Psychology, 49*, 607–627.

Sternberg, R. J., Grigorenko, E. L., & Singer, J. L. (2004). *Creativity: From potential to realization.* Washington, DC: American Psychological Association.

Tan, C. S., & Qu, L. (2012). Generality and specificity: Malaysian undergraduate students' self-reported creativity. *International Journal of Creativity & Problem Solving, 22*, 19–30.

Tang, C., Baer, J., & Kaufman, J. C. (2015). Implicit theories of creativity in computer science in the United States and China. *Journal of Creative Behavior, 49*, 137–156.

Wai, J., Lubinski, D., & Benbow, C. P. (2005). Creativity and occupational accomplishments among intellectually precocious youth: An age 13 to age 33 longitudinal study. *Journal of Educational Psychology, 97*, 484–492.

Werner, C. H., Tang, M., Kruse, J., Kaufman, J. C., & Spörrle, M. (2014). The Chinese version of the Revised Creativity Domain Questionnaire (CDQ-R): First evidence for its factorial validity and systematic association with the Big Five. *Journal of Creative Behavior, 48*, 254–275.

Yue, X. D., & Rudowicz, E. (2002). Perception of the most creative Chinese by undergraduates in Beijing, Guangzhou, Hong Kong, and Taipei. *Journal of Creative Behavior, 36*, 88–104.

Zhang, L. F., & Fan, W. (2007). Do modes of thinking predict career interest types among Chinese university students? *Thinking Skills and Creativity, 2*, 118–127.

Measures of Creativity

"As we all know, true creativity comes from simple formulas and the memorization of data." (Hoffman & Rudoren, 2007, front matter)

Many people have a gut reaction about studying and measuring creativity; one of my favorites is from Sherry Lansing, a one-time CEO of Paramount Pictures and a University of California regent. "You can evaluate grammar, punctuation, and spelling, but not creativity," she told the *Chronicle of Higher Education* (Hoover, 2002). "How would *Ulysses* be graded on the SAT? How would Faulkner have been graded?"

The thought of grading a future Faulkner (or Mozart or Picasso) does indeed sound absurd. Of course, the idea of "grading" a future Einstein or Bill Gates is a little absurd, too, yet we still have an awful lot of science and math questions on the SATs, GREs, and AP tests that aim to do this Herculean task.

So how do we measure creativity? I briefly mentioned divergent thinking in the last chapter. Now we're going to dive in, because after more than 60 years, divergent thinking tests are still the most common way that creativity is measured (Callahan, Hunsaker, Adams, Moore, & Bland, 1995; J. C. Kaufman, Plucker, & Baer, 2008).

TORRANCE TESTS OF CREATIVE THINKING AND OTHER DIVERGENT THINKING TESTS

Guilford (1950, 1967) derived the core ideas behind divergent thinking as well as many popular measures. Getzels and Jackson (1962) and Wallach and Kogan (1965) were other early pioneers of such measures; their contributions are essential but often overlooked. There was one key pioneer behind divergent thinking assessment, however, who put all of the pieces into place and advocated for creativity his entire life. I am speaking of E. Paul Torrance, author of the Torrance Tests of Creative Thinking (TTCT; Torrance, 1974, 2008). If Guilford kick-started the field of creativity and its scientific study, then Torrance served as its beloved international champion. Beyond simply being translated into other languages and adopted for other cultures, the Torrance approach is a driving force in how creativity is conceived around the world (e.g., J. C. Kaufman & Sternberg, 2006).

So what is a divergent thinking test like? Well, if you're in the mood for playing along at home, take out a pen and some scrap paper and give yourself 3 minutes to answer this question: *What would happen if we didn't need sleep?*

It's either been 3 minutes or you didn't feel inspired. Before we look at what you wrote (or thought), let's explore the basic structure of the TTCT; then we will discuss how Guilford conceptualized divergent production and its influence on how the tests are scored today.

The current TTCT (Torrance, 2008) are divided into two separate tests, Figural and Verbal.

The Figural test includes three subtests:

- *Picture Construction*: Given a basic shape, you are asked to expand on it to create a picture.

- *Picture Completion*: You are asked to finish and title incomplete drawings.
- *Lines/Circles*: You are asked to modify many different series of lines or circles into different objects or shapes.

The Verbal test of the TTCT has six subtests. The first three are considered part of Ask-and-Guess:

- *Ask-and-Guess*: Each of the following three subtests begins when you are shown an ambiguous picture.
  - *Asking*: You ask as many questions as you can about the picture.
  - *Guessing Causes*: You list as many possible causes as you can for the pictured action.
  - *Guessing Consequences*: You list as many possible consequences as you can for the pictured action.
- *Product Improvement*: You are asked to make changes to improve a toy.
- *Unusual Uses*: Given a typical, ordinary item (a box or a pen), you are asked to think of as many different possible uses for it as you can.
- *Just Suppose*: As in the earlier question about sleep, you are asked to "just suppose" about an unlikely hypothetical situation and list as many ramifications as possible.

Although they are considered two tests that form a larger battery, the Figural and Verbal tests barely correlate ($r = .06$; Cramond, Matthews-Morgan, Bandalos, & Zuo, 2005). People often treat them as if they are interchangeable, but they're not. Most studies just use one of the tests, not both, yet if they had used the other part of the battery, the results would likely be different. Kim's (2011b) study of creativity declining, which grabbed a *Newsweek* cover before it was published, only looked at Figural, not Verbal. A subsequent study concluded that the specific domain of creativity that is studied determines whether increased or decreased creativity is found over time (Weinstein, Clark, DiBartlomomeo, & Davis, 2014), with some aspects of written creativity showing decline and some aspects of visual artistic creativity showing improvement. The issues of domain and measurement are reasons why I hesitate to overinterpret Kim's finding quite yet.

DIVERGENT THINKING SCORING

How are these measures scored? Some of the answer lies in Guilford's (1950, 1967) original conception of divergent thinking. Although he had many different ideas about it (which makes sense, given that having many different ideas is a sign of divergent thinking), much of Guilford's work can be boiled down to four key components. The first one, fluency, is derived by counting all of your ideas. Think about your response to the question about not needing sleep. Did you come up with five possible results? Ten? Fifteen? I can't translate your number into a creativity score, but with the correct (and copyrighted) tables, you would be assigned a score.

Let's examine just what a fluency score does and does not represent. If I asked you another standard type of divergent thinking question (from the Unusual Uses category), I might ask you to name uses for a brick. Maybe you'd mention that you could use it as a weapon, to build a house, as a paperweight, as a doorstop, as a kitchen tool, or as a parking brake. One singer-songwriter, Bill Berry, wrote a whole song called "The Brick," in which he rattles off the many possible things you can do with a brick (Schock, 1998). Your fluency score would simply be how many different things you named, as long as they are relevant to the question (so if you said "Kentucky smells like mayonnaise," you would not get credit). However, if you say that you would use a brick to build an apartment, a condominium, a house, a shack, a wall, a fence—they all would count. It is important to note that an answer must be reasonable.

In the original version of *Creativity 101*, I said that saying you'd use a brick to fly to Spain would count for your fluency score. But, in fact, that's not true. As my colleague Bonnie Cramond has explained, it would only count if the respondent could give a reasonable way that you could use a brick to fly to Spain (her examples include threatening the pilot with a brick or selling bricks to purchase a ticket, which are both brilliant).

Flexibility looks at how many different types of ideas you have according to the number of categories in which they could be classified. Let's go back to not needing sleep. Maybe you said that people wouldn't need pajamas. That would count for both fluency and flexibility. But let's say that you also said that people wouldn't need pillows, bed sheets, mattresses, or blankets. All of these answers work just fine for fluency. Yet they all represent the same category, not needing sleep-related objects. You would only get credit for one category for flexibility. Although flexibility is still included in the Verbal subtests, it is no longer scored for the Figural subtests.

Originality is being able to produce the most unusual ideas. You might have said, for example, that if people didn't need sleep, then they would have less physical intimacy (i.e., sex). It's a perfectly good response, and usually gets a good laugh from people, but it's also one that many people might suggest (an equal number of people also suggest more physical intimacy, incidentally; one way or another, it's all about sex).

I actually speak out of expertise. Usually, the sleep example is the one I use in my talks that I give about creativity, which means that I've heard from probably 15,000 people. I know more about what might happen if people didn't need sleep than anyone has the right to know (and, indeed, I will be well prepared if such an occurrence transpires). People say that more work would be done (because there would be more time to work), that less work would be done (because people would be tired), that there would be more crime, less crime, happier people, sadder people, and so on. I've only encountered a few truly original responses. One of my favorites was when I discussed this concept in a theater class in Taiwan. One student said, "If we didn't need sleep, then clearly we are Martians, and therefore the differences that would exist would be the differences between ourselves and Martians."

One simple way of measuring originality is asking many people the same question and seeing how many times people give a certain response. If your response is rarely (or never) given, then it is more original. How, you may ask, can someone distinguish answers that are original from answers that are just plain weird? This question can be answered both practically—in terms of how the Torrance Tests would handle it—and in a more philosophical way. The people who score the Torrance Tests are specifically trained to distinguish responses that are truly original from those that are just bizarre, and they've demonstrated strikingly high reliability at doing so. The training materials are detailed and highly specific about what constitutes a relevant response.

As a more introspective question, though, where is the line between being original and crazy? Someone might suggest that not needing sleep would make everyone love the rock group Scissor Sisters. That response would be thrown out when the test was scored, but what is your own opinion? Before you picked up this book, would you have called that response creative or original? What if someone wrote, "If people didn't need sleep, then binky rollo ponga zennadril?"

It's also worth noting that there are many situations where original ideas are not necessarily the best ideas. My first PhD student, Lamies Nazzal, used an engineering prompt for her dissertation about how to handle a situation where your house is costing too much to heat. Some of the responses that were considered original (both relevant and rarely given) were not particularly helpful (such as "wear sweatpants during the winter"). I'll discuss this concept more in Chapter 11, but there are times when the tried-and-true is not only acceptable but preferable. If I cut my finger, I'd rather get the best answer about how to medically tend to it, although the most creative answer might entertain me as I slowly bleed to death.

Back to Guilford's model, the final component is elaboration. To review, fluency is the ability to produce a great number of ideas, flexibility is the ability to produce many different types of ideas, and originality is the ability to produce the most unusual ideas. Elaboration is the ability to develop these ideas. You say that people would get into more violent fights if there was no sleep? Okay, explain why and how. Elaboration is not scored for the Verbal subtests, but is included in the Figural subtests—and it is easier to conceptualize in drawing. If you drew a picture of a person, what's the level of detail—is your person wearing a watch? Does the person have earlobes? Shoelaces? Elbows? Obviously, levels of cognitive development come into play here, too.

One example to distinguish the four components, adapted from J. C. Kaufman, Plucker, et al. (2008), might be if your significant other wants to go out to eat and asks you to come up with different possible restaurants. You might come up with a huge list of different restaurants (high fluency), you might come up with a wide range of food styles (high flexibility), you might think up a few restaurants that most people wouldn't have known (high originality), or you might focus on one restaurant but give your significant other a very thorough rundown of the menu, ambiance, location, and Yelp or Zagat reviews (high elaboration). Or, if you have two boys, you might just laugh and order pizza.

Moving beyond Guilford, the Figural subtests of the TTCT can also be scored for two additional dimensions. Resistance to Premature Closure refers to whether, when given incomplete figures to modify, you keep the figures open or closed. Rooted in Gestalt psychology, it measures a person's ability to delay the urge to quickly close off an incomplete figure. Watch people doodle. Many people create figures and then will right away close them off, color them in, and frame the drawing. People who are high on this ability are more likely to have an open mind and can resist jumping to conclusions (Kim, 2006). Abstractness of Titles assesses the degree to which the titles that you assign to your pictures go beyond simply labeling what is happening (Kim, 2006). In other words, do you call your picture "Contentment" or "Dog Eating Peanut Butter"?

Torrance (1974, 2008) provided extensive reliability and validity data in the technical-norms manual of the TTCT. Torrance and his colleagues typically gave the TTCT and compared the scores (usually with solid correlations) to other measures of creativity, or else they showed that gifted students scored higher on the TTCT than non-gifted students. Torrance and Safter (1989) used one of the subtests ("Just Suppose") to conduct a long-range study looking at predictive validity. They found a solid relationship to self-reported creative achievement after more than 20 years. Plucker (1999) reanalyzed data from a different Torrance longitudinal study and found that scores on the Verbal test (but not the Figural) were much more predictive of how people differed in creative achievement than were traditional IQ tests. Runco, Millar, Acar, and Cramond (2010) conducted a 50-year follow-up of a longitudinal study begun by Torrance himself; they found moderate correlations between TTCT scores and personal achievement (but not public achievement). There have been a multitude of studies that have shown relationships between the TTCT and various other indices of creativity (see Kim, 2011a, 2011c).

Nonetheless, the validity and reliability of the TTCT specifically and divergent thinking in general are quite controversial. Part of me hates this part of the book, because I have tremendous respect for Torrance as a man and as a scholar. But the criticisms are real. Some claim that the procedures for interpreting scores are not backed up by factor analysis (Heausler & Thompson, 1988); others have commented on the overly strong relationship between fluency and originality scores (e.g., Dixon, 1979). Still others point to how easy it is to change scores with different instructions (Lissitz & Willhoft, 1985), although any standardized test should have the same instructions; if the SATs were given telling some people "Hey, screw it, it's a meaningless test," then scores would likely change as well. Perhaps most critically, the predictive validity of the tests has been sharply challenged, although this issue remains highly debated (see Baer, 2011a, 2011b, for a summary of his arguments).

In response, a number of alternate scoring methods for divergent thinking tests have been proposed. Some ways use statistical analysis. For example, Snyder, Mitchell, Bossomaier, and Pallier (2004) suggested giving more weight to responses from categories that are strikingly different compared to responses from within the same category. Plucker, Qian, and Wang (2011) compared several different scoring methods for divergent thinking tests and found that using a percentage (by dividing originality scores by fluency scores) provided the best results.

Other methods examine the responses in a different way. Silvia, Martin, and Nusbaum (2009) suggested a "snapshot" method of scoring in which raters assigned a holistic score to an entire set of responses. Similarly, Silvia et al. (2008; see also Silvia, 2011) used subjective evaluation of divergent thinking items, in which people identified their two best ideas. Raters then gave their opinions on the creativity of these specific ideas. Benedek, Mühlmann, Jauk, and Neubauer (2013) found strong validity when only considering the three most creative ideas produced in only 2 minutes. Such limitations can both reduce the number of responses that need to be rated and lower originality's confounding relationship with fluency. It is interesting to note a new study by Reiter-Palmon and Arreola (2015) that compared how people asked to generate one idea compared with those asked to generate multiple ideas. The multiple-response folks were more likely to come up with a superoriginal idea, but the single-response people were more likely to generate more original, complex, elaborate, and higher-quality ideas.

Beyond the specific critiques (and potential solutions) of divergent thinking, there is a deeper issue: Creativity is not only divergent thinking. This ability—to come up with many different responses, with outrageously innovative responses, and so on—is incredibly important. It's a cornerstone of creativity. But it's not all that creativity can be. This criticism can be levied at many constructs—intelligence, as we shall see in Chapter 7, is comprised of much more than the exact things that IQ tests measure.

Some people act as if creativity began and ended with Guilford and Torrance. They're wrong. As is often the case, much of the problem lies in the distance between prophet and disciples. Torrance, along with his colleagues, argued for using several different methods to assess creativity (Cramond, Matthews-Morgan, Torrance, & Zuo, 1999) and called for tests to be developed that extend beyond verbal and figural creativity (Torrance & Cramond, 2002). Teachers or administrators who rely *only* on the TTCT (or a similar instrument) are missing out on the complete "creativity" picture. Torrance himself would've likely been the first one to argue this point.

There's an argument I like to call the "breakfast cereal problem" that I've used before in discussing IQ tests (J. C. Kaufman & Kaufman, 2015). Think about Lucky Charms cereal (which is, of course, magically delicious). Lucky Charms cereal is designed to be part of a complete, nutritious breakfast, as they always show in commercials, surrounded by orange juice and scrambled eggs and a muffin. But in real life, many children may simply chow down on three bowls of Lucky Charms and nothing else. It's easy and tastes good. I sharply criticize the misuse of the TTCT. I still have critiques of the test itself, but it is important to distinguish an instrument's intentions from its actual use.

So what else is there? The most similar test—which is subject to many of the same criticisms as divergent thinking tests without anywhere near the positive aspects—is the Remote Associates Test (Mednick, 1968).

REMOTE ASSOCIATES TEST (RAT)

The foundation of the Remote Associates Test (RAT) is the associative theory (Mednick, 1962, 1968), which argues that creative people will be able to make associations between more remote concepts. An instant response to hearing the word *cow*, for example, might be to think of grass (which cows eat), or milk (which cows produce), or bulls (with which cows discuss philosophy). Upon further thought, maybe you can connect cows with all sorts of things—cow's milk is used to make cheese, and goats are creatures that also produce milk, and both "holy cow" and "don't have a cow" are somewhat dated popular expressions. Similarly, connecting the word *dog* with *cat* is a much more straightforward connection than thinking of *dogwood* or *colorblind*.

The RAT (Mednick, 1968) attempts to measure this theory by presenting three seemingly unrelated words and seeing if people can derive a fourth word that connects them. The original test had 30 items. The original RAT is not often used, but it is quite common for studies to use one of the various updates by different authors (and sometimes called the Compound Remote Associates Task) to both include additional items and to correct some out-of-date slang (see Bowden & Jung-Beeman, 2003, an essential compilation). An example of a recent problem is *sleeping, bean*, and *trash*. What word connects them (look away and think . . . now look back)? It's *bag*. Sleeping bag, bean bag, and trash bag are all common phrases (although bean bags have, sadly, slipped in popularity since my childhood).

The RAT is the source of one of my solidly embarrassing graduate school moments; my professor was presenting on the RAT and I was zoning out or doodling. I missed him say that he was going to present us with items that were unsolvable (I don't remember exactly why he gave us these items; I told you, I wasn't paying attention). One of the items caught my attention, and in the throes of puzzle-solving bliss, I shouted out the answer at the top of my lungs: "Fish!" Alas, it wasn't. I still sometimes yell out, "Fish!" although at least now I *know* I'm being odd.

The RAT is most often used to study problem solving and creative thinking (Ansburg, 2000; Beeman & Bowden, 2000; Storm, Angello, & Bjork, 2011). It is a common choice because, bluntly, it's quick and easy. Because there is a "right answer," it is much easier to score than any other creativity assessment; you can also administer many items in a short period of time. There are some circumstances in which the need for brevity outweighs the other concerns; a prime example is the creativity research by neuroscientists (see, e.g., essays in Vartanian, Bristol, & Kaufman, 2013). If a participant has to be in heavy machinery or attached to electrodes, a quick test is essential.

However, the RAT is one of the poorer creativity measures out there. It has long been accused of being heavily influenced by verbal abilities and intelligence (Katz, 1983), and C. Lee and Therriault (2013) found that RAT scores were much more associated with working memory and intelligence than with divergent thinking. It can be argued that these results simply indicate that the RAT is a measure of convergent thinking (C. Lee, Huggins, & Therriault, 2014). Thus, given the quite strong overlap with intelligence, the RAT can only be recommended for its simplicity.

CONSENSUAL ASSESSMENT TECHNIQUE (CAT)

One of the most exciting ways (to me) to measure creativity can also, alas, be a gigantic pain in the butt. It seems almost too simple—ask people to do something creative (anything), and then have experts tell you how creative it is. The general concept has been around for quite a while (e.g., Cattell, Glascock, & Washburn, 1918; Getzels & Csikszentmihalyi, 1976), but Amabile (1982, 1996) refined it into a method called the Consensual Assessment Technique (CAT).

What does the CAT entail? The first part is gathering the material. You have your participants produce something creative. These tend to be aesthetic products; past studies have examined collages (Amabile, 1996; Hennessey, Kim, Guomin, & Weiwei, 2008), short stories and poetry (Baer, Kaufman, & Riggs, 2009; J. C. Kaufman, Gentile, & Baer, 2005), photo captions (J. C. Kaufman, Lee, Baer, & Lee, 2007), photographic essays (Dollinger, 2007), designs (Haller, Courvoisier, & Cropley, 2010), dramatic performance (Myford, 1989), and music compositions (Hickey, 2001; Priest, 2006). However, the CAT has also been used in such domains as writing mathematical problems and equations (Baer, 1994), responding to science-based questions about an animal's habitat (J. C. Kaufman, Evans, & Baer, 2010), devising strategic military plans (McClary, 1999), teaching designs

(Cheng, 2015), cooking a chicken dish (Horng & Lin, 2009), and solving everyday problems (Reiter-Palmon, Mumford, O'Connor Boes, & Runco, 1997). It could conceivably be used in any domain.

Once you have a bunch of poems or drawings or submarines, you gather appropriate experts (I will explore this issue in a moment) and ask them to assign a rating for each piece. For example, they might use a scale of 1 to 6, where 1 means the piece is not at all creative and 6 means it is extremely creative. The experts do not discuss the rating process with one another in any way. This part may be counterintuitive (wouldn't the ratings be better if the experts discussed their opinions?), but it is essential. Hekkert and van Wieringen (1998) examined how art experts evaluated work both independently and after discussions. They found that after discussions, the consensus usually only reflected the original opinion of one (likely vocal) expert.

Another rule in using the CAT is that the products are compared to one another instead of an ideal. Otherwise, someone being forced to rate 400 poems written by second graders might assign them all scores of 1 or 2; after all, even the best second-grade poet is probably pretty bad. In addition the raters use their own judgment based on their ideas of what creativity means in that particular domain. By comparing products to one another, the CAT can work with any sample, from young kids to people with intellectual difficulties.

A great deal of past research (e.g., Amabile, 1996; Baer, 1993, 1998; Baer, Kaufman, & Gentile, 2004; Baer et al., 2009) has shown that experts agree at a strikingly high rate. Indeed, the first time I ever used this methodology (Baer et al., 2004), I had to rerun the statistics just to make sure there wasn't a mistake. This high level of agreement is called high interrater reliability.

This agreement occurs under many different situations. For example, raters tend to agree across cultures. Several studies have looked at judgments of creative work by both Chinese and American raters (e.g., Chen et al., 2002; Niu & Sternberg, 2001; Rostan, Pariser, & Gruber, 2002). Generally, the cultures agreed with each other. Niu and Sternberg (2001) found that Chinese judges generally gave higher scores, yet, conversely, when Hong and Lee (2015) compared East Asian nonexpert raters to Caucasian American nonexperts, there was the reverse effect. The finding of judges agreeing on creativity across culture has also been found with Japanese and Americans

(Child & Iwao, 1968) and Greeks and Americans (Haritos-Fatouros & Child, 1977). Hennessey et al. (2008) found solid reliability in judges in America, Saudi Arabia, South Korea, and China.

In a cross-cultural study of what variables affect a person's ratings, Paletz and Peng (2008) asked students from Japan, China, and the United States to rate products (either a meal or a textbook). Raters from all three countries valued novelty; however, Chinese raters placed less importance on appropriateness. In separately rating a product's desirability (as opposed to creativity), Chinese raters were more impacted by novelty.

Kozbelt and Serafin (2009; see also Serafin, Kozbelt, Seidel, & Dolese, 2011) took an interesting approach by having artists and nonartists assess in-progress stages of drawings; they call this process dynamic evaluation. The artists preferred original work, whereas the nonartists were more impressed with realism. The other cool finding was that the ratings of the finished drawings were more related to the in-progress ratings in less creative works. In other words, you can better predict how good a piece of art will be midway through its creation if it's just so-so. More creative artwork can suddenly improve by leaps and bounds, making it harder to tell its end quality in the middle.

In addition to studying creativity ratings across cultures, other studies have examined creativity ratings across one person's work. One study (J. C. Kaufman et al., 2007) looked at captions written to a series of 12 different photographs. Four experts rated these captions for creativity. J. C. Kaufman et al. (2007) found that not only did the experts agree on their ratings, but they also agreed across captions. In other words, if they thought that Joe Smith's caption for photograph #1 was creative, they also thought that his caption for photograph #10 was creative (without knowing it was the same person).

The reason why this finding is important is that if you're evaluating a lot of creative work, there's always the chance that some prompts may yield higher creativity than others. If I ask you to write a short story about "greed" or about "the sensation of biting into a chicken bone and hurting your front tooth that you had replaced a year ago," the odds are that people will write more creative stories about "greed."

If your instinct, incidentally, was to pick the longer topic as being able to inspire more creativity, I think that you're wrong. The topic itself was creative (or at least different), but it would result in a long stream of very similar stories (how many different ways can you bite into a chicken bone?). Consider the (humorous) example of a bad creative writing prompt: "A husband and a wife are meeting in a restaurant to finalize the impending divorce. Write the scene from the point of view of the busboy snorting cocaine in the restroom" (Wiencek, 2008). In fact, Medeiros, Partlow, and Mumford (2014) found that there is an optimal level of constraint for creativity. Some constraint is beneficial to creativity (consistent with Stokes, 2005, 2007; Haught, 2015), but too many constraints can cause overload and reduce creativity.

Jeffries (2015) examined the impact of the instructions given to experts before ratings. He found higher agreement when experts were told not to consider technical proficiency (as per Baer, 1993) than when this point was not included (as in other CAT studies, such as J. C. Kaufman, Baer, Cole, & Sexton, 2008).

WHO'S AN EXPERT?

The next question is what constitutes an expert. What, for example, would I be qualified to rate? I can make a solid case for my being an expert in creativity. I can make a decent case for my expertise in noncognitive constructs in general (such as personality), as well as cognitive psychology. Speaking a little more broadly, I'm perhaps an expert in psychology. I'm a musical theater buff, and some of my favorite shows are lesser-known works such as *Birds of Paradise*, *Weird Romance*, and *The Fix*. Does that make me an expert? Indeed, my own musical, *Discovering Magenta*, was initially written before I began studying creativity and then got its New York City premiere in 2015—did I magically become an expert opening night?

Similarly, I love dogs and spend many hours with them each day—am I an expert? The question becomes where to draw the line. I'm certainly an expert on my dogs (Pandora, Kirby, and Sweeney), and by extension I've learned about a wide variety of dopey hound dogs. But I'm only vaguely aware that Chihuahuas are little yippy things that don't like me.

Who should rate a child's drawings for creativity? Is the best choice her teacher, her mom, herself, her friends, a professional artist, a graduate student in art history, an art gallery owner, an editor of a children's art journal, Banksy, someone who collects children's art, or a creativity specialist? One could make a case for all of these people being some type of expert in rating this child's drawings.

As you may remember, expertise research suggests that it takes about 10 years from someone first entering a field to that person making any kind of substantial contribution (Ericsson, Roring, & Nandagopal, 2007; Hayes, 1989). In these 10 years, the future expert learns the basics of the domain, obsessively practices, and learns the practical issues that can't be taught in a book. These 10 years are different from an apprenticeship (the way that old-time shoemakers may have learned their trade); these expert-shaping years are times of active experimentation and new ideas (Gardner, 1993). Reaching a level of greatness may require another 10 years or more (S. B. Kaufman & Kaufman, 2007; Simonton, 2000).

It is interesting to note that the 10-year rule is also pretty consistent, regardless of when someone first enters a field. Mozart, for example, began composing when he was only 5 years old, in 1761, and his first major composition, "Exsultate, Jubilate," debuted in 1773. Steven Spielberg shot his first home movies (such as *Escape to Nowhere* and *Battle Squad*) around 1961, when he was 15 years old. His first significant movie, *Duel*, was released in 1971, when he was 25. *Jaws* was released 4 years later.

Going back to the question of expertise and being able to assess creativity, most of the potential raters we've discussed would have 10 years of expertise, with the exception of the child herself, her friends, and (likely) her parents. A number of studies have suggested that different types of experts will agree with one another. For example, creativity researchers, English teachers, and professional writers/editors all agreed with one another in their assessment of eighth-grade creative writing (Baer et al., 2004, 2009).

Is it really that important for the raters to be experts? It would certainly be much easier if anyone could assess creativity—it's much harder to find experts than to corral folks from off the street. In a way, it comes down to whether creativity should be measured with the logic of the Oscars (gifted practitioners), the New York Film Critics

Circle Awards (very knowledgeable people), the Golden Globes (a handful of foreign journalists), or the People's Choice Awards (anyone and everyone).

So the first question is whether novices and experts agree. If I ask people off the street and English literature PhDs to assess the same poems and they show perfect agreement, then I don't need the experts—it's just more work on my part as a creativity researcher. It's the same logic that says that if a professional plumber and my 8-year-old son do the same quality job fixing the toilet, then I should hire my son, whom I can pay in Lunchables.

The research that compares pure novices and experts is, alas, discouraging. Novices consistently show much worse agreement than do experts, whether they are evaluating flower designs (S. Lee, Lee, & Young, 2005), poetry (J. C. Kaufman, Baer, et al., 2008), short stories (J. C. Kaufman, Baer, & Cole, 2009), or mousetrap designs (J. C. Kaufman, Baer, Cropley, Reiter-Palmon, & Sinnett, 2013). This lack of agreement can be partially remedied by using a large amount of novices—without getting too technical, the more raters you have, the higher the reliability becomes. So, for example, combining the ratings of 100 novices is roughly as valuable as combining the ratings of 10 experts.

Unfortunately, there is a further complication, which is that novices and experts don't necessarily agree with one another. At a certain level, it makes sense. Adam Sandler and Charlie Sheen are unlikely to be honored with Oscars and Emmys. What the general population is looking for in a creative product is likely quite different than what someone working in that area would seek. As *Mad Magazine* argues, "There's a reason McDonald's doesn't put tarragon on their Big Macs" (Devlin, 2006, p. 48).

S. Lee et al. (2005), for example, found that their experts (professional artists who worked in flower design) could distinguish different flower designs, whereas the novices (undergraduate students) could not. In J. C. Kaufman, Baer, et al. (2008), novices (undergraduate students) agreed with the experts (poets) at only $r = .22$ in their poetry ratings. For short stories, the agreement was notably better at $r = .71$ (J. C. Kaufman et al., 2009); one reason could be that the average person is more likely to have experience in reading short stories than poetry.

Beyond mere agreement, novices and experts may be interpreting creative work differently. Several studies have found that experts with art training viewed paintings as being more complex, varied, interesting, and distinct than did novices without any training (Locher, Smith, & Smith, 2001; Millis, 2001; Silvia, 2006). Further, experts and novices react emotionally differently to art, and novices rely on their emotions more when they judge art (Leder, Gerger, Dressler, & Schabmann, 2012). Müller, Höfel, Brattico, and Jacobsen (2010) physiologically measured how experts and novices responded to music. Experts and novices showed different brain responses to different types of chord progressions. Their results suggested that experts are better at perceiving music and can more easily switch between types of listening modes.

Are there differences among novice raters? Tan et al. (2015) had novices rate creatures built out of Legos. It is interesting to note that the novices' majors (art, computer science, or psychology) did not relate to how they assigned ratings. Those judges who were more agreeable or self-reported higher everyday creativity tended to give higher ratings.

Alas, novices do not seem to be equivalent to experts for the purposes of judging creative work. What J. C. Kaufman and Baer (2012) have proposed is that whereas novice raters are not qualified, people with a certain amount of expertise may do just fine. We called these people "quasi-experts"—those who are clearly more experienced than a novice, yet would not be recognized as experts (and have likely spent fewer than 10 years engaged in deliberate practice).

A pair of studies that utilized the International Movie Database (IMDb.com) can help illustrate. First, Plucker, Holden, and Neustadter (2008) compared movie reviews from professional critics (experts) to ratings by IMDb users. These users range from movie buffs to professionals to teenagers who stumbled on the website; in general, however, they are a decent representation of quasi-experts. Plucker, Kaufman, Temple, and Qian (2009) extended the original study to also include novices (undergraduate students with no particular experience with film). The experts (critics) showed the strongest reliability, followed by the quasi-experts (IMDb users), and then the novices (students). The IMDb users were highly correlated with both students (.65) and critics (.72). However, the correlation between critics and students was notably lower (.43). As an interesting addendum, though, this distinction may not matter in how reviews impact people. Bad reviews diminish viewer enjoyment, regardless of whether it's an online nut or a respected professional critic (Jacobs, Heuvelman, Ben Allouch, & Peters, 2015).

J. C. Kaufman et al. (2013) compared novices, quasi-experts, and experts across two domains, creative writing and engineering. For creative writing, they used professional writers as experts and examined many different groups of quasi-experts—English teachers early in their careers, advanced undergraduates or graduate students with creativity research experience, people studying to be elementary school teachers, and people studying to be English teachers. For engineering, professional engineers were the experts (unsurprisingly), and engineering students were the quasi-experts. For writing, all of the quasi-experts were appropriate raters for the short stories, with high interrater reliability and high correlations with the experts. For the engineers, the experts and novices did not particularly agree. Although the quasi-experts showed decent agreement with the experts, they showed equally strong agreement with the novices.

Other studies have showed that quasi-experts are reasonable if imperfect substitutes for experts. J. C. Kaufman et al. (2005) utilized gifted novices (high school students who had been singled out for their creative writing ability); their ratings of poetry and stories showed strong agreement with expert judgments. Hekkert and van Wieringen (1996) compared expert, quasi-expert, and novice assessment of art; the three groups agreed on some types of art (figurative) but not others (abstract). Experts and novices were far apart in how much they liked abstract paintings, with the quasi-experts in the middle.

Another approach is to see if novices can be trained to rate creativity such that they are closer to experts. Much early work with this technique was flawed (J. C. Kaufman & Baer, 2002, 2012). A recent study, though, used much more rigorous methods and did show that novices could improve when they received interactive feedback from an expert (Storme, Myszkowski, Çelik, & Lubart, 2014).

There needs to be more work on nonartistic domains. Simonton (2009) argues for a hierarchy within domains, with "hard sciences" (such as physics or mathematics) at the pointy top of the pyramid, "soft sciences" (such as psychology or sociology) in the middle, and arts and humanities at the bottom. Some of the variables that

Simonton uses in his model include the level of domain agreement. If people show a consensus about which components are needed to produce new and good work, then it is likely that most experts possess this knowledge. Novices without such expertise would be at an even greater disadvantage for these domains than for domains in which there is a high level of disagreement even at the expert level. This concept is also consistent with Amabile's (1983) suggestion that the more esoteric or specialized the field, the more narrow the range of possible experts. In other words, there may be nuclear physics equations that could only be evaluated for creativity by 20 experts; to everyone else, they would just be mumbo-jumbo. But a much larger group of possible experts could evaluate a painting or story. Of course, there is always subjectivity—just because experts agree does not mean they agree for the right reasons, and I will discuss some potential biases later in the book.

LOOKING AHEAD

There are other tests that measure creativity, but most are either a variation on divergent thinking or use some type of raters. For example, the Evaluation of Potential Creativity (EPoC; Lubart, Besançon, & Barbot, 2011) has begun to be used in some studies and may be promising, but is still largely rooted in a mix of divergent thinking scoring and raters (with a similar verbal/artistic split as the Torrance tests). Another test, based on the Geneplore model, is the Finke Creative Invention Task (Finke, 1990), which is clever (people are asked to make inventions with specific named objects) but also requires raters for scoring. There are also self-report measures, which I discuss later; these can range from actually grading your own abilities to seeing whether you have a creative personality. What is a creative personality? I am glad you asked! We will kick off Part II, The Creative Individual, with a look at creativity and personality.

REFERENCES

Amabile, T. M. (1982). Children's artistic creativity detrimental effects of competition in a field setting. *Personality and Social Psychology Bulletin*, 8, 573–578.

Amabile, T. M. (1983). *The social psychology of creativity.* New York, NY: Springer-Verlag.

Amabile, T. M. (1996). *Creativity in context: Update to "The Social Psychology of Creativity."* Boulder, CO: Westview Press.

Ansburg, P. I. (2000). Individual differences in problem solving via insight. *Current Psychology, 19,* 143–146.

Baer, J. (1993). *Creativity and divergent thinking: A task-specific approach.* Hillsdale, NJ: Erlbaum.

Baer, J. (1994). Divergent thinking is not a general trait: A multi-domain training experiment. *Creativity Research Journal, 7,* 35–46.

Baer, J. (1998). The case for domain specificity in creativity. *Creativity Research Journal, 11,* 173–177.

Baer, J. (2011a). How divergent thinking tests mislead us: Are the Torrance Tests still relevant in the 21st century? *Psychology of Aesthetics, Creativity, and the Arts, 5,* 309–313.

Baer, J. (2011b). Four (more) arguments against the Torrance Tests. *Psychology of Aesthetics, Creativity, and the Arts. 5,* 316–317.

Baer, J., Kaufman, J. C., & Gentile, C. A. (2004). Extension of the consensual assessment technique to nonparallel creative products. *Creativity Research Journal, 16,* 113–117.

Baer, J., Kaufman, J. C., & Riggs, M. (2009). Rater-domain interactions in the Consensual Assessment Technique. *International Journal of Creativity & Problem Solving, 19,* 87– 92.

Beeman, M. J., & Bowden, E. M. (2000). The right hemisphere maintains solution-related activation for yet-to-be-solved problems. *Memory & Cognition, 28*(7), 1231–1241.

Benedek, M., Mühlmann, C., Jauk, E., & Neubauer, A. C. (2013). Assessment of divergent thinking by means of the subjective top-scoring method: Effects of the number of top-ideas and time-on-task on reliability and validity. *Psychology of Aesthetics, Creativity, and the Arts, 7,* 341–349.

Bowden, E. M., & Jung-Beeman, M. (2003). One hundred forty-four compound remote associate problems: Short insight-like problems with one-word solutions. *Behavioral Research, Methods, Instruments, and Computers, 35,* 634–639.

Callahan, C. M., Hunsaker, S. L., Adams, C. M., Moore, S. D., & Bland, L. C. (1995). Instruments used in the identification of gifted and talented students. *American Educational Research Journal, 45,* 150–165.

Cattell, J., Glascock, J., & Washburn, M. F. (1918). Experiments on a possible test of aesthetic judgment of pictures. *American Journal of Psychology,* 333–336.

Chen, C., Kasof, J., Himsel, A. J., Greenberger, E., Dong, Q., & Xue, G. (2002). Creativity in drawing of geometric shapes: A cross-cultural examination with the consensual assessment technique. *Journal of Cross-Cultural Psychology, 33,* 171–187.

Cheng, V. M. (2015). Consensual assessment of creativity in teaching design by supportive peers—its validity, practicality, and benefit. *Journal of Creative Behavior.* Advance online publication. doi:10.1002/jocb.125

Child, I. L., & Iwao, S. (1968). Personality and esthetic sensitivity: Extension of findings to younger age and to different culture. *Journal of Personality and Social Psychology, 8,* 308.

Cramond, B., Matthews-Morgan, J., Bandalos, D., & Zuo, L. (2005). A report on the 40-year follow-up of the Torrance Tests of Creative Thinking: Alive and well in the new millennium. *Gifted Child Quarterly, 49,* 283–291.

Cramond, B., Matthews-Morgan, J., Torrance, E. P., & Zuo, L. (1999). Why should the Torrance Tests of Creative Thinking be used to access creativity? *Korean Journal of Thinking & Problem Solving, 9,* 77–101.

Devlin, D. (2006). You can write the next American Idol single. *Mad Magazine, 466,* 48.

Dixon, J. (1979). Quality versus quantity: The need to control for the fluency factor in originality scores from the Torrance Tests. *Journal for the Education of the Gifted, 2,* 70–79.

Dollinger, S. J. (2007). Creativity and conservatism. *Personality and Individual Differences, 43,* 1025–1035.

Ericsson, K. A. Roring, R. W., & Nandagopal, K. (2007). Giftedness and evidence for reproducibly superior performance: An account based on the expert-performance framework. *High Ability Studies, 18,* 3–56.

Finke, R. A. (1990). *Creative imagery: Discoveries and inventions in visualization.* Hillsdale, NJ: Erlbaum.

Gardner, H. (1993). *Creating minds.* New York, NY: Basic Books.

Getzels, J. W., & Csikszentmihalyi, M. (1976). *The creative vision.* New York, NY: Wiley.

Getzels, J. W., & Jackson, P. W. (1962). *Creativity and intelligence: Explorations with gifted students.* New York, NY: Wiley.

Guilford, J. P. (1950). Creativity. *American Psychologist, 5,* 444–454.

Guilford, J. P. (1967). *The nature of human intelligence.* New York, NY: McGraw-Hill.

Haller, C. S., Courvoisier, D. S., & Cropley, D. H. (2010). Correlates of creativity among visual art students. *International Journal of Creativity & Problem Solving, 20,* 53–71.

Haritos-Fatouros, M., & Child, I. L. (1977). Transcultural similarity in personal significance of esthetic interests. *Journal of Cross-Cultural Psychology, 8,* 285–298.

Haught, C. (2015). The role of constraints in creative sentence production. *Creativity Research Journal, 27,* 160–166.

Hayes, J. R. (1989). Cognitive processes in creativity. In J. A. Glover, R. R. Ronning, & C. R. Reynolds (Eds.), *Handbook of creativity* (pp. 135–145). New York, NY: Plenum Press.

Heausler, N. L., & Thompson, B. (1988). Structure of the Torrance Tests of Creative Thinking. *Educational and Psychological Measurement, 48,* 463–468.

Hekkert, P., & Van Wieringen, P. C. W. (1996). Beauty in the eye of expert and nonexpert beholders: A study in the appraisal of art. *American Journal of Psychology, 109,* 389–407.

Hekkert, P., & Van Wieringen, P. C. W. (1998). Assessment of aesthetic quality of artworks by expert observers: An empirical investigation of group decisions. *Poetics, 25,* 281–292.

Hennessey, B. A., Kim, G., Guomin, Z., & Weiwei, S. (2008). A multi-cultural application of the Consensual Assessment Technique. *International Journal of Creativity & Problem Solving, 18,* 87–100.

Hickey, M. (2001). An application of Amabile's consensual assessment technique for rating the creativity of children's musical compositions. *Journal of Research in Music Education, 49,* 234–244.

Hoffman, E., & Rudoren, G. (2007). *Comedy by the numbers.* San Francisco, CA: McSweeney's Quarterly Concern.

Hong, S. W., & Lee, J. S. (2015). Nonexpert evaluations on architectural design creativity across cultures. *Creativity Research Journal, 27,* 314–321.

Hoover, E. (2002). SAT is set for an overhaul, but questions linger about the test. *Chronicle of Higher Education,* A35–A36.

Horng & Lin, 2009 Horng, J.-S., & Lin, L. (2009). The development of a scale for evaluating creative culinary products. *Creativity Research Journal, 21,* 54–63.

Jacobs, R. S., Heuvelman, A., Ben Allouch, S., & Peters, O. (2015). Everyone's a critic: The power of expert and consumer reviews to shape readers' post-viewing motion picture evaluations. *Poetics.* Advance online publication. doi:10.1016/j.poetic.2015.07.002

Jeffries, K. K. (2015). A CAT with caveats: Is the Consensual Assessment Technique a reliable measure of graphic design creativity? *International Journal of Design Creativity and Innovation.* Advance online publication. doi: 10.1080/21650349.2015.1084893

Katz, A. N. (1983). Creativity and individual differences in asymmetric cerebral hemispheric functioning. *Empirical Studies of the Arts, 1,* 3–16.

Kaufman, J. C., & Baer, J. (2002). Could Steven Spielberg manage the Yankees?: Creative thinking in different domains. *Korean Journal of Thinking & Problem Solving, 12,* 5–15.

Kaufman, J. C., & Baer, J. (2012). Beyond new and appropriate: Who decides what is creative? *Creativity Research Journal, 24,* 83–91.

Kaufman, J. C., Baer, J., & Cole, J. C. (2009). Expertise, domains, and the Consensual Assessment Technique. *Journal of Creative Behavior, 43,* 223–233.

Kaufman, J. C., Baer, J., Cole, J. C., & Sexton, J. D. (2008). A comparison of expert and nonexpert raters using the Consensual Assessment Technique. *Creativity Research Journal, 20*, 171–178.

Kaufman, J. C., Baer, J., Cropley, D. H., Reiter-Palmon, R., & Sinnett, S. (2013). Furious activity vs. understanding: How much expertise is needed to evaluate creative work? *Psychology of Aesthetics, Creativity, and the Arts, 7*, 332–340.

Kaufman, J. C., Evans, M. L., & Baer, J. (2010). The American Idol Effect: Are students good judges of their creativity across domains? *Empirical Studies of the Arts, 28*, 3-17.

Kaufman, J. C., Gentile, C. A., & Baer, J. (2005). Do gifted student writers and creative writing experts rate creativity the same way? *Gifted Child Quarterly, 49*, 260–265.

Kaufman, J. C., & Kaufman, A. S. (2015). It can be very tempting to throw out the baby with the bathwater: A father-and-son commentary on "Does IQ really predict job performance?" *Applied Developmental Science, 19*, 176–181.

Kaufman, J. C., Lee, J., Baer, J., & Lee, S. (2007). Captions, consistency, creativity, and the consensual assessment technique: New evidence of validity. *Thinking Skills and Creativity, 2*, 96–106.

Kaufman, J. C., Plucker, J. A., & Baer, J. (2008). *Essentials of creativity assessment*. New York, NY: Wiley.

Kaufman, J. C., & Sternberg, R. J. (Eds.). (2006). *The international handbook of creativity*. New York, NY: Cambridge University Press.

Kaufman, S. B., & Kaufman, J. C. (2007). Ten years to expertise, many more to greatness: An investigation of modern writers. *Journal of Creative Behavior, 41*, 114–124.

Kim, K. H. (2006). Is creativity unidimensional or multidimensional? Analyses of the Torrance Tests of Creative Thinking. *Creativity Research Journal, 18*, 251–259.

Kim, K. H. (2011a). The APA 2009 Division 10 debate: Are the Torrance tests still relevant in the 21st century? *Psychology of Aesthetics, Creativity, and the Arts, 5*, 302–308.

Kim, K. H. (2011b). The creativity crisis: The decrease in creative thinking scores on the Torrance Tests of Creative Thinking. *Creativity Research Journal, 23*, 285–295.

Kim, K. H. (2011c). Proven reliability and validity of the Torrance Tests of Creative Thinking (TTCT). *Psychology of Aesthetics, Creativity, and the Arts, 5*, 314–315.

Kozbelt, A., & Serafin, J. (2009). Dynamic evaluation of high- and low-creativity drawings by artist and nonartist raters. *Creativity Research Journal, 21*, 349–360.

Leder, H., Gerger, G., Dressler, S. G., Schabmann, A. (2012). How art is appreciated. *Psychology of Aesthetics, Creativity, and the Arts, 6*, 1–10.

Lee, C. S., Huggins, A. C., & Therriault, D. J. (2014). Examining internal and external structure validity evidence of the Remote Associates Test. *Psychology of Aesthetics, Creativity, and the Arts, 8*, 446–460.

Lee, C. S., & Therriault, D. J. (2013). The cognitive underpinnings of creative thought: A latent variable analysis exploring the roles of intelligence and working memory in three creative thinking processes. *Intelligence, 41*, 306–320.

Lee, S., Lee, J., & Young, C.-Y. (2005). A variation of CAT for measuring creativity in business products. *Korean Journal of Thinking and Problem Solving, 15*, 143–153.

Lissitz, R. W., & Willhoft, J. L. (1985). A methodological study of the Torrance Tests of creativity. *Journal of Educational Measurement, 22*, 1–11.

Locher, P. J., Smith, J. K., & Smith, L. F. (2001). The influence of presentation format and viewer training in the visual arts on the perception of pictorial and aesthetic qualities of paintings. *Perception, 30*, 449–465.

Lubart, T., Besançon, M., & Barbot, B. (2011). *Évaluation du potentiel créatif (EPoC)*. Paris, France: Hogrefe France.

McClary, R. B. (1999). *An investigation into the relationship between tolerance of ambiguity and creativity among military officers.* Unpublished doctoral dissertation, Kansas State University, Manhattan, KS.

Medeiros, K. E., Partlow, P. J., & Mumford, M. D. (2014). Not too much, not too little: The influence of constraints on creative problem solving. *Psychology of Aesthetics, Creativity, and the Arts, 8*, 198–210.

Mednick, S. A. (1962). The associative basis of the creative process. *Psychological Review, 69*, 220–232.

Mednick, S. A. (1968). The Remote Associates Test. *Journal of Creative Behavior, 2*, 213–214.

Millis, K. (2001). Making meaning brings pleasure: The influence of titles on aesthetic experience. *Emotion, 1*, 320–329.

Müller, M., Höfel, L., Brattico, E., & Jacobsen, T. (2010). Aesthetic judgments of music in experts and laypersons—An ERP study. *International Journal of Psychophysiology, 76*, 40–51.

Myford, C. M. (1989). *The nature of expertise in aesthetic judgment: Beyond inter-judge agreement.* Unpublished doctoral dissertation, University of Georgia, Athens, GA.

Niu, W., & Sternberg, R. J. (2001). Cultural influence of artistic creativity and its evaluation. *International Journal of Psychology, 36*, 225–241.

Paletz, S. B. F., & Peng, K. (2008). Implicit theories of creativity across cultures: Novelty and appropriateness in two product domains. *Journal of Cross-Cultural Psychology, 39*, 286–302.

Plucker, J. A. (1999). Is the proof in the pudding? Reanalyses of Torrance's (1958 to present) longitudinal study data. *Creativity Research Journal, 12,* 103–114.

Plucker, J. A., Holden, J., & Neustadter, D. (2008). The criterion problem and creativity in film: Psychometric characteristics of various measures. *Psychology of Aesthetics, Creativity, and the Arts, 2,* 190–196.

Plucker, J. A., Kaufman, J. C., Temple, J. S., & Qian, M. (2009). Do experts and novices evaluate movies the same way? *Psychology & Marketing, 26,* 470–478.

Plucker, J. A., Qian, M., & Wang, S. (2011). Is originality in the eye of the beholder? Comparison of scoring techniques in the assessment of divergent thinking. *Journal of Creative Behavior, 45,* 1–22.

Priest, T. (2006). Self-evaluation, creativity, and musical achievement. *Psychology of Music, 34,* 47–61.

Reiter-Palmon, R., & Arreola, N. J. (2015). Does generating multiple ideas lead to increased creativity? A comparison of generating one idea vs. many. *Creativity Research Journal, 27,* 369–374.

Reiter-Palmon, R., Mumford, M. D., O'Connor Boes, J., & Runco, M. A. (1997). Problem construction and creativity: The role of ability, cue consistency and active processing. *Creativity Research Journal, 10,* 9–23.

Rostan, S. M., Pariser, D., & Gruber, H. E. (2002). A cross-cultural study of the development of artistic talent, creativity and giftedness. *High Ability Studies, 13,* 123–155.

Runco, M. A., Millar, G., Acar, S., & Cramond, B. (2010). Torrance tests of creative thinking as predictors of personal and public achievement: A fifty-year follow-up. *Creativity Research Journal, 22,* 361–368.

Schock, H. (1998). *Becoming remarkable.* Nevada City, CA: Blue Dolphin Publishing.

Serafin, J., Kozbelt, A., Seidel, A., & Dolese, M. (2011). Dynamic evaluation of high- and low-creativity drawings by artist and nonartist raters: Replication and methodological extension. *Psychology of Aesthetics, Creativity, and the Arts, 5,* 350–359.

Silvia, P. J. (2006). Artistic training and interest in visual art: Applying the appraisal model of aesthetic emotions. *Empirical Studies of the Arts, 24,* 139–161.

Silvia, P. J. (2011). Subjective scoring of divergent thinking: Examining the reliability of unusual uses, instances, and consequences tasks. *Thinking Skills and Creativity, 6,* 24–30.

Silvia, P. J., Martin, C., & Nusbaum, E. C. (2009). A snapshot of creativity: Evaluating a quick and simple method for assessing divergent thinking. *Thinking Skills and Creativity, 4,* 79–85.

Silvia, P. J., Winterstein, B. P., Willse, J. T., Barona, C. M., Cram, J. T., Hess, K. I., . . . Richard, C. A. (2008). Assessing creativity with divergent thinking tasks: Exploring the reliability and validity of new subjective scoring methods. *Psychology of Aesthetics, Creativity, and the Arts, 2,* 68–85.

Simonton, D. K. (2000). Creative development as acquired expertise: Theoretical issues and an empirical test. *Developmental Review, 20*, 283–318.

Simonton, D. K. (2009). Varieties of (scientific) creativity: A hierarchical model of disposition, development, and achievement. *Perspectives on Psychological Science, 4*, 441–452.

Snyder, A., Mitchell, J., Bossomaier, T., & Pallier, G. (2004). The creativity quotient: An objective scoring of ideational fluency. *Creativity Research Journal, 16*, 415–420.

Stokes, P. D. (2005). *Creativity from constraints: The psychology of breakthrough.* New York, NY: Springer Publishing Company.

Stokes, P. D. (2007). Using constraints to generate and sustain novelty. *Psychology of Aesthetics, Creativity, and the Arts, 1*, 107–113.

Storm, B. C., Angello, G., & Bjork, E. L. (2011). Thinking can cause forgetting: Memory dynamics in creative problem solving. *Journal of Experimental Psychology: Learning, Memory, and Cognition, 37*, 1287–1293.

Storme, M., Myszkowski, N., Çelik, P., & Lubart, T. (2014). Learning to judge creativity: The underlying mechanisms in creativity training for non-expert judges. *Learning and Individual Differences, 32*, 19–25.

Tan, M., Mourgues, C., Hein, S., MacCormick, J., Barbot, B., & Grigorenko, E. (2015). Differences in judgments of creativity: How do academic domain, personality, and self-reported creativity influence novice judges' evaluations of creative productions? *Journal of Intelligence, 3*, 73–90.

Torrance, E. P. (1974). *Torrance Tests of Creative Thinking. Directions manual and scoring guide, verbal test booklet B.* Bensenville, IL: Scholastic Testing Service.

Torrance, E. P. (2008). *The Torrance Tests of Creative Thinking: Norms-Technical Manual Figural (Streamlined) Forms A & B.* Bensenville, IL: Scholastic Testing Service.

Torrance, E. P., & Cramond, B. (2002). Needs of creativity programs, training, and research in the schools of the future. *Research in the Schools, 9*, 5–14.

Torrance, E., & Safter, H. T. (1989). The long range predictive validity of the Just Suppose Test. *Journal of Creative Behavior, 23*, 219–223.

Vartanian, O., Bristol, A. S., & Kaufman, J. C. (2013). *Neuroscience of creativity.* Cambridge, MA: MIT Press.

Wallach, M. A., & Kogan, N. (1965). *Modes of thinking in young children: A study of the creativity-intelligence distinction.* New York, NY: Holt Rinehart & Winston.

Weinstein, E. C., Clark, Z., DiBartlomomeo, D. J., & Davis, K. (2014). A decline in creativity? It depends on the domain. *Creativity Research Journal, 26*, 174–184.

Wiencek, D. (2008). Thirteen writing prompts. In McSweeney's (Eds.), *The McSweeney's joke book of book jokes* (pp. 37–39). New York, NY: Vintage.

The Creative
Individual

Creativity and Personality

There are many different personality theories, but the one that is most commonly used in current research (and one that is backed up by a ton of data) is the Five Factor theory of personality (Goldberg, 1992; Hofstee, de Raad, & Goldberg, 1992). The Five Factor theory reduces all of the different possible personality variables into five broad factors. These factors are sometimes called the "Big Five," kind of like the Five Families in *The Godfather* but with more data and fewer button men. Each of these five factors represents a continuum of behavior, traits, and inclinations. The Big Five, which I will discuss in more detail, are extraversion, neuroticism, agreeableness, conscientiousness, and openness to experience. DeYoung's (2006, 2015) Cybernetic Big Five begins with two overarching hierarchical factors, plasticity (comprised of extraversion and openness) and stability (comprised of neuroticism, agreeableness, and conscientiousness), with the specific aspects of the Big Five below and then the specific facets (as I will discuss) underneath. The hierarchical factor of plasticity is more related to creativity (Silvia et al., 2009).

Each dimension of the factors is morally the same (being an introvert is not inherently better or worse than being an extrovert). Most organizations would nonetheless view specific patterns of scores as being more positive than others, although the truth is more nuanced (Kyllonen, Walters, & Kaufman, 2005; McCrae & Costa, 1997). For example, extraversion (which is the opposite pole of introversion) refers to the extent to which a person is gregarious and assertive (DeYoung, 2015). It is traditionally a desired trait, but it can also imply that someone is superficial or obnoxious. Another factor is neuroticism, which is more commonly labeled by its more positive side, emotional stability (perhaps a nod to Woody Allen's diminished popularity). Agreeableness is being friendly and good-natured, although there may be a twinge of passivity, naiveté, or dullness mixed in. Conscientiousness taps into one's discipline, rule orientation, and integrity; it is consistently the personality factor most associated with academic achievement (Conrad & Patry, 2012; Poropat, 2009) and workplace performance (Brown, Lent, Telander, & Tramayne, 2011). The less positive spin on being conscientious is that it comes with a certain air of drudgery (one former colleague used to explain it to me as "the people who enjoy doing their taxes"). Finally, openness to experience (sometimes just called openness) represents one's intellectual and experiential curiosity—how much someone is interested in cognitive exploration (DeYoung, 2014).

There are some popular personality measures that use different theories, such as Eysenck's Personality Questionnaire, which looks at extraversion and neuroticism as well as psychoticism (which encompasses aggression, egocentrism, and dogmatism; Eysenck, Eysenck, & Barrett, 1985). Others use their own categorization system, such as the 16 Personality Factor Questionnaire (16 PF), the Minnesota Multiphasic Personality Inventory (MMPI), and the Myers–Briggs, but I'm going to stick to the Big Five for the sake of simplicity (and better data). I will, however, explore potential expansions or modifications of the Big Five.

OPENNESS TO EXPERIENCE: DUH

The personality factor most associated with creativity is openness to experience. Indeed, one way that researchers study creativity is by giving creative personality tests. The questions on these tests tend to be strikingly similar to the kinds of questions used to measure openness to experience. They usually ask you to rate how much you agree with these types of statements:

1. I have a good imagination.
2. I enjoy playing with my ideas.
3. Going to an art museum sounds like a fun time.
4. Gosh, I like thinking deep thoughts.
5. I bet it would be fun to make up a story and see where it takes me.
6. My waffles are better than store-bought waffles.

I made up the last one (although if you said it was true, contact me care of the publisher—but with an actual waffle; recipes are useless to me). The first five are pretty typical of what creative personality tests are like. Indeed, my friend Maciej Karwowski reminded me of a classic bit by the late Colin Martindale (1989), who noted that measures of openness to experience seem so much more related to being creative than to being open that it was a cause for debate why the factor wasn't just called creativity.

It is unsurprising, therefore, that there is a near-universal finding that openness to experience is related to a wide variety of creativity measures, ranging from self-reports of creative activities (Ivcevic & Mayer, 2009; Jauk, Benedek, & Neubauer, 2014), particularly in the arts (Hong, Peng, & O'Neil, 2014); to verbal creativity (King, McKee-Walker, & Broyles, 1996); being in a traditionally creative profession (Domino, 1974) or major (Furnham & Crump, 2013; Silvia et al., 2009); self-rated creativity (Furnham, 1999); creative identity and self-efficacy (Karwowski & Lebuda, 2015; Karwowski, Lebuda, Wisniewska, & Gralewski, 2013); divergent thinking tests (McCrae, 1987; Sánchez-Ruiz, Hernández-Torrano, Pérez-González, Batey, & Petrides, 2011); and rated creativity in stories (Wolfradt & Pretz, 2001), autobiographical photo essays (Dollinger & Clancy, 1993), and metaphors (Silvia & Beaty, 2012).

Groups that are more open to experience are also more creative—although the most creativity is found in groups filled with people spanning across a diverse range of openness to experience (Schilpzand, Herold, & Shalley, 2011). It can also be predictive over many years; people who were more tolerant at age 27 were more likely to have creative accomplishments at the age of 72 (Feist & Barron, 2003). Indeed, although the creative personality can stay consistent over the life span, there are ebbs and flows; a cross-sectional study of four age groups found that older adults perceived both gains and losses in the creative personality as they got older (Hui et al., 2014).

Just when you might be thinking, "Hey, this stuff actually makes sense," I'm about to make it complicated. If you want to hold on to that feeling of "I get it!" then I will not hold it against you if you skip ahead to the next heading. I won't make you feel guilty over how many hours I've spent submerged in the personality literature trying to make sense of all of the details when I could've been watching reruns of the *Twilight Zone.*

Okay, for the hard-core folks: in the most common personality assessments, openness to experience has been split into subcomponents (Costa & McCrae, 1992) such as openness to fantasy (a good imagination), aesthetics (artistic), feelings (experiencing and valuing feelings), actions (trying new things, many interests), ideas (curious, smart, likes challenges), and values (unconventional, liberal).

Some of the subcomponents are obviously related to creativity because they *are* creativity. The connection for others may be less initially straightforward. For example, think about people who would be very high on the actions subcomponent. It is easy to imagine these folks enjoying eating new foods or learning a new language. It certainly makes sense that they would also be creative, but the connection is less direct; the most obvious associations would be with things like sensation seeking or risk taking. Similarly, values and feelings also make sense but are less obvious (there are many creative people who are straitlaced, calm, and conservative). However, there is research supporting this connection. Students who self-rated themselves as more conservative (in the social/political sense) reported fewer creative accomplishments and produced photo essays rated as less creative than those produced by their more liberal classmates (Dollinger, 2007). In addition, Kenett, Anaki, and Faust

(2015) found that creative people were better able to handle and understand unconventional stimuli.

McCrae (1987) looked at the subcomponents and their relationship to several different divergent thinking measures (mostly looking at some aspect of fluency). All subcomponents were significantly correlated; the smallest correlation was found for actions. These relationships stayed significant (although weakened) even when McCrae controlled for vocabulary and education. In Dollinger and Clancy's (1993) study of personality and autophotobiographical essays (telling your story through photographs), the aesthetics facet was significantly linked to creativity for both men and women, and the ideas facet was also associated with creativity in women.

Perrine and Brodersen (2005) examined openness to experience, interests, and artistic versus scientific creativity (all via survey measures). Five of the six subcomponents were related to artistic creativity (all but values), with aesthetics showing the strongest relationship. Only ideas and values were related to scientific creativity. When interests were included, the results stayed consistent. Artistic interests help to predict artistic creativity and investigative interests help to predict scientific creativity.

A similar way of thinking about the openness-to-experience factor can be found in Zuckerman's (1994) work on sensation seeking. Just as openness to experience is made up of one part creativity and one part risk taking, so is sensation seeking a comparable mix. His dimensions are boredom susceptibility (intolerance for being bored), disinhibition (taking social risks, such as excessive alcohol intake or one-night stands), experience seeking (needing new experiences, which can include art or museums), and thrill and adventure seeking (taking physical risks, such as bungee-jumping). Indeed, sensation seeking has been found to relate to creativity (Oral, 2008; Rawlings, Twomey, Burns, & Morris, 1998).

The relationship between openness and creativity has many further nuances. There are interactions with domain. Benedek, Borovnjak, Neubauer, and Kruse-Weber (2014) compared different types of musicians and found that jazz musicians were more open to experience than were classical musicians (and were higher on divergent thinking). Similarly, Fink and Woschnjak (2011) found that modern/contemporary dancers were more open to experience than were ballet and jazz/musical dancers. Maslej, Rain, Fong, Oatley, and Mar (2014) compared writers and nonwriters; the writers were higher on both the ideas and aesthetics facets of openness (and overall openness to experience).

Being open to new experiences may also help creative people be more productive. King et al. (1996) found that people who were creative and high on openness to experience were more likely to report creative accomplishments. Those people who were creative and low on openness to experience, however, showed comparatively few creative accomplishments. In a different study, Jauk et al. (2014) found that openness and creative potential predicted participating in creative activities, whereas actual creative achievement was predicted by participation in creative activities and intelligence.

This general finding of the power of openness to experience mostly extends across domains, even the nonartistic ones. In a clever study, Christensen, Drewsen, and Maaløe (2014) scoured job ads for the adjectives used to describe the ideal employee; businesses specifically seeking creative workers used adjectives strongly related to openness. Feist (1998) conducted an extensive meta-analysis, in which many different empirical studies are studied together to look for larger patterns. In looking at the relationship between personality and creativity, he found that creative scientists were more open to experience than were less creative scientists, and artists were more open to experience than nonartists. Grosul and Feist (2014) tested professional scientists and found that openness predicted creativity as measured by publications and citations. It is interesting to note, though, that a recent study of Chinese high school students found openness associated with self-reported creative accomplishments in music, art, and writing but not science or technology (Hong et al., 2014).

DeYoung, Quilty, and Peterson (2007) demonstrated in a series of studies that each of the Big Five can be split into two distinct factors. They tested 15 different measures of openness to experience and found that it was best explained by two subfactors: intellect and openness. Building off of this work within the openness factor, Nusbaum and Silvia (2011b) examined the relationship between openness, intellect, fluid intelligence (reasoning and spatial abilities), and creativity (as measured by self-reported creative activities and accomplishments). As predicted, openness (but not intellect) predicted creativity, and intellect (but not openness) predicted fluid intelligence.

S. B. Kaufman (2013) took this line of analysis even further. He used multiple personality measures to derive a four-factor model of openness beyond the openness/intellect split. The two openness-related factors were affective engagement (in other words, how involved you are with your own emotions and feelings) and aesthetic engagement (think of a search for beauty). The two intellect-related factors were intellectual engagement (the search for truth and the love of ideas) and explicit cognitive ability (traditional IQ-like measures).

Using the Creative Achievement Questionnaire (Carson, Peterson, & Higgins, 2005), S. B. Kaufman (2013) found domain differences based on the openness/intellect factor. The findings make sense. Intellectual engagement was related to inventions and science, and explicit cognitive ability was positively related to science and, curiously, negatively related to cooking (does this introduce a stereotype of the dumb cook?). Affective engagement was positively related to music, dance, humor, theater/film, and overall creative achievement (and negatively related to science). Aesthetic engagement was related to visual arts, music, dance, theater/film, and overall creative achievement. A follow-up study with a large sample also found the broad connection between openness and artistic accomplishments and intellect and scientific accomplishments (S. B. Kaufman et al., 2015). Intellect was also found to be related to both intelligence and divergent thinking.

A theoretical expansion of the intellect part of the openness/intellect factor is the Theoretical Intellect Framework (Mussel, 2013). It breaks down intellect into two dimensions, operation and focus. Focus is more rooted in motivation (whether we are driven to seek or conquer). There are three operations: think (reasoning and drawing conclusions), learn (acquiring knowledge), and create (exactly what it sounds like). Mussel, McKay, Ziegler, Hewig, and Kaufman (2015) found that most self-reported creativity ratings were most associated with the create operation, but performance-based measures (a rated photo caption) and remote associate items were most associated with think.

A different take on the openness factor was introduced by Connelly, Ones, Davies, and Birkland (2014). First, they identified 11 traits within openness, which represent a similar-but-different list to Costa and McCrae's subcomponents: aesthetics, fantasy, innovation, introspection, openness to emotions, openness to sensations, variety seeking, autonomy (i.e., independence), nontraditionalism (i.e., liberal and nondogmatic), tolerance, and thrill seeking. Next they conducted a meta-analysis and singled out four of these traits as being distinct from both one another and the other personality factors; these remaining four were called facets.

Connelly et al. (2014) found four facets. Three of the four facets seem roughly analogous to S. B. Kaufman's (2013) four subfactors; what Connelly et al. dub aestheticism, openness to sensations, and introspection seem very similar to S. B. Kaufman's aesthetic engagement, affective engagement, and intellectual engagement. That two totally unrelated studies both came up with these three core components reinforces their importance. The differences emerged in the fourth factor; whereas S. B. Kaufman's work pointed to explicit cognitive ability, Connelly et al. found nontraditionalism.

This divergence is rooted in a broader difference in data interpretation. On one hand, Connelly et al. (2014) compare their aestheticism and openness to sensations to De Young et al.'s (2007) openness and their introspection and nontraditionalism to De Young et al.'s intellect. On the other hand, they ultimately end up arguing against DeYoung et al.'s (2007; DeYoung, 2014, 2015) split of openness and intellect; instead, intellect is placed under openness. Without focusing on the statistical issues, I conceptually like DeYoung et al.'s approach more from a theoretical perspective. That said, it would be fun (well, to me, but I'm a boring guy) to see how the Connelly et al. model would predict different measures and models of creativity.

Where does all of this research take us? The biggest common theme is that the connection between openness to experience and creativity is quite strong and consistently shown. But the relationship is also more complex than many have thought (including myself in the first edition of this book). A recurring pattern that pops up in this field (and, perhaps, all fields) is that two complex constructs with many possible dimensions and measurements can seem to relate positively or negatively or strongly or weakly or not at all, depending on the specific nitty-gritty details.

CONSCIENTIOUSNESS: HUH?

Openness to experience is clearly related to creativity; the devil is in the details. The research on conscientiousness, however, is more complex. Part of the issue is a strong domain interaction. As measured by traditional Big Five measures, creativity in the arts has shown a negative relationship to conscientiousness. In other words, creative artists tend to not be conscientious (reminding me of the old joke about the difference between a drummer and a pizza—which is that a pizza can feed a family of four).

This finding (about conscientiousness, not drummers and pizza) has been shown with creativity ratings on stories (Wolfradt & Pretz, 2001), biographical data (Walker, Koestner, & Hum, 1995), and an arts-based creativity measure (Furnham, Zhang, & Chamorro-Premuzic, 2006). Similarly, Lievens, Coetsier, De Fruyt, and De Maeseneer (2002) found that arts majors were less conscientious than other majors and J. C. Kaufman (2002) found that creative writers were less conscientious than journalists. Feist's (1998) meta-analysis found that artists were less conscientious than nonartists, and Fink and Woschnjak (2011) found that modern/contemporary dancers were less conscientious than ballet and jazz/musical dancers.

Conversely, Feist (1998) also found that scientists were much more conscientious than nonscientists. This finding has been mirrored in college major choice; those whose majors were related to science, technology, engineering, and math (STEM) fields were not only more conscientious than arts majors, but also notably more conscientious than social science majors. Although not using a traditional measure of Big Five conscientiousness, Furnham and Crump (2013) relatedly found that science majors were more rule conscious and perfectionist than arts majors.

It is interesting to note, however, that being a scientist is not the same as being a creative scientist. Feist's (1998) same meta-analysis showed that creative scientists were not necessarily more conscientious than less creative scientists. In fact, only four studies found a link between low conscientiousness and high creativity in scientists, although the effect was strong.

103

Chamorro-Premuzic (2006) conducted an interesting study looking at how creative thinking and conscientiousness differed in predicting student success. He found that creativity was associated with how well students performed on their dissertations, whereas conscientiousness was more associated with performance on exams. Creative students tended to prefer oral exams, group projects, and working on their dissertations; more conscientious students preferred multiple-choice and essay exams. Moutafi, Furnham, and Paltiel (2004) suggest that less intelligent people may overcompensate by being very conscientious in order to be successful. Perhaps a similar relationship exists with creativity; creative students enjoy activities that allow them to be creative and set their own timetable, whereas less creative students may emphasize tasks that they can accomplish via sheer willpower (such as studying for exams).

What does this all mean? In the arts, creative people are much less conscientious. In the sciences, there is an overwhelming tendency in general for conscientiousness; your average scientist is likely more conscientious than your average artist (and they pay us to figure out this stuff). But when you're looking within the domain, just at scientists, the factor doesn't particularly help and may hurt. Interestingly, King et al. (1996) found that conscientiousness helped less creative people produce more creative accomplishments. Putting this and Feist's meta-analysis together, perhaps genuinely creative scientists don't need to be as conscientious as people who are making advances with more sweat and late nights than moments of inspiration.

It is also important to look beyond just the arts and sciences. People with enterprising interests (i.e., business oriented) tend to be more conscientious (Larson, Rottinghaus, & Borgen, 2002). Yet just as with science, more likely to do something isn't the same as being more creative at it. George and Zhou (2001) studied openness to experience and conscientiousness in organizations, and they found that a supervisor's feedback and the structure of the task were essential in relating the two personality factors to creative behavior on the job. In situations where people received positive feedback from supervisors and had an open-ended task, those who were high on openness to experience produced more creative results. When a person's work is closely monitored, then people who are high on conscientiousness will produce less creative results. In addition, people who are highly conscientious may be more likely to nitpick, be generally unhelpful, and create a negative work environment; these factors then interact to produce a strikingly low level of creativity.

Conscientiousness is typically associated with positive work outcomes (i.e., people showing up for work on time and getting projects completed by deadline), so this type of negative finding is fairly unusual. It is interesting to note that a different study in the workplace, Gelade's (1997) investigation of advertising and design workers, also found a negative relationship between creativity and conscientiousness (and a positive relationship with neuroticism, extraversion, and openness to experience).

Another nuance is that just as openness to experience can be split into openness and intellect, conscientiousness can be divided, also. One aspect is being industrious and focused on achievement, and the other is being orderly and dependable (Roberts, Chernyshenko, Stark, & Goldberg, 2005; DeYoung et al., 2007). If a conscientious kid gets her homework handed in on time, then the industrious one is doing it to get the A, whereas the orderly one is doing it because that's what she's supposed to do. Generally, however, the industrious facet is more associated with actual classroom achievement (Corker, Oswald, & Donnellan, 2012).

Some meta-analyses have suggested that industriousness is related to creativity but orderliness is not (Hough, 1992; Barrick & Mount, 1991). Reiter-Palmon, Illies, and Kobe-Cross (2009) found evidence that a cooperative suppression effect happens with creativity and conscientiousness. Sadly, "cooperative suppression effect" is not a ska band but is instead a statistical term that refers to a very complicated situation that I'm not going to try to completely explain. In essence, industriousness and orderliness are connected to each other (which makes sense, because they both form the larger conscientiousness factor). Industriousness is positively correlated with creativity and orderliness is (slightly) negatively correlated with creativity, but because they are usually measured as one thing (conscientiousness) and not separately, it looks like a nonexistent relationship. It's kind of like if you love peanut butter but dislike bananas, so a peanut butter and banana sandwich is just a nothing concept to you—it doesn't make you want to throw up, but it doesn't sound too good, either.

I would be very curious to see more in-depth investigations of the arts versus the sciences on industriousness and orderliness. My personal guess is that people in the arts are strongly negatively correlated with orderliness but are slightly positively related to industriousness, thereby causing the domain effect. The role of persistence in creativity— plugging away and doing the work needed to succeed—is understudied. Interestingly, people actually tend to underestimate the role that persistence plays in creative performance (Lucas & Nordgren, 2015).

THE REST: MEH

Of the remaining three personality factors, one of them— neuroticism—opens up a can of worms that I'll discuss later when I go into mental health. Creativity and any aspect of mental illness becomes a volatile topic that deserves its own chapter (or its own book; see J. C. Kaufman, 2014), if only to sort out the actual data from the many strongly held opinions and personal feelings. Neuroticism's two facets are withdrawal and volatility (DeYoung, 2015).

The fourth factor, extraversion, is probably linked with creativity. Certainly, extraversion was shown to be related to creativity measured through fantasy stories rated for creativity (Martindale & Dailey, 1996); in an analysis of biographical data, controlling for academic accomplishments (King et al., 1996); through self-reported creative behaviors (Furnham & Bachtiar, 2008); and with divergent thinking tests (Batey, Chamorro-Premuzic, & Furnham, 2009; Furnham & Nederstrom, 2010).

Other studies have compared different types of creativity. Students with performing arts experience were more extraverted than those with visual arts experience or no creativity-relevant experience (Silvia et al., 2008), and arts majors were more extraverted than conventional majors (Silvia & Nusbaum, 2012). Similarly, S. B. Kaufman et al. (2015) found that extraversion was more related to arts-related creative achievement than sciences-related creative achievement. Yet Roy (1996) found that the artists were more introverted than nonartists. Several other studies (most notably Matthews, 1986; McCrae, 1987) found no significant relationship at all. Feist's (1998) meta-analysis showed that scientists were much more introverted than nonscientists—but *creative* scientists were more extraverted than less creative scientists. There was a small effect for artists being more extraverted than nonartists.

DeYoung's (2015) two facets of extraversion are enthusiasm and assertiveness; one of the few studies to look at facets in extraversion and creativity was Maslej et al.'s (2014) study of writers; there was no difference in assertiveness, but writers showed higher levels of activity (the label used in this study as opposed to enthusiasm) than nonwriters.

The fifth factor, agreeableness, has inspired fewer studies, although they general imply it's not too fun to hang out with creative folk, particularly if they like science. The two facets of agreeableness are compassion and politeness (DeYoung, 2015); it is mostly the politeness facet that is (negatively) related to creativity. Broadly, Feist's (1998) meta-analysis found that creative scientists were less agreeable than less creative scientists (see also Feist, 1993, who specifically found links to arrogance and hostility), and artists were less agreeable than nonartists (see also Burch, Pavelis, Hemsley, & Corr, 2006). Honesty/humility was also negatively correlated with self-reported creative accomplishments (Silvia, Kaufman, Reiter-Palmon, & Wigert, 2011; see also King et al., 1996). In business, Hunter and Cushenbery (2014) studied teams and found that disagreeable people's ideas were no more original than other people's ideas, but they were more likely to be adopted by the team. Yet this effect was minimized when the environment was supportive of new ideas.

That said, many positive personal attributes are associated with creativity, as I'll discuss later. Batey and Furnham (2006) suggest that although artistic and scientific creativity may be negatively associated with agreeableness, everyday creativity is positively associated.

Nothing's ever simple.

DeYoung (2006, 2014, 2015) and S. B. Kaufman (2013), of course, are not the only people to blend or split different factors of personality to present new models. Fürst, Ghisletta, and Lubart (2014) suggest three factors: plasticity, divergence, and convergence. Plasticity is comprised of extraversion, openness, and inspiration;

divergence encompasses nonconformity, distraction, disagreeableness, and low conscientiousness; and convergence includes critical sense, persistence, and precision. Plasticity and divergence are both related to idea generation, which in Fürst et al.'s model leads to both everyday creative intensity and achievement. Convergence is linked with idea selection, which leads to everyday creativity achievement.

LOOKING AHEAD

We'll dive into creativity and motivation, which can also look straightforward or thorny depending on your perspective.

REFERENCES

Barrick, M. R., & Mount, M. K. (1991). The Big Five personality dimensions and job performance: A meta-analysis. *Personnel Psychology, 44*, 1–26.

Batey, M., Chamorro-Premuzic, T., & Furnham, A. (2009). Intelligence and personality as predictors of divergent thinking: The role of general, fluid and crystallised intelligence. *Thinking Skills and Creativity, 4*, 60–69.

Batey, M., & Furnham, A. (2006). Creativity, intelligence and personality: A critical review of the scattered literature. *Genetic, Social, and General Psychology Monographs, 132*, 355–429.

Benedek, M., Borovnjak, B., Neubauer, A. C., & Kruse-Weber, S. (2014). Creativity and personality in classical, jazz and folk musicians. *Personality and Individual Differences, 63*, 117–121.

Brown, S. D., Lent, R. W., Telander, K., & Tramayne, S. (2011). Social cognitive career theory, conscientiousness, and work performance: A meta-analytic path analysis. *Journal of Vocational Behavior, 79*, 81–90.

Burch, G. S. J., Pavelis, C., Hemsley, D. R., & Corr, P. J. (2006). Schizotypy and creativity in visual artists. *British Journal of Psychology, 97*, 177–190.

Carson, S. H., Peterson, J. B., & Higgins, D. M. (2005). Reliability, validity and factor structure of the Creative Achievement Questionnaire. *Creativity Research Journal, 17*, 37–50.

Chamorro-Premuzic, T. (2006). Creativity versus conscientiousness: Which is a better predictor of student performance? *Applied Cognitive Psychology, 20*, 521–531.

Christensen, B. T., Drewsen, L. K., & Maaløe, J. (2014). Implicit theories of the personality of the ideal creative employee. *Psychology of Aesthetics, Creativity, and the Arts, 8,* 189–197.

Connelly, B. S., Ones, D. S., Davies, S. E., & Birkland, A. (2014). Opening up openness: A theoretical sort following critical incidents methodology and a meta-analytic investigation of the trait family measures. *Journal of Personality Assessment, 96,* 17–28.

Conrad, N., & Patry, M. W. (2012). Conscientiousness and academic performance: A mediational analysis. *International Journal for the Scholarship of Teaching and Learning, 6,* 1–13.

Corker, K. S., Oswald, F. L., & Donnellan, M. B. (2012). Conscientiousness in the classroom: A process explanation. *Journal of Personality, 80,* 995–1028.

Costa, P. T., & McCrae, R. R. (1992). *NEO PI–R: Professional manual.* Odessa, FL: Psychological Assessment Resources.

DeYoung, C. G. (2006). Higher-order factors of the Big Five in a multi-informant sample. *Journal of Personality and Social Psychology, 91,* 1138–1151.

DeYoung, C. G. (2014). Openness/Intellect: A dimension of personality reflecting cognitive exploration. In M. L. Cooper & R. J. Larsen (Eds.), *APA handbook of personality and social psychology: Personality processes and individual differences* (Vol. 4, pp. 369–399). Washington, DC: American Psychological Association.

DeYoung, C. G. (2015). Cybernetic Big Five theory. *Journal of Research in Personality, 56,* 33–58.

DeYoung, C. G., Quilty, L. C., & Peterson, J. B. (2007). Between facets and domains: 10 aspects of the Big-Five. *Journal of Personality and Social Psychology, 93,* 880–896.

Dollinger, S. J. (2007). Creativity and conservatism. *Personality and Individual Differences, 43,* 1025–1035.

Dollinger, S. J., & Clancy, S. M. (1993). Identity, self, and personality: II. Glimpses through the autophotographic eye. *Journal of Personality and Social Psychology, 64,* 1064–1071.

Domino, G. (1974). Assessment of cinematographic creativity. *Personality and Social Psychology, 30,* 150–154.

Eysenck, S. B., Eysenck, H. J., & Barrett, P. (1985). A revised version of the psychoticism scale. *Personality and Individual Differences, 6,* 21–29.

Feist, G. J. (1993). A structural model of scientific eminence. *Psychological Science, 4,* 366–371.

Feist, G. J. (1998). A meta-analysis of personality in scientific and artistic creativity. *Personality and Social Psychology Review, 2,* 290–309.

Feist, G. J., & Barron, F. (2003). Predicting creativity from early to late adulthood: Intellect, potential and personality. *Journal of Research in Personality, 37,* 62–88.

Fink, A., & Woschnjak, S. (2011). Creativity and personality in professional dancers. *Personality and Individual Differences, 51,* 754–758.

Furnham, A. (1999). Personality and creativity. *Perceptual and Motor Skills, 88,* 407–408.

Furnham, A., & Bachtiar, V. (2008). Personality and intelligence as predictors of creativity. *Personality & Individual Differences, 45,* 613–617.

Furnham, A., & Crump, J. (2013). The sensitive, imaginative, articulate art student and conservative, cool, numerate science student: Individual differences in art and science students. *Learning and Individual Differences, 25,* 150–155.

Furnham, A., & Nederstrom, M. (2010). Ability, demographic and personality predictors of creativity. *Personality and Individual Differences, 48,* 957–961.

Furnham, A., Zhang, J., & Chamorro-Premuzic, T. (2006). The relationship between psychometric and self-estimated intelligence, creativity, personality, and academic achievement. *Cognition and Personality, 25,* 119–145.

Fürst, G., Ghisletta, P., & Lubart, T. (2014). Toward an integrative model of creativity and personality: Theoretical suggestions and preliminary empirical testing. *Journal of Creative Behavior.* Advance online publication. doi:10.1002/jocb.71

Gelade, G. (1997). Creativity in conflict: The personality of the commercial creative. *Journal of Genetic Psychology, 165,* 67–78.

George, J. M., & Zhou, J. (2001). When openness to experience and conscientiousness are related to creative behavior: An interactional approach. *Journal of Applied Psychology, 86,* 513–524.

Goldberg, L. R. (1992). The development of markers for the Big Five factor structure. *Psychological Assessment, 4,* 26–42.

Grosul, M., & Feist, G. J. (2014). The creative person in science. *Psychology of Aesthetics, Creativity, and the Arts, 8,* 30–43.

Hofstee, W. K. B., de Raad, B., & Goldberg, L. R. (1992). Integration of the Big Five and circumplex approaches to trait structure. *Journal of Personality and Social Psychology, 63,* 146–163.

Hong, E., Peng, Y., & O'Neil, H. J. (2014). Activities and accomplishments in various domains: Relationships with creative personality and creative motivation in adolescence. *Roeper Review, 36,* 92–103.

Hough, L. M. (1992). The "Big Five" personality variable construct confusion: Description versus prediction. *Human Performance, 5,* 139–155.

Hui, A., Yeung, D. Y., Sue-Chan, K., Chan, K. , Hui, D. C. K., & Cheng, S. T. (2014). Gains and losses in creative personality as perceived by adults across the lifespan. *Developmental Psychology, 50,* 709–713.

Hunter, S. T., & Cushenbery, L. (2014). Is being a jerk necessary for original-ity? Examining the role of disagreeableness in the sharing and utiliza-tion of original ideas. *Journal of Business and Psychology.* Advance online publication. doi:10.1007/s10869-014-9386-1

Ivcevic, Z., & Mayer, J. D. (2009). Mapping dimensions of creativity in the life-space. *Creativity Research Journal, 21,* 152–165.

Jauk, E., Benedek, M., & Neubauer, A. C. (2014). The road to creative achieve-ment: A latent variable model of ability and personality predictors. *European Journal of Personality, 28,* 95–105.

Karwowski, M., & Lebuda, I. (2015). The Big Five, the Huge Two, and creative self-beliefs: A meta-analysis. *Psychology of Aesthetics, Creativity, and the Arts.* Advance online publication. doi:10.1037/aca0000035

Karwowski, M., Lebuda, I., Wisniewska, E., & Gralewski, J. (2013). Big Five personality factors as the predictors of creative self-efficacy and creative personal identity: Does gender matter? *Journal of Creative Behavior, 47,* 215–232.

Kaufman, J. C. (2002). Narrative and paradigmatic thinking styles in cre-ative writing and journalism students. *Journal of Creative Behavior, 36,* 201–220.

Kaufman, J. C. (Ed.). (2014). *Creativity and mental illness.* New York, NY: Cambridge University Press.

Kaufman, S. B. (2013). Opening up openness to experience: A four-factor model and relations to creative achievement in the arts and sci-ences. *Journal of Creative Behavior, 47,* 233–255.

Kaufman, S. B., Quilty, L. C., Grazioplene, R. G., Hirsh, J. B., Gray, J. R., Peterson, J. B., & DeYoung, C. G. (2015). Openness to experience and intellect differentially predict creative achievement in the arts and sci-ences. *Journal of Personality.* Advance online publication. doi:10.1111/jopy.12156

Kenett, Y. N., Anaki, D., & Faust, M. (2015). Processing of unconventional stimuli requires the recruitment of the non-specialized hemisphere. *Frontiers in Human Neuroscience, 9,* 32.

King, L. A., McKee-Walker, L., & Broyles, S. J. (1996). Creativity and the Five Factor model. *Journal of Research in Personality, 30,* 189–203.

Kyllonen, P. C., Walters, A. M., & Kaufman, J. C. (2005). Noncognitive con-structs and their assessment in graduate education. *Educational Assess-ment, 10,* 153–184.

Larson, L. M., Rottinghaus, P. J., & Borgen, F. H. (2002). Meta-analyses of Big Six interests and Big Five personality factors. *Journal of Vocational Behav-ior, 61,* 217–239.

Lievens, F., Coetsier, P., De Fruyt, F., & De Maeseneer, J. (2002). Medical students' personality characteristics and academic performance: A Five-Factor model perspective. *Medical Education, 36,* 1050–1056.

Lucas, B. J., & Nordgren, L. F. (2015). People underestimate the value of persistence for creative performance. *Journal of Personality and Social Psychology, 109*, 232–243.

Martindale, C. (1989). Personality, situation, and creativity. In J. A. Glover, R. R. Ronning, & C. R. Reynolds (Eds.), *Handbook of creativity* (pp. 211–232). New York, NY: Plenum Press.

Martindale, C., & Dailey, A. (1996). Creativity, primary process cognition and personality. *Personality and Individual Differences, 20*, 409–414.

Maslej, M. M., Rain, M., Fong, K., Oatley, K., & Mar, R. A. (2014). The hierarchical personality structure of aspiring creative writers. *Creativity Research Journal, 26*, 192–202.

Matthews, G. (1986). The interactive effects of extraversion and arousal on performance: Are creativity tests anomalous? *Personality and Individual Differences, 7*, 751–761.

McCrae, R. R. (1987). Creativity, divergent thinking, and openness to experience. *Journal of Personality and Social Psychology, 52*, 1258–1265.

McCrae, R. R., & Costa, P. T., Jr. (1997). Personality trait structure as a human universal. *American Psychologist, 52*, 509–516.

Moutafi, J., Furnham, A., & Paltiel, L. (2004). Why is conscientiousness negatively correlated with intelligence? *Personality and Individual Differences, 37*, 1013–1022.

Mussel, P. (2013). Intellect: A theoretical framework for personality traits related to intellectual achievements. *Journal of Personality and Social Psychology, 104*, 885–906.

Mussel, P., McKay, A. S., Ziegler, M., Hewig, J., & Kaufman, J. C. (2015). Predicting creativity based on the facets of the Theoretical Intellect Framework. *European Journal of Personality, 29*, 459–467.

Nusbaum, E. C., & Silvia, P. J. (2011). Are openness and intellect distinct aspects of openness to experience? A test of the O/I model. *Personality and Individual Differences, 51*, 571–574.

Oral, G. (2008). Sensation seeking and creativity in prospective educators and musicians. *International Journal of Creativity & Problem Solving, 18*, 81–86.

Perrine, N. E., & Brodersen, R. (2005). Artistic and scientific creative behavior: Openness and the mediating role of interests. *Journal of Creative Behavior, 39*, 217–236.

Poropat, A. E. (2009). A meta-analysis of the five-factor model of personality and academic performance. *Psychological Bulletin, 135*, 322–338.

Rawlings, D., Twomey, F., Burns, E., & Morris, S. (1998). Personality, creativity and aesthetic preference: Comparing psychoticism, sensation seeking, schizotypy and openness to experience. *Empirical Studies of the Arts, 16*, 153–178.

Reiter-Palmon, R., Illies, J. J., & Kobe-Cross, L. M. (2009). Conscientiousness is not always a good predictor of performance: The case of creativity. *International Journal of Creativity & Problem Solving, 19,* 27–45.

Roy, D. D. (1996). Personality model of fine artists. *Creativity Research Journal, 9,* 391–394.

Sánchez-Ruiz, M. J., Hernández-Torrano, D., Perez-González, J. C., Batey M., & Petrides, K. V. (2011). The relationship between trait emotional intelligence and creativity across subject domains. *Motivation & Emotion, 35,* 461–473.

Schilpzand, M. C., Herold, D. M., & Shalley, C. E. (2011). Members' openness to experience and teams' creative performance. *Small Group Research, 42,* 55–76.

Silvia, P. J., & Beaty, R. E. (2012). Making creative metaphors: The importance of fluid intelligence for creative thought. *Intelligence, 40,* 343–351.

Silvia, P. J., Kaufman, J. C., Reiter-Palmon, R., & Wigert, B. (2011). Cantankerous creativity: Honesty-Humility, Agreeableness, and the HEXACO structure of creative achievement. *Personality and Individual Differences, 51,* 687–689.

Silvia, P. J., & Nusbaum, E. C. (2012). What's your major? College majors as markers of creativity. *International Journal of Creativity and Problem Solving, 22,* 31–44.

Silvia, P. J., Nusbaum, E. C., Berg, C., Martin, C., & O'Connor, A. (2009). Openness to experience, plasticity, and creativity: Exploring lower-order, higher-order, and interactive effects. *Journal of Research in Personality, 43,* 1087–1090.

Silvia, P. J., Winterstein, B. P., Willse, J. T., Barona, C. M., Cram, J. T., Hess, K. I., . . . Richard, C. A. (2008). Assessing creativity with divergent thinking tasks: Exploring the reliability and validity of new subjective scoring methods. *Psychology of Aesthetics, Creativity, and the Arts, 2,* 68–85.

Walker, A. M., Koestner, R., & Hum, A. (1995). Personality correlates of depressive style in autobiographies of creative achievers. *Journal of Creative Behavior, 29,* 75–94.

Wolfradt, U., & Pretz, J. E. (2001). Individual differences in creativity: Personality, story writing, and hobbies. *European Journal of Personality, 15,* 297–310.

Zuckerman, M. (1994). *Behavioral expressions and biosocial bases of sensation seeking.* New York, NY: Cambridge University Press.

Creativity and Motivation

Just as I did with personality, I'm going to cram an entire century's worth of copious research into a manageable discussion by mostly focusing on one key issue: intrinsic versus extrinsic motivation and their relationship to creativity. As with the Big Five of personality, it is a bit more complex than it sounds, and I will similarly hint at some of this nuance.

Someone who is intrinsically motivated is performing an activity because he or she enjoys it or gets personal meaning out of it. In contrast, extrinsic motivation is doing something for an external reason, such as grades, money, or praise (Deci & Ryan, 1985, 2010; Ryan & Deci, 2000). It's as simple as that. You are driven to do something because you like to do it and believe it has great worth, or because you are getting paid in some way. Neither one is inherently better or worse. There are some times when it's hard to be intrinsically motivated, like when you have to clean toilets. There are some aspects of cleaning toilets that might inspire intrinsic motivation—a pride in one's accomplishments, a strong work ethic, and so on. But the experience itself is unlikely to be in itself rewarding. If you are cleaning a toilet, either you want a specific outcome (such as your bathroom not smelling bad) or someone is giving you money.

Some activities are easy to categorize—I play with my dog Kirby because I love doing it. Nobody's paying me anything (or if they are, Kirby's funneling away the money to a Swiss bank account and not telling me). When I was in graduate school, I would occasionally volunteer to do MRI studies in which I had my brain scanned while I performed some random task. I chose to do these studies because of the $40 they were paying me, which translated into about eight eggplant-sausage calzones at Town Pizza (at least back in the day). But other things are somewhere in the middle. I often enjoy teaching, but I would be unlikely to do it for free. Certainly, I would never offer to grade papers or midterms—particularly multiple-choice tests that involve repetitive circling of answers—if I weren't getting paid for teaching the class. Yet I love mentoring students and have often worked with them in circumstances where I wasn't getting any specific benefits.

Here's where it gets tricky, too—why am I writing this book? It's certainly not for the money. Any academic-oriented book that isn't self-help or an introductory psychology textbook doesn't make enough money to pay more than minimum wage per hour worked. Yet extrinsic motivation can be praise ("Dr. Kaufman," said in an alluring voice, "I really enjoyed your book about creativity") or external evaluations and reviews. Perhaps if writing this book were a purely intrinsically motivated task done for the sheer joy of writing it, it wouldn't matter if anyone ever read it. I could write it and then delete the files off my computer (although my editor would rightfully kill me).

In revising this book, there are some aspects I love and some that feel like work. Going back and rereading what I've written to make sure it makes sense and doesn't have glaring mistakes is a bit of a drudge. Thinking of examples or discovering some of the cool work that's been done since the first edition came out (or stuff I just missed the first go-round) is fun.

Choice is often seen as a big part of intrinsic motivation (Cordova & Lepper, 1996). It's harder to love something when you're forced to do it. Curiously, the importance of choice is mostly a Western phenomenon; choice was much less of a determinant of intrinsic motivation for Asian children than their American counterparts (Iyengar & Lepper, 1999). In fact, when people role-played scenarios that emphasized a more collectivist mentality, choice played a smaller role in intrinsic motivation (Hagger, Rentzelas, Chatzisarantis, 2014). Relatedly, Paletz, Peng, and Li (2011) gave Chinese, Japanese, and American students pairs of professions and asked them to pick which one was more creative. Asian students were more likely to select professions that expressed creativity externally, through their experiences (such as a scientist or an inventor). In contrast, American students chose professions that showed creativity in internal ways, through their disposition (such as being a philosopher or a spiritual person).

If choice may or may not be related to what motivates us, depending on the culture, our goals are definitely a key aspect (Barron & Harackiewicz, 2001; To, Fisher, Ashkanasy, & Rowe, 2012). There are learning goals (also called mastery goals) in which you do something because of the learning you achieve while doing it. You might take a night course in Spanish or Introduction to Tiramisu because you want the knowledge from the course. You don't really care whether you get an A or an A–. Another type of goal is the performance goal—you are focused on how well you perform a task and are less concerned with how much you learn while doing so (Midgely, 2014). If you need to pass an exam to get out of taking Remedial Math, you care much more about doing well on the exam than about learning from it. Taking your driver's test is another good example; if you were anything like me, you wanted to pass the test with the very specific goal of getting your license. Performance goals can be further split into two types: performance-prove, in which you want to show that you can do well, and performance-avoid, in which you want to avoid looking incompetent.

Your goals shift with the task. Let's take cooking, for example. Sometimes you might want to learn new things and try cooking a new dish. You care less about the success of the actual product than the new techniques or combinations that you can apply to future meals (for example, salmon and honey don't usually mix). Other times, you might cook to impress someone, and it's more important to you for the meal to turn out perfectly than for you to learn something. Indeed, you would probably be more likely to use a tried-and-true recipe than experiment.

Learning goals are associated with intrinsic motivation. If your goal from a task is to learn how to do something, then you are more likely to be doing it out of enjoyment or for the meaning of the activity. Performance goals are associated with extrinsic motivation. If your goal is to get a perfect final product, you are more likely to be doing this task for a reward or external value. These connections aren't too shocking.

Sometimes our goals and motivations shift with the task, but there are also consistencies in how we approach things. Dweck (1986, 2000) argued that the main reason why people have different goal orientations is due to how they view psychological attributes such as intelligence or personality, which she calls their mindset. For example, some people have a fixed view of intelligence—either you're smart or you're dumb, and you have what you have. Other people have a malleable view of intelligence; if you keep trying, you can get smarter and succeed. Let's imagine two people, Dawna and Don. When Dawna has trouble doing something, she sees it as a chance to grow and get better. When Don encounters problems, he assumes that he's hit the ceiling for his brain (Miele, Finn & Molden, 2011).

Your mindset and your goals have different types of impact based on your ability. If you have learning goals and a malleable mindset, it doesn't matter how much ability you have; your goal is, after all, to get better. It's equally possible to improve when you're starting from a place of poor ability (Elliott & Dweck, 1988). If you have performance goals and a fixed mindset along with high ability, then you're usually going to do pretty well, also. If you want to write a great poem or give a great speech or juggle 10 chainsaws, *and* you are high in poem-writing, speech-giving, or chainsaw-juggling ability, then the world will be a happy place. The problems come up, however, when you have performance goals and run into a snag. If you feel like you aren't good enough, you are much more likely to give up. This situation produces a learned-helplessness type of response

(Elliot & Church, 1997; Middleton & Midgley, 1997). Analysis of the two types of performance goals has indicated that performance-avoid goals are related to poor performance (Cellar et al., 2011).

Another potential problem is that rewards can have a hidden cost (Lepper & Greene, 1975; Lepper, Greene & Nisbett, 1973). If you offer people a reward to do something that they already find interesting, then you may *decrease* intrinsic motivation. If you enjoy drawing pictures and I start giving you money for drawing pictures, then you may choose to draw fewer pictures for your own enjoyment. According to this theory, offering extensive praise, rewards, or performance incentives may backfire with already dedicated and passionate workers and students (e.g., Kohn, 1993). One application of this general principle, by the way, is how to train your dog not to bark. If your dog barks a lot and you want her to stop, start rewarding the barking behavior. Dog barks, give her a biscuit. Dog barks, give her another biscuit. Your dog will eventually be trained that she should get a biscuit for barking, and she will slowly stop giving you the barking behavior for free. Little does she know, however, that you have again proved your intellectual dominance and fooled her (although your dog does know where you keep the cheese; she's just slowly waiting for the right opportunity to embezzle said cheese and move to Guam, under the mistaken illusion that Guam has a cheese-based economy).

CREATIVITY AND INTRINSIC MOTIVATION

So we have intrinsic motivation, learning goals, and a malleable mindset on one side, and extrinsic motivation, performance goals, and a fixed mindset on the other side, suited up and ready to do battle. It will likely not come as a surprise that creativity tends to be associated with the intrinsic-learning-malleable side. Indeed, the idea that feeling passionately about something leads you to be more creative seems almost simplistic. One time, I was being interviewed for Spanish television about creativity. Right as the segment was ending, the journalist summed up (very nicely, actually) everything I had just said, and then asked me for any final thoughts. I was a bit stymied—anything that came to mind was something that he had just said. The only thing that popped into my brain was "Love what you do." Afterward, I was kicking myself for how corny it sounded (although nothing new entered my head), but the basic mantra holds true.

Much of the research on this area has been conducted by Teresa Amabile and her colleagues (Amabile, 1979, 1982, 1983a, 1983b, 1996; Amabile & Gitomer, 1984; Amabile, Hennessey, & Grossman, 1986; Amabile, Hill, Hennessey, & Tighe, 1994). I will highlight a few of the key studies here. I will first say that the basic idea that intrinsic motivation is associated with higher creativity is reasonably established. For example, a recent meta-analysis of 20 years' worth of studies found that product creativity and intrinsic motivation had an average correlation of $r = .30$ (de Jesus, Rus, Lens, & Imaginário, 2013). This correlation is higher than that for most studies on intelligence and creativity, for example. The debate and intricacies are focused on the underlying reasons and whether and how extrinsic motivation is necessarily bad.

One line of research has tried to induce intrinsic motivation to see if it makes people more creative and extrinsic motivation to see if it makes people less creative. In one classic study, Amabile (1985) studied the effects of an intrinsic versus extrinsic motivational orientation on creative-writing graduate and undergraduate students. She asked the students to first write a poem to establish a baseline of creative writing. She then gave them a list of reasons for writing. One group received lists that stressed extrinsic motivation (i.e., "You want your writing teachers to be favorably impressed with your writing talent," "You know that many of the best jobs available require good writing skills"), while another group received lists that emphasized intrinsic motivation (i.e., "You enjoy the opportunity for self-expression," "You like to play with words"). The students ranked these reasons and then wrote a second poem. The poems were rated according to the Consensual Assessment Technique described in Chapter 4. The students given the list of intrinsic reasons, as well as a control group that received no lists, showed no significant difference in the ratings of creativity. The students given the extrinsic list, however, were rated significantly lower on the second poem.

In a related vein, Greer and Levine (1991) found that students given an intrinsic motivation introduction wrote poems that were judged to be more creative than those produced by a control group. Stanko-Kaczmarek (2012) used a similar method with artists; the folks who received the intrinsic instructions reported being in a better mood and thought they did more creative work than did the extrinsic folks.

Prabhu, Sutton, and Sauser (2008) found the same pattern of intrinsic motivation being positively associated with creativity and extrinsic motivation negatively associated. They also examined personality; intrinsic motivation helped mediate the relationship between openness to experience and creativity. This relationship makes sense given the common ground between intrinsic motivation and openness to experience (liking challenges, being emotional, having many interests).

Why does intrinsic motivation help creativity? One explanation is that it frees people from concerns about the context of a situation (Amabile, Goldfarb, & Brackfield, 1990). This freedom then allows people to focus on the primary task at hand—whether writing a poem or developing a new product. Another possibility is the depth of interest. For example, Ruscio, Whitney, and Amabile (1998) examined which task behaviors best predicted creativity across three domains (problem solving, visual art, and writing). The most important indicator was found to be a participant's involvement in the task, which is also a crucial component of intrinsic motivation. Like many of these studies, these aren't shocking concepts—if you're more involved in a task, it makes sense that you'd be more creative.

One way to think about the link between intrinsic motivation and creativity is in Csikszentmihalyi's (1990, 1996) conception of Flow, or optimal experience. Flow represents the sensations and feelings that come when someone is actively engaged in an intense, favorite pursuit. You must feel like your abilities are a match for the potential challenges of the situation to enter the Flow state—someone who never played the piano would not enter Flow when trying to master Rachmaninov, and a concert pianist would not enter Flow trying to play "Mary Had a Little Lamb" (Csikszentmihalyi, 1990; Csikszentmihalyi & Csikszentmihalyi, 1988). Csikszentmihalyi and colleagues' early studies on Flow asked participants to wear electronic paging devices. The participants were then beeped at random times (during the day, not at 3 a.m.) and asked to fill out forms that asked what they were doing and how they were feeling (Csikszentmihalyi, Rathunde, & Whalen, 1996; Prescott, Csikszentmihalyi, & Graef, 1981). With this technique, Csikszentmihalyi and colleagues were able to determine when people were being creative and in Flow. Later methodologies usually consisted of interviewing well-known creators (Csikszentmihalyi, 1996).

People like being in Flow because it's fun. Some people enter Flow with strenuous physical pursuits; a runner's high (so I'm told) is exhilarating. Other people enter Flow with creative activity. It's a glorious moment of losing track of time and place and being completely absorbed in something. It's easy to get so involved in studying this topic that you forget to take a step back and remember the pure joy of creation. It's also important to remember the pleasure of creativity when we discuss its dark side later in the book.

CREATIVITY AND EXTRINSIC MOTIVATION: EVALUATION

Why does extrinsic motivation potentially hurt creativity? One proposed reason is the threat of evaluation. In general, if people are expecting that their creativity output is going to be judged or evaluated, they are less creative (Amabile, 1979, 1996) and they feel less competent (King & Gurland, 2007).

Chamorro-Premuzic and Reichenbacher (2008) looked at the interaction between personality and threat of evaluation; in their study, both openness to experience and extraversion predicted creativity regardless of whether the participants thought they would be evaluated. People who were low on emotional stability did worse in the evaluation threat condition, although much of this correlation was due to introversion (i.e., neurotic, introverted people did particularly poorly when they thought their work would be evaluated).

Personality is not the only additional factor to consider. Another issue may be whether a person is specifically trying to be creative. A pair of studies by Shalley (1995) found that for people working alone with the specific goal of being creative, the expectation of evaluation led to more creative work. She argued that this expectation of creativity, along with the knowledge that their work would be judged, might lead people to better focus on the task. Delving further, Shalley and Perry-Smith (2001) outlined two types of potential evaluations, controlling and informational. Controlling evaluation emphasizes the specific task performance, triggering extrinsic motivation. Informational evaluation is more concerned with feedback and the chance to learn, and thus increases intrinsic motivation. They found that informational evaluation led to more creative ideas (and higher levels of intrinsic motivation) than did controlling evaluation.

Even within this moderating variable of the type of evaluation, however, is another moderating variable, like nesting dolls. People with a high need for structure (who would have a low tolerance for ambiguity) need feedback so much that the impact of informational versus controlling evaluation does not come into play (Slijkhuis, Rietzschel, & Van Yperen, 2013). They want an answer—any answer—and simply knowing feedback is coming will help with the unpleasant nature of uncertainty. I am reminded of the first time I ever asked out a girl; she responded that her parents wouldn't let her go out (this happened a number of years ago). I persisted and asked, "Well, hypothetically, if they would let you go out—would you go out with me?" There was a noticeable pause, and then ". . . No." Sometimes it is best not to know.

Finally, there may be a key gender difference in evaluation and creativity. J. Baer (1997) asked eighth graders to write original poems and stories and either told them they wouldn't be evaluated or that they would be (and emphasized the evaluation). The poems and stories were rated using the Consensual Assessment Technique, and there was a significant gender-by-motivational-interaction effect. For boys, there was virtually no difference in creativity ratings under intrinsic and extrinsic conditions, but for the girls these differences were quite large. J. Baer (1998) replicated this finding in a follow-up study with students of the same age; once again, the negative impact of both rewards and anticipated evaluation were shown to be largely confined to female subjects. Similarly Conti, Collins, and Picariello (2001) found that girls were less creative in competitive situations and boys were more creative in competitive situations. M. Baer, Vadera, Leenders, and Oldham (2014) examined this question within the context of group creativity and found the same pattern; they also found that within-group collaboration was an underlying reason for these effects.

CREATIVITY AND EXTRINSIC MOTIVATION: REWARDS

A more slippery slope and cause for debate is the role of rewards and creativity. One perspective firmly backs up the idea of the hidden cost of rewards. Amabile et al. (1986) looked at the effect of reward on student creative performance. They had a "reward" and a "no-reward" condition, and then had a second condition as to how the task was presented—"work," "play," or no label. In the "reward" condition, the children were offered the use of a Polaroid camera, a desirable activity for these children, if they would promise to tell a story later. In the "no-reward" condition, the children were also allowed the use of a Polaroid camera, but this was presented as merely another task, not as a reward for future activity. After the children in all conditions took photographs, they were then asked to tell a story, based on a picture book. In the "work" condition, the storytelling task was labeled "work," whereas in the "play" task it was labeled "play." The "no-label" condition did not use a label for the storytelling activity. These stories were then judged by outside raters. Children told more creative stories if they were in the "no-reward" condition, whereas no significant effect was found for the task-labeling condition (Amabile et al., 1986).

In a different study by the same lab, participants received intrinsic motivation training (such as directed discussion sessions that focused on intrinsic reasons for performing the task in question) before performing a task and receiving a reward. For these trained people, receiving a reward did not have a negative effect on creativity (Hennessey, Amabile, & Martinage, 1989). A later study was less optimistic, finding that even with tasks set in a context that emphasized intrinsic motivation, rewards had a negative impact on performance (Cooper, Clasen, Silva-Jalonen, & Butler, 1999). Hennessey (2015) examined how rewards impact creativity across cultures and different types of problems. Results did not yield fully consistent patterns but, as she noted in the paper, there is no reason to doubt the positive power of intrinsic motivation.

Over the last couple of decades, the perspective on rewards has gradually shifted in many quarters. There may be particular circumstances when they can harm creativity, but there are many more when they have no effect or can even help. Cameron and Pierce (1994) conducted a meta-analysis of 96 experimental studies involving the effects of reward on intrinsic motivation, and found that the only negative effect came from a reward being tangible, expected, and given for the performance of a simple task. Eisenberger and Cameron (1996) argued that rewards (which result in extrinsic motivation) are not necessarily detrimental to performance. They stated that the detrimental effects occur under restricted and avoidable conditions, and that rewards can often have a positive effect on creativity.

Subsequent studies indicated that intrinsic motivation and creativity were not necessarily negatively affected by a reward (particularly a verbal reward). Creativity could actually be improved if the reward was presented in a less salient manner, especially in tasks requiring divergent thinking (Eisenberger & Selbst, 1994). Indeed, rewards have been shown to increase creativity when individuals received training in divergent thinking or if instructions emphasized the need for creativity (Eisenberger, Armeli, & Pretz, 1998) or if students had prior experience with creative activity (Eisenberger, Haskins, & Gambleton, 1999). Eisenberger and Rhoades (2001) discovered that employees offered more creative suggestions at work with the promise of a reward—if an intrinsic interest in the activity was already present. Similarly, Malik, Butt, and Choi (2015) found that rewards increased creativity if employees had high creative self-efficacy and valued the rewards.

Eisenberger and Shanock (2003), in reviewing the many studies on the harm or benefits of reward, conclude that much of the debate is surrounding methodological issues. Rewarding creative performance, they argue, increases both intrinsic motivation and creativity; rewarding conventional performance decreases both intrinsic motivation and creativity.

CREATIVITY AND EXTRINSIC MOTIVATION: NUANCES OF REWARDS AND EVALUATION

Rewards and evaluation may interact in how they impact creativity. For example, Friedman (2009) argues that the way that reward is framed is critical to understanding its potential impact on creativity. In his study, people wrote titles for a story and had a possible reward that was either presented as something to be gained (i.e., if your title is among the most creative, you will get a bonus) or not (i.e., if your title is among the least creative, you won't get diddly); there was also a third group that served as a control (the control group never gets the good stuff). People were most creative when there was a reward that was tied to creativity (as in past studies) yet when it was not presented as a specific possible gain. In other words, seeing it as gain-based meant participants were perpetually thinking, "I've got to be in the top half to get my bonus," whereas the nongain group just thought "I'll do okay as long as I don't completely suck."

A thorough meta-analysis by Byron and Khazanchi (2012) added support for the idea that rewards that are explicitly tied to creative work can enhance creativity. In this circumstance, rewards can give people permission to be creative. This positive impact is particularly true when there is more choice (it is worth noting that most of the studies included in the meta-analysis were from Western samples, so it is unclear if this finding would also be true in Eastern cultures). They also found that positive feedback that was specifically focused on the creative task also enhanced creativity.

When I concluded this section in the first edition, I said it was complicated but intrinsic motivation was certainly preferable. And it's hard to argue with that basic statement—people who are intrinsically motivated to do something will likely be more creative. Yet in the real world, we need things like rewards and evaluation. Not giving students grades may help their creativity, but it will also not help them when they're trying to get into college (unless it is a small liberal arts one). As I read the evidence, under the right circumstances and in optimal conditions, they're not necessarily creativity killers.

Amabile (1997) suggested that entrepreneurial creativity existed within a motivational synergy. In other words, if you already have a keen personal interest in a topic (high intrinsic motivation), then the promise of rewards for something that is consistent with your abilities (extrinsic motivation) could spur you on to even higher levels of creativity. Nearly 20 years later, this concept still makes sense to me (and a hat tip to Maciej Karwowski for reminding me of this work and similar work he has done in Polish). In an ideal world, we would get to choose what we would like to do and how we would like to express our creativity. Alas, as Mamet (1987) said in his classic *House of Games*, we all have to live in an imperfect world. Indeed, as I am writing this sentence, my back hurts and I have had too little sleep. We need rewards and evaluation for many things—in school and at work and in life—and there are times that they will hurt people's creativity. We can minimize the impact by optimizing the classroom or organizational climate (as I will discuss later in the book), but sometimes the forces of societal expectations, group needs, and general indifference will combine to squash someone's creative fervor.

GOALS, MINDSETS, AND CREATIVITY

Conceptually, learning goals, malleable mindsets, and intrinsic motivation seem to be consistent with one another, just as performance goals, fixed mindsets, and extrinsic motivation would align together. Yet although there is extensive research on motivation and creativity, the work on mindsets, goals, and creativity is still sparse. Kaufman, Reiter-Palmon, and Royston (2015) reviewed the studies on learning goal orientation and creativity and found great inconsistency. Some studies show a relationship but others do not. Much of this work is done in an organizational setting, meaning that goal orientation is usually one component in a larger model that will often include leadership styles and team behavior (e.g., Gong, Kim,

Lee, & Zhu, 2013). This circumstance is neither good nor bad, but makes it harder to discern the specific role that goal orientation plays in creativity.

How about mindset? People who have a malleable view of intelligence tend to have the same view of creativity (Yamazaki & Kumar, 2013). There have been a couple of studies that show support for a malleable mindset being associated with creativity. O'Connor, Nemeth, and Akutsu (2013) found that people with a malleable creativity mindset tended to have higher self-reported creativity, higher divergent thinking scores, and more interest in creativity. People primed to have a more malleable mindset scored higher on a divergent thinking measure. Karwowski (2014) found that people with a malleable mindset were better at solving insight problems and were more likely to see creativity as part of their self-concept.

BEYOND INTRINSIC AND EXTRINSIC

Just as the Big Five is an accurate but simplified way of thinking about personality, so too is intrinsic and extrinsic motivation. Much of the work on motivation hasn't been applied to creativity yet, so I will primarily focus on what has. A recent and very promising theory is the 4-G approach. Forgeard and Mecklenburg (2013) integrate intrinsic and extrinsic motivation with the idea of the intended beneficiary. If I do an activity, am I thinking mostly of how it impacts me (self-oriented) or an audience (other-oriented)? This concept is rooted in the idea of prosocial motivation (Grant & Berry, 2011), or doing things to help other people. Having an audience in mind doesn't have to be purely altruistic, of course. Theoretically, you could be completely other-oriented in figuring out how to harm a larger number of people.

Forgeard and Mecklenburg (2013) propose a 4-G approach: growth, gain, guidance, and giving, each representing a reason why we engage in creative activity. The two self-oriented motivations are in essence intrinsic and extrinsic; growth is the personal enjoyment of the creative process, and gain is being driven by traditional rewards. Guidance, similar to mentorship, is the pleasure of offering one's creative talents to help someone else nurture and grow. Giving is when you use your creativity to help other people; it is still extrinsic motivation because there is a specific, tangible outcome involved (even if it is not personally beneficial).

Cooper and Jayatilaka (2006) propose a third type of motivation to go along with intrinsic and extrinsic: obligation motivation. Although also tied to extrinsic factors (like rewards), the question of task performance is less important. People driven by obligation motivation simply need to complete the task; how well they do is immaterial. Cooper and Jayatilaka examined how intrinsic, extrinsic, and obligation motivation impacted group creativity; they found that obligation showed a similar pattern as intrinsic motivation, despite appearing to have the same roots as extrinsic. They argued that people may feel more freedom when motivated by obligation because they just need to focus on participating and not on their actual performance.

Another model of creativity and motivation was proposed by Unsworth (2001). She examined the interaction between the type of problem (open or closed) and the reason for engagement (internal or external), resulting in four types of creativity. First is responsive creativity, which is handling a specific problem for an external reason—such as finding a new way to fix a leaky sink. Next is expected creativity, which is being asked to produce something creative, so that the way you create may be inspired but it is in response to a given prompt (much the way that I ask my participants in studies to write a poem or draw a picture—they can do what they want, but it's still part of a study). Then there is contributory creativity, in which your reasons for helping are your own, but the problem to be solved is set—for example, if someone asks your help in brainstorming a solution to a crisis. Finally, Unsworth proposes proactive creativity, in which you actively seek a new problem to solve for your own reasons. It is this last category that holds the most possibility for true greatness.

Unsworth's approach emphasizes the idea of creativity requirements—namely, whether we see what we are doing as needing creativity. If supervisors believe that the job requires creativity, then the employees tend to be more creative (Scott & Bruce, 1994), even when intrinsic motivation is controlled (Yuan & Woodman, 2010). Robinson-Morral, Reiter-Palmon, and Kaufman (2013) found that people with strong beliefs in their own creativity who also believed their job demanded creativity were the most creative. Even people who did not particularly think of themselves as being creative were able to be creative if they felt their job required it.

Joy (2005, 2012) has proposed the idea of innovation motivation, which is comprised of both feeling the need to be different and expecting that acting in an innovative way will be rewarding. Measures of both of these facets of innovation motivation are solidly correlated with intelligence, openness, and several measures of creativity (Joy, in press).

LOOKING AHEAD

At this point you might be thinking, those wacky creativity researchers— they can disagree about everything! To which I would agree, and then introduce you to the topic of creativity and intelligence.

REFERENCES

Amabile, T. M. (1979). Effects of external evaluation on artistic creativity. *Journal of Personality and Social Psychology, 37,* 221–233.

Amabile, T. M. (1982). Children's artistic creativity: Detrimental effects of competition in a field setting. *Personality and Social Psychology Bulletin, 8,* 573–578.

Amabile, T. M. (1983a). *The social psychology of creativity.* New York, NY: Springer-Verlag.

Amabile, T. M. (1983b). The social psychology of creativity: A componential conceptualization. *Journal of Personality and Social Psychology, 45,* 357–376.

Amabile, T. M. (1985). Motivation and creativity: Effects of motivational orientation on creative writers. *Journal of Personality and Social Psychology, 48,* 393–399.

Amabile, T. M. (1996). *Creativity in context: Update to "The Social Psychology of Creativity."* Boulder, CO: Westview Press.

Amabile, T. M. (1997). Entrepreneurial creativity through motivational synergy. *Journal of Creative Behavior, 31,* 18–26.

Amabile, T. M., & Gitomer, J. (1984). Children's artistic creativity: Effects of choice in task materials. *Personality and Social Psychology Bulletin, 10,* 209–215.

Amabile, T. M., Goldfarb, P., & Brackfield, S. C. (1990). Social influences on creativity: Evaluation, coaction, and surveillance. *Creativity Research Journal, 3,* 6–21.

Amabile, T. M., Hennessey, B. A., & Grossman, B. S. (1986). Social influences on creativity: The effects of contracted-for reward. *Journal of Personality and Social Psychology, 50,* 14–23.

Amabile, T. M., Hill, K. G., Hennessey, B. A., & Tighe, E. M. (1994). The Work Preference Inventory: Assessing intrinsic and extrinsic motivational orientations. *Journal of Personality and Social Psychology, 66,* 950–967.

Baer, J. (1997). Gender differences in the effects of anticipated evaluation on creativity. *Creativity Research Journal, 10,* 25–31.

Baer, J. (1998). The case for domain specificity in creativity. *Creativity Research Journal, 11,* 173–177.

Baer, M., Vadera, A. K., Leenders, R. J., & Oldham, G. R. (2014). Intergroup competition as a double-edged sword: How sex composition regulates the effects of competition on group creativity. *Organization Science, 25,* 892–908.

Barron, K. E., & Harackiewicz, J. M. (2001). Achievement goals and optimal motivation: Testing multiple goal models. *Journal of Personality and Social Psychology, 80*(5), 706.

Byron, K., & Khazanchi, S. (2012). Rewards and creative performance: A meta-analytic test of theoretically derived hypotheses. *Psychological Bulletin, 138,* 809–830.

Cameron, J., & Pierce, W. D. (1994). Reinforcement, reward, and intrinsic motivation: A meta-analysis. *Review of Educational Research, 64,* 363–423.

Cellar, D. F., Stuhlmacher, A. F., Young, S. K., Fisher, D. M., Adair, C. K., Haynes, S., & Riester, D. (2011). Trait goal orientation, self-regulation, and performance: A meta-analysis. *Journal of Business and Psychology, 26,* 467–483.

Chamorro-Premuzic, T., & Reichenbacher, L. (2008). Effects of personality and threat of evaluation on divergent and convergent thinking. *Journal of Research in Personality, 42,* 1095–1101.

Conti, R., Collins, M., & Picariello, M. (2001). The impact of competition on intrinsic motivation and creativity: Considering gender, gender segregation, and gender role orientation. *Personality and Individual Differences, 30,* 1273–1289.

Cooper, B. L., Clasen, P., Silva-Jalonen, D. E., & Butler, M. (1999). Creative performance on an inbasket exercise: Effects of inoculation against extrinsic reward. *Journal of Managerial Psychology, 14,* 39–56.

Cooper, R. B., & Jayatilaka, B. (2006). Group creativity: The effects of extrinsic, intrinsic, and obligation motivations. *Creativity Research Journal, 18,* 153–172.

Cordova, D. I., & Lepper, M. R. (1996). Intrinsic motivation and the process of learning: Beneficial effects of contextualization, personalization, and choice. *Journal of Educational Psychology, 88*, 715.

Csikszentmihalyi, M. (1990). *Flow: The psychology of optimal experience.* New York, NY: Harper & Row.

Csikszentmihalyi, M. (1996). *Creativity: Flow and the psychology of discovery and invention.* New York, NY: HarperCollins.

Csikszentmihalyi, M., & Csikszentmihalyi, I. S. (1988). *Optimal experience.* New York, NY: Cambridge University Press.

Csikszentmihalyi, M., Rathunde, K. R., & Whalen, S. (1997). *Talented teenagers: The roots of success and failure.* New York, NY: Cambridge University Press.

Deci, E. L., & Ryan, R. M. (1985). *Intrinsic motivation and self-determination in human behavior.* New York, NY: Plenum.

Deci, E. L., & Ryan, R. M. (2010). *Self-determination.* New York, NY: Wiley.

De Jesus, S. N., Rus, C., Lens, W., & Imaginário, S. (2013). Creativity and intrinsic motivation: A meta-analysis of the studies between 1990–2010. *Creativity Research Journal, 25*, 80–84.

Dweck, C. S. (1986). Motivational processes affecting learning. *American Psychologist, 41*, 1040–1048.

Dweck, C. S. (2000). *Self-theories: Their role in motivation, personality and development.* Philadelphia, PA: Taylor & Francis.

Eisenberger, R., Armeli, S., & Pretz, J. (1998). Can the promise of reward increase creativity? *Journal of Personality and Social Psychology, 74*, 704–714.

Eisenberger, R., & Cameron, J. (1996). Detrimental effects of reward: Reality or myth? *American Psychologist, 51*, 1153–1166.

Eisenberger, R., Haskins, F., & Gambleton, P. (1999). Promised reward and creativity: Effects of prior experience. *Journal of Experimental Social Psychology, 35*, 308–325.

Eisenberger, R., & Rhoades, L. (2001). Incremental effects of reward on creativity. *Journal of Personality and Social Psychology, 81*, 728–741.

Eisenberger, R., & Selbst, M. (1994). Does reward increase or decrease creativity? *Journal of Personality and Social Psychology, 66*, 1116–1127.

Eisenberger, R., & Shanock, L. (2003). Rewards, intrinsic motivation, and creativity: A case study of conceptual and methodological isolation. *Creativity Research Journal, 15*, 121–130.

Elliot, A. J., & Church, M. A. (1997). A hierarchical model of approach and avoidance achievement motivation. *Journal of Personality and Social Psychology, 72*, 218–232.

Elliot, S., & Dweck, C. S. (1988). Goals: An approach to motivation and achievement. *Journal of Personality and Social Psychology, 54*, 5–12.

Forgeard, M. J. C., & Mecklenburg, A. C. (2013). The two dimensions of motivation and a reciprocal model of the creative process. *Review of General Psychology, 17*, 255–266.

Friedman, R. S. (2009). Reinvestigating the effects of promised reward on creativity. *Creativity Research Journal, 21*, 258–264.

Gong, Y., Kim, T. Y., Lee, D. R., & Zhu, J. (2013). A multilevel model of team goal orientation, information exchange, and creativity. *Academy of Management Journal, 56*, 827–851.

Grant, A. M., & Berry, J. W. (2011). The necessity of others is the mother of invention: Intrinsic and prosocial motivations, perspective-taking, and creativity. *Academy of Management Journal, 54*, 73–96.

Greer, M., & Levine, E. (1991). Enhancing creative performance in college students. *Journal of Creative Behavior, 25*, 250–255.

Hagger, M. S., Rentzelas, P., & Chatzisarantis, N. L. (2014). Effects of individualist and collectivist group norms and choice on intrinsic motivation. *Motivation and Emotion, 38*, 215–223.

Hennessey, B. A. (2015). Reward, task motivation, creativity, and teaching: Towards a cross-cultural examination. *Teachers College Record, 117*, 1–28.

Hennessey, B. A., Amabile, T. M., & Martinage, M. (1989). Immunizing children against the negative effects of reward. *Contemporary Educational Psychology, 14*, 212–227.

Iyengar, S. S., & Lepper, M. R. (1999). Rethinking the value of choice: A cultural perspective on intrinsic motivation. *Journal of Personality and Social Psychology, 76*, 349–366.

Joy, S. P. (2005). Innovation motivation and artistic creativity. *Journal of Creative Behavior, 39*, 35–56.

Joy, S. P. (2012). Origins of originality: Innovation motivation and intelligence in poetry and comics. *Empirical Studies of the Arts, 30*, 195–213.

Joy, S. P. (in press). Innovation motivation: A social learning model of originality. In G. J. Feist, R. Reiter-Palmon, & J. C. Kaufman (Eds.), *Cambridge handbook of creativity and personality research*. New York, NY: Cambridge University Press.

Karwowski, M. (2014). Creative mindset: Measurement, correlates, consequences. *Psychology of Aesthetics, Creativity, and the Arts, 8*, 62–70.

Kaufman, J. C., Reiter-Palmon, R., & Royston, R. (2015). What we want impacts how we create: Creativity, motivation, and goals. In R. Wegerif, L. Li, & J. C. Kaufman (Eds.), *The Routledge international handbook of research on teaching thinking* (pp. 181–190). London, England: Routledge.

King, L. A., & Gurland, S. T. (2007). Creativity and experience of a creative task: Person and environment effects. *Journal of Research in Personality, 41*, 1252–1259.

Kohn, A. (1993). *Punished by rewards*. Boston, MA: Houghton Mifflin.

Lepper, M. R., & Greene, D. (1975). Turning play into work: Effects of adult surveillance and extrinsic rewards on children's intrinsic motivation. *Journal of Personality and Social Psychology, 31,* 479–486.

Lepper, M. R., Greene, D., & Nisbett, R. E. (1973). Undermining children's intrinsic interest with extrinsic reward: A test of the "overjustification" hypothesis. *Journal of Personality and Social Psychology, 28,* 129–137.

Malik, M. A. R., Butt, A. N., & Choi, J. N. (2015). Rewards and employee creative performance: Moderating effects of creative self-efficacy, reward importance, and locus of control. *Journal of Organizational Behavior, 36,* 59–74.

Mamet, D. (1987). *House of games: A screenplay*. New York, NY: Grove Press.

Middleton, M. J., & Midgley, C. (1997). Avoiding the demonstration of lack of ability: An underexplored aspect of goal theory. *Journal of Educational Psychology, 89,* 710–718.

Midgley, C. (Ed.). (2014). *Goals, goal structures, and patterns of adaptive learning*. London, England: Routledge.

Miele, D. B., Finn, B., & Molden, D. C. (2011). Does easily learned mean easily remembered? It depends on your beliefs about intelligence. *Psychological Science, 22,* 320–324.

O'Connor, A. J., Nemeth, C. J., & Akutsu, S. (2013). Consequences of beliefs about the malleability of creativity. *Creativity Research Journal, 25,* 155–162.

Paletz, S. B. F., Peng, K., & Li, S. (2011). In the world or in the head: External and internal implicit theories of creativity. *Creativity Research Journal, 23,* 83–98.

Prabhu, V., Sutton, C., & Sauser, W. (2008). Creativity and certain personality traits: Understanding the mediating effect of intrinsic motivation. *Creativity Research Journal, 20,* 53–66.

Prescott, S., Csikszentmihalyi, M., & Graef, R. (1981). Environmental effects on cognitive and affective states: The experiential time sampling approach. *Social Behavior and Personality, 9,* 23–32.

Robinson-Morral, E. J., Reiter-Palmon, R., & Kaufman, J. C. (2013). The interactive effects of self-perceptions and job requirements on creative problem solving. *Journal of Creative Behavior, 47,* 200–214.

Ruscio, J., Whitney, D. M., & Amabile, T. M. (1998). Looking inside the fishbowl of creativity: Verbal and behavioral predictors of creative performance. *Creativity Research Journal, 11,* 243–263.

Ryan, R. M., & Deci, E. L. (2000). Intrinsic and extrinsic motivations: Classic definitions and new directions. *Contemporary Educational Psychology, 25,* 54–67.

Scott, S. G., & Bruce, R. A. (1994). Determinants of innovative behavior: A path model of individual innovation in the workplace. *Academy of Management Journal, 38,* 1442–1465.

Shalley, C. (1995). Effects of coaction, expected evaluation, and goal setting on creativity and productivity. *Academy of Management Journal, 38,* 483–503.

Shalley, C. E., & Perry-Smith, J. E. (2001). Effects of social-psychological factors on creative performance: The role of informational and controlling expected evaluation and modeling experience. *Organizational Behavior and Human Decision Processes, 84,* 1–22.

Slijkhuis, J. M., Rietzschel, E. F., & Van Yperen, N. W. (2013). How evaluation and need for structure affect motivation and creativity. *European Journal of Work and Organizational Psychology, 22,* 15–25.

Stanko-Kaczmarek, M. (2012). The effect of intrinsic motivation on the affect and evaluation of the creative process among fine arts Students. *Creativity Research Journal, 24,* 304–310.

To, M. L., Fisher, C. D., Ashkanasy, N. M., & Rowe, P. A. (2012). Within-person relationships between mood and creativity. *Journal of Applied Psychology, 97,* 519–612.

Unsworth, K. (2001). Unpacking creativity. *Academy of Management Review, 26,* 289–297.

Yamazaki, S., & Kumar, V. K. (2013). Implicit theories of intelligence and creative ability: Relationships with academic risk-taking and academic stress. *International Journal of Creativity & Problem Solving, 23,* 25–39.

Yuan, F., & Woodman, R. W. (2010). Innovative behavior in the workplace: The role of performance and image outcome expectations. *Academy of Management Journal, 53,* 323–342.

Creativity and Intelligence

reativity and intelligence, like bacon and eggs, certainly seem like they should go together (with less cholesterol). But exactly how they do, or whether intelligence is part of creativity or creativity is part of intelligence, is still debated. At one point in time, a "threshold" theory was popular (e.g., Barron, 1963; Getzels & Jackson, 1962), which argued that creativity and intelligence are positively related up until an IQ of approximately 120. After that point, for people of extremely high intelligence, the relationship is minor. In more recent years, however, as our conceptions of both intelligence and creativity have grown more sophisticated, this theory has fallen out of favor. Some recent studies show support for the threshold theory (Jauk, Benedek, Dunst, & Neubauer, 2013) and others do not (Preckel, Holling, & Wiese, 2006). Karwowski and Gralewski (2013) found that whether the threshold hypothesis was supported or not depended on the exact way that it was defined and on the statistical techniques used.

As Plucker and Renzulli (1999) argue (and is still true today), it is not so much that we need to figure out whether intelligence and creativity are related, but how they are related. Indeed, it is a perpetual question as to whether we should be discussing how intelligence fits into models of creativity or how creativity fits into models of intelligence (Sternberg & O'Hara, 1999).

One problem with delving deeply into the matter is that both intelligence and creativity are nuanced beasts. We've already covered the measurement problems inherent in creativity, as well as questions about domains, levels of eminence, and other distractions. Intelligence has its own gristle, as we shall soon see (for a deeper look at intelligence, see Plucker & Esping, 2014). If we look at studies that conceptualize intelligence as g (or a general construct, as I discussed earlier), there is usually a mild but significant positive relationship (Barron & Harrington, 1981; Wallach & Kogan, 1965). Kim (2005) conducted an extensive meta-analysis of 21 studies containing more than 45,000 participants and using multiple measures of IQ and creativity. She found very small positive correlations ($r = .17$) between measures of intellectual ability (designed to measure g) and creativity (primarily divergent thinking).

However, Silvia (2008a, 2008b) argues that the relationship is underestimated because we are limited by looking at observable scores (i.e., performance on an intelligence test). Indeed, he has done some even more recent work with colleagues (which I will discuss soon) that shows the constructs may be much more closely related than we have thought (see, e.g., Silvia, 2015). Another way of considering the relationship between the two constructs is presented by Jung (2014), who suggests that if intelligence is problem solving at an everyday level (e.g., S. B. Kaufman, DeYoung, Reis, & Gray, 2011), then creativity may be problem solving for less common occurrences (e.g., Simonton, 2011).

It is also essential to explore in more detail what we mean by intelligence. Just as creativity is more than just divergent thinking, so is intelligence more than just g. I will discuss some different theories of intelligence and how creativity plays a role in each of them. In many ways, creativity grew out of intelligence research, from the early days of Galton, Binet, and Spearman to Guilford's (1967) Structure of Intellect model, which yielded the concept of divergent and convergent thinking. Unfortunately, most intelligence scholars (both before and after Guilford) have not placed such a high importance on creativity within their theories (J. C. Kaufman, Kaufman, & Plucker, 2013).

SUCCESSFUL INTELLIGENCE

The theory of intelligence that most prominently features creativity is Sternberg's (1996) theory of successful intelligence. An earlier version of this theory, the Triarchic Theory of Intelligence (Sternberg, 1985a), argued that there were three intelligences: analytic (which is what traditional intelligence tests measured), creative, and practical (or "street smarts").

The revised theory comprises three subtheories. The *componential* subtheory outlines the mental mechanisms used in planning, carrying out, and evaluating intelligent behavior (and, I suppose, dumb behavior). The *experiential* subtheory includes the way that people adjust to novelty and automatize information processing (in other words, how you learn to do a complicated activity, such as driving, without having to actively think about it all the time). Finally, the *contextual* subtheory is focused on how we adapt to, select, and shape our real-world environment (Sternberg, Kaufman, & Grigoreko, 2008). Creativity is most present in the experiential subtheory, particularly in how we react to new and different ideas.

An expanded version of successful intelligence is Sternberg's (2003, 2007) WICS model (it is alternately called a model of leadership or education), which stands for Wisdom, Intelligence, Creativity, Synthesized. It builds off of both the Triarchic Theory and the tenets of successful intelligence, adding wisdom as the key additional piece.

Sternberg's measures of successful intelligence (including creativity) predict college success more accurately than standard admissions tests, and differences by ethnicity are significantly reduced (Sternberg, 2006, 2008; Sternberg & Coffin, 2010). I discuss these and similar findings later in the book. Sternberg has also used the successful intelligence model to offer educational interventions in which instruction was aligned with different components of the model. Some interventions showed notable success (e.g., Grigorenko, Jarvin, & Sternberg, 2002; Sternberg, Jarvin, & Grigorenko, 2011). However, a huge study drawing on nearly 8,000 students spread out across the United States found that successful intelligence instructional interventions often outperformed the control condition, but the effects were inconsistent and nowhere near as strong as in past studies (Sternberg et al., 2014). Such discouraging findings may be most attributable, however, to just how hard it is to upscale successful educational interventions.

MULTIPLE INTELLIGENCES

Gardner's well-known theory of multiple intelligences (1999, 2006) does not specifically address creativity in the same way that it does not address the idea of g; it is a different approach to intelligence. There is surprisingly little research that explicitly studies creativity and multiple intelligences. However, his eight intelligences (interpersonal, intrapersonal, spatial, naturalistic, language, logical-mathematical, bodily-kinesthetic, and musical) certainly seem to require varying levels of creativity. Gardner (1993) has also written books with case studies of eminent creative individuals who embody his intelligences (Freud, Einstein, Picasso, Stravinsky, T. S. Eliot, Martha Graham, and Gandhi). Certainly, his conception of intelligence is "creativity friendly."

CHC THEORY: *Gf* AND *Gc*

The theory of intelligence that is most frequently used in the construction of IQ tests is the Cattell–Horn–Carroll (CHC) theory, a synthesis of the Cattell–Horn theory of fluid and crystallized intelligence (Horn & Cattell, 1966) and Carroll's (1993) Three-Stratum Theory.

Both theories started from the same initial point, Spearman's (1904) g-factor theory. You may remember g theory from earlier in the book (or as the star of *Die Hard*—no, wait, that was Bruce Willis;

I get them confused). Although Cattell/Horn and Carroll took different paths from the idea of *g*, they ended up with strikingly consistent conclusions about what the spectrum of cognitive abilities looks like. Horn and Cattell split *g* into two parts: fluid intelligence (*Gf*), the ability to apply a variety of mental operations to solve novel problems, ones that don't benefit from past learning or experience, and crystallized intelligence (*Gc*), the breadth and depth of a person's accumulated knowledge of a culture and the ability to use that knowledge to solve problems (Horn & Cattell, 1966).

Although Horn expanded the model (as I will discuss) and the integration of Horn–Cattell with Carroll led to further refinements, it is especially important to understand *Gf* and *Gc* if we want to analyze intelligence's relationship with creativity. One way to distinguish and explain the two types of intelligences is to look at how we age—which also helps explain some of the creative trajectories I discussed earlier.

As you may remember, Simonton's (1994, 1997) work noted that individuals in some creative fields (such as mathematics and physics) peak particularly young. Someone's first notable contribution (not necessarily a best work) happens at an even younger age. Most mathematicians have made their first mark on the field by their 25th birthday. It is quite rare for someone over 40 to make a major discovery in theoretical physics. Why? There are, of course, many possible reasons for these patterns of decline; one is rooted in *Gf–Gc*.

A. S. Kaufman (2000, 2001; see also A. S. Kaufman, 2009) used data from three different editions of the Wechsler Adult Intelligence Scales to compare people across different age cohorts. A. S. Kaufman controlled for educational level, thereby accounting for the big difference in graduation rates in age (regardless of whether it was the "Greatest Generation," it was never known as the "Best-Educated Generation"). What he found was a little scary. First, the good news: *Gc* maintains pretty well. Crystallized intelligence peaks around ages 45 to 54, and doesn't get depressingly low until about age 80. This bit of information should be quite encouraging—you'll likely remember reading about this study for a mighty long time. The bad news: *Gf* peaks around 20 to 24, and starts dropping at a rate of about 5 IQ points a decade. Scores are notably lower by age 40. If you're in your late 20s or older, then your ability to problem solve

141

and deal with new stimuli is dropping *as you read these words*. This is not necessarily the best news for someone contemplating a creative career change.

It is possible that the drops in fluid intelligence may be counterbalanced by other factors (such as experience) that enable people to stay at least somewhat successful with advancing age. Ng and Feldman (2008) conducted a large meta-analysis that studied job performance and age; one of their 10 dimensions of job performance was creativity. They found no relationship between age and creativity when measured either as a self-report or when measured by supervisor ratings. Remember, though, that the studies were conducted at the workplace, so the upper age limit was 59 years old.

Roskos-Ewoldsen, Black, and McCown (2008) looked at creativity as measured by both the Torrance Tests and a creative invention task. They found no age differences on the Torrance Tests, but they did find that younger adults (aged 18–22) outperformed older adults (aged 61–86) on the creative invention task. However, these differences disappeared when they accounted for differences in working memory. It may be that declines in working memory and Gf make it difficult for older people to make unique contributions in certain fields. In contrast, the steadiness of Gc may be the reason why some people in occupations, such as historians and philosophers, can peak well into their fifth decade (Simonton, 1989, 2012). Other studies of creativity across the life span in average people have found that most people peak in divergent thinking and creative production around the age of 40, but remain somewhat stable until age 70 (Palmiero, 2015). In comparing younger versus older adults on both verbal and figural divergent thinking tests, the only significant difference was that older people showed lower fluency on the figural test (Palmiero, Di Giacomo, & Passafiume, 2014). An interesting addition to this discussion is to consider what people think will happen. One study found that young people thought that creativity declined sharply with age, but middle-aged and older people thought that creativity did not start to decline until much later. In addition, older people thought creativity began to truly develop much later in life as well (Hui et al., 2014).

In the early stages of the Cattell–Horn Gf–Gc theory, Gf (fluid intelligence) was hypothesized to be closely linked to creativity

(Cattell & Butcher, 1968). Such a relationship is no longer explicitly part of the model. Nevertheless, many studies have examined the creativity–intelligence connection through a Gf–Gc lens. In my opinion, one of the most thorough studies was by Sligh, Conners, and Roskos-Ewoldsen (2005), who used an individually administered IQ test (Kaufman Adolescent and Adult Intelligence Test [KAIT]; A. S. Kaufman & Kaufman, 1993) and a creative invention task (in which people would use shapes to create a possible object, and then name and describe the invention; see Finke, 1990). They found that Gc showed the same moderate and positive relationship to creativity as in past studies with g. In contrast, Gf was more related to creativity in people with higher IQs.

Most of the other studies that have examined Gf–Gc and creativity have used group-administered intelligence tests. Such tests work well for research but have less clinical or psychoeducational relevance (A. S. Kaufman & Lichtenberger, 2006). These studies have shown mixed results. Batey, Furnham, and Safiullina (2010) found that Gf—and not Gc—predicted performance on a divergent thinking fluency task. Gf was also found to significantly predict both creative metaphor production (Silvia & Beaty, 2012) and ideational behavior (Batey, Chamorro-Premuzic, & Furnham, 2010). Yet Batey, Chamorro-Premuzic, and Furnham (2009) found that Gc was more tied to divergent thinking fluency scores than were Gf, a g-based ability measure, and personality scores; Cho, Nijenhuis, van Vianen, Kim, and Lee (2010) found comparable results.

Some new work has looked at the underlying mechanisms between these relationships. Gilhooly, Fioratou, Anthony, and Wynn (2007) argue that divergent thinking is essentially an executive cognitive function. Nusbaum and Silvia (2011) examined this idea empirically by looking at the role that Gf and strategy use played in divergent thinking tasks. They found that Gf did predict creativity—but it also predicted who would benefit most from using a new strategy for the divergent thinking tasks. People with high Gf improved even more with an efficient strategy.

Beaty and Silvia (2012) looked further at Gf's role in divergent thinking. They asked people to do divergent thinking tests over 10 minutes. Not surprisingly, people had more creative ideas with more time. Yet people with higher Gf scores showed much less improvement—their initial ideas were quite creative, and having more time to think of new ideas made less of an impact. People with lower *Gf* scores needed the extra time to reach their creative potential. Remember, as my friend Zorana Ivcevic Pringle points out, that the sample is college students, so even people with "low" *Gf* scores aren't dumb.

An interesting suggestion posed by Batey and Furnham (2006) is that the role of *Gf* and *Gc* in creativity may shift across the life span of a creative person. *Gf*, they argue, might be more important in early stages, such as mini-c and little-c (Beghetto & Kaufman, 2007, 2014; J. C. Kaufman & Beghetto, 2009). Conversely, a later-career creator (who might be in Pro-c) may rely more on *Gc*—and, I would add, some other dimensions of the CHC model (as I will discuss).

Benedek, Jauk, Sommer, Arendasy, and Neubauer (2014) examined the underlying executive functions behind both divergent thinking and *Gf*. They studied three types of executive functions (Miyake & Friedman, 2012): updating (effectively managing one's short-term memory by replacing outdated information with more relevant stuff), shifting (being flexible enough to shift between types of tasks, such as determining whether number–letter pairs are either odd or even or a vowel or a consonant), and inhibition. Inhibition is the ability to not say the obvious response, such as in the Stroop task; you might be shown the name of a color ("blue") in the shade of a different color (pink) and then asked to say the shade of the color while ignoring the word. Benedek et al. found that only the executive function of updating predicted *Gf*, and both updating and inhibition predicted divergent thinking.

Now if you've paying exceptionally close attention, you might remember that disinhibition (or low levels of inhibition) is related to sensation seeking, which is related to creativity. Having disinhibition has been suggested to relate to creativity (Martindale, 1999). There is also a very closely related concept of latent inhibition; if regular inhibition is being able to filter out the dominant response, then latent inhibition is the broader ability to filter out anything that seems irrelevant. Some studies also show that low levels of latent inhibition are associated with openness to experience and creativity—as well as schizotypy, which is a whole different can of worms that awaits in the next chapter (Carson, 2011).

But here we have a finding that inhibition can help creativity. It's not a single result, either; a different study found a similar connection using a Stroop-like task (Edl, Benedek, Papousek, Weiss, & Fink, 2014). In addition, another way of examining inhibition is to have people randomly generate sequences of one-digit numbers (3, 7, 2, 9, 1, 4) and see if they can avoid the trap of using patterns (such as 2, 4, 6, 8 or 1, 1, 2, 3, 5, 8, for all the Fibonacci fans out there). Again, inhibition is associated with greater divergent thinking (Benedek, Franz, Heene, & Neubauer, 2012; Zabelina, Robinson, Council, & Bresin, 2012).

What gives? I'm not smart enough to answer, but luckily Mathias Benedek was kind enough to not only coach me on this topic but also suggest a possible answer. He notes that Zabelina, O'Leary, Pornpattananangkul, Nusslock, and Beeman (2015) studied disinhibition (they call it leaky sensory gating, which is a much cooler term) with an auditory task that measured ERPs (if you know what that means, great; if you don't, join me in the corner). They found that inhibition was positively associated with divergent thinking, but disinhibition was positively associated with real-world creative achievements. Divergent thinking tasks, with a specific goal and a time limit, may benefit from the ability to hyperfocus and blot out distracting thoughts. In the real world, though, this lack of filter (particularly when paired with higher intelligence; Peterson, Smith, & Carson, 2002) can lead to higher levels of creativity. It is important to note that it is entirely out of your control whether you have a leaky filter and cannot ignore irrelevant noise or whether you have high inhibition and can block everything but the main task. It is essential to keep remembering this point as we later discuss these issues and mental health.

CHC THEORY: THE FULL MODEL

The full CHC model expands on Gf–Gc and adds a number of additional intelligences. Horn continued to expand and tinker with the model through the 1980s and 1990s, only bothering to write down his thoughts in a few chapters with his graduate students at the time

(Horn & Hofer, 1992; Horn & Noll, 1997). Indeed, I had the good fortune to have John Horn as my undergraduate advisor, and the sheer number of ideas he had was astounding. He was fascinated by ideas and much less concerned with writing them down or publishing them; we're lucky we have what exists.

The original Cattell–Horn model, Horn's expansion, and Carroll's work were integrated into one large model with additional factors beyond Gc and Gf (Flanagan, Ortiz, & Alfonso, 2013). These factors included Gq (quantitative knowledge, typically related to math), Grw (reading and writing), Gsm (short-term memory, although when measured it is closer to working memory), Gv (visual processing), Ga (auditory processing), Glr (long-term storage and retrieval), Gs (processing speed), and Gt (decision speed/reaction time).

In this expanded model, creativity is primarily related to long-term storage and retrieval (Glr), which is defined as the ability to store information in long-term memory and then be able to retrieve it when needed (Flanagan et al., 2013). You use Glr when you learn the name of your son's third-grade teacher and then again when you are able to remember the name of your own third-grade teacher. You are still using Glr when you help your son with his homework and can recall your own long-ago knowledge of the state capitals and then link this memory of Hartford being the capital of Connecticut with last night's news story about the Mark Twain house in Hartford. The connection of Glr to creativity may seem tenuous, but remember Mednick's (1968) associative theory. Being able to make remote associations requires the ability to dredge things out of your long-term memory when you need them. Those "aha" moments of insight often occur when past knowledge is considered in a new way. As an example, imagine if I ask you for a straightforward explanation of why three pieces of coal, a carrot, and a scarf might be sitting on someone's front lawn. If you can produce the right answer ("a melted snowman"), it is because you're combining old knowledge ("snowmen are made with coal, carrots, and scarves") with this new information. You need both the knowledge and a good memory to make this connection. It may seem to be less creative to dig out a response from memory versus coming up with a new idea. Silvia, Nusbaum, and Beaty (2015) compared divergent thinking responses that were old and remembered with those that were spontaneously produced. The "old" ideas were judged by external raters to be less creative—but there was no difference between how both "old" and "new" responses predicted other creativity-related abilities (such as openness).

Glr has two distinct components: *learning efficiency* (how well you can both learn and retain new information) and *fluency* (your ability to rapidly recall many things). Continuing the spiraling hierarchy, there are then further "narrow abilities" that comprise these components (Schneider & Flanagan, 2015; Schneider & McGrew, 2012). One of these narrow abilities is idea production, which can encompass fluency, flexibility, and originality (J. C. Kaufman, Kaufman, & Lichtenberger, 2011). These may sound a bit familiar, especially if you can use your own *Glr* to remember Chapter 4 of this book (and the part about divergent thinking).

Gabora (2010) has proposed that analytic thought activates standard neurons (dog–cat type associations), whereas associative thought triggers additional neurons (which she dubs "neurds"). The "neurds" that are activated bring with them the associations most relevant for the specific context. So, for example, the connection between *dog* and *cat* is pretty straightforward, whereas that for *dog* and *colorblind* is more remote. If you hear the word *dog* in a situation that makes you think about vision, the "neurds" that carry the "dogs are colorblind" concept might be prompted. This act of engaging in associative thought may actually give you bonus cognitive capacity.

In addition, increasing specific aspects of your memory can boost your creativity. People who received instructions on how to better remember specific details about a recent life event performed better on a divergent thinking task than controls (Madore, Addis, & Schacter, 2015).

Part of using your memory to be more creative also means knowing (perhaps subconsciously) what information to let go. Retrieval-induced forgetting is when the act of remembering a particular piece of information causes related information to be forgotten or harder to retrieve (MacLeod & Macrae, 2001). Bristol and Viskontas (2016) connect this process with reduced cortical inhibition and argue that people who are less prone to retrieval-induced forgetting will also be more creative. Yet, in my continuing goal of making the research literature as confusing and disjointed as possible, I will point out that a different study by Storm, Angello, and Bjork (2011) found that when people take the Remote Associates Test they are more likely to forget other common associated words. This tendency, called goal-directed forgetting (Bjork, Bjork, & Anderson, 1998), is linked to better creative problem solving. Storm and Patel (2014), across four experiments, also found this effect with a divergent thinking test. They had people study some common potential uses for household objects (such as buckets or spoons), then later had them generate many different uses for those same objects (as in an Alternate Uses test). The people who were able to come up with the most creative responses were those who could forget the original common uses they had studied. As with love, there are times when it is good to remember and times when it is good to forget.

In a nice case of theory mirroring the actual research, however, there are several studies that suggest that *Glr* is empirically related to creativity. Avitia and Kaufman (2014) compared rated creative performance in drawing and writing with scores on *Glr* (as measured by four subtests from the Kaufman Assessment Battery for Children–II; A. S. Kaufman & Kaufman, 2004) and *Gc*. Creative writing (curiously) showed no association with either *Glr* or *Gc*; drawing was significantly related with *Glr*, and this relationship was stronger for *Glr* than for *Gc*.

Silvia, Beaty, and Nusbaum (2013) examined how divergent thinking performance related to multiple verbal fluency tests (representing the fluency-related, lower-order *Glr* factors). Silvia et al. found that the primary *Glr* factor had a significant effect on both originality and fluency (as did *Gf*). In a similar vein, Benedek, Könen, and Neubauer (2012) showed that cognitive tasks that are comparable to *Glr*, such as associative fluency, were strongly related with divergent thinking measures. Another study by Benedek and Neubauer (2013) suggested that the key variable related to creativity was not the way that people stored information, but rather how effectively they could draw information from memory. Beaty, Silvia, Nusbaum, Jauk, and Benedek (2014) explored how *Glr* and *Gc* interact with creativity and semantic differences; think of Mednick's (1968) associational theory—larger semantic differences represent a more remote association. Only *Glr* and larger semantic differences predicted more creative responses to a divergent thinking item, whereas all three predicted the fluency of responses. Similarly, Kenett, Anaki, and Faust (2014) compared the semantic memory networks of people who were high or low on creativity. Less creative people had more rigid networks that were more likely to break off into subcomponents. Consistent with Mednick's (1962) ideas, the more that a person's network is broken apart, the harder it is to retrieve an appropriate memory to help solve a creative problem (imagine picking up a ball from your lawn compared to chasing a ball that has rolled down the gutter).

Glr is not the only additional CHC component to be connected with creativity. Martindale (1999) proposed a differential relationship between *Gs* (processing speed) and creativity, and his theory has been tested out (Dorfman, Martindale, Gassimova, & Vartanian, 2008; Vartanian, Martindale, & Kwiatkowski, 2007). According to Martindale's model, people who are creative vary in their speed of information processing. Early in the creative problem-solving stage, when interference from distracting information is typically high, their breadth of attention is wider, allowing a larger amount of information to be processed. This in turn lowers processing speed. Later, when the problem space is better understood and interference is reduced, their attention span becomes narrower and their reaction time is therefore quicker. To test this theory, Vartanian, Martindale, and colleagues administered two different types of reaction-time tasks to their participants. One set of tasks included high levels of ambiguity and interference, whereas the reverse was true for the other set of tasks. As predicted, across both studies creative participants were slower in the former set of tasks but faster in the latter set of tasks. Importantly, Martindale argued that in creative people this variability in processing speed is not regulated purposefully, but rather happens in reaction to features of the problem space. In other words, creative people reflexively exhibit greater sensitivity to levels of ambiguity and interference in the problem space than do noncreative people.

There is also some reason to believe that other factors may be related. *Grw* (reading and writing) has been proposed to include some creativity-relevant abilities, particularly divergent production (J. C. Kaufman et al., 2011). In addition, *Gsm* (short-term memory) may have a connection. In one in-depth investigation, cellists with higher working memory were able to better improvise, and working memory was separately associated with higher levels of originality (De Dreu, Nijstad, Baas, Wolsink, & Roskes, 2012).

THE PASS MODEL

Although most current studies of intelligence and creativity use either g or the CHC model, these are by no means the only approaches to warrant discussion. The Planning, Attention, Simultaneous, and Successive (PASS) theory (Das, Naglieri, & Kirby, 1994) is a cognitive-processing approach rooted in the neuropsychological work of Luria (1970). According to this model, there are three functional units in the brain. The first unit is responsible for focused and sustained attention. The second unit receives and stores information, with both simultaneous and successive (or sequential) processing. Simultaneous processing is integrating information together; pieces are synthesized together much as one might appreciate a painting all at once. Successive processing is interpreting each piece of individual information separately, in sequential fashion. Think about how you would want to get directions to an unknown place. If you want someone to draw you a map, then you prefer simultaneous processing—seeing everything together. If you want someone to write out line-by-line directions ("Turn right on Outer Highway 10, then turn left in front of the monster truck dealership"), then you prefer successive processing. If you prefer to have a GPS use maps, directions, and vocal instructions to tell you what to do, then you're simply lazy.

The third functional unit is responsible for decision making, self-monitoring behavior, and planning. It is this last ability, planning, that has been hypothesized to be related to creativity (Naglieri & Kaufman, 2001). People who spent time planning and replanning a project were more productive and more creative (Redmond, Mumford, & Teach, 1993), consistent with the already-discussed research on problem recognition and creativity. Finally, mind-wandering has been proposed to play a crucial role in both planning and creativity (Mooneyham & Schooler, 2013). The connection with creativity may seem straightforward (mind-wandering can occur during the incubation stage of the creative problem-solving process and is generally associated with imagination). Planning can come about, Mooneyham and Schooler argue, because many of the thoughts that people have when mind-wandering are future-oriented thoughts. Someone starting to lose attention during a meeting may be thinking of a fantastic story or be calculating weekend plans.

CREATIVITY AND ABILITY TESTS

Although creativity is certainly related to many theories of intelligence, it is not particularly present on any major IQ test battery (J. C. Kaufman et al., 2011). Indeed, creativity can actually hurt performance on some tests. For example, one subtest on the Wechsler Adult Intelligence Scale–IV is Similarities. An example of a question (not a real one) is "What do a dodo bird and a dinosaur have in common?" A 2-point response would likely be, "They are both extinct." A 1-point response might be, "They are both animals." Yet if you answered in a completely novel (yet appropriate) way with "They were both characters in Disney movies" [*Alice in Wonderland* and *Toy Story*], then you would earn a score of 0.

Consider *New York Times* bestselling author Daniel Tammet's beautiful comment on this phenomenon: "You can imagine all kinds of wonderfully poetic, interesting, creative responses to that kind of question but if it's not simply and bluntly that they're both living things, something that is so trivially true that most people wouldn't even think of it... they would be marked down if they didn't say it as the answer. The other answer, which is more interesting and creative than the actual response expected, gets zero marks" (quoted in S. B. Kaufman, 2009, n. p.). This way of inadvertently punishing creative responses may be a reason why the correlations between creativity and intelligence seem lower than you might think.

The absence of creativity on standardized IQ and ability tests is noticed by the average Joe. Layperson conceptions of intelligence typically include problem solving and verbal fluency as key components, both of which are associated with creativity (Sternberg, 1985b; Sternberg, Conway, Ketron, & Bernstein, 1981). Of the top

100 liberal arts colleges, 46 do not require the SAT ("Colleges and Universities," 2015), with at least one college, Bates, citing as a reason that students who do not submit SAT scores are more likely to pursue original and creative activities (Bates College Office of Communications and Media Relations, 2004).

KNOWLEDGE AND ACADEMIC ACHIEVEMENT

As I will discuss later when I go into creativity, fairness, and admissions, the argument for including creativity in the college admissions process is that it doesn't overlap terribly well with existing measures. Early critics of the SATs and their ilk actually highlighted the tests' low correlations with divergent thinking as a major anti-testing argument (Wallach & Wing, 1969; Wing & Wallach, 1971).

Most studies that actually look at how standardized tests relate to creativity find the same low correlations that are found with intelligence—a pattern that makes sense given that standardized tests are highly related to IQ (Frey & Detterman, 2004; Koenig, Frey, & Detterman, 2008). These low levels (correlations ranging from $r = .20$ to $r = .26$) have been found in studies that have compared SAT or ACT results with such creativity measures as rated drawings and photographs and self-reported creative behaviors (Dollinger, 2011), and a rated imagination task and self-reported creative accomplishments (Dollinger & Skaggs, 2011). The GREs have also been shown to correlate with self-reported creativity (Powers & Kaufman, 2004). Kuncel, Hezlett, and Ones (2001) used a meta-analysis to argue that the Miller Analogies Test not only predicts academic performance, but also creativity (and job performance, career potential, and perhaps the ability to regenerate limbs like a newt).

A similar relationship has been found between school GPA and creativity (Grigorenko et al., 2009). Some studies have found that although creativity does predict GPA, other variables do it better or more directly, such as cognitive style (Niaz, Nunez, & Pineda,

2000), mental speed and short-term memory (Vock, Preckel, & Holling, 2011), or reasoning ability (Freund & Holling, 2008).

In the Grigorenko et al. (2009) study, private school students who performed well on two creativity tasks (writing and science) also had higher GPAs. The creative science task significantly predicted first-year GPA, although the creative writing task did not. In addition, a rated creativity score (by admissions officers) was not predictive of first-year GPA, either. Grigorenko et al. (2009) argue that the admissions ratings' lack of predictive validity is a sign that performance-based tests are needed (there is also the question of whether admissions officers qualify as genuine expert raters). Altman (1999) looked at divergent thinking and GPA and found a bimodal distribution; creativity was most associated with grades in early courses and very advanced courses. It is also interesting to note that Gralewski and Karwowski (2012) found that the relationship between GPA and creativity was much stronger in big schools and in schools located in bigger cities. They hypothesize it may be because in bigger cities students may have larger numbers of weak social relationships, which could spur a wider variety of possible ideas.

A different approach is to see whether standardized test scores predict later creative achievement; a series of longitudinal studies on this topic has been conducted on gifted 13-year-olds who were administered the SAT and then followed years later. The SAT scores of these children, who had taken the tests so much earlier than most kids, predicted a wide range of adult achievement years later—which extended to creativity-related success within their fields (Wai, Lubinski, & Benbow, 2005). Indeed, math SAT scores predicted scientific creative accomplishment, such as patents or publications (Park, Lubinski, & Benbow, 2007), and higher scores predicted more creative achievement even when academic degrees were controlled (Park, Lubinski, & Benbow, 2008). In addition, verbal SAT scores specifically predicted artistic creative accomplishment (Kell, Lubinski, & Benbow, 2013). Higher spatial ability above and beyond high SAT scores further predicted creativity in technological fields (Kell, Lubinski, Benbow, & Steiger, 2013).

We've been talking about knowledge in terms of school-based learning, but there are many types of knowledge. It can also refer to someone's everyday knowledge of a particular topic. Some scholars have argued that too much knowledge can stifle creativity because it can lead to inflexibility (e.g., Frensch & Sternberg, 1989). However, Bilalić, McLeod, and Gobet (2008) questioned whether expertise truly came with such negative side effects. They found that although some expert chess players were inflexible, they were more likely to be flexible if they had an even greater level of expertise. Such findings indicate that the rigid-expert stereotype may be an urban myth.

Another way that knowledge may hinder creativity is via the path-of-least-resistance model (Ward, 1995; Ward, Dodds, Saunders, & Sifonis, 2000; Ward & Kolomyts, 2010). According to this model, people will tend to rely on standard examples within a domain to generate new ideas in that same domain. So if I ask you to name a color, you're more likely to say "blue" than "magenta." If I ask you to name an old-time baseball Hall-of-Famer, you're more likely to say "Babe Ruth" than "Tris Speaker." This principle extends to how we use our imaginations. Tom Ward and his colleagues have done much of this work. For example, Ward (1994) asked students to imagine animal life on other planets, and found that nearly everyone used Earth-based animal characteristics (such as eyes and legs) as a basis for their alien creatures. These results held even when students were asked to describe alien animals that were extremely different from Earth beings (Ward & Sifonis, 1997), and similar patterns emerged for a variety of different concepts (such as food or tools; Ward, Patterson, Sifonis, Dodds, & Saunders, 2002). Dow (2015) applied this concept to accidental plagiarism (cryptomnesia, which should mean something cooler). Across several studies, she found that providing examples increased the odds of accidental plagiarism, especially for novices and those under high cognitive load.

In addition, we're also more likely to use recently primed words; Ward and Wickes (2009) asked people to rate either fruit (such as apples, bananas, figs, and plantains) or tools (such as screwdrivers, wrenches, pitchforks, and rakes) on how pleasing they were. They were then asked to do a creative generation task involving either fruit or tools. What they found, in essence, was that people were lazy in two different ways. People were more likely to use a fruit or tool in the generation task if they had just seen it in their rating task. But people were also more likely to use popular items—so apples and bananas showed up more than figs and plantains, and screwdrivers and wrenches made more appearances than pitchforks and rakes.

This same phenomenon can be found in how we behave in teams. When people in a group feel that they are similar to others in the group, they are more likely to behave in a way that reflects the group's beliefs. Adarves-Yorno, Postmes, and Haslam (2007) first primed either social (group) identity or personal identity. With social identity primed, people were creative in ways consistent with group behavior and rated other people's work as more creative when it was consistent with group norms. When personal identity was primed, people were more willing to be creative in different ways than the group; they also gave higher ratings to creative work that disobeyed group norms. A second study had people work by themselves after group norms were established; with social identity primed, people were creative in a manner aligned with the group—even when they were working all by themselves. The power of the social norm is another force in following the path of least resistance.

Why do we fall into this path of least resistance? Well, it's easier. We tend to do things that are easier (and cheaper). It is possible to break out of this mindset, particularly if you are given instructions that encourage you to think more abstractly about the task (Ward, Patterson, & Sifonis, 2004). Even then, however, you might need to be careful about abstract thinking; sometimes it can lead to original ideas that aren't very practical. Ward (2008) followed up this idea with an experiment that found that people who designed new sports based on known ones (such as soccer) came up with ideas that were rated less original but more playable than people who thought more abstractly. As any of us who admit to seeing the movie *BASEketball* can attest (hey, it starred Oscar-winner Ernest Borgnine—how was I supposed to know?), an original sport does not always translate into a sport you'd want to play (or watch).

On the opposite pole, countering stereotypes can prime creative thinking. Godlowska, Crisp, and Labuschagne (2013) gave people prompts that made them think in nonstereotypical ways (such as picturing a hippie lawyer) and saw an increase in cognitive flexibility. Indeed, Godlowska and Crisp (2013) found that some of the same interventions that can increase tolerance can also increase creativity. These results held particularly true for people with low needs for structure (Gocłowska, Baas, Crisp, & De Dreu, 2014). Along the same lines, another study found that people who believe in racial stereotypes (which can reflect a rigid view of humankind) are less creative—regardless of whether they are in the cultural majority or minority (Tadmor, Chao, Hong, & Polzer, 2013). We will return to some of these themes later in the book, in Chapter 9.

CREATIVITY AND LEARNING DISABILITIES

An additional way of considering how creativity relates to intellectual abilities is to consider how creativity is connected to learning disabilities (LD). It is first important to note that learning disabilities are not the same as intellectual disabilities; you can be gifted and have learning disabilities. If this topic is of interest, I would strongly recommend my friend Scott Barry Kaufman's book *Ungifted* (2013).

Enrichment programs can improve creativity for both gifted students and students with LD (Baum, 1988; Nogueira, 2006). Differences in creativity may vary; one study found that elementary school children with LD engaged in less task persistence than controls and, consequently, scored lower on the Torrance Tests of Creative Thinking (TTCT) in elaboration. On the other three components of the TTCT, however, there were no differences between students with LD and controls (Argulewicz, Mealor, & Richmond, 1979). Another study of gifted children with and without LD found no differences in creativity (Woodrum & Savage, 1994). Conversely, children with LD (who were not categorized as gifted) produced more original responses than controls on a divergent thinking task (N. L. Kaufman & Kaufman, 1980).

Cox and Cotgreave (1996) examined human figure drawings by 10-year-old children with mild learning disabilities (MLD) and 6- and 10-year-old children without MLD. The drawings by the children with MLD were easily distinguished from drawings by the other 10-year-olds but not the group of 6-year-olds. This finding implies that although the children with MLD may be developing artistic and creative abilities at a slower rate, the development still approaches a normal pattern.

Dyslexia is another learning disability that is associated with creativity. Dyslexics scored higher than controls on both verbal and figural divergent thinking tasks (Everatt, 1997). Scholars have suggested creativity as being one way to help identify gifted children with dyslexia (LaFrance, 1997) and to reduce frustration and improve self-perceptions (Burrows & Wolf, 1983). Yet a recent study of adults with developmental dyslexia showed no advantage in creativity (Łockiewicz, Bogdanowicz, & Bogdanowicz, 2014).

Another learning disability with a relationship to creativity is Williams syndrome. Children with Williams syndrome are developmentally delayed and often have profound disabilities in spatial cognition (Bellugi, Lichtenberger, Jones, Lai, & St. George, 2000). Yet children with Williams syndrome have exceptional narrative skills for their cognitive ability level. Although their syntax was simpler and they were more likely to make errors in morphology than average children, they also used more evaluative devices and—of most interest for creativity studies—used much more elaboration in their narratives (Losh, Bellugi, Reilly, & Anderson, 2000). Between these narrative skills and the hypersociability associated with Williams syndrome, these children often engage in storytelling (Jones et al., 2000). And while their stories use less complex syntax as compared with the stories of average children, they are much *more* complex (and more expressive) than the stories of children with similar cognitive abilities with Down syndrome (Reilly, Klima, & Bellugi, 1990). There is also some evidence that children with Williams syndrome have better musical ability than their cognitive patterns would predict. They were able to keep rhythm as well as nonimpaired controls, and their mistakes were more likely to be related to the original beat—in other words, their mistakes could theoretically be considered an act of creative improvisation (Levitin & Bellugi, 1998).

There has also been work looking at creativity across the autism spectrum. Children on the spectrum were better able to be creative with reality-based prompts than with prompts purely rooted in imaginary ideas (Craig & Baron-Cohen, 1999), although they scored lower than children with MLD and a control group. In another line of research, Diener, Wright, Smith, and Wright (2014) developed a visual-spatial measure of creativity designed for students on the autism spectrum.

157

In a related fashion, researchers studied the human figure drawings of children with Down syndrome (Cox & Maynard, 1998). Although children with Down syndrome scored lower than both age-mates and younger children, it is interesting to note that their drawings did not differ when drawn from a model or drawn from imagination, whereas both groups of children without Down syndrome improved when drawing from a model. This finding may indicate that creative processes are a comparative strength for children with Down syndrome.

Dykens, Schwenk, Maxwell, and Myatt (2007) administered semiprojective tests to people with Williams, Down, and Prader–Willi syndromes. They used a sentence completion task (i.e., "I like to _____") and a three-wishes task (i.e., "What would you do with three wishes?"). Although those were not measures of creativity, these tests did allow participants to display their imaginative ability and self-perceptions (the study itself examined the contents of their responses, not the creativity of these responses). Another study examined play and imagination in children with autism and Prader–Willi syndrome (Zyga, Russ, Ievers-Landis, & Dimitropoulos, 2014); both groups showed impairment in their creative abilities but were nonetheless able to play and demonstrate their imaginative thinking.

The learning disability with the most notable connection to creativity is attention deficit hyperactivity disorder (ADHD). Gifted and talented students are often diagnosed with ADHD (Baum & Olenchak, 2002; Silverman, 2009). One reason may be found in Dąbrowski's (1964) ideas about development. He outlined five overexcitabilities: psychomotor, sensual, imaginational, intellectual, and emotional (Daniels & Piechowski, 2009). Children with overexcitabilities may be greatly stimulated and seem to overreact or show too much energy. Yet these children may also be exceptionally intelligent or creative. Rinn and Reynolds (2012) argue that gifted children with overexcitabilities may display very similar behavior as children with ADHD; in an exploratory study they found that there were, indeed, significant relationships between different overexcitabilities and different facets of ADHD. Such overlap, Rinn and Reynolds say, may lead to misdiagnosis.

Several scholars have proposed that the behaviors and characteristics associated with ADHD, such as sensation seeking, stimulation seeking, and a greater use of imagery, are highly similar to creative behaviors (Cramond, 1994; Shaw, 1992). High-IQ children with ADHD scored higher on tests of figural creativity than high-IQ children without ADHD (Shaw & Brown, 1990). A study of adults with ADHD found that they performed better than controls on a divergent thinking task, which requires more diffuse thinking, but worse on the Remote Associates Test, which requires more focused thinking (White & Shah, 2006). A follow-up study (White & Shah, 2011) replicated the divergent thinking finding and added that adults with ADHD reported more creative achievements than those without ADHD.

Abraham, Windmann, Siefen, Daum, and Güntürkün (2006) found that adolescents with ADHD had creative strengths and weakness as compared with controls; they were better at overcoming constraints, but performed worse when asked to create a functional invention. Similarly, Fugate, Zentall, and Gentry (2013) compared gifted children with and without the characteristics of ADHD. Children with the ADHD characteristics showed poorer working memory but increased creativity.

Healey and Rucklidge (2006) found that although 40% of a creative group showed symptoms of ADHD, none met the level for actual diagnosis. Healey (2014), in reviewing the literature, argues that although there are notable similarities between ADHD and creativity, creative children tend to score notably better on IQ, processing speed, and social and emotional functioning as compared with children with ADHD. She concludes that most creative kids likely do not have ADHD, and most kids with ADHD are likely not especially creative. But creative kids with ADHD symptoms may warrant interventions even if these symptoms do not reach the level of a diagnosis (Healey, 2014).

THINKING STYLES

Thinking styles (also called cognitive styles) are a different beast altogether—they're not cognitive abilities, but rather preferences for how people like to use these abilities (Sternberg, 1999; Zhang & Sternberg, 2006). Thinking styles are how we tend to solve problems and interpret information. Perhaps the most classic theory of thinking styles is field dependence versus independence. People who rely on the context of a situation, or external cues, are called field dependent, whereas people who rely more on internal cues and focus on specific details are called field independent (Witkin & Goodenough, 1981). Although there are indications that people who are more field independent are also more creative (Miller, 2007), this theory is not heavily studied today. One reason is that some have argued that field independence is too similar to fluid intelligence (Sternberg & Grigorenko, 1997).

A different theory, Sternberg's (1999) Mental Self Government (MSG), has three primary functional components: legislative, executive, and judicial. Legislative thinkers prefer to create things and to be self-directed. Executive thinkers prefer to follow directions, to carry out orders, and to work under a great deal of structure. Judicial thinkers like to judge and evaluate things. Indeed, legislative thinkers do tend to be more creative (Davis, Kaufman, & McClure, 2011; J. C. Kaufman, 2002).

Within the MSG theory there are a number of subcomponents. There are four different forms: monarchic (focusing on one thing at a time), hierarchical (focusing attention on multiple tasks with a set priority), oligarchic (focusing attention on multiple tasks without a set priority), and anarchic (working on tasks with no system). There are two levels, local and global; local focuses on attention to details, and global looks at the big picture. The levels are comparable to Bruner's (1986) distinction between narrative and paradigmatic thought. Paradigmatic thought is logical and scientific, whereas narrative thought seeks connections and sees the world as a story. If paradigmatic thought is concerned with capturing "what is," then narrative thought is focused more on "what may be." Going further into the MSG theory, there are two scopes; internal is more geared to working independently, whereas external is linked to working with people. Finally, there are two leanings, liberal (preferring novelty and ambiguity) and conservative (following rules and procedures).

Zhang and Sternberg (2006) have integrated the MSG theory and others into a threefold model of intellectual styles. Type I thinkers are the creative thinkers, with the pattern of legislative, judicial, global, and hierarchical (and field-independent) styles. Type II thinkers are more conventional (executive, local, monarchic, and conservative), whereas Type III thinkers are more realistic (oligarchic, anarchic, internal, external). Zhu and Zhang (2011) used the Investment Theory framework (Sternberg & Lubart, 1995) to compare how people perceive creativity with their preferred thinking style. Type I thinkers tend to emphasize thinking and motivation as being important for creativity, Type II thinkers focus on knowledge and intelligence, and Type III thinkers place greater value on the role of the environment.

LOOKING AHEAD

So far in our analysis of the creative person, we've looked at several aspects. Personality is who people are, motivation is why they do something, and intelligence is the horsepower behind how they do it. Mental health is a little trickier—some argue that it's what enables people to be creative, others argue it's what prevents people from being creative, still others argue there is little relationship, and others just enjoy arguing.

REFERENCES

Abraham, A., Windmann, S., Siefen, R., Daum, I., & Güntürkün, O. (2006). Creative thinking in adolescents with attention deficit hyperactivity disorder (ADHD). *Child Neuropsychology, 12*, 111–123.

Adarves-Yorno, I., Postmes, T., & Haslam, S. A. (2007). Creative innovation or crazy irrelevance? The contribution of group norms and social identity to creative behavior. *Journal of Experimental Social Psychology, 43*, 410–416.

Altman, W. S. (1999). *Creativity and academic success.* Unpublished dissertation, Cornell University, Ithaca, NY.

Argulewicz, E. N., Mealor, D. J., & Richmond, B. O. (1979). Creative abilities of learning disabled children. *Journal of Learning Disabilities, 12*, 21–24.

Avitia, M. J., & Kaufman, J. C. (2014). Beyond g and c: The relationship of rated creativity to long-term storage and retrieval (Glr). *Psychology of Aesthetics, Creativity, and the Arts, 8*, 293.

Barron, F. (1963). *Creativity and psychological health.* Princeton, NJ: D. Van Nostrand Company.

Barron, F., & Harrington, D. M. (1981). Creativity, intelligence, and personality. *Annual Review of Psychology, 32,* 439–476.

Bates College Office of Communications & Media Relations. (2004). 20 years of optional SATs. *Bates News.* Retrieved from http://www.bates.edu/news/2004/10/01/sats-at-bates

Batey, M., Chamorro-Premuzic, T., & Furnham, A. (2009). Intelligence and personality as predictors of divergent thinking: The role of general, fluid and crystallised intelligence. *Thinking Skills and Creativity, 4,* 60–69.

Batey, M., Chamorro-Premuzic, T., & Furnham, A. (2010). Individual differences in ideational behavior: Can the big five and psychometric intelligence predict creativity scores? *Creativity Research Journal, 22,* 90–97.

Batey, M., & Furnham, A. (2006). Creativity, intelligence and personality: A critical review of the scattered literature. *Genetic, Social, and General Psychology Monographs, 132,* 355–429.

Batey, M., Furnham, A., & Safiullina, X. (2010). Intelligence, general knowledge and personality as predictors of creativity. *Learning and Individual Differences, 20,* 532–535.

Baum, S. M. (1988). An enrichment program for gifted learning disabled students. *Gifted Child Quarterly, 32,* 226–230.

Baum, S. M., & Olenchak, F. R. (2002). The alphabet children: GT, ADHD, and more. *Exceptionality, 10,* 77–91.

Beaty, R. E., & Silvia, P. J. (2012). Why do ideas get more creative across time? An executive interpretation of the serial order effect in divergent thinking tasks. *Psychology of Aesthetics, Creativity, and the Arts, 6,* 309–319.

Beaty, R. E., Silvia, P. J., Nusbaum, E. C., Jauk, E., & Benedek, M. (2014). The roles of associative and executive processes in creative cognition. *Memory & Cognition, 42,* 1186–1197.

Beghetto, R. A., & Kaufman, J. C. (2007). Toward a broader conception of creativity: A case for "mini-c" creativity. *Psychology of Aesthetics, Creativity, and the Arts, 1,* 73–79.

Beghetto, R. A., & Kaufman, J. C. (2014). Classroom contexts for creativity. *High Ability Studies, 25,* 53–69.

Bellugi, U., Lichtenberger, E. O., Jones, W., Lai, Z., & St. George, M. (2000). The neurocognitive profile of Williams syndrome: A complex pattern of strengths and weaknesses. *Journal of Cognitive Neuroscience, 12,* 7–29.

Benedek, M., Franz, F., Heene, M., & Neubauer, A. C. (2012). Differential effects of cognitive inhibition and intelligence on creativity. *Personality and Individual Differences, 53,* 480–485.

Benedek, M., Jauk, E., Sommer, M., Arendasy, M., & Neubauer, A. C. (2014). Intelligence, creativity, and cognitive control: The common and differential involvement of executive functions in intelligence and creativity. *Intelligence, 46*, 73–83.

Benedek, M., Könen, T., & Neubauer, A. C. (2012). Associative abilities underlying creativity. *Psychology of Aesthetics, Creativity, and the Arts, 6*, 273–281.

Benedek, M., & Neubauer, A. C. (2013). Revisiting Mednick's Model on creativity-related differences in associative hierarchies. Evidence for a common path to uncommon thought. *Journal of Creative Behavior, 47*, 273–289.

Bilalić, M., McLeod, P., & Gobet, F. (2008). Inflexibility of experts—Reality or myth? Quantifying the Einstellung effect in chess masters. *Cognitive Psychology, 56*, 73–102.

Bjork, E. L., Bjork, R. A., & Anderson, M. C. (1998). Varieties of goal-directed forgetting. In J. M. Golding & C. MacLeod (Eds.), *Intentional forgetting: Interdisciplinary approaches* (pp. 103–137). Hillsdale, NJ: Erlbaum.

Bristol, A. S., & Viskontas, I. V. (2016). Dynamic processes within associative memory stores: Piecing together the neural basis of creative cognition. In J. C. Kaufman & J. Baer (Eds.), *Creativity and reason in cognitive development* (2nd ed., pp. 187–210). New York, NY: Cambridge University Press.

Bruner, J. (1986). *Actual minds, possible worlds.* Cambridge, MA: Harvard University Press.

Burrows, D., & Wolf, B. (1983). Creativity and the dyslexic child: A classroom view. *Annals of Dyslexia, 33*, 269–274.

Carroll, J. B. (1993). *Human cognitive abilities: A survey of factor-analytic studies.* New York, NY: Cambridge University Press.

Carson, S. H. (2011). Creativity and psychopathology: A shared vulnerability model. *Canadian Journal of Psychiatry/La Revue Canadienne De Psychiatrie, 56*, 144–153.

Cattell, R. B., & Butcher, H. (1968). *The prediction of achievement and creativity.* Indianapolis, IN: Bobbs-Merrill.

Cho, S. H., Nijenhuis, J. T., Vianen, A. E., Kim, H. B., & Lee, K. H. (2010). The relationship between diverse components of intelligence and creativity. *Journal of Creative Behavior, 44*, 125–137.

Colleges and universities that do not use SAT/ACT scores for admitting substantial numbers of students into Bachelor Degree programs. (2015, Summer). *Fairtest.org.* Retrieved from http://www.fairtest.org/university/optional

Cox, M. V., & Cotgreave, S. (1996). The human figure drawings of normal children and those with mild learning difficulties. *Educational Psychology, 16*, 433–438.

Cox, M. V., & Maynard, S. (1998). The human figure drawings of children with Down syndrome. *British Journal of Developmental Psychology, 16*, 133–137.

Craig, J., & Baron-Cohen, S. (1999). Creativity and imagination in autism and Asperger syndrome. *Journal of Autism and Developmental Disorders, 29*, 319–326.

Cramond, B. (1994). Attention-deficit hyperactivity disorder and creativity: What is the connection? *Journal of Creative Behavior, 28*, 193–210.

Dąbrowski, K. (1964). *Positive disintegration.* Boston, MA: Little, Brown, and Company.

Daniels, S., & Piechowski, M. M. (2009). Embracing intensity: Overexcitability, sensitivity, and the developmental potential of the gifted. In S. Daniels & M. M. Piechowski (Eds.), *Living with intensity* (pp. 3–19). Scottsdale, AZ: Great Potential Press.

Das, J. P., Naglieri, J. A., & Kirby, J. R. (1994). *Assessment of cognitive processes: The PASS theory of intelligence.* Boston, MA: Allyn & Bacon.

Davis, C. D., Kaufman, J. C., & McClure, F. H. (2011). Non-cognitive constructs and self-reported creativity by domain. *Journal of Creative Behavior, 45*, 188–202.

De Dreu, C. K. W., Nijstad, B. A., Baas, M., Wolsink, I., & Roskes, M. (2012). Working memory benefits creative insight, musical improvisation, and original ideation through maintained task-focused attention. *Personality and Social Psychology Bulletin, 38*, 656–669.

Diener, M. L., Wright, C. A., Smith, K. N., & Wright, S. D. (2014). An assessment of visual-spatial creativity in youth with autism spectrum disorder. *Creativity Research Journal, 26*, 328–337.

Dollinger, S. J. (2011). 'Standardized minds' or individuality? Admissions tests and creativity revisited. *Psychology of Aesthetics, Creativity, and the Arts, 5*, 329–341.

Dollinger, S. J., & Skaggs, A. (2011). Does the ACT predict "Inside the Box" thinking or creativity?: Creative characters in the personality imagination exercise. *Imagination, Cognition and Personality, 31*, 199–216.

Dorfman, L., Martindale, C., Gassimova, V., & Vartanian, O. (2008). Creativity and speed of information processing: A double dissociation involving elementary versus inhibitory cognitive tasks. *Personality and Individual Differences, 44*, 1382–1390.

Dow, G. T. (2015). Do cheaters never prosper? The impact of examples, expertise, and cognitive load on cryptomnesia and inadvertent self-plagiarism of creative tasks. *Creativity Research Journal, 27*, 47–57.

Dykens, E., Schwenk, M., Maxwell, M., & Myatt, B. (2007). The Sentence Completion and Three Wishes tasks: Windows into the inner lives of people with intellectual disabilities. *Journal of Intellectual Disability Research, 51,* 588–597.

Edl, S., Benedek, M., Papousek, I., Weiss, E. M., & Fink, A. (2014). Creativity and the Stroop interference effect. *Personality and Individual Differences, 69,* 38–42.

Everatt, J. (1997). The abilities and disabilities associated with adult developmental dyslexia. *Journal of Research in Reading, 20,* 13–21.

Finke, R. A. (1990). *Creative imagery: Discoveries and inventions in visualization.* Hillsdale, NJ: Erlbaum.

Flanagan, D. P., Ortiz, S. O., & Alfonso, V. C. (2013). *Essentials of cross-battery assessment* (3rd ed.). New York, NY: Wiley.

Frensch, P. A., & Sternberg, R. J. (1989). Expertise and intelligence thinking: When is it worse to know better? In R. J. Sternberg (Ed.), *Advances in the psychology of human intelligence* (Vol. 5, pp. 157–188). Hillsdale, NJ: Erlbaum.

Freund, P. A., & Holling, H. (2008). Creativity in the classroom: A multilevel analysis investigating the impact of creativity and reasoning ability on GPA. *Creativity Research Journal, 20,* 309–318.

Frey, M. C., & Detterman, D. K. (2004). Scholastic assessment or g? The relationship between the SAT and general cognitive ability. *Psychological Science, 15,* 373–378.

Fugate, C. M., Zentall, S. S., & Gentry, M. (2013). Creativity and working memory in gifted students with and without characteristics of attention deficit hyperactive disorder: Lifting the mask. *Gifted Child Quarterly, 57,* 234–246.

Gabora, L. (2010). Revenge of the "neurds": Characterizing creative thought in terms of the structure and dynamics of human memory. *Creativity Research Journal, 22,* 1–13.

Gardner, H. (1993). *Creating minds.* New York, NY: Basic Books.

Gardner, H. (1999). *Intelligence reframed: Multiple intelligences for the 21st century.* New York, NY: Basic Books.

Gardner, H. (2006). *Five minds for the future.* Cambridge, MA: Harvard Business School Press.

Getzels, J. W., & Jackson, P. W. (1962). *Creativity and intelligence: Explorations with gifted students.* New York, NY: Wiley.

Gilhooly, K. J., Fioratou, E., Anthony, S. H., & Wynn, V. (2007). Divergent thinking: Strategies and executive involvement in generating novel uses for familiar objects. *British Journal of Psychology, 98,* 611–625.

Gocłowska, M. A., Baas, M., Crisp, R. J., & De Dreu, C. K. W. (2014). Whether social schema violations help or hurt creativity depends on need for structure. *Personality and Social Psychology Bulletin, 40,* 959–971.

Gocłowska, M. A., & Crisp, R. J. (2013). On counter-stereotypes and creative cognition: When interventions for reducing prejudice can boost divergent thinking. *Thinking Skills and Creativity, 8*, 72–79.

Gocłowska, M. A., Crisp, R. J., & Labuschagne, K. (2013). Can counter-stereotypes boost flexible thinking? *Group Processes & Intergroup Relations, 16*, 217–231.

Gralewski, J., & Karwowski, M. (2012). Creativity and school grades: A case from Poland. *Thinking Skills and Creativity, 7*, 198–208.

Grigorenko, E. L., Jarvin, L., Diffley, R., Goodyear, J., Shanahan, E., & Sternberg, R. J. (2009). Are SATS and GPA enough? A theory-based approach to predicting academic success in secondary school. *Journal of Educational Psychology, 101*, 964–981.

Grigorenko, E. L., Jarvin, L., & Sternberg, R. J. (2002). School-based tests of the Triarchic Theory of Intelligence: Three settings, three samples, three syllabi. *Contemporary Educational Psychology, 27*, 167–208.

Guilford, J. P. (1967). *The nature of human intelligence.* New York, NY: McGraw-Hill.

Healey, D. (2014). Attention-deficit/hyperactivity disorder (ADHD) and creativity: Ever the twain shall meet? In J. C. Kaufman (Ed.), *Creativity and mental illness* (pp. 236–251). New York, NY: Cambridge University Press.

Healey, D., & Rucklidge, J. J. (2006). An investigation into the relationship among ADHD symptomatology, creativity, and neuropsychological functioning in children. *Child Neuropsychology 12*, 421–438.

Horn, J. L., & Cattell, R. B. (1966). Refinement and test of the theory of fluid and crystallized intelligence. *Journal of Educational Psychology, 57*, 253–270.

Horn, J. L., & Hofer, S. M. (1992). Major abilities and development in the adult period. In R. J. Sternberg & C. A. Berg (Eds.), *Intellectual development* (pp. 44–99). New York, NY: Cambridge University Press.

Horn, J. L., & Noll, J. (1997). Human cognitive capacities: Gf-Gc theory. In D. P. Flanagan, J. L., Genshaft, & P. L. Harrison (Eds.), *Life-span developmental psychology: Research and theory* (pp. 423–466). New York, NY: Academic Press.

Hui, A., Yeung, D. Y., Sue-Chan, K., Chan, K. , Hui, D. C. K., & Cheng, S. T. (2014). Gains and losses in creative personality as perceived by adults across the lifespan. *Developmental Psychology, 50*, 709–713.

Jauk, E., Benedek, M., Dunst, B., & Neubauer, A. C. (2013). The relationship between intelligence and creativity: New support for the threshold hypothesis by means of empirical breakpoint detection. *Intelligence, 41*, 212–221.

Jones, W., Bellugi, U., Lai, Z., Chiles, M., Reilly, J., Lincoln, A., & Adolphs, R. (2000). Hypersociability in Williams syndrome. *Journal of Cognitive Neuroscience, 12,* 30–46.

Jung, R. E. (2014). Evolution, creativity, intelligence, and madness: "Here be dragons." *Frontiers in Psychology, 5,* 784.

Karwowski, M., & Gralewski, J. (2013). Threshold hypothesis: Fact or artifact? *Thinking Skills and Creativity, 8,* 25–33.

Kaufman, A. S. (2000). Seven questions about the WAIS-III regarding differences in abilities across the 16 to 89 year life span. *School Psychology Quarterly, 15,* 3–29.

Kaufman, A. S. (2001). WAIS-III IQs, Horn's theory, and generational changes from young adulthood to old age. *Intelligence, 29,* 131–167.

Kaufman, A. S. (2009). *IQ testing 101.* New York, NY: Springer Publishing Company.

Kaufman, A. S., & Kaufman, N. L. (1993). *Kaufman Adolescent and Adult Intelligence Test (KAIT).* Circle Pines, MN: American Guidance Service.

Kaufman, A. S., & Kaufman, N. L. (2004). *Kaufman Assessment Battery for Children* (2nd ed.). Circle Pines, MN: American Guidance Service.

Kaufman, A. S., & Lichtenberger, E. O. (2006). *Assessing adult and adolescent intelligence* (3rd ed.). New York, NY: John Wiley.

Kaufman, J. C. (2002). Narrative and paradigmatic thinking styles in creative writing and journalism students. *Journal of Creative Behavior, 36,* 201–220.

Kaufman, J. C., & Beghetto, R. A. (2009). Beyond big and little: The Four C Model of Creativity. *Review of General Psychology, 13,* 1–12.

Kaufman, J. C., Kaufman, S. B., & Lichtenberger, E. O. (2011). Finding creativity on intelligence tests via divergent production. *Canadian Journal of School Psychology, 26,* 83–106.

Kaufman, J. C., Kaufman, S. B., & Plucker, J. A. (2013). Contemporary theories of intelligence. In D. Reisberg (Ed.), *Oxford handbook of cognitive psychology* (pp. 811–822). Oxford, England: Oxford University Press.

Kaufman, N. L., & Kaufman, A. S. (1980). Creativity in children with minimal brain dysfunction. *Journal of Creative Behavior, 14,* 73.

Kaufman, S. B. (2009). Conversations on creativity with Daniel Tammet— Part IV, IQ and human intelligence. *Psychology Today.* Retrieved from https://www.psychologytoday.com/blog/beautiful-minds/200912/conversations-creativity-daniel-tammet-part-iv-iq-and-human-intelligence

Kaufman, S. B. (2013). *Ungifted: Intelligence redefined.* New York, NY: Basic Books.

Kaufman, S. B., DeYoung, C. G., Reis, D. L., & Gray, J. R. (2011). General intelligence predicts reasoning ability even for evolutionarily familiar content. *Intelligence, 39,* 311–322.

Kell, H. J., Lubinski, D., & Benbow, C. P. (2013). Who rises to the top? Early indicators. *Psychological Science, 24*, 648–659.

Kell, H. J., Lubinski, D., Benbow, C. P., & Steiger, J. H. (2013). Creativity and technical innovation: Spatial ability's unique role. *Psychological Science, 24*, 1831–1836.

Kenett, Y. N., Anaki, D., & Faust, M. (2014). Investigating the structure of semantic networks in low and high creative persons. *Frontiers in Human Neuroscience, 8*, 407.

Kim, K. H. (2005). Can only intelligent people be creative? A meta-analysis. *Journal of Secondary Gifted Education, 16*, 57–66.

Koenig, K. A., Frey, M. C., & Detterman, D. K. (2008). ACT and general cognitive ability. *Intelligence 36*, 153–160.

Kuncel, N. R., Hezlett, S. A., & Ones, D. S. (2001). A comprehensive meta-analysis of the predictive validity of the Graduate Record Examinations. *Psychological Bulletin, 127*, 162–181.

LaFrance, E. B. (1997). The gifted/dyslexic child: Characterizing and addressing strengths and weaknesses. *Annals of Dyslexia, 47*, 163–182.

Levitan, D. J., & Bellugi, U. (1998). Musical abilities in individuals with Williams syndrome. *Music Perception, 15*, 357–398.

Lockiewicz, K., Bogdanowicz, K. M., & Bogdanowicz, M. (2014). Psychological resources of adults with developmental dyslexia. *Journal of Learning Disabilities, 47*, 543–555.

Losh, M., Bellugi, U., Reilly, J., & Anderson, D. (2000). Narrative as a social engagement tool: The excessive use of evaluation in narratives from children with Williams syndrome. *Narrative Inquiry, 10*, 265–290.

Luria, A. R. (1970). The functional organization of the brain. *Scientific American, 222*, 66–78.

MacLeod, M. D., & Macrae, C. N. (2001). Gone but not forgotten: The transient nature of retrieval-induced forgetting. *Psychological Science, 12*, 148–152.

Madore, K. P., Addis, D. R., & Schacter, D. L. (2015). Creativity and memory: Effects of an episodic-specificity induction on divergent thinking. *Psychological Science*. Advance online publication. doi:10.1177/0956797615591863

Martindale, C. (1999). Biological bases of creativity. In R. J. Sternberg (Ed.), *Handbook of creativity* (pp. 137–152). New York, NY: Cambridge University Press.

Mednick, S. A. (1962). The associative basis of the creative process. *Psychological Review, 69*, 220–232.

Mednick, S. A. (1968). The Remote Associates Test. *Journal of Creative Behavior, 2*, 213–214.

Miller, A. L. (2007). Creativity and cognitive style: The relationship between field-dependence-independence, expected evaluation, and creative performance. *Psychology of Aesthetics, Creativity, and the Arts, 1*, 243–246.

Miyake, A., & Friedman, N. P. (2012). The nature and organization of individual differences in executive functions: Four general conclusions. *Current Directions in Psychological Science, 21*, 8–14.

Mooneyham, B. W., & Schooler, J. W. (2013). The costs and benefits of mind-wandering: A review. *Canadian Journal of Experimental Psychology/Revue Canadienne de Psychologie Expérimentale, 67*, 11–18.

Naglieri, J. A., & Kaufman, J. C. (2001). Understanding intelligence, giftedness, and creativity using PASS theory. *Roeper Review, 23*, 151–156.

Ng, T. W., & Feldman, D. C. (2008). The relationship of age to ten dimensions of job performance. *Journal of Applied Psychology, 93*, 392–423.

Niaz, M., Nunez, G. S., & Pineda, I. R. (2000). Academic performance of high school students as a function of mental capacity, cognitive style, mobility-fixity dimension, and creativity. *Journal of Creative Behavior, 34*, 18–29.

Nogueira, S. M. (2006). MORCEGOS: A Portuguese enrichment program of creativity pilot study with gifted students and students with learning difficulties. *Creativity Research Journal, 18*, 45–54.

Nusbaum, E. C., & Silvia, P. J. (2011). Are intelligence and creativity really so different?: Fluid intelligence, executive processes, and strategy use in divergent thinking. *Intelligence, 39*, 36–45.

Palmiero, M. (2015). The effects of age on divergent thinking and creative objects production: A cross-sectional study. *High Ability Studies, 96*, 93–104.

Palmiero, M., Di Giacomo, D., & Passafiume, D. (2014). Divergent thinking and age-related changes. *Creativity Research Journal, 26*, 456–460.

Park, G., Lubinski, D., & Benbow, C. P. (2007). Contrasting intellectual patterns predict creativity in the arts and sciences: Tracking intellectually precocious youth over 25 years. *Psychological Science, 18*, 948–952.

Park, G., Lubinski, D., & Benbow, C. P. (2008). Ability differences among people who have commensurate degrees matter for scientific creativity. *Psychological Science, 19*, 957–961.

Peterson, J. B., Smith, K. W., & Carson, S. (2002). Openness and extraversion are associated with reduced latent inhibition: Replication and commentary. *Personality and Individual Differences, 33*, 1137–1147.

Plucker, J. A., & Esping, A. (2014). *Intelligence 101*. New York, NY: Springer Publishing Company.

Plucker, J. A., & Renzulli, J. S. (1999). Psychometric approaches to the study of human creativity. In R. J. Sternberg (Ed.), *Handbook of creativity* (pp. 35–61). New York, NY: Cambridge University Press.

Powers, D. E., & Kaufman, J. C. (2004). Do standardized tests penalize deep-thinking, creative, or conscientious students? Some personality correlates of Graduate Record Examinations test scores. *Intelligence, 32*, 145–153.

Preckel, F., Holling, H., & Wiese, M. (2006). Relationship of intelligence and creativity in gifted and non-gifted students: An investigation of threshold theory. *Personality and Individual Differences, 40*, 159–170.

Redmond, M. R., Mumford, M. D., & Teach, R. (1993). Putting creativity to work: Effects of leader behavior on subordinate creativity. *Organizational Behavior and Human Decision Processes, 55*, 120–151.

Reilly, J., Klima, E. S., & Bellugi, U. (1990). Once more with feeling: Affect and language in atypical populations. *Development and Psychopathology, 2*, 367–391.

Rinn, A. N., & Reynolds, M. J. (2012). Overexcitabilities and ADHD in the gifted: An examination. *Roeper Review, 34*, 38–45.

Roskos-Ewoldsen, B., Black, S. R., & McCown, S. M. (2008). Age-related changes in creative thinking. *Journal of Creative Behavior, 42*, 33–57.

Schneider, W. J., & Flanagan, D. P. (2015). The relationship between theories of intelligence and intelligence tests. In S. Goldstein, D. Princiotta, & J. A. Naglieri (Eds.), *Handbook of intelligence* (pp. 317–340). New York, NY: Springer.

Schneider, W. J., & McGrew, K. (2012). The Cattell-Horn-Carroll model of intelligence. In D. Flanagan & P. Harrison (Eds.), *Contemporary intellectual assessment* (3rd ed., pp. 99–144). New York, NY: Guilford.

Shaw, G. A. (1992). Hyperactivity and creativity: The tacit dimension. *Bulletin of the Psychonomic Society, 30*, 157–160.

Shaw, G. A., & Brown, G. (1990). Laterality and creativity concomitants of attention problems. *Developmental Neuropsychology, 6*, 39–56.

Silverman, L. K. (2009). *Giftedness 101*. New York, NY: Springer Publishing Company.

Silvia, P. J. (2008a). Another look at creativity and intelligence: Exploring higher-order models and probable confounds. *Personality and Individual Differences, 44*, 1012–1021.

Silvia, P. J. (2008b). Creativity and intelligence revisited: A latent variable analysis of Wallach and Kogan (1965). *Creativity Research Journal, 20*, 34–39.

Silvia, P. J. (2015). Intelligence and creativity are pretty similar after all. *Educational Psychology Review, 27*, 1–8.

Silvia, P. J., & Beaty, R. E. (2012). Making creative metaphors: The importance of fluid intelligence for creative thought. *Intelligence, 40*, 343–351.

Silvia, P. J., Beaty, R. E., & Nusbaum, E. C. (2013). Verbal fluency and creativity: General and specific contributions of broad retrieval ability (Gr) factors to divergent thinking. *Intelligence, 41*, 328–340.

Silvia, P. J., Nusbaum, E. C., & Beaty, R. E. (2015). Old or new? Evaluating the old/new scoring method for divergent thinking tasks. *Journal of Creative Behavior*. Advance online publication. doi:10.1002/jocb.101

Simonton, D. K. (1989). Age and creative productivity: Nonlinear estimation of an information-processing model. *International Journal of Aging and Human Development, 29*, 23–37.

Simonton, D. K. (1994). *Greatness: Who makes history and why.* New York, NY: Guilford Press.

Simonton, D. K. (1997). Creative productivity: A predictive and explanatory model of career trajectories and landmarks. *Psychological Review, 104*, 66–89.

Simonton, D. K. (2011). Creativity and discovery as blind variation and selective retention: Multiple-variant definitions and blind-sighted integration. *Psychology of Aesthetics, Creativity, and the Arts, 5*, 222–228.

Simonton, D. K. (2012). Citation measures as criterion variables in predicting scientific eminence. *Measurement: Interdisciplinary Research and Perspectives, 10*, 170–171.

Sligh, A. C., Conners, F. A., & Roskos-Ewoldsen, B. (2005). Relation of creativity to fluid and crystallized intelligence. *Journal of Creative Behavior, 39*, 123–136.

Spearman, C. (1904). "General Intelligence," objectively determined and measured. *American Journal of Psychology, 15*, 201–292.

Sternberg, R. J. (1985a). *Beyond IQ: A triarchic theory of human intelligence.* New York, NY: Cambridge University Press.

Sternberg, R. J. (1985b). Implicit theories of intelligence, creativity, and wisdom. *Journal of Personality and Social Psychology, 49*, 607–627.

Sternberg, R. J. (1996). *Successful intelligence.* New York, NY: Simon & Schuster.

Sternberg, R. J. (1999). *Thinking styles.* New York, NY: Cambridge University Press.

Sternberg, R. J. (2003). *WICS: Wisdom, intelligence, and creativity, synthesized.* Cambridge, England: Cambridge University Press.

Sternberg, R. J. (2006). Creating a vision of creativity: The first 25 years. *Psychology of Aesthetics, Creativity, and the Arts, S*, 2–12.

Sternberg, R. J. (2007). A systems model of leadership: WICS. *American Psychologist, 62*, 34–42.

Sternberg, R. J. (2008). Applying psychological theories to educational practice. *American Educational Research Journal, 45*, 150–165.

Sternberg, R. J., & Coffin, L. A. (2010). Admitting and developing "new leaders for a changing world." *New England Journal of Higher Education, 24*, 12–13.

Sternberg, R. J., Conway, B. E., Ketron, J. L., & Bernstein, M. (1981). People's conceptions of intelligence. *Journal of Personality and Social Psychology, 41*, 37–55.

Sternberg, R. J., & Grigorenko, E. L. (1997). Are cognitive styles still in style? *American Psychologist, 52*, 700–712.

Sternberg, R. J., Jarvin, L., Birney, D. P., Naples, A., Stemler, S. E., Newman, T., . . . Grigorenko, E. L. (2014). Testing the theory of successful intelligence in teaching grade 4 language arts, mathematics, and science. *Journal of Educational Psychology, 106,* 881–899.

Sternberg, R. J., Jarvin, L., & Grigorenko, E. L. (2011). *Explorations of giftedness.* New York, NY: Cambridge University Press.

Sternberg, R. J., Kaufman, J. C., & Grigorenko, E. L. (2008). *Applied intelligence.* New York, NY: Cambridge University Press.

Sternberg, R. J., & Lubart, T. I. (1995). *Defying the crowd.* New York, NY: Free Press.

Sternberg, R. J., & O'Hara, L. A. (1999). Creativity and intelligence. In R. J. Sternberg (Ed.), *Handbook of creativity* (pp. 251–272). New York, NY: Cambridge University Press.

Storm, B. C., Angello, G., & Bjork, E. L. (2011). Thinking can cause forgetting: Memory dynamics in creative problem solving. *Journal of Experimental Psychology: Learning, Memory, and Cognition, 37,* 1287–1293.

Storm, B. C., & Patel, T. N. (2014). Forgetting as a consequence and enabler of creative thinking. *Journal of Experimental Psychology: Learning, Memory, and Cognition, 40,* 1594–1609.

Tadmor, C. T., Chao, M. M., Hong, Y. Y., & Polzer, J. T. (2013). Not just for stereotyping anymore: Racial essentialism reduces domain-general creativity. *Psychological Science, 24,* 99–105.

Vartanian, O., Martindale, C., & Kwiatkowski, J. (2007). Creative potential, attention, and speed of information processing, *Personality and Individual Differences, 43,* 1470–1480.

Vock, M., Preckel, F., & Holling, H. (2011). Mental abilities and school achievement: A test of a mediation hypothesis. *Intelligence, 39,* 357–369.

Wai, J., Lubinski, D., & Benbow, C. P. (2005). Creativity and occupational accomplishments among intellectually precocious youth: An age 13 to age 33 longitudinal study. *Journal of Educational Psychology, 97,* 484–492.

Wallach, M. A., & Kogan, N. (1965). *Modes of thinking in young children: A study of the creativity-intelligence distinction.* New York, NY: Holt Rinehart & Winston.

Wallach, M. A., & Wing, C. W. (1969). *The talented student: A validation of the creativity-intelligence distinction.* New York, NY: Holt Rinehart & Winston.

Ward, T. B. (1994). Structured imagination: The role of category structure in exemplar generation. *Cognitive Psychology, 27,* 1–40.

Ward, T. B. (1995). What's old about new ideas. In S. M. Smith, T. B. Ward, & R. A. Finke (Eds.), *The creative cognition approach* (pp. 157–178). Cambridge, MA: MIT Press.

Ward, T. B. (2008). The role of domain knowledge in creative generation. *Learning and Individual Differences, 18,* 363–366.

Ward, T. B., Dodds, R. A., Saunders, K. N., & Sifonis, C. M. (2000). Attribute centrality and imaginative thought. *Memory & Cognition, 28,* 1387–1397.

Ward, T. B., & Kolomyts, Y. (2010). Cognition and creativity. In J. C. Kaufman & R. J. Sternberg (Eds.), *Cambridge handbook of creativity* (pp. 93–112). New York, NY: Cambridge University Press.

Ward, T. B., Patterson, M. J., & Sifonis, C. M. (2004). The role of specificity and abstraction in creative idea generation. *Creativity Research Journal, 16*, 1–9.

Ward, T. B., Patterson, M. J., Sifonis, C. M., Dodds, R. A., & Saunders, K. N. (2002). The role of graded category structure in imaginative thought. *Memory & Cognition, 30*, 199–216.

Ward, T. B., & Sifonis, C. M. (1997). Task demands and generative thinking: What changes and what remains the same? *Journal of Creative Behavior, 31*, 245–259.

Ward, T. B., & Wickes, K. N. (2009). Stable and dynamic properties of category structure guide imaginative thought. *Creativity Research Journal, 21*, 15–23.

White, H. A., & Shah, P. (2006). Training attention-switching ability in adults with ADHD. *Journal of Attention Disorders, 10*, 44–53.

White, H. A., & Shah, P. (2011). Creative style and achievement in adults with attention-deficit/hyperactivity disorder. *Personality and Individual Differences, 50*, 673–677.

Wing, C. W., & Wallach, M. A. (1971). *College admissions and the psychology of talent.* Oxford, England: Holt Rinehart & Winston.

Witkin, H. A., & Goodenough, D. R. (1981). *Cognitive styles: Essence and origins, field dependence and field independence.* New York, NY: International University Press.

Woodrum, D. T., & Savage, L. B. (1994). Children who are learning disabled/gifted: Where do they belong? *Educational Research, 36*, 83–89.

Zabelina, D. L., O'Leary, D., Pornpattananangkul, N., Nusslock, R., & Beeman, M. (2015). Creativity and sensory gating indexed by the P50: Selective versus leaky sensory gating in divergent thinkers and creative achievers. *Neuropsychologia, 69*, 77–84.

Zabelina, D. L., Robinson, M. D., Council, J. R., & Bresin, K. (2012). Patterning and nonpatterning in creative cognition: Insights from performance in a random number generation task. *Psychology of Aesthetics, Creativity, and the Arts, 6*, 137–145.

Zhang, L. F., & Sternberg, R. J. (2006). *The nature of intellectual styles.* Mahwah, NJ: Erlbaum.

Zhu, C., & Zhang, L. F. (2011). Thinking styles and conceptions of creativity among university students. *Educational Psychology, 31*, 361–375.

Zyga, O., Russ, S., Ievers-Landis, C. E., & Dimitropoulos, A. (2015). Assessment of pretend play in Prader–Willi syndrome: A direct comparison to autism spectrum disorder. *Journal of Autism and Developmental Disorders, 45*, 975–987.

Creativity and Mental Health

I n the first edition, this chapter was called "Does Creativity Have a Dark Side?" I had written the first four chapters, and I came up to this one, and I was so eager to tackle it that I promptly put the book down for 2 years. It's a contentious topic and one that somehow is still a hot topic. I've shifted my approach a bit to look at the bigger picture of mental health, placing the work on malevolent creativity later in the book.

Some people believe that creativity and mental illness are not connected at all; others argue that there is a particular connection between bipolar disorder (also called manic depression) and creativity or schizophrenia and creativity; still others just prefer their creative geniuses to be stark-raving, ear-cutting crazy. Robert Downey, Jr., an Oscar-nominated actor and general superstar, has a history of arrest for prescription and illegal drug abuse and gun possession (among other things). Now drug- and alcohol-free, he has said, "My vice, it seems now, is creativity" (Stoynoff, 2008).

The "mad genius" concept has been proposed by such luminaries as Plato and Aristotle (Becker, 2014). One of the first researchers to study creativity did so to address this question (Lombroso, 1894). By the year 1800, according to Simonton (1994), this stereotype had become dogma. Most people today still accept this connection as a truth, and it is sometimes called the "lone nut" view of creativity (Plucker, Beghetto, & Dow, 2004). Curiously, the mad genius idea is endorsed most strongly by those who see themselves as very creative and those who do not see themselves as creative at all (Kaufman, Bromley, & Cole, 2006).

As usual, the truth is both less sensational and more complex than the quick stereotypes, which is why people are usually quite happy to stop at stereotypes. The first questions that must be addressed, however, are (a) what do we mean by creativity, and (b) what do we mean by mental illness? These distinctions are more than semantics. Arguing that creative genius is more likely to be associated with bipolar disorder is radically different than predicting that your brother who writes stories is likely to end up a little weird. Indeed, throughout the muddy research, discordant studies are lumped together oddly. Studies of famous poets who committed suicide are used by some to prove the same point as studies on how the average college student performs on measures of divergent thinking and anxiety.

Such comparisons are akin to finding one paper that connects the smell of buttered popcorn with increased sadness in parrots and a different paper that shows that finches that eat grapes are more likely to smile and coming away from the whole mess by concluding that birds are emotionally invested in their food. Well, perhaps, but does this synthesis give us any useful information? Or does it actively confuse the issue?

In an ideal world, this question would be addressed by giving in-depth clinical interviews and extensive and validated assessments to a huge sample of creative individuals that wildly range from Nobel Prize–winning chemists to published poets to a group of graduate students recommended by their advisors as being particularly creative. We'd also have huge control groups to compare them with people who might or might not be especially creative: people who like collecting string or very young children or people who shop at Costco or people who take more than two naps a day. We would test so many people that we would have a huge range of creative abilities and mental health represented.

In the real world, however, famous and accomplished people don't like psychologists, and often with good reason. We ask a lot of questions and take up a lot of time, and we usually don't have good things to offer, like money or candy. The kinds of questions that would need to be asked for this type of a study would be intrusive, embarrassing, and generally unappealing. It may not be surprising that most studies of creative genius are conducted on dead people, who complain less.

Before we start a survey of the research that has been done, some basic facts: Approximately 1 in 5 people (18.5%) in America (18 years or older) suffers from mental illness, as defined by the latest version of the *Diagnostic and Statistical Manual of Mental Disorders* (5th ed.; *DSM-5*; American Psychiatric Association, 2013). About 1 in 25 people (4.2%; same population) have a severe mental illness (such as bipolar disorder or schizophrenia; National Institute of Mental Health [NIMH], n.d.) Without these rates in mind, any comparisons become meaningless. A wonderful Yiddish proverb says, "For example is not proof." It is easy to anecdotally pick out 10 or 20 or 200 instances of people who are creative and mentally ill. I could just as easily pull out a list of people who are creative and short: Michael J. Fox, Dr. Ruth, Prince, Henri de Toulouse-Lautrec, my wife, Tom Cruise, Peter Dinklage. Therefore, I could argue, creative people are short. That doesn't make it true.

There are many important distinctions to make, from type of illness to level of eminence to method of study. Perhaps the most important is: What question are you actually asking? Do you want to know if the mad genius stereotype is true, or if people with mental illness are also more likely to be creative, of if the everyday schnook who is more creative will therefore be more likely to be mentally ill? These are all radically different questions. For a much more in-depth look, I've edited a book of essays specifically on this topic (Kaufman, 2014). What I will present here is a highlight, synthesis, and interpretation of what's out there.

THE BIG THREE STUDIES THAT EVERYONE CITES

I will start with three "classic" studies of creativity and mental illness. I call them classic because they're the same ones that everyone always cites, not because they are necessarily good. The first is Jamison (1993), and it's noteworthy that this reference is a book, not an article. She reports a variety of work here, including one small study she did (Jamison, 1989), but the book is primarily a mix of anecdotes, opinions, and stories. Her focus is on the connection between bipolar disorder and creativity. Jamison (1997) later wrote a bestselling memoir about her own struggle with the illness.

The second is Andreasen (1987), who used structured interviews to analyze 30 creative writers, 30 matched controls, and first-degree relatives of each group. The writers had a higher rate of mental illness, with a particular tendency toward bipolar and other affective disorders. The writers' first-degree relatives were more likely to both be creative and have affective disorders. This study is bafflingly again in the public eye despite no additional data being reported (Andreasen, 2014), and Andreasen presents the facts as though the creativity–mental illness debate has ended (Bartlett, 2014). Such a position is a great misrepresentation of both relevant data and the general opinion of the field. I find it highly unfortunate that Andreasen (and Jamison) have reached such a wide audience, leading to widespread misinformation. Their messages easily lead to the assumption that all levels of creativity are associated with mental illness (not true at all), as opposed to the much more narrow finding that genius-level creative people are more likely to be mentally ill (which has been shown, albeit in a much more nuanced and specific way).

The third major work is Ludwig (1995), who utilized the historiometric technique. Although developed centuries ago, historiometrics has been pioneered in the modern age by Dean Keith Simonton (1990, 1994, 2009a). Traditional research involves reading biographies of eminent people and noting life events (marriages, tragedies, winning prizes, battling sea monsters) to gain insight into broader issues of creativity or genius. A typical study might analyze the word content of a president's inaugural address or categorize the themes present in Shakespearean sonnets (Simonton, 1990). Ludwig conducted a massive investigation of over 1,000 eminent individuals who were the subjects of major biographies written between 1960 and 1990. Among many other discoveries, he found a higher incidence of mental illness among people in artistic professions (e.g., writing, art, and theater) than in nonartistic professions (e.g., business, politics, and science).

All three studies have come under serious criticism. Rothenberg (1990), for example, argues that Andreasen's control group was not well matched to the writers chosen; the creative group was comprised of faculty members from the creative writing department, whereas the control group had a wide mix of people. Andreasen was the sole interviewer, with no corroborating opinions about the mental health of the writers. Schlesinger (2009, 2012, 2014) has devoted extensive output to highlighting the flaws of these three studies (which she calls the "wobbly tripod," 2014, p. 64). In addition to the critiques just listed, she notes that Andreasen knew her participants personally and extrapolated her results to the general population without just cause. She points out that Jamison simply counted whether a person was treated for mood disorder as evidence of such a disorder existing, and criticizes Ludwig's research for the way the people studied were categorized and the many ambiguous or unclear aspects of the methodology. Personally, I do find value in Ludwig's research despite its flaws; I think there is much of interest. In contrast, I think that Jamison and Andreasen's work has little to offer the debate besides noise, and few recent serious discussions mention them at all.

These three studies are far from the last word, of course. There have been hundreds more, with often contradictory findings.

EMINENT CREATORS AND MENTAL ILLNESS

Historiometrics and Big-C

Many of the studies of Big-C creators are historiometric, akin to Ludwig's work. Some such studies claim that eminent creators show higher rates of mental illness. Such studies have explored links between jazz musicians and psychopathology (Wills, 2003), eminent male artists and writers and personality disorders (Post, 1994), and writers and affective disorders (Post, 1996). Ludwig (1998), in a later historiometric study, found that artistic creators showed higher rates of mental illness that those in other occupations.

Another strand of research has looked at how creative domains differ in rates of mental illness. I've done some work in this area, looking mostly at writers. For example, female poets were significantly more likely to suffer from mental illness (as measured by suicide attempts, hospitalizations, or specific periods of depression that warranted discussion in a brief biography) than other types of women writers (fiction writers, playwrights, and nonfiction writers) and male writers (fiction writers, poets, playwrights, and nonfiction writers; Kaufman, 2001a). An additional study looked only at women and compared poets with journalists, politicians, actresses, novelists, and visual artists. Again, poets were significantly more likely to have mental illness than any other group (Kaufman, 2001a). This finding was dubbed the "Sylvia Plath Effect." Additional studies have also found that eminent poets were more likely than other writers to be mentally ill (Kaufman, 2005) and show cognitive distortion (Thomas & Duke, 2007).

Writers additionally have a shorter life span than people in other occupations, including other artistic-related occupations (Cassandro, 1998; Kaun, 1991; Ludwig, 1995; Simonton, 1975). A large-scale study of almost 2,000 American, Chinese, Turkish, and Eastern European writers found that, on average, poets died younger than fiction writers and nonfiction writers across all four cultures (Kaufman, 2003). Earlier studies (e.g., Ludwig, 1995; Simonton, 1975) also found poets to die the youngest of all writers. It is important to note that general creativity (as associated with openness to experience) is *not* associated with earlier mortality (Roberts, Kuncel, Shiner, Caspi, & Goldberg, 2007).

Other research has looked at how the actual language writers use can be associated with mental health. Stirman and Pennebaker (2001) found that suicidal poets were likely to use words associated with the self (as opposed to the collective) in their poetry, as opposed to nonsuicidal poets. The authors of the study suggested that this tendency revealed an inward focus and lack of social integration. Forgeard (2008) examined the linguistic patterns of eminent writers who were either bipolar, unipolar, or neither; bipolar writers used more death-related words than did unipolar writers, whereas unipolar writers were less likely than the controls to use self-related words. Her findings are somewhat consistent with Stirman and Pennebaker in that unipolar depressives are less likely

180

to commit suicide than bipolar depressives (who used more self-associated words). Djikic, Oatley, and Peterson (2006) did a neat study that explored linguistic patterns of creative writers and physicists; the writers used more emotion-related words and—specifically—more negative-emotion words (i.e., related to anger, anxiety, or depression). This finding doesn't necessarily mean that writers feel these emotions more, just that they are more likely to use these words.

There are a lot of problems with historiometric work, often depending on the competence of the researcher. Some might diagnose eminent creators not based on objective criteria (such as the number of times someone attempted suicide) but on subjective criteria (such as the tone of a private letter). I know I wouldn't want my own life to be interpreted so closely. George Carlin once talked about a criminal who had a "history of questionable behavior" and wondered which of us would not qualify as having such a background.

Another problem is that no one ever wrote a biography of a creative person because that person was so gosh-darn normal. Indeed, normal people can seem boring, at least as subjects of biographies. If I want to sell books—or get published—I'll write about the most bizarre people I can find. So if a researcher is using biographies to get information about a creator, these biographies may not be perfectly objective. Creative people who are bizarre or weird or suffer from mental illness make for more compelling stories than creative people who are boring, work hard, and have happy marriages. There may be more biographies available for that kind of creative genius than for happy, well-adjusted creative geniuses (Silvia & Kaufman, 2010).

Similarly, it is impossible to compare, let's say, 100 legendary poets and 100 legendary shepherds because no one is writing the biographies of the shepherds. Another problem is sample selection—drawing from a specific, well-defined set of people is great. Picking out 50 poets or 50 musicians and then analyzing their lives begs the question of how these people were chosen. If you're picking out data points (or people) selectively, you can tell any story you want.

All of that said, I find that when the researchers are careful and do not over-claim or over-extrapolate, the evidence is hard to completely ignore. I wish that Simonton had done more studies on the topic. Although he has written extensively on the matter (e.g., Simonton,

2009, 2014a), it has only been very recently that he has studied the matter in earnest, although he has been making up for lost time. One excellent study (Simonton, 2014c) examines how the relationship between mental illness and eminence varies by domain. For writers and artists, higher rates of mental illness are associated with higher rates of eminence (also found by Kaufman, 2001b; Ludwig, 1995). But scientists, composers, and thinkers showed specific peaks in the relationship between creative accomplishment and mental illness. These peaks represent what Simonton (2014c) calls the "optimal amounts of psychopathy" (p. 57). Scientists had a particularly sharp peak, indicating that those with severe illness were notably less accomplished than those with no illness. In other recent work, Damian and Simonton (2014) examined eminent African Americans and found comparable relationships as past studies on majority cultures (for example, artists and writers showed higher levels of mental illness than scientists). Finally, Simonton (2014b) uses mathematical laws that I won't begin to explain to show how creative geniuses might be more mentally ill yet creativity and positive mental health may be nonetheless related, a point I will delve into later.

Empirical Studies of Pro-C

Not all studies of eminent creators are historiometric, nor are they all solely aimed at Big-C. A growing number of investigations have looked at professional creators. Some studies are by the usual suspects. For example, Jamison (1989) interviewed 47 British artists and writers and found that a significantly higher percentage of them suffered from some form of mental illness, particularly from affective disorders (such as bipolar), than would be expected from population rates. It is worth noting again, though, that this study is flawed—as Schlesinger (2014) points out, Jamison didn't have a control group and selected which 47 creators she interviewed; it is hard to put too much stock in these results. Ludwig (1994) studied 59 female writers and 59 matched controls, and found that the writers were more likely to have mental illness, including mood disorders (including bipolar) and general anxieties.

Studies of Pro-c creators (whether or not examining mental health) are rare. Curiously, two of the few such studies were

182

unpublished dissertations. Staltaro (2003) looked at 43 published poets and found that approximately one-third had a history of at least one psychiatric condition, and more than half had been in therapy (this is notably higher than population rates). But poets did not score significantly higher than the norm on a measure of current depression. Colvin (1995) studied gifted student musicians with matched controls; the musicians had more mood disorders.

Nettle (2006) examined poets, mathematicians, visual artists, and average people, finding higher levels of schizotypy in poets and visual artists and lower levels in mathematicians. Another study that found domain-based differences was that by Rawlings and Locarnini (2008), who gave measures of subclinical psychosis and autism to artists and scientists. In the artist group, creativity was linked to schizotypy and hypomania. In the scientist group, these connections were not found; however, a slight connection was found between creativity and autistic tendencies.

Several studies have used personality measures, such as the Minnesota Multiphasic Personality Inventory (MMPI) or the Eysenck Personality Questionnaire (EPQ), which measure aspects of personality that can overlap with mental illness. The best-known line of research in this vein is by legendary researcher Frank Barron (1969), who tested many prominent and creative individuals throughout his work with the Institute for Personality Assessment and Research. Most creators scored higher on the pathology-related scales of the MMPI—yet also scored higher on health-related and ego strength scales. Such seeming disparities capture the enigmas inherent in the creativity–mental illness question (and, perhaps, in studying creativity itself). One of Barron's well-known quotes (and a favorite of my friend Zorana Ivcevic Pringle) is that a creative person is "at once naïve and knowledgeable . . . more primitive and more cultured, more constructive and more destructive, occasionally crazier and yet adamantly saner than the average person" (1963, p. 224).

An inventive yet flawed methodology that has enabled the study of Pro-c creators is the use of Swedish registries to examine occupation and mental health diagnoses (Kyaga et al., 2011, 2013). First, they found that people with bipolar disorder and (healthy) relatives of people with schizophrenia or bipolar were more likely to have creative occupations (Kyaga et al., 2011). In a second, larger study, they examined a wider array of disorders (Kyaga et al., 2012). Only bipolar disorder was associated with having a creative occupation; other diagnoses, such as schizophrenia, depression, anxiety, alcoholism, and autism, were not. The only specific occupation to be associated with a wide array of diagnoses was writing, consistent with the Sylvia Plath Effect and other historiometric studies. It is worth noting here that you may remember me drumming home the point that any occupation can be a creative one—there are creative plumbers and creative electricians and creative financial planners. Although the Kyaga studies have many plusses, the sole use of occupation as a metric for creativity is a strong caution.

A brief tangent is that most of these studies (indeed, most of *all* studies) show a relationship—which is not the same as a causal relationship. Things can be related for many reasons. A quick trip to Tyler Vigen's terrific website Spurious Correlations, for example, tells us that per capita consumption of cheese has correlated an astounding $r = .95$ over the last 10 years with the number of people who died by getting tangled in their bed sheets. Similarly, the number of films that Nicholas Cage makes per year has correlated $r = .86$ with the number of female editors on the *Harvard Law Review* (Vigen, 2015). Clearly, you can take any series of numbers (or lists of creative people) and argue *anything*. These examples are not to call into question all data analysis, of course—but one needs to be an informed consumer. Just as if you didn't know how to pick out a good grapefruit, you would ask someone, so, too, if you don't know anything about statistics (and it is okay if you don't), then you should at least seek out an expert opinion if you want to truly consider past research in this area.

EVERYDAY CREATORS AND MENTAL ILLNESS

A much more common approach is to look at everyday people and give them measures of creativity and mental health. Typically, researchers look at what are called subclinical disorders—in other words, they're not clinically significant.

Subclinical Versus Clinical Disorders

For example, hypomania is related to bipolar disorder (there are periods of elevated mood, but these are less intense and shorter), yet it does not necessarily lead to a diagnosis of "mentally ill." People with minor hypomania may be more creative (Furnham, Batey, Anand, & Manfield, 2008; Lloyd-Evans, Batey, & Furnham, 2006). Zabelina, Condon, and Beeman (2014) found that when divergent thinking was scored according to the manual (in which fluency, or the number of responses, strongly influences the results), there was no relationship between creativity and hypomania. When the same test was scored with raters using the Consensual Assessment Technique, thereby not weighing the quantity of responses, there was a relationship.

The question of whether the hypomania findings extend to bipolar disorder is debatable. Richards, Kinney, Lunde, Benet, and Merzel (1988) looked at 17 people with bipolar disorder, 16 people with severe mood swings (cyclothymes), 11 normal first-degree relatives, and 33 controls. They found higher creativity levels (as measured by a Lifetime Creativity Scale) in the 33 people with mental illness and their relatives, as compared with the controls. Strong et al. (2007) studied creativity and personality in bipolar and unipolar depressives, as well as controls from creative and noncreative disciplines. They found two distinct factors; one was strongly based in neuroticism and mood disorders (cyclothymia and dysthymia), whereas the other was comprised mostly of openness to experience and creativity. Although both factors were related to self-report measures of creativity, neither factor was related to scores on the Torrance Tests.

All diagnoses are also not created equal. People with extreme bipolar disorder may be less creative (see Richards & Kinney, 1990). For example, Rubenstein (2008) compared the divergent thinking scores of psychiatric inpatients who were diagnosed with schizophrenia, major depression, anxiety, or a personality disorder (narcissistic, borderline, or schizoid). The people with schizophrenia had significantly and notably lower fluency scores (the number of responses) than the other groups; no groups differed in originality.

It is also important to bring in the trait-versus-state distinction. You can have a trait (you may tend to crave cheese dipped in

185

chocolate) but you may or may not be in that current state (you may not be in the mood at this moment for cheese dipped in chocolate). Similarly, you might be an angry or anxious person in general or you might be angry or anxious at this particular moment in time. Vellante et al. (2011) found that students in traditionally creative majors were more likely to have temperaments that were irritable, rapidly cycling, or manic—yet they were not in more active distress. So, for example, it is possible that creative people may be more likely to have subclinical disorders, yet they could still be most creative when they are feeling the healthiest. Similarly, Wadeson (1980) found that bipolar patients going through depression and unipolar depressive patients had similar painting styles, with fewer colors; bipolar patients in a manic stage used more colors and were more expressive.

Taylor (under review), in an extensive review of creativity and mood disorders, found that everyday creative people demonstrated very slightly higher levels of mood disorders than less creative people (except for dysthymic disorder, which was negatively related to creativity). People with mood disorders, however, were not more creative than those without mood disorders. There was a slight domain effect, with creativity in math-related areas being less related to mood disorders and both verbal and visual creativity being more related.

Another subclinical disorder linked to creativity is schizotypy (Abraham & Windmann, 2008; Karimi, Windmann, Güntürkan, & Abraham 2007). Schizotypy is a disorder that is closer to a personality trait than a mental illness (Kwapil, Barrantes-Vidal, & Silvia, 2008). Symptoms of schizotypy can be similar to creativity, such as highly original and sudden new thoughts. Schizotypy and creativity can have some of the same cognitive and emotional underpinnings, such as heightened emotion (Fisher et al., 2004). Yet schizotypy has different types; positive schizotypy is more likely to include magical thinking, impulsive behavior, unusual experiences, and nonconformity, whereas negative schizotypy is closer to withdrawn behavior and anhedonia (Acar & Sen, 2013; Claridge, 1997).

There are also neuropsychological connections in the discussion of creativity and schizotypy. Fink et al. (2014) used functional magnetic resonance imaging (fMRI) techniques to examine brain activity in people with high and low levels of schizotypy. All participants were given two tasks: an Alternate Uses task to measure idea generation and a variation in which people were asked to think of common uses for an object (to serve as a control task). Without going into the details of the specific brain areas, the same patterns were found in both people engaged in idea generation and people with high levels of schizotypy.

Burch, Pavelis, Hemsley, and Corr (2006) found visual artists to be higher on both schizotypy and creativity than nonartists. What I found particularly interesting, though, was that the artists produced more responses designed to shock and provoke (e.g., you could "have sex on" a chair or "snort coke" off a knife). Typical creativity tests (such as those used in this study) reward antisocial or odd behavior as much as they reward specifically creative behavior. It may not be that bizarre, then, that people who score high on creativity tests also demonstrate antisocial or unusual behavior. Such a finding could be more a statement on the creativity test used than any deeper insights into antisocial behavior and real creativity.

The relationship between schizotypy and creativity is not uncontested. Miller and Tal (2007) found that although both openness to experience and intelligence predicted verbal and drawing creativity, neither positive nor negative schizotypy did so (although positive schizotypy was slightly correlated with creativity). Further, the relationship between schizotypy and creativity has been shown to vary by culture (Landgraf et al., 2015).

It is crucial, even though numerous studies have found a relationship between schizotypy and creativity, that the strength of the connection is not overblown. Acar and Sen (2013) conducted a meta-analysis and found that the average effect size was pretty weak ($r = .07$). The type of schizotypy was the key determining factor (as opposed to how creativity was measured or other variables). Positive and impulsive schizotypy ($r = .14$) and unspecified schizotypy ($r = .11$), were significantly related to creativity. However, negative schizotypy and anhedonia (the inability to feel pleasure—and also the original title of Woody Allen's *Annie Hall*) actually had a negative relationship with creativity ($r = -.09$).

It is further important to note that (similar to hypomania versus bipolar disorder) people with actual schizophrenia tend to be less creative than control groups, perhaps because their thought disorders decrease the coherent cognitive abilities needed for creativity (Abraham, Windmann, McKenna, & Güntürkün, 2007). The specific diagnosis may matter. In a different (and somewhat contradictory) study, Keefe and Magaro (1980) gave measures of divergent thinking to 40 people: 10 with paranoid schizophrenia, 10 with nonparanoid schizophrenia, 10 nonpsychotic psychiatric patients, and 10 controls. Those with nonparanoid schizophrenia earned higher divergent thinking scores than the other three groups. Merten and Fischer (1999) compared a group of writers and actors with both schizophrenics and controls. Both the creative and the schizophrenic groups gave more responses to a word-association task, but the writers and actors gave responses that were more relevant and were better able to evaluate their performance.

In another interesting study, Kinney, Richards, Lowing, LeBlanc, and Zimbalist (2001) tested adults who were born to parents with schizophrenia and adopted by parents without schizophrenia and compared them with adults born to and adopted by parents without schizophrenia. They found that (consistent with other studies) people with schizotypy or related disorders were more creative than those without the disorder—but the presence of schizophrenia in biological parents did not have an impact on creativity.

Many other subclinical disorders have been studied. Silvia and Kimbrel (2010) found negligible effects for anxiety, depression, and social anxiety on creativity. Byron and Khazanchi (2011) conducted an extensive meta-analysis examining the relationship between anxiety and creativity, and (as with hypomania) the state-versus-trait distinction came into play. Broadly, anxiety was negatively related to creative performance. But trait anxiety showed a stronger negative relationship to creativity than did state anxiety. Anxiety was especially negatively related to creativity tasks that were verbal and complex.

Latent Inhibition And Shared Vulnerabilities

You hopefully remember the idea of inhibition from the discussion on creativity and intelligence (Chapter 7). This concept comes into play here; an extensive body of work suggests that people with schizophrenia and those suffering from schizophrenic-like disorders (such as schizotypy) have lower levels of latent inhibition—in other words, they are not as good at filtering out irrelevant information. Peterson and Carson (2000) found that lower latent inhibition was strongly associated with higher levels of openness to experience.

Additionally, as I mentioned earlier, they further found (Peterson, Smith, & Carson, 2002) that lower latent inhibition in highly intelligent individuals is correlated to higher levels of creativity. They suggest that intelligence may be used as a mechanism to handle the many different stimuli that a person with low levels of latent inhibition may be forced to encounter—intelligence may serve as a coping device, so to speak. A further possibility is that perhaps higher intelligence allows better management of potentially dangerous impulses. Fink, Slamar-Halbedl, Unterrainer, and Weiss (2012) compared actors, students (serving as controls), and people with drug addictions. They found that both the actors and the addicts showed high creativity, low latent inhibition, and high psychoticism.

Carson (2011, 2014) integrates these studies and ideas to argue for a shared vulnerability model. She sets out three shared traits that both creativity and psychopathology have in common. One, of course, is latent inhibition. The second shared trait is a preference for novelty, which is one of the key aspects of openness to experience. Creative people tend to seek new experiences and sensations—yet sensation seeking is also related to less-desirable behaviors, such as gambling and substance use (Leeman, Hoff, Krishnan-Sarin, Patock-Peckham, & Potenza, 2014). It is also related to suicidal ideation (Ortin, Lake, Kleinman, & Gould, 2012), aggression (Wilson & Scarpa, 2011), and bipolar disorder (Bøen et al., 2015).

The third shared trait is hyperconnectivity—areas in the brain being linked that are not usually linked. Hyperconnectivity was found in musicians with absolute pitch (Loui, Li, Hohmann, & Schlaug, 2011). It is also often associated with synesthesia, which is when your senses cross over (Zamm, Schlaug, Eagleman, & Loui, 2013). You might see colors in music or smell sounds. Synesthesia has been long associated with creativity (Ramachandran & Hubbard, 2001). For example, people with synesthesia scored higher on the Remote Associates Test (Ward, Thompson-Lake, Ely, & Kaminski, 2008) and are overrepresented among art students (Rothen & Meier, 2010). Some people with synesthesia have a conceptual association and others actually perceive colors; it is the people who truly see the colors who are more likely to be creative (Domingo, Lalwani, Boucher, & Tartar, 2010).

There are additional factors that can either help protect people with these shared traits or put them further at risk of illness (Carson,

2011, 2014). Having a high IQ and good working memory can serve as protective factors, whereas a lower IQ and a poor working memory are risk factors. Another protective factor is cognitive flexibility, the ability to switch approaches and focus on different aspects of a problem. It often requires breaking patterns, and potentially even breaking social norms or standard ways of doing things (Ritter et al., 2012). Cognitive flexibility allows us to think of new ways to use old materials; think of furniture made out of broken crates or jewelry made out of typewriter keys. Cognitive flexibility also prevents functional fixedness, in which one continues to pursue strategies or solutions even after it is clear they are not working (Agogué, Poirel, Pineau, Houdé, & Cassotti, 2014; Öllinger, Jones, & Knoblich, 2008).

We usually think of being persistent as a good thing, but functional fixedness is persevering past the point of good sense. It's getting stuck and being unwilling to figure out ways of getting unstuck. In the 2014 National League Championship Series, for example, two different baseball managers were pitted against each other: Bruce Bochy and Mike Matheny. Bochy went against the book and made decisions based on choosing the best possible pitcher for the situation. In comparison, Matheny was handcuffed. Matheny refused to bring in his closer in a tie-game situation in game 5—showing functional fixedness. As a result, he left his best pitcher on the bench and brought in a different pitcher to give up the winning home run that ended the series (Keown, 2014).

There are several other models that examine traits that might be linked with both creativity and mental illness. One emphasizes egocentrism and perceptual processing (Winston, Tarkas, & Maher, 2014). Another one focuses on the personality construct of openness (DeYoung, Grazioplene, & Peterson, 2012). Two components of openness that are the most disparate are intellect and apophenia (seeing patterns in meaningless arrangements of information). So Dave might be very high on intellect and low on apophenia and Nate might be very high on apophenia and low on intellect, but both would be high in openness. Comparable to Carson's model, DeYoung and colleagues thus argue that the specific way that a person is open to experience helps determine if that person is more likely to be smart or apophenic (i.e., a bit wacky).

190

BEYOND CREATIVITY AND MENTAL ILLNESS

If you're feeling confused after reading about all of these studies, I understand. If you want a simple take-home point, you won't find one, because I don't think there is one yet, other than "take everything with a grain of salt." For a topic that inspires so much general interest, there is a lot of sloppy work and many inconsistent findings. It's part of the problem of seeing how two fuzzy constructs relate to each other.

It's also important to note that the issue of creativity and mental health doesn't stop with studying specific disorders or illnesses. I'll wrap up the chapter with a discussion of creativity and mood. I'll revisit the issue from the exact opposite perspective, the healing power of creativity, in Chapter 12.

Creativity and Mood

Although we tend to think of ourselves as being in a "good" mood or a "bad" mood, the researchers who actually study mood prefer the terms "positive" and "negative." A large body of research has found that positive mood can have beneficial influences on creative performance. The initial work was conducted by the late Alice Isen and colleagues (Estrada, Isen, & Young, 1994; Isen, Daubman, & Nowicki, 1987; Isen, Labroo, & Durlach, 2004). Typically, some participants would be put in a positive mood (for example, they might watch a funny movie or receive candy). Then they would do a problem-solving task or divergent thinking test, and often perform better than controls.

Amabile, Barsade, Mueller, and Staw (2005) studied the relationship of creativity and mood on employees. They e-mailed daily questionnaires asking participants to answer questions about the day's events (similar to the methodology used in Csikszentmihalyi's early Flow studies). These narratives were then coded for both creative and affective thought. In addition, the creative performances of these employees were rated by their peers on a monthly basis. There were significant relationships across multiple measures between being in a positive mood and higher creative performance (self- and peer-evaluated). There was no relationship between creative performance and being in a negative mood. Amabile et al. (2005) strongly emphasized the connection between positive mood and creativity to the point of arguing that the role of positive affect needs to be better incorporated into our current conceptions of creativity.

Other studies have suggested that the relationship may be more complex. Hirt, Levine, McDonald, Melton, and Martin (1997) argue for a hedonic contingency theory explanation for the positive mood–creativity relationship. People in a happy mood want to maintain their happy mood and will consciously behave in a way that will keep them happy. People in a sad mood, however, are not so careful, because most activities are likely to improve their mood (Wegener & Petty, 2001). Therefore, people in a happy mood, when faced with a divergent thinking type of task, try to make the task as fun and enjoyable as possible by being more creative.

Hirt, Devers, and McCrea (2008) manipulated people's beliefs in whether or not their moods could be changed. People typically believe moods are changeable, which makes sense; a good mood can quickly turn bad if someone kicks you in the shins or makes fun of your outfit. With no manipulation, people were generally more creative if they were in a good mood. However, when people were convinced that their moods could be frozen, Hirt et al. (2008) found no connection between mood and creativity. Such work is reminiscent of Dweck's (2000) mindset studies; if you believe that your ability cannot change, you are more prone to give up.

Despite the established link indicating that positive moods lead to higher creative performance, there is some evidence that clashes with this type of straightforward takeaway message (things are never so simple). For example, Kaufmann and Vosburg (1997) found that positive moods actually inhibited creative performance when there was no external feedback (i.e., participants had to decide for themselves if their performance was good enough; there were no real-world checks to gauge the creativity or quality of their solutions). In fact, Kaufmann (2003) argues that negative moods such as anger or sadness can be beneficial for creativity under certain circumstances. In one study, Kaufmann and Vosburg (2002) looked at positive and negative mood in creative problem solving. Interestingly, they found that a positive mood led to better scores in early idea production (similar to past findings, most recently Gasper, 2004). A negative mood, however, led to better scores in later idea production (see also Verleur, Verhagen, & Heuvelman, 2007).

Kaufmann and Kaufmann (2014), synthesizing the literature, argue that people in a good mood may be less cautious and come up with many different ideas right away (and these ideas may be shallower and inspire overconfidence). People in a bad mood are more likely to brood, analyze, and ruminate. They will be less satisfied with their responses and will keep persisting after the happy-go-lucky folks are done. One implication of this effect is that positive mood may be better when there are fewer constraints on the solution—in other words, when many different attempts at solving a problem will be the most helpful. Indeed, De Dreu, Nijstad, and Baas (2011) had people who tended more toward positive affect solve a problem that was either broadly or narrowly defined. These people were more creative and showed higher cognitive flexibility—but only on the broad problem.

This concept is consistent with the dual pathway to creativity model posed by Nijstad, De Dreu, Rietzschel, and Baas (2010). They argue that when positive moods are activated, you can be more creative because of higher cognitive flexibility. When negative moods are activated, you can be more creative because of persistence. Conversely, De Dreu, Baas, and Nijstad (2008), in a key paper I will discuss in a moment, suggest another possibility. The mood-contingency idea proposes that people in a positive mood are more careful when engaged in a task, so that a positive mood is connected with cognitive flexibility and associative thinking. These abilities may allow someone to connect with creative ideas quickly, whereas the persistence that comes with rumination or brooding takes more time.

The research on mood has spawned different and often outright contradictory findings; both positive and negative mood seem to both help and hurt creativity. Baas, De Dreu, and Nijstad (2008) conducted an in-depth meta-analysis to probe deeper into the paradox of positive versus negative mood. They use a framework in which moods aren't just simply "positive" or "negative." Moods can also be either activating or deactivating; for example, activating positive moods would be feeling happy or elated, whereas deactivating positive moods would be calm, serene, or relaxed. On the other side, negative moods can also be either activating (such as anger) or deactivating (such as sadness). These negative moods can also have a motivational drive, which emphasize promotion (or approach) or prevention (or avoidance). Promotion seeks nurturance, whereas prevention seeks security. So, for example, a student trying to get an A in a class may have a promotion focus (in that the student is motivated to achieve success) or a prevention focus (in that the student is motivated to avoid failure). If the student gets the A, then the student sees himself or herself as having achieved success, as the student has reached an "ideal" goal (representing hopes and aspirations). If the student sees himself or herself as having avoided failure, the student has reached an "ought" goal (representing responsibilities and duties). Having a promotion focus and succeeding results in joy; failure can lead to dejection or sadness. Having a prevention focus can lead to relaxed contentment with success and anxiety with failure (Higgins, 2006; Higgins, Shaw, & Friedman, 1997).

As Baas et al. (2008) categorized these negative moods, they found that deactivating negative moods included being sad, discouraged, or disappointed. Activating negative moods could be prevention focused (such as feeling uneasy, tense, fear, or disgust) or promotion focused (such as anger and frustration). They found that positive activating moods enhanced creativity (although the impact of mood on creativity decreased as people spent more time engaged in the creative task). In contrast, positive deactivating moods had no relationship with creativity. Among negative moods, deactivating moods had no relationship with creativity. In this meta-analysis, they found that prevention-focused negative moods were negatively related to creativity, and limited studies showed that promotion-focused negative moods were positively related. In other words, being happy or angry can make you more creative, being relaxed will likely show no impact, and being sad or fearful can make your ideas more structured (Baas, De Dreu, & Nijstad, 2012). Consistent with these results, Gaspar and Middlewood (2014) found that when a promotion focus was emphasized (regardless of positive or negative affect), people did better on a creativity-related association task. They found that the effects in part were rooted in people with a promotion focus wanting to seek out new experiences (which, as you hopefully remember, is a key component of the openness facet of openness to experience).

Another study by the same team (Baas, De Dreu, & Nijstad, 2011b) suggested that activation is more important than focus. If you're feeling stressed, then it is better (for your creativity) for you to continue to feel that way than for you to seek relief and good cheer. Highly activated states—which include both happiness and anger— are associated with creativity (De Dreu et al., 2008). A further study specifically on anger (Baas, De Dreu, & Nijstad, 2011a) confirms that angry people are more creative than sad or mood-neutral people at first—but anger consumes more cognitive resources than sadness, so creative production declines more rapidly in angry people than in sad people. Even fear, which I just wrote was not particularly associated with creativity, can serve its purpose. Baas and De Dreu (2013) examined the role of threat and creativity. People were better able to access their ideas in domains related to the threat, leading to higher creativity (and reminiscent of the connection between *Glr* and creativity discussed in Chapter 7). However, the creativity had to be seen as serving a function.

A recent study that used the Experience Sampling Method repeatedly tested college students through their cell phones to ask about their activities, mood, and personality (Silvia et al., 2014). Similar to the Amabile et al. (2005) study, they actually tapped into out-of-the-lab, real-world creative behavior; these types of results are, in my opinion, particularly powerful. What did they find? Consistent with Baas et al. (2008), positive and active moods predicted creativity. In addition, openness was strongly linked with actual creative behavior; this connection is unsurprising, but higher conscientiousness also increased the chance of doing something creative. Overall, their participants were engaged in a creative activity 22% of the time when they were surveyed.

Other studies have examined how mood interacts with disposition and personality. Forgeard (2011) found that preexisting mood determined how emotion induction interacted with creativity. People who were naturally not depressed produced captions that were rated as being more creative when they had negative mood induced than when they had positive or neutral mood induced. People who tended toward depression showed no such effect. Leung et al. (2014), curiously, found nearly opposite results; people who were higher on neuroticism were more creative when induced to recall a negative event (although it is important to note the distinction between neuroticism and depression). Leung et al. (2014) further found that intrinsic motivation and task enjoyment mediated this relationship (in other words, broadly, neurotic people enjoyed thinking about negative events, and this enjoyment helped them be more creative).

Creativity and Emotional Intelligence

Emotional intelligence (EI), often considered a component of positive mental health, has a nuanced relationship with creativity. When EI was first conceived, a key ability was being able to utilize EI. One of the four elements of this ability was creative thinking (Salovey & Mayer, 1990). Current models do not emphasize the relationship between EI and creativity, although using one's emotions to think more creatively is still a component (Mayer & Salovey, 1997). It is also worth noting that in Guilford's full Structure of Intellect model (the one with 120 possibilities), one of the areas of content was behavioral—in other words, interacting with people. Like creativity, EI has measurement issues rooted in how it is conceptualized. Most tests are self-report and based on the idea that EI is a trait, like being conscientious. These tests tend to overlap with personality measures; more importantly, EI was conceived as an ability, more akin to having a strong vocabulary. Ability-based tests tend to be both more expensive and time-consuming.

Strong empirical research examining the connection between EI and creativity is surprisingly scarce. Ivcevic, Brackett, and Mayer (2007) examined EI (measured as an ability), creativity, and emotional creativity. Emotional creativity is being able to experience and express combinations of emotions that are new, appropriate, and genuine (Averill, 1999, 2004). They found that self-reported emotional creativity correlated with both self-reported creative behavior and a variety of creative performance measures. However, an ability measure of emotional creativity correlated only with one self-report measure of emotional creativity. EI was not related to any of the creativity measures.

Certainly, components associated with EI are connected with creativity. Carmeli, McKay, and Kaufman (2014) connected trait-based

EI to creativity via the moderators of generosity and vigor. Parke, Seo, and Sherf (2015) found that two specific components of trait-based EI, emotion regulation and emotion facilitation, were associated with being creative at work. Hoffman and Russ (2012) discovered that pretend play in elementary school children was associated with both creativity and with emotion regulation, which is also consistent with Yeh's (2008) study that found that emotion regulation was related to creativity in young children. Sanchez-Ruiz, Hernandez-Torrano, Perez-Gonzalez, Batey, and Petrides (2011) found domain-specific nuances to the relationship between EI and creativity; for example, self-control was positively correlated to creative personality in scientists but negatively correlated with divergent thinking performance in artists.

My colleague Jessica Hoffman suggests that EI, particularly emotion regulation, may explain some of the discrepancies in the research on creativity and mood or emotions. People who are particularly good at being in charge of their emotions may resist most mood inductions; a sad movie won't necessarily make them sad, and writing about their happiest moment won't necessarily make them happy. Such folks are often considered noise and lumped with the people who just weren't paying attention. Indeed, it's acceptable practice to not use data from people for whom the mood induction didn't work. But maybe instead of just representing error, these people are high in EI (or, specifically, emotion regulation), in which case these are important individual differences that should be considered.

As my friend Zorana Ivcevic Pringle explains it, the relationship between EI abilities and creativity is likely to be complex. EI by itself does not make a person more creative. The ability to accurately perceive, understand, or regulate emotions does not provide original ideas. However, these abilities can be helpful in actualizing one's creative potential. In a recent study, Ivcevic and Brackett (2015) found that emotion regulation ability, a component of EI, is associated with higher creativity in individuals who are relatively high in openness to experience (which, as you may remember from Chapter 5, is closely associated with creativity). High emotion regulation ability increases persistence in the face of obstacles and passion for one's interests, which in turn predict higher creativity.

FINAL THOUGHTS ON A COMPLICATED TOPIC

Richards (2007) makes an interesting point as she discusses her Richards et al. (1988) study, which found higher levels of creativity in patients with mental illness: "It is ironic that work I have done . . . has been cited to support this negativity, although we, the researchers, think it is quite the opposite. We investigated the possibility that everyday creativity might carry a compensatory advantage" (p. 28).

My own work (Kaufman, 2001a, 2001b, 2003, 2005; Kaufman & Baer, 2002b) is often held up as evidence that creative people are more likely to be mentally ill, even though I never actually said that, nor would I say that today. I began my own work being interested in writers; I entered information initially on many, many writers using many different categories—mentors, best works, age of first publication, as well as mental illness. I didn't (and don't) claim to be a diagnostician; I only entered basic information focused on a yes–no dichotomy for the presence of possible mental illness. What I actually found was that eminent poets, especially female poets, were more likely to be mentally ill *than other types of writers*. In my second experiment, I found that eminent female poets were more likely to be mentally ill *than other eminent women*. This parallel finding struck me as interesting, so I published it. Unexpectedly, the media caught on to my finding that poets die young (Lee, 2004), and I wasted some of my 15 minutes of fame trying to explain this odd finding in the world press. Even an anonymous caption-writer at CNN.com got into the act, writing, "This study found this/ Haiku holds the threat of death/ Write prose live longer."

Most people misunderstood. I wasn't saying that *all* poets die young, or *all* poets were mentally ill, and I only studied very eminent poets. People posted online comments about how poetry was hazardous to your health, and so-and-so wrote poetry so she or he would die soon, and so on. It surprised me how much it struck a nerve. Some people were genuinely upset and felt stigmatized, and I felt bad. Especially because the main comparison I made was between poets, novelists, playwrights, and nonfiction writers, I was

198

surprised there weren't an equal number of journalists gloating on-line. Most people, either to prove a point or to help them react in fury, assumed I was arguing that all poets were nuts, and therefore creative people in general were crazy.

It reminds me of what I call the WGASA factor, which is named after the (now defunct) WGASA Bush Line at the Wild Animal Park in San Diego. The park was trying to figure out what to call the monorail, which takes visitors on a tour of most of the animals and is a key part of the park experience. After a long time of debating and getting nowhere, one zoo executive wrote down in frustration, "WGASA." If you ask workers at the park today, they will either say they don't know what it stands for, or that it's an African word that means something like "happiness," or that it's for "World's Greatest Animal Show Anywhere." In fact, the acronym stands for something quite different. Upon reviewing entries to name the new monorail, supposedly one beleaguered Wild Animal Park executive just wrote WGASA on a chalkboard, referencing a common expression they would use (Mikkelson & Mikkelson, 2015): "Who gives a spit any-how?" (the actual word is a little coarser). I have often felt that a lot of psychology—a lot of life, really—can suffer from the WGASA sentiment. It is easy to do research on any topic and lose sight of the purpose or the point; I can't be the only professor to be stumped by a student asking me why a particular study or theory is impor-tant. It is almost easier to specialize in things that the average per-son will never care about or understand. Studying something that inspires interest (or anger or fear or inspiration) brings with it a certain weight.

Indeed, I think there is a corollary to the WGASA factor, which states that research should ideally lead to more potential positive outcomes than negative outcomes. Obviously, this rule can't always be true—but there are certainly areas of research (such as the count-less studies that emphasize one group's superiority to another) that seem destined to cause harm and to hurt people, with little ben-efit. I think that some research on creativity and mental illness can certainly help—but psychologists who are interested in these areas should make sure they are not glorifying illness, stigmatizing creative people, or generally causing havoc in the name of truth or headlines, whichever comes first.

LOOKING AHEAD

This discussion is an ideal setup for sliding away from the specifics of the creative individual and into some bigger questions about creativity. We'll start with the question of admissions, hiring, and fairness.

REFERENCES

Abraham, A., & Windmann, S. (2008). Selective information processing advantages in creative cognition as a function of schizotypy. *Creativity Research Journal, 20,* 1–6.

Abraham, A., Windmann, S., McKenna, P., & Güntürkün, O. (2007). Creative thinking in schizophrenia: The role of executive dysfunction and symptom severity. *Cognitive Neuropsychiatry, 12,* 235–258.

Acar, S., & Sen, S. (2013). A multilevel meta-analysis of the relationship between creativity and schizotypy. *Psychology of Aesthetics, Creativity, and the Arts, 7,* 214–228.

Agogué, M., Poirel, N., Pineau, A., Houdé, O., & Cassotti, M. (2014). The impact of age and training on creativity: A design-theory approach to study fixation effects. *Thinking Skills and Creativity, 11,* 33–41.

Amabile, T. M., Barsade, S. G., Mueller, J. S., & Staw, B. M. (2005). Affect and creativity at work. *Administrative Science Quarterly, 50,* 367–403.

American Psychiatric Association. (2013). *Diagnostic and statistical manual of mental disorders* (5th ed.). Arlington, VA: American Psychiatric Publishing.

Andreasen, N. C. (1987). Creativity and mental illness. *American Journal of Psychiatry, 144,* 1288–1292.

Andreasen, N. C. (2014). Secrets of the creative brain. *The Atlantic.* Retrieved from http://www.theatlantic.com/features/archive/2014/06/secrets-of-the-creative-brain/372299

Averill, J. R. (1999). Individual differences in emotional creativity: Structure and correlates. *Journal of Personality, 67,* 331–371.

Averill, J. R. (2004). A tale of two snarks: Emotional intelligence and emotional creativity compared. *Psychological Inquiry, 15,* 228–233.

Baas, M., & De Dreu, C. (2013). *Functional creativity: When creativity helps to avoid threats.* Paper presented at the Society for Experimental Social Psychology, Berkeley, CA.

Baas, M., De Dreu, C., & Nijstad, B. A. (2012). Emotions that associate with uncertainty lead to structured ideation. *Emotion, 12,* 1004–1014.

Baas, M., De Dreu, C. K., & Nijstad, B. A. (2008). A meta-analysis of 25 years of mood-creativity research: Hedonic tone, activation, or regulatory focus? *Psychological Bulletin, 134,* 779–806.

Baas, M., De Dreu, C. K., & Nijstad, B. A. (2011a). When prevention promotes creativity: The role of mood, regulatory focus, and regulatory closure. *Journal of Personality and Social Psychology, 100,* 794–809.

Baas, M., De Dreu, C. K., & Nijstad, B. A. (2011b). Creative production by angry people peaks early on, decreases over time, and is relatively unstructured. *Journal of Experimental Social Psychology, 47,* 1107–1115.

Barron, F. (1963). *Creativity and psychological health.* Princeton, NJ: D. Van Nostrand Company.

Barron, F. (1969). *Creative person and creative process.* New York, NY: Holt Rinehart & Winston.

Bartlett, T. (2014). Madness and the muse; we're captivated by the idea of the troubled genius. But is it a fiction? *Chronicle of Higher Education.* Retrieved from http://chronicle.com/article/Madnessthe-Muse/148845

Becker, G. (2014). A socio-historical overview of the creativity-pathology connection: From antiquity to contemporary times. In J. C. Kaufman (Ed.), *Creativity and mental illness* (pp. 3–24). New York, NY: Cambridge University Press.

Bøen, E., Hummelen, B., Elvsåshagen, T., Boye, B., Andersson, S., Karterud, S., & Malt, U. F. (2015). Different impulsivity profiles in borderline personality disorder and bipolar II disorder. *Journal of Affective Disorders, 170,* 104–111.

Burch, G. S. J., Pavelis, C., Hemsley, D. R., & Corr, P. J. (2006). Schizotypy and creativity in visual artists. *British Journal of Psychology, 97,* 177–190.

Byron, K., & Khazanchi, S. (2011). A meta-analytic investigation of the relationship of state and trait anxiety to performance on figural and verbal creative tasks. *Personality and Social Psychology Bulletin, 37,* 269–283.

Carmeli, A., McKay, A. S., & Kaufman, J. C. (2014). Emotional intelligence and creativity: The mediating role of generosity and vigor. *Journal of Creative Behavior, 48,* 290–309.

Carson, S. H. (2011). Creativity and psychopathology: A shared vulnerability model. *Canadian Journal of Psychiatry/La Revue Canadienne De Psychiatrie, 56,* 144–153.

Carson, S. H. (2014). Cognitive disinhibition, creativity, and psychopathology. In D. K. Simonton (Ed.), *The Wiley handbook of genius* (pp. 198–221). New York, NY: Wiley-Blackwell.

Cassandro, V. J. (1998). Explaining premature mortality across fields of creative endeavor. *Journal of Personality, 66,* 805–833.

Claridge, G. E. (1997). *Schizotypy: Implications for illness and health*. Oxford, England: Oxford University Press.

Colvin, K. (1995). *Mood disorders and symbolic function: An investigation of object relations and ego development in classical musicians*. Unpublished doctoral dissertation, California School of Professional Psychology, San Diego, CA.

Damian, R. I., & Simonton, D. K. (2014). Diversifying experiences in the development of genius and their impact on creative cognition. In D. K. Simonton (Ed.), *The Wiley handbook of genius* (pp. 375–393). Oxford, England: Wiley-Blackwell.

De Dreu, C. K. W., Baas, M., & Nijstad, B. A. (2008). Hedonic tone and activation in the mood-creativity link: Towards a dual pathway to creativity model. *Journal of Personality and Social Psychology, 94*, 739–756.

De Dreu, C. K. W., Nijstad, B. A., & Baas, M. (2011). Behavioral activation links to creativity because of increased cognitive flexibility. *Social Psychological and Personality Science, 2*, 72–80.

DeYoung, C. G. (2006). Higher-order factors of the Big Five in a multi-informant sample. *Journal of Personality and Social Psychology, 91*, 1138–1151.

Djikic, M., Oatley, K., & Peterson, J. B. (2006). The bitter-sweet labor of emoting: Linguistic analysis of writers and physicists. *Creativity Research Journal, 18*, 191–197.

Domingo, S., Lalwani, L. N., Boucher, L., & Tartar, J. L. (2010). Individuals with grapheme-color associations exhibit creativity. *Imagination, Cognition and Personality. 30*, 289–299.

Dweck, C. S. (2000). *Self-theories: Their role in motivation, personality and development*. Philadelphia, PA: Taylor & Francis.

Estrada, C., Isen, A. M., & Young, M. J. (1994). Positive affect influences creative problem solving reported source of practice satisfaction in physicians. *Motivation and Emotion, 18*, 285–299.

Fink, A., Slamar-Halbedl, M., Unterrainer, H.-F., & Weiss, E. M. (2012). Creativity: Genius, madness or a combination of both? *Psychology of Aesthetics, Creativity, and the Arts, 6*, 11–18.

Fink, A., Weber, B., Koschutnig, K., Benedek, M., Reishofer, G., Ebner, F., . . . Weiss, E. M. (2014). Creativity and schizotypy from the neuroscientific perspective. *Cognitive, Affective, and Behavioral Neuroscience, 14*, 378–387.

Fisher, J. E., Mohanty, A., Herrington, J. D., Koven, N. S., Miller, G. A., & Heller, W. (2004). Neuropsychological evidence for dimensional schizotypy: Implications for creativity and psychopathology. *Journal of Research in Personality, 38*, 24–31.

Forgeard, M. J. C. (2008). Linguistic styles of eminent writers suffering from unipolar and bipolar mood disorder. *Creativity Research Journal, 20*, 81–92.

Forgeard, M. J. C. (2011). Happy people thrive on adversity: Pre-existing mood moderates the effect of mood inductions on creativity. *Personality and Individual Differences, 51*, 904–909.

Furnham, A., Batey, M., Anand, K., & Manfield, J. (2008). Personality, hypomania, intelligence and creativity. *Personality and Individual Differences, 44*, 1060–1069.

Gasper, K. (2004). Permission to seek freely? The effect of happy and sad moods on generating old and new ideas. *Creativity Research Journal, 16*, 215–229.

Gasper, K., & Middlewood, B. L. (2014). Approaching novel thoughts: Understanding why elation and boredom promote associative thought more than distress and relaxation. *Journal of Experimental Social Psychology, 52*, 50–57.

Higgins, E. T. (2006). Value from hedonic experience and engagement. *Psychological Review, 113*, 439–460.

Higgins, E. T., Shah, J. Y., & Friedman, R. (1997). Emotional responses to goal attainment: Strength of regulatory focus as moderator. *Journal of Personality and Social Psychology, 72*, 515–525.

Hirt, E. R., Devers, E. E., & McCrea, S. M. (2008). I want to be creative: Exploring the role of hedonic contingency theory in the positive mood-cognitive flexibility link. *Journal of Personality and Social Psychology, 94*, 214–230.

Hirt, E. R., Levine, G M., McDonald, H. E., Melton, R. J., & Martin, L. L. (1997). The role of mood in qualitative aspects of performance. *Journal of Experimental Social Psychology, 33*, 602–629.

Hoffmann, J., & Russ, S. (2012). Pretend play, creativity, and emotion regulation. *Psychology of Aesthetics, Creativity, and the Arts, 6*, 175–184.

Isen, A. M., Daubman, K. A., & Nowicki, G. P. (1987). Positive affect facilitates creative problem solving. *Journal of Personality and Social Psychology, 52*, 1122–1131.

Isen, A. M., Labroo, A. A., & Durlach, P. (2004). An influence of product and brand name on positive affect: Implicit and explicit measures. *Motivation and Emotion, 28*, 43–63.

Ivcevic, Z., & Brackett, M. (2015). Predicting creativity: Interactive effects of openness to experience and emotion regulation ability. *Psychology of Aesthetics, Creativity, and the Arts, 9*, 480–487.

Ivcevic, Z., Brackett, M. A., & Mayer, J. D. (2007). Emotional intelligence and emotional creativity. *Journal of Personality, 75*, 199–235.

Jamison, K. R. (1989). Mood disorders and patterns of creativity in British writers and artists. *Psychiatry, 52*, 125–134.

Jamison, K. R. (1993). *Touched with fire: Manic-depressive illness and the artistic temperament.* New York, NY: Free Press.

Jamison, K. R. (1997). *An unquiet mind: A memoir of moods and madness.* London, England: Picador.

Karimi, Z., Windmann, S., Güntürkün, O., & Abraham, A. (2007). Insight problem solving in individuals with high versus low schizotypy. *Journal of Research in Personality, 41*, 473–480.

Kaufman, J. C. (2001a). Genius, lunatics, and poets: Mental illness in prize-winning authors. *Imagination, Cognition, and Personality, 20*, 305–314.

Kaufman, J. C. (2001b). The Sylvia Plath Effect: Mental illness in eminent creative writers. *Journal of Creative Behavior, 35*, 37–50.

Kaufman, J. C. (2003). The cost of the muse: Poets die young. *Death Studies, 27*, 813–822.

Kaufman, J. C. (2005). The door that leads into madness: Eastern European poets and mental illness. *Creativity Research Journal, 17*, 99–103.

Kaufman, J. C. (Ed.). (2014). *Creativity and mental illness.* New York, NY: Cambridge University Press.

Kaufman, J. C., & Baer, J. (2002). I bask in dreams of suicide: Mental illness and poetry. *Review of General Psychology, 6*, 271–286.

Kaufman, J. C., Bromley, M. L., & Cole, J. C. (2006). Insane, poetic, lovable: Creativity and endorsement of the "mad genius" stereotype. *Imagination, Cognition, and Personality, 26*, 149–161.

Kaufmann, G., & Kaufmann, A. (2014). When good is bad and bad is good: Mood, bipolarity, and creativity. In J. C. Kaufman (Ed.), *Creativity and mental illness* (pp. 205–235). New York, NY: Cambridge University Press.

Kaufmann, G., & Vosburg, S. K. (1997). "Paradoxical" mood effects on creative problem-solving. *Cognition and Emotion, 11*, 151–170.

Kaufmann, G., & Vosburg, S. K. (2002). The effects of mood on early and late idea production. *Creativity Research Journal, 14*, 317–330.

Kaun, D. E. (1991). Writers die young: The impact of work and leisure on longevity. *Journal of Economic Psychology, 12*, 381–399.

Keefe, J. A., & Magaro, P. A. (1980). Creativity and schizophrenia: An equivalence of cognitive processing. *Journal of Abnormal Psychology, 89*, 390–398.

Keown, T. (2014, October 17). *Bruce Bochy: Outside the box.* Retrieved from http://espn.go.com/mlb/playoffs/2014/story/_/id/11717586/mlb-bruce-bochy-postsreason-success-not-book

Kinney, D. K., Richards, R., Lowing, P. A., LeBlanc, D., & Zimbalist, M. E. (2001). Creativity in offspring of schizophrenic and control parents: An adoption study. *Creativity Research Journal, 13*, 17–25.

Kwapil, T. R., Barrantes-Vidal, N., & Silvia, P. J. (2008). The dimensional structure of the Wisconsin schizotypy scales: Factor identification and construct validity. *Schizophrenia Bulletin, 34*, 444–457.

Kyaga, S., Landén, M., Boman, M., Hultman, C. M., Långström, N., & Lichtenstein, P. (2013). Mental illness, suicide and creativity: 40-year prospective total population study. *Journal of Psychiatric Research, 47*, 83–90.

Kyaga, S., Lichtenstein, P., Boman, M., Hultman, C. M., Långström, N., & Landén, M. (2011). Creativity and mental disorder: Family study of 300,000 people with severe mental disorder. *British Journal of Psychiatry, 199*, 373–379.

Landgraf, S., Ilinykh, A., Haller, C. S., Shemelina, O., Cropley, D., von Treskow, I., . . . van der Meer, E. (2015). Culture makes the differences: The "creativity-schizotypy" association varies between Germans and Russians. *International Journal of Creativity & Problem Solving, 25*, 35–60.

Lee, F. R. (2004, April 24). Going early into that good night. *New York Times*, Arts pp. 1, 4.

Leeman, R. F., Hoff, R. A., Krishnan-Sarin, S., Patock-Peckham, J. A., & Potenza, M. N. (2014). Impulsivity, sensation seeking and part-time job status in relation to substance use and gambling in adolescents. *Journal of Adolescent Health, 54*, 460–466.

Leung, A. K. -Y., Liou, S., Qiu, L., Kwan, L. Y-Y., Chiu, C-Y., & Yong, J. C. (2014). The role of instrumental emotion regulation in the emotions-creativity link: How worries render neurotic individuals more creative. *Emotion, 14*, 845–856.

Lloyd-Evans, R., Batey, M., & Furnham, A. (2006). Bipolar disorder and creativity: Investigating a possible link. *Advances in Psychology Research, 40*, 111–142.

Lombroso, C. (1894). *The man of genius*. London, England: Walter Scott.

Loui, P., Li, H., Hohmann, A., & Schlaug, G. (2011). Enhanced cortical connectivity in absolute pitch musicians: A model for local hyperconnectivity. *Journal of Cognitive Neuroscience, 23*, 1015–1026.

Ludwig, A. M. (1994). Mental illness and creative activity in female writers. *American Journal of Psychiatry, 151*, 1650–1656.

Ludwig, A. M. (1995). *The price of greatness*. New York, NY: Guilford Press.

Ludwig, A. M. (1998). Method and madness in the arts and sciences. *Creativity Research Journal, 11*, 93–101.

Mayer, J. D., & Salovey, P. (1997). What is emotional intelligence? In P. Salovey & D. J. Sluyter (Eds.), *Emotional development and emotional intelligence: Educational implications* (pp. 3–34). New York, NY: HarperCollins.

Merten, T., & Fischer, I. (1999). Creativity, personality and word association responses: Associative behaviour in forty supposedly creative persons. *Personality and Individual Differences, 27*, 933–942.

Mikkelson, B., & Mikkelson, D. P. (2015). WGASA. *Snopes.* Retrieved from http://www.snopes.com/business/names/wgasa.asp

Miller, G. F., & Tal, I. R. (2007). Schizotypy versus openness and intelligence as predictors of creativity. *Schizophrenia Research, 93,* 317–324.

National Institute of Mental Health. (n.d.). *Any mental illness among adults.* Retrieved from http://www.nimh.nih.gov/health/statistics/prevalence/ any-mental-illness-ami-among-adults.shtml

Nettle, D. (2006). Schizotypy and mental health amongst poets, visual artists, and mathematicians. *Journal of Research in Personality, 40,* 876–890.

Nijstad, B. A., De Dreu, C. K., Rietzschel, E. F., & Baas, M. (2010). The dual pathway to creativity model: Creative ideation as a function of flexibility and persistence. *European Review of Social Psychology, 21,* 34–77.

Öllinger, M., Jones, G., & Knoblich, G. (2008). Investigating the effect of mental set on insight problem solving. *Experimental Psychology, 55,* 269–282.

Ortin, A., Lake, A. M., Kleinman, M., & Gould, M. S. (2012). Sensation seeking as risk factor for suicidal ideation and suicide attempts in adolescence. *Journal of Affective Disorders, 143,* 214–222.

Parke, M. R., Seo, M., & Sherf, E. N. (2015). Regulating and facilitating: The role of emotional intelligence in maintaining and using positive affect for creativity. *Journal of Applied Psychology, 100,* 917–934.

Peterson, J. B., & Carson, S. (2000). Latent inhibition and openness to experience in a high-achieving student population. *Personality and Individual Differences, 28,* 323–332.

Peterson, J. B., Smith, K. W., & Carson, S. (2002). Openness and extraversion are associated with reduced latent inhibition: Replication and commentary. *Personality and Individual Differences, 33,* 1137–1147.

Plucker, J. A., Beghetto, R. A., & Dow, G. (2004). Why isn't creativity more important to educational psychologists? Potential, pitfalls, and future directions in creativity research. *Educational Psychologist, 39,* 83–96.

Post, F. (1994). Creativity and psychopathology: A study of 291 world-famous men. *British Journal of Psychiatry, 165,* 22–34.

Post, F. (1996). Verbal creativity, depression and alcoholism: An investigation of one hundred American and British writers. *British Journal of Psychiatry, 168,* 545–555.

Ramachandran, V. S., & Hubbard, E. M. (2001). Synaesthesia—A window into perception, thought, and language. *Journal of Consciousness Studies, 8,* 3–34.

Rawlings, D., & Locarnini, A. (2008). Dimensional schizotypy, autism, and unusual word associations in artists and scientists. *Journal of Research in Personality, 42,* 465–471.

Richards, R. L. (2007). Everyday creativity: Our hidden potential. In R. Richards (Ed.), *Everyday creativity and new views of human nature* (pp. 25–54). Washington, DC: American Psychological Association.

Richards, R. L., & Kinney, D. K. (1990). Mood swings and creativity. *Creativity Research Journal, 3*, 202–217.

Richards, R. L., Kinney, D. K., Lunde, I., Benet, M., & Merzel, A. P. C. (1988). Creativity in manic-depressives, cyclothemes, their normal relatives, and control subjects. *Journal of Abnormal Psychology, 97*, 281–288.

Ritter, S. M., Damian, R. I., Simonton, D. K., van Baaren, R. B., Strick, M., Derks, J., & Dijksterhuis, A. (2012). Diversifying experiences enhance cognitive flexibility. *Journal of Experimental Social Psychology, 48*, 961–964.

Roberts, B. W., Kuncel, N. R., Shiner, R., Caspi, A., & Goldberg, L. R. (2007). The power of personality: The comparative validity of personality traits, socioeconomic status, and cognitive ability for predicting important life outcomes. *Perspectives on Psychological Science, 2*, 313–345.

Rothen, N., & Meier, B. (2010). Higher prevalence of synaesthesia in art students. *Perception, 39*, 718–720.

Rothenberg, A. (1990). *Creativity and madness: New findings and old stereotypes.* Baltimore, MD: Johns Hopkins University Press.

Rubinstein, G. (2008). Are schizophrenic patients necessarily creative? A comparative study between three groups of psychiatric inpatients. *Personality and Individual Differences, 45*, 806–810.

Salovey, P., & Mayer, J. D. (1990). Emotional intelligence. *Imagination, Cognition and Personality, 9*, 185–211.

Sanchez-Ruiz, M. J., Hernandez-Torrano, D., Perez-Gonzalez, J. C., Batey, M., & Petrides, K. V. (2011). The relationship between trait emotional intelligence and creativity across subject domains. *Motivation & Emotion, 35*, 461–473.

Schlesinger, J. (2009). Creative mythconceptions: A closer look at the evidence for "mad genius" hypothesis. *Psychology of Aesthetics, Creativity, and the Arts, 3*, 62–72.

Schlesinger, J. (2012). *The insanity hoax: Exposing the myth of the mad genius.* New York, NY: Shrinktunes Media.

Schlesinger, J. (2014). Building connections on sand: The cautionary chapter. In J. C. Kaufman (Ed.), *Creativity and mental illness* (pp. 60–76). New York, NY: Cambridge University Press.

Silvia, P. J., Beaty, R. E., Nusbaum, E. C., Eddington, K. M., Levin-Aspenson, H., & Kwapil, T. R. (2014). Everyday creativity in daily life: An experience-sampling study of "little c" creativity. *Psychology of Aesthetics, Creativity, and the Arts, 8*, 183–188.

Silvia, P. J., & Kaufman, J. C. (2010). Creativity and mental illness. In J. C. Kaufman & R. J. Sternberg (Eds.), *Cambridge handbook of creativity* (pp. 381–394). New York, NY: Cambridge University Press.

Silvia, P. J., & Kimbrel, N. A. (2010). A dimensional analysis of creativity and mental illness: Do anxiety and depression symptoms predict creative cognition, creative accomplishments, and creative self-concepts? *Psychology of Aesthetics, Creativity, and the Arts, 4*, 2–10.

Simonton, D. K. (1975). Age and literary creativity: A cross-cultural and transhistorical survey. *Journal of Cross-Cultural Psychology, 6*, 259–277.

Simonton, D. K. (1990). *Psychology, science, and history: An introduction to historiometry.* New Haven, CT: Yale University Press.

Simonton, D. K. (1994). *Greatness: Who makes history and why.* New York, NY: Guilford Press.

Simonton, D. K. (2009). *Genius 101.* New York, NY: Springer Publishing Company.

Simonton, D. K. (2014a). The mad (creative) genius: What do we know after a century of historiometric research? In J. C. Kaufman (Ed.), *Creativity and mental illness* (pp. 25–41). New York, NY: Cambridge University Press.

Simonton, D. K. (2014b). The mad-genius paradox: Can creative people be more mentally healthy but highly creative people more mentally ill? *Perspectives on Psychological Science, 9*, 470–480.

Simonton, D. K. (2014c). More method in the mad-genius controversy: A historiometric study of 204 historic creators. *Psychology of Aesthetics, Creativity, and the Arts, 8*, 53–61.

Staltaro, S. O. (2003). *Contemporary American poets, poetry writing, and depression.* Unpublished doctoral dissertation, Alliant International University, Fresno, CA.

Stirman, S. W., & Pennebaker, J. W. (2001). Word use in the poetry of suicidal and non-suicidal poets. *Psychosomatic Medicine, 63*, 517–523.

Stoynoff, N. (2008, May 19). Robert Downey, Jr. *People*, pp. 81–83.

Strong, C. M., Nowakowska, C., Santosa, C. M., Wang, P. W., Kraemer, H. C., & Ketter, T. A. (2007). Temperament-creativity relationships in mood disorder patients, healthy controls and highly creative individuals. *Journal of Affective Disorders, 100*, 41–48.

Taylor, C. L. (under review). *Beyond vague and definitive maybes: A meta-analysis of the link between creativity and mood disorder.*

Thomas, K., & Duke, M. P. (2007). Depressed writing: Cognitive distortions in the works of depressed and non-depressed. *Psychology of Aesthetics, Creativity, and the Arts, 1*, 204–218.

Vellante, M., Zucca, G., Preti, A., Sisti, D., Rocchi, M. B. L., Akiskal, K. K., & Akiskal, H. S. (2011). Creativity and affective temperaments in non-clinical professional artists: An empirical psychometric investigation. *Journal of Affective Disorders, 135*, 28–36.

Verleur, R., Verhagen, P. W., & Heuvelman, A. (2007). Can mood-inducing videos affect problem-solving activities in a web-based environment? *British Journal of Educational Technology, 38*, 1010–1019.

Vigen, T. (2015). *Spurious correlations*. New York, NY: Hachette Books.

Wadeson, H. (1980). *Art psychotherapy*. New York, NY: Wiley.

Ward, J., Thompson-Lake, D., Ely, R., & Kaminski, F. (2008). Synaesthesia, creativity and art: What is the link? *British Journal of Psychology, 99*, 127–141.

Wegener, D. T., & Petty, R. E. (2001). Understanding effects of mood through the elaboration likelihood and flexible correction models. In L. L. Martin & G. L. Clore (Eds.), *Theories of mood and cognition* (pp. 177–210). Mahwah, NJ: Erlbaum.

Wills, G. I. (2003). A personality study of musicians working in the popular field. *Personality and Individual Differences, 5*, 359–360.

Wilson, L. C., & Scarpa, A. (2011). The link between sensation seeking and aggression: A meta-analytic review. *Aggressive Behavior, 37*, 81–90.

Winston, C. N., Tarkas, N. J., & Maher, H. (2014). Eccentric or egocentric? Preoperational features in schizotypic and creative adults. *Psychology of Aesthetics, Creativity, and the Arts, 8*, 413–422.

Yeh, Y. C. (2008). Age, emotion regulation strategies, temperament, creative drama, and preschoolers' creativity. *Journal of Creative Behavior, 42*, 293–293.

Zabelina, D. L., Condon, D., & Beeman, M. (2014). Do dimensional psychopathology measures relate to creative achievement or divergent thinking? *Frontiers in Psychology, 5*. doi:10.3389/fpsyg.2014.01029

Zamm, A., Schlaug, G., Eagleman, D. M., & Loui, P. (2013). Pathways to seeing music: Enhanced structural connectivity in colored-music synesthesia. *NeuroImage, 74*, 359–366.

The Big Picture

Creativity and Admissions, Hiring, and Fairness

ow do we decide who gets into college or who gets hired? I'll tackle college admissions first. In some situations, admissions are straightforward to the point of simplicity (or idiocy) itself. Many colleges use a formula. Multiply your GPA by your SAT score; if you're above a specific line, you're in, and if you're below the line, you're out. Certainly, many programs look beyond GPA and test scores; examples of other commonly used tools include letters of recommendation, personal statements, or statements of goals (Briel et al., 2000). But GPA and SAT or GRE scores tend to be the key (Zwick, 2013). Some elite colleges may also use interviews (Soares, 2012). You might think that the criteria get more in depth as you advance through the academic system, but that's not necessarily true. Surveys of psychology graduate admissions committees have found that the two most important criteria for graduate admissions are undergraduate

GPA and GRE scores (Keith-Spiegel, Tabachnick, & Spiegel, 1994; Landrum, Jeglum, & Cashin, 1994).

Does this emphasis on test scores work? It's a tricky question. A long stream of studies has demonstrated that the GREs are a perfectly good predictor of graduate school grades (e.g., Kuncel & Hezlett, 2007; Kuncel, Hezlett, & Ones, 2001; Sackett, Borneman, & Connelly, 2008). Yet are grades the best outcome variable? J. C. Kaufman and Agars (2009) argue it is essential to broaden the criteria for what we want to predict and begin to look at real-world variables. Sternberg and Williams (1997) conducted a small study to look at these questions; they found that GRE scores predicted first-year grades—but little else. GRE scores did not, for example, predict advisor ratings of the quality of a student's teaching, research, or dissertation (it is worth pointing out, however, that the study suffered from a restriction-of-range problem—in other words, there was less variation because everyone was smart). Remember, too, Chamorro-Premuzic's (2006) study that associated creativity with both dissertation quality and preference.

It is tempting to argue that the GREs and SATs are unnecessarily narrow or not indicative of full student potential. But the people who make these tests are not stupid; if it were easy to add a construct such as creativity to a standardized test, it would be done. We've discussed the hazards of measuring creativity at all. One other deterring factor is the general belief (true or not) that creativity tests are susceptible to coaching and faking (Kyllonen, Walters, & Kaufman, 2014). Is such a concern reasonable?

There is a clearly desired outcome (which school would explicitly look for an uncreative student?). Any self-report or personality-style test could be coached or faked; most items are not intended to be deceptive. There are some potential solutions (such as forced choice, in which you pick between two equally desirable statements), but it's a perpetual issue. Similarly, any measure of divergent thinking could be theoretically coached. Just by reading this book, you understand (or may dimly recall) the underlying scoring mechanisms and could therefore practice to improve your fluency or originality. It is important to note that the Torrance Tests of Creative Thinking (TTCT) are no more susceptible than any other divergent thinking measure. Indeed, one study found that TTCT-specific training was no more effective than general creativity training or even no training; all groups slightly improved on a second test-taking (Fairweather, Cramond, & Landis, 2015).

Researchers at the Educational Testing Service, the company that creates the GREs and is involved in the creation of the SATs, have been considering measures of creativity for over 50 years (Stewart, 1953). Frederiksen (1959; Frederiksen & Evans, 1974; Frederiksen, Evans, & Ward, 1975) developed and tested a measure of scientific creativity to see how many hypotheses someone could generate in response to a graph or chart. Although ETS still occasionally uses this task in research studies (now adapted for computer use), the measure has yet to make it onto the actual test. One reason is likely its extremely low correlation with the rest of the test (Bennett & Rock, 1995).

It's a safe bet that the last Number 2 pencil will have been ground to a nub by a nervous test-taker before creativity blasts its way onto a big-bucks group test. ETS would likely argue that the two are not mutually exclusive, and as you hopefully remember from Chapter 6, there are a myriad of studies that show solid correlations between standardized tests (and GPA) and creativity. This relationship is unsurprising given creativity's connection with intelligence.

Regardless, seeking creativity from standardized tests may be like seeking an emotional commitment from a warthog—you are left heartbroken and empty, and the warthog is vaguely aware that something important has happened. How else might creativity enter the admissions field (and should it do so in the first place)?

GIFTEDNESS AND CREATIVITY

One school admissions area that already uses creativity is gifted admissions—which students are chosen to enter gifted classes, programs, or after-school activities. The federal government has actually proposed its own definition of giftedness, the Marland definition, which about half of all schools use (which makes it the most commonly used definition; Callahan, Hunsaker, Adams, Moore, & Bland, 1995). This view argues that giftedness and talent are most present in six areas: general intellectual ability, specific academic aptitude, creative or productive thinking, leadership ability, visual and performing arts, and psychomotor ability (Marland, 1972). It has continued to be tweaked and updated (McClain & Pfeiffer, 2012).

Each state has its own definition of giftedness that it may use. Most are variations of the Marland definition. McClain and Pfeiffer (2012) surveyed all of the states' definitions and found that 27 states included creativity in their definition in 2010 (it was 30 states in 2000, which is an unsettling trend). For comparison's sake, 45 include intelligence, and 39 include high achievement.

The second most used mechanism for determining giftedness is to simply use an IQ cut-off score, which is a fine measure of IQ but, of course, not a particularly good measure of creativity (Hunsaker & Callahan, 1995). Indeed, it is commonplace for a student to be recommended for gifted services but to be denied if the student's IQ score is 1 point lower than the cut-off (McClain & Pfeiffer, 2012; Pfeiffer, 2008). To foreshadow the last section of this chapter, I will go on a very brief tangent. There may be societal roots in this conception that reveal an ugly past, even if many who simply use IQ today are unaware. Many point to the explosion in creativity work in America in the 1950s as being greatly due to *Sputnik*, when the Russians seemed to beating our heinies at space exploration (A. J. Cropley & D. H. Cropley, 2009; D. H. Cropley, 2015).

Certainly, there is much truth to this connection for both creativity and giftedness. But for giftedness . . . that's not all. Many have also pointed to a different milestone in the 1950s as being the key to the giftedness explosion: school integration. Some gifted and talented programs were initially established as a way to keep schools segregated after the courts ordered them to be integrated (Ford, 2003). A common argument is that IQ-based definitions are used for giftedness programs to this day to help enforce this separation (e.g., Baldwin, 2011). A pioneer at pressing this point and broadening conceptions of giftedness to include creativity (and thereby better integrate gifted programs) was E. Paul Torrance (Grantham, 2013).

Another commonly used definition is Renzulli's three-ring definition. Renzulli (1978) proposed that there are two types of giftedness: *high-achieving ("schoolhouse") giftedness* and *creative-productive giftedness*. High-achieving giftedness is more analytic in nature; someone with high-achieving giftedness would be a good test-taker.

Creative-productive giftedness emphasizes generation and production (similar to Guilford's work discussed earlier in the book). Unlike many theorists, Renzulli has ardently sought to apply his ideas to the classroom. Much of his work is directly aimed at teachers (e.g., Renzulli, 1994; Renzulli, Gentry, & Reis, 2014). His Enrichment Triad Model (Renzulli, 1977, Reis & Renzulli, 2003) proposes three key E's for the kind of investigative learning that can help enrich the student experience: enjoyment, engagement, and enthusiasm. The three types of enrichment that he proposes are Type I, which exposes students to new ideas and concepts; Type II, which targets how students think and feel; and Type III, which gives the student an active role in exploring a particular passion (Renzulli, 2012).

Most schools that use the Marland or Renzulli definitions include some kind of creativity assessment, often the Torrance tests or a Guilford-based measure or a ratings checklist, such as the Scales for Rating the Behavioral Characteristics of Superior Students (SRBCSS; Renzulli et al., 2004). Other schools use some variant of the Consensual Assessment Technique (CAT) methodology with expert ratings; such schools include the Governor's School of the Arts and Gifted and Talented programs in Washington County, Maryland (Baer & McKool, 2009).

Unfortunately, not all schools are careful in their creativity assessment. As mentioned, some schools use group-based intelligence or achievement tests to score student creativity, which seems a rather poor choice (Callahan et al., 1995; see longer discussion in J. C. Kaufman, Plucker, & Baer, 2008). I would suggest that people particularly interested in giftedness check out (as I've mentioned before) Scott Barry Kaufman's *Ungifted* (2013), or Steven Pfeiffer's *Essentials of Gifted Assessment* (2015), or the Psych 101 Series' own *Giftedness 101* by Linda Silverman (2009).

HIGHER EDUCATION ADMISSIONS

Creativity-related assessments are often part of university admissions for arts-based schools, such as Julliard, or art-related departments (such as New York University's Tisch School of the Arts). Rated creative performance and artistic portfolios are often a major component of their admissions. Most schools that do not focus on the arts do not look at creativity, although there are some exceptions. One of the leaders in this area is Robert Sternberg.

As mentioned earlier, Sternberg and his colleagues have studied how college admissions would be impacted by supplemental measures of successful intelligence (such as practical intelligence and creativity). These assessments are based on Sternberg's work on open-ended creativity assessments. Specifically, Sternberg and colleagues (Sternberg, 2008; Sternberg & the Rainbow Project Collaborators, 2006) used three types of open-ended measures. Students are asked to write captions to a cartoon, write short stories based on titles like "The Octopus's Sneakers," and tell stories based on a selected series of images. These responses are then evaluated using a similar methodology as the CAT. Performance is then rated by trained judges for cleverness, humor, originality, and task appropriateness (for the cartoons), and originality, complexity, emotional evocativeness, and descriptiveness for both written and oral stories (Sternberg & Lubart, 1995; Sternberg & the Rainbow Project Collaborators, 2006).

In a related vein, Sternberg's team created "augmented" versions of the Advanced Placement (AP) Test for Psychology, Statistics, and Physics that assessed the information via analytic, creative, practical, and memory-based subscales (Stemler, Grigorenko, Sternberg, & Jarvin, 2006; Stemler, Sternberg, Grigorenko, Jarvin, & Sharpes, 2009). This first phase of the project, conducted at many different universities, was called the "Rainbow Project."

Sternberg continued this work at Tufts University and beyond (Sternberg, 2010; Sternberg, Bonney, Gabora, & Merrifield, 2012; Sternberg & Coffin, 2010). He called his work with these new measures (based on his successful intelligence and WICS [Wisdom, Intelligence, Creativity, Synthesized] models and including creativity) the "Kaleidoscope Project." Similar to earlier work, students write stories (with titles like "Confessions of a Middle School Bully"), describe an alternate history in which Rosa Parks gave up her seat on the bus, and design and advertise new products. These measures were included (optionally) in the 2006–2007 application for the 15,000 students who applied to arts, sciences, and engineering at Tufts.

The results from these extensive implementations are both fascinating and encouraging. Sternberg's measures (not only of creativity, but for all components of successful intelligence) predict college success more accurately than standard admissions tests. In addition, and I'm going to come back to this, ethnic differences were significantly reduced (Sternberg, 2006; Sternberg & the Rainbow Project Collaborators, 2006; Stemler et al., 2006). At Tufts, the quality of applicants rose (indeed, despite de-emphasizing SAT scores, the average SAT scores of applicants increased), and minority admissions went up (Sternberg, 2008).

It is interesting to note that even within the creativity realm there are critics of Sternberg's approach, despite the results. These essays are "probably not the right way to assess . . . creativity, in my view," Howard Gardner told National Public Radio (Smith, 2007). Gardner goes on to argue that personal, one-on-one interviews would be the best way to get such information. Yet it would be hard to imagine an interview having any real scientific rigor. Indeed, job interviews tend to not give particularly valuable information, although there are several ongoing efforts to improve the process (Hamdani, Valcea, & Buckley, 2014). Further, personal interviews would represent an enormous investment in assessing creativity—think of the costs of interviewing every applicant to try to tap into such a nuanced construct. I worry that such criticisms will simply make it less likely that any school would actually take such an initiative in the first place.

Other schools are slowly starting to include creativity as an additional admissions tool. Jean Pretz, for example, has led a research-based effort at Elizabethtown College. One early study has shown that the traditional admissions components were only weakly related to the creativity measures (Pretz & Kaufman, 2015).

With enough effort, creativity *can* be part of the admissions process. Yet *should* creativity be part of the admissions process? Certainly, most graduate schools that ask letters of recommendation to rate or describe different traits in prospective students include creativity as one of the many variables (Walters, Plante, Kyllonen, Kaufman, & Gallagher, 2004). A now-discontinued product from ETS (which, many iterations earlier, I actually helped develop) is the Personal Potential Index (PPI), which is a standardized letter of recommendation for professors and other recommenders to fill out for graduate school applicants (Kyllonen, 2008). Six key abilities are highlighted on the PPI, including Knowledge/Creativity (combined as a single factor).

When faculty members are asked which factors are important for success in graduate school, creativity invariably is included (Walpole, Burton, Kanyi, & Jackenthal, 2001). Many schools specify on their admissions websites that they may look for creativity either in the entire application packet or in specific essay responses. Of course, it remains an open question whether an admission counselor's idea of creativity would include an essay written in iambic pentameter, a response given as a scientific formula, or a computer program that installs malware into the system of any school that rejects the applicant.

Yet it is interesting to note that some schools that do not specifically seek creative applications (unlike Tufts or Elizabethtown) may be turned off by such quirky demonstrations. Indeed, in a discussion of whether creative gimmicks help applicants, Debra Shaver, Smith College's director of admissions, admitted, "It certainly entertains the staff, but it doesn't help the student get in" (Wertheimer, 2008). Indeed, the consensus emerged that most clever and uncommon additions to the traditional application will be of minimal assistance. It may even backfire, as in the student who sent in a photograph of herself riding a bicycle naked; the committee felt it reflected poor judgment (in fact, as my friend Vlad Glăveanu noted, you could argue that the photograph was original, but not appropriate—and thus not creative).

Some admissions officers noted that there were fewer of these displays in recent years, perhaps because of the fear of seeming too unusual. "I regret that sense that an applicant has to come across as a perfectly polished product at the age of 17," Duke University director of undergraduate admissions Christoph Guttentag told the *Boston Globe*, "because they're not" (Wertheimer, 2008). Such panic can particularly be seen in those who want to be doctors. David Muller (2013) wrote in the *New England Journal of Medicine* that the "current model has perpetuated 'Premed syndrome,' a culture of aggressive competition for grades that conflicts with the precepts of medical professionalism: academic and intellectual rigor, creative thinking, collaboration, and social conscience" (p. 1568).

There is a rising tide against this status quo. The American Psychological Association's Coalition for Psychology in Schools and Education (2015) produced a position paper on 20 psychological principles that impact preK–12 teaching and learning, and the eighth principle is that creativity can be fostered. The Partnership for 21st Century Skills has its own 4-C model in which it argues for four key skills that all students should be able to master: collaboration, communication, critical thinking, and creativity. As this movement and the many creativity advocates gain popularity, there may eventually be enough impetus to change. Certainly, creativity in education has been a go-to topic for TED talks and media outlets such as *Newsweek* and the *Wall Street Journal*. It makes for good reading, and it's a fun way to bash schools without having to suggest practical, doable changes.

But in the meantime, things stay the same. With a few notable exceptions, incorporating creativity into admissions for higher education is greeted in the same way as an admonition to include leafy green vegetables with dinner. It's certainly a good idea, and if it could magically happen it would be great . . . but in real life, it's easier warming up our SAT scores with leftover corn or mashed potatoes. It doesn't help that creativity assessments, like daily fresh servings of kale, require effort, can be inconsistent in quality, and are more accessible for the rich. Are things any different in organizations?

THE HIRING PROCESS

Both education and business play great lip service to creativity (and innovation). Puccio and Cabra (2010) review the literature on creativity and organizations and do a nice job of highlighting how every couple of years, a new report from industry emphasizes the importance of creativity. As they discuss, the U.S. Labor Department, Dell, Microsoft, and Verizon are just a few of the influential groups to endorse the power of innovation. They report several studies and surveys of executives who consistently list creativity or innovation as a top priority.

Mind you, I'm not saying at all that such endorsements are bad things—they're terrific. And businesses are usually better at putting their pocketbooks where their praise is, with many consultants making a fine living on advising companies how to make their workplace more supportive of creativity (and I'm one of them, except for the fine-living bit). Are such good intentions reflected in the hiring process?

Just as each school has its own admissions process, so too does each company have its own personnel selection process. Schmidt and Hunter (1998), in a classic overview of the research literature on personnel selection, identify 19 types of assessments that are most commonly used for hiring. By far the most commonly used is some measure of general mental ability (GMA), which is sometimes called cognitive ability (but is basically the same as intelligence). These could include IQ tests, although they are more likely to be a group assessment instead of an individually administered measure. The Wonderlic is a famous example of a workplace test because it is used by the National Football League (NFL; Solomon, Haase, & Kuhn, 2013).

Another popular assessment is what is called a work sample test. These are simulations of actual job duties; if someone is applying for a car mechanic job, the company might ask the person to actually repair a broken car. For the NFL, in addition to the Wonderlic, players trying out were asked to run, jump, lift weights, and show off moves (Kuzmits & Adams, 2008).

There are many inbox exercises or problem-solving tests that pose hypothetical questions that are similar to the kind an actual worker might face. For example, perhaps you are asked what you would do if a client demands a solution by the next morning but you know it will be impossible to produce quality results before next week. These types of tests might be short answer or multiple choice (such as, would you [a] explain the situation to the client; [b] hurry the work to get some type of product to the client; or [c] tell the client to choke on his own vomit?).

Both GMA and work sample tests show a very strong relationship to job performance (Schmidt & Hunter, 1998). Personality tests are also very commonly used (unlike in school admissions), and conscientiousness is by far the factor that is most desired and most predictive of job performance (Hough, 1992; Mount & Barrick, 1995). There is some debate about whether it is better to use the nuance of the facets of conscientiousness or the broad factor (e.g., Paunonen, Rothstein, & Jackson, 1999), although recent work suggests that the facets are only helpful in specific situations and

222

may actually hide a connection with the broader factor (Salgado, Moscoso, & Berges, 2013). Conscientiousness is such the dominant factor that most companies seek that sometimes they only give measures of this specific factor and don't bother with the rest of the Big Five (the Paltry Four?).

A different selection measure related to conscientiousness is an integrity test. These tests may directly ask someone's views on honest behavior, past experiences with being dishonest, and whether the test-taker thinks that most people are dishonest (Wanek, Sackett, & Ones, 2003), with the underlying idea that people tend to be consistent between behavior and thought (the whole cognitive dissonance thing) and people who think "Hey, dishonest people are cool" are more likely to steal staplers. Another approach is to give a personality-based test and look for traits associated with honesty (such as social conformity—raising a creativity-related question that will fully poke its head out later in the book). Both ways show reasonable validity (Van Iddekinge, Roth, Raymark, & Odle-Dusseau, 2012).

So where does creativity come in amid all of this hoo-ha? Certainly, when organizations utilize personality tests, openness to experience is one of the factors and is considered a positive, desirable quality (Moy & Lam, 2004). In addition, measures that are used for personnel selection can be used to incorporate creativity, from interviews to biographical data to reference letters. Yet Hough and Dilchert (2010) argue that openness (let alone creativity) may be harder to assess from an interview than other factors. Similarly, supervisor or peer ratings are another common measure, and creativity can be included among this information, although Hunter, Cushenbery, and Freidrich (2012) caution that bosses may not always actually see creativity happening among the lower-level riffraff (they don't use that word).

Many companies interested in creativity will have their own methods they use (and likely secret ones). These may include questions to be asked during interviews, problem-solving tasks, or a specific psychometric measure. This measure may be made in-house, custom designed, or ordered commercially.

What commercial measures might companies choose from? It's a mixed bag. There are many out there. Some we have already discussed (such as the TTCT and other divergent thinking measures). One promising new development in the commercial realm is Mark

Runco's Runco Creativity Assessment Battery (rCAB), which incorporates automatic computerized scoring (e.g., Acar & Runco, 2014, 2015).

What of non–divergent thinking tests? Some, such as the Basadur Profile products (e.g., the Creative Problem Solving Profile [CPSP] Inventory), are rooted in empirical work (Basadur & Gelade, 2005; Basadur, Gelade, & Basadur, 2014). Some are questionable and hard to decipher from cryptic yet impressive-looking websites. Regardless, however, there are few published studies on the specific efficacy of any of these tests.

It speaks to a larger issue that with the exception of tests rooted in Guilford and Torrance, there are strikingly few creativity tests that have been successful in both the financial and academic realms. There are many commercial consulting companies; some have grown out of research, such as Creative Problem Solving (CPS; Isaksen & Treffinger, 2004), but others are snake oil salespeople. Taking a step back, it is surprising at how poorly creativity tests stack up against intelligence, personality, and even emotional intelligence tests.

This whole section is starting to feel incredibly depressing, and yet there is reason for hope. Including creativity as part of the personnel selection process does pay dividends if a company values the construct (Hunter et al., 2012). Even simple things such as using multiple sources when recruiting is associated with enhanced organizational innovation (Jiang, Wang, & Zhao, 2012). Further, scholars are aware of this issue; Montag, Maertz, and Baer (2012) offer a thorough model of workplace creativity with a focus on the criteria used, as opposed to the usual emphasis on creativity as a predictor.

THE ELEPHANT IN THE ROOM: ETHNICITY AND GENDER

Murphy, Cronin, and Tam (2003) surveyed organizational psychologists and found consensus that GMA tests were valid and useful—yet there was still controversy over how much organizations rely on these tests. Why? It's the same reason why the use of IQ tests, the Wonderlic, and the SATs causes vigorous debate: There are notable differences by ethnicity and gender on many of these instruments. Specifically, African Americans and Hispanic Americans receive lower scores on such major IQ tests as the Woodcock–Johnson (Edwards & Oakland, 2006) and the Wechsler Adult Intelligence Scale (Weiss, Chen, Harris, Holdnack, & Saklofske, 2010). Further, such differences persist on major standardized tests such as the SATs or GREs (e.g., Bleske-Rechek & Browne, 2014). Minorities score lower on the Wonderlic as well (Lyons, Hoffman, & Michel, 2009).

The differences between males and females are not as large for intelligence tests as the differences found between different ethnic groups, although males tend to obtain higher scores on tasks involving mental rotation (S. B. Kaufman, 2007), and females tend to obtain higher scores on verbal tests (Hedges & Nowell, 1995). Males tend to outscore females on the SAT, GRE, Graduate Management Admissions Test (GMAT), and AP exams, particularly on the quantitative sections or those related to science, technology, engineering, and math (STEM; Ackerman, Kanfer, & Calderwood, 2013); such trends have persisted even as women are more represented in STEM fields (Bleske-Rechek & Browne, 2014).

The reasons behind these differences are the source of much contention. Some researchers argue that these measures reflect actual differences (e.g., Herrnstein & Murray, 1994; Jensen, 1998). Others point to the discrepancy between socioeconomic status and opportunities across ethnicities (Sternberg, 1996), whereas still others argue that current ability measures do not incorporate enough aspects of intelligence to truly reflect a person's "global" ability (Sternberg, Kaufman, & Grigorenko, 2008).

Women tend to get better grades than men despite the reverse trend on standardized tests (Hyde & Kling, 2001; Noftle & Robins, 2007). Suggested reasons for this discrepancy have included women being less likely to guess on high-stakes testing (Baldiga, 2014), women being more likely to use slower but more accurate strategies for solving problems (Gallagher & DeLisi, 1994), and the role that conscientiousness plays in women getting strong grades (Kling, Noftle, & Robins, 2013). I also can't help but note that girls' scores on pretend play and divergent thinking predicted (4 years later) their mathematical achievement (Wallace & Russ, 2015).

It is important to note that basic differences in means across groups do not by themselves mean a test is biased. It is too easy to say that if one ethnicity, gender, or culture scores better on a test, then the test is just bad. Indeed, it is possible to create a test that seems fair but is biased. For example, let's say that I want to test your knowledge of cities. I ask you to estimate the population of Birmingham, Tuscaloosa, Decatur, Mobile, Huntsville, Auburn, and Montgomery. As you may realize, all of these cities are in Alabama. People from Alabama would therefore (probably) do better on this test than people from California or New York. If my intention was to measure general knowledge of cities (or American cities), then I have not succeeded.

Imagine that there is a magical "true score" that someone might have on any test—whether of intelligence or soccer-playing ability or height or knowledge of Sylvester Stallone comedies—that would represent your individual ability and somehow ignore the role of context. There are many reasons why you might not get your "true score" any time you take a test; usually you'd get a lower score. Maybe you're tired or distracted or sad or focused on the attractive person sitting in front of you. Psychometricians consider a measure to be fair to the extent that it minimizes systematic error in true-score estimation as a function of group membership. If a test consistently assigns certain groups (such as women or minorities) lower scores than their true scores, then the test should be considered biased (Mackintosh, 2011). Let me explain this concept a bit more, as it can be convoluted and counter-intuitive.

A fair test of vocabulary would mean that the only reasons why anyone would do better than someone else would either be because the person had a better vocabulary or because of random chance. For example, maybe you saw an Aaron Sorkin show such as *The Newsroom* the night before the test and you learned all sorts of new words. You might do better than your friend who would usually know more words, but seeing the television show was an example of random error. What wouldn't be random error would be if your verbal test truly assessed verbal ability in Caucasians but was actually measuring something quite different (such as exposure to American culture) in a Hispanic American population (Reynolds, 2000). The Alabama–California difference isn't random error—it's based on geography.

Going back to the Cattell–Horn–Cattel (CHC) theory of intelligence, think about *Gf* (fluid intelligence/solving novel problems).

If I want to test *Gf,* I might present a series of new problems to solve. Maybe I'll ask you to solve a lateral thinking puzzle (e.g., DeBono, 1992). These puzzles are ambiguous or unlikely situations or dilemmas that have a specific answer that can be deduced through a back-and-forth dialogue (Sloane, 1992). Maybe the puzzle I ask you to solve is the first one I ever solved, which my brother asked me 20 years ago:

A man walks into a restaurant and orders albatross soup. He takes one bite, then pulls out a gun and kills himself. Why?

It would take me another 30 pages to present a typical back-and-forth conversation (or it would take you several hours of guessing), so I will cut to the answer—he is a man who was a sailor, and was in a shipwreck. He was blinded, and his brother was killed. Another sailor fed him, telling him he was eating albatross soup. After being rescued, he tried albatross soup and it tasted different—and he realized he had eaten his brother's body. So he kills himself.

Not going into the absurdity of the question or the further questions of whether this actually measures fluid intelligence, let's explore how your response might be affected. Maybe you have read *Rime of the Ancient Mariner* or otherwise know that the albatross is a seafaring bird. In this case, the puzzle might be easier for you—and be tapping more into *Gc* (crystallized intelligence/acquired knowledge). Or perhaps you have solved other, similar puzzles, in which case the concept would make more sense. In the most extreme situation, maybe you solved the puzzle the day before when someone else asked you, and you are simply remembering the answer. In this case, you are using *Glr* (long-term storage and retrieval). The same question can produce different results depending on which people are answering it, and the test is not always purely at fault.

I've already discussed (in Chapter 7) how creative people may miss some items on IQ tests because they are creative. Others have taken this argument and specifically applied it to African Americans. They argue that differences on some IQ or achievement subtests, such as those involved in remembering the details of a story, may show larger differences between African Americans and Caucasians in part because African Americans approach the task differently (Heath, 1983; see Manly et al., 1998). This theory argues that Caucasians approach the task as the test-makers intended—by trying to memorize as many appropriate details as possible and stick to the presented story; in contrast, African Americans may put more emphasis on telling the story creatively. Indeed, another possible negative outcome is that African Americans will be penalized for creative behavior in the classroom. Baldwin (2003) argues that teachers and other authority figures may mistake creativity in African American students as unruly or disruptive behavior.

Baldwin (2001) also analyzed a list of creative traits and abilities. These abilities included well-researched aspects, such as being open to experience or having high divergent thinking ability, and more theoretical aspects, such as being anti-authoritarian, having a "zany" sense of humor, and having a low tolerance for boredom (Clark, 1988). Many of these abilities, Baldwin (2001) argued, are sometimes seen as being inappropriate—and often found in African Americans. These ideas are consistent with Shade's (1986) theory of an African American cognitive style. Her research with tests of cognitive style found that African Americans were more likely to be spontaneous, flexible, and open-minded. In contrast, Caucasians were more regulated and structured. Jenkins (2005) further proposes that African Americans throughout history have used their imagination and creativity to bolster their resiliency.

Another possibility for why there are ethnic and gender differences on ability and achievement measures is stereotype threat. Many studies have suggested that individuals feel stress when placed in a situation where they run the risk of confirming a negative stereotype about their group (e.g., ethnicity). This stress often causes poor performance (Steele & Aronson, 1995). Stereotypes about intelligence are widely known, even among people who are targets of the stereotypes and who do not endorse them (Devine, 1989). As a result, for example, an African American test-taker may worry about confirming negative stereotypes, which causes added stress—and, by extension, a lower performance on the test. Schmader and Johns (2003) argue that stereotype threat causes reduced working memory.

What may then occur is that members of ethnicities that have traditionally scored lower on IQ tests may experience "disidentification" in this domain—in other words, they gradually remove this domain (in this case, analytic and other "IQ test" types of abilities) from their conception of self (Crocker & Major, 1989; Steele, 1997). Instead of identifying themselves with these types of abilities, some people may instead identify themselves with other important cognitive abilities that are not associated with IQ tests. It may not shock you when I suggest that one of these abilities might be creativity.

How do our self-perceptions compare to what others think? Consider the competence–warmth stereotype (Fiske, Cuddy, Glick, & Xu, 2002), in which high-status people are seen as competent and those lower in status who are perceived as noncompetitive are seen as warm. Warmth is the less-valued attribute given as a runner-up prize to people (particularly women) who aren't seen as a threat. Are we more likely to see a member of a minority group as "creative" because we don't think it is as important as being smart? These are scary but important things to think about.

Are standardized tests accurate for everyone equally? Well, no. The SATs are more accurate in predicting first-year college GPA for Caucasians than African Americans (Mattern, Patterson, Shaw, Kobrin, & Barbuti, 2008), Hispanic Americans (Ramist, Lewis, & McCamley-Jenkins, 1994), and Asian Americans (Mattern et al., 2008). It is particularly poor at predicting first-year GPA for African American men (Bridgeman, McCamley-Jenkins, & Ervin, 2000). Hiring measures tend to have better validity, even the GMA measures; even if minorities score lower (as for the Wonderlic and NFL players), the accuracy of prediction is consistent by ethnicity (Gill & Brajer, 2012).

What can we do about this issue? The issue of some groups receiving lower scores may be due to broad and deeply ingrained societal problems. But the question of trying to make admissions and hiring measures fairer doesn't need to involve changing the whole world (as much as such a change would be a good thing). It can be as relatively simple as administering additional measures that may tap into other aspects of ability not assessed by the usual components of the admissions or hiring process. Again, it will likely not shock you that I would propose creativity to be an ideal match. Let's explore ethnic and gender differences on measures of creativity.

Ethnic Differences and Creativity

I've broadly adapted this section from J. C. Kaufman (2010), and if you are dying to see the numbers involved, I'd refer you to that paper. Most studies of ethnic differences in creativity have used divergent thinking tests. There tend to be few differences in divergent thinking

229

between African Americans and Caucasians in both children (Glover, 1976b; Iscoe & Pierce-Jones, 1964) and adults (Glover, 1976a). A few investigations found some (small) differences favoring African Americans. For example, Torrance (1971, 1973) found that African American children scored higher on the TTCT than Caucasian children on the Figural tests in fluency, flexibility, and originality; Caucasians scored higher on Figural elaboration and all Verbal subtests. The initial sample compared African American children in Georgia with children of higher socioeconomic status in Minnesota. When a subsequent study also used Caucasians from Georgia, all differences were significantly reduced; geography may have equally played a role.

Price-Williams and Ramirez (1977) found an interesting ethnicity and gender interaction. African American males and Hispanic American males outperformed Caucasian males on the fluency subscale of the Unusual Uses Test (results for flexibility were slightly in favor of African American and Hispanic American males). The results were reversed for females. Caucasians outperformed African Americans and Hispanic Americans on fluency and flexibility.

Comparisons of divergent thinking in Hispanic Americans and Caucasians tend to find different results depending on whether the measure is verbal or nonverbal. For example, Argulewicz and Kush (1984) found that Caucasians scored higher than Hispanic Americans on three of four TTCT Verbal forms, but there were no significant differences on the Figural forms. A wide body of studies indicates that bilingual students (specifically those who speak each language equally well) may have an advantage in creative abilities (Ghonsooly & Showqi, 2012; Lee & Kim, 2011). One recent study found differences in domain-specific creativity tests (verbal and mathematics) but not a general test (Leikin & Tovli, 2014).

Kharkurin (2012) outlined several reasons why being multilingual would increase creativity. One is that speaking multiple languages seems to increase intellectual capacity. Second, and more important, being multilingual involves the use of more elaborate cognitive structures and results in enhanced cognitive flexibility. Kharkurin offers several issues that challenge research in this area, ranging from an overreliance on divergent thinking measures (and the possibility that any benefits could be restricted to divergent thinking) to the fact that getting a genuinely random sample of multilinguals is nearly impossible. Random samples occur when someone is just as likely to be placed in one group as another group, and a person is either multilingual or not; you can't snap your fingers and have these people become multilingual for your study. He concludes that multilingualism is an advantage, but it is possible to get these same types of advantages in many different ways.

It is also possible that people who are multiracial may have a comparable leg up for being creative (Gaither, 2015). One study found that multiracials primed to think about their racial identity were more creative than those who were not primed, as well as monoracials asked to think about their racial identity (Gaither, Remedios, Sanchez, & Sommers, 2015). Tendayi Viki and Williams (2014) noted that the more multiracial individuals were able to integrate their different racial identities, the higher they scored on measures of creativity.

There are many studies on divergent thinking differences between Eastern and Western cultures. Jellen and Urban (1989) administered a measure of creative thinking and drawing to children from several different countries. They found that, in general, individuals from Western countries (such as Germany, England, and the United States) scored higher than those from Eastern countries (such as China and India). Zha, Walczyk, Griffith-Ross, Tobacyk, and Walczyk (2006) found that although Chinese graduate students outperformed their American counterparts on the GRE, American graduate students scored higher on four out of five measures of divergent thinking. In general, most studies find that individuals from Western cultures receive higher scores on creativity assessments than do those from Eastern cultures; I discuss the underlying reasons in Chapter 10. Of course, many studies show opposite or mixed findings; for example, Jaquish and Ripple (1984) found that Westerners outperformed Easterners on the Verbal portion of the TTCT but Easterners outperformed Westerners on the Figural component.

Fewer studies have compared Asian Americans to Americans of different ethnicities on divergent thinking tasks. Yoon (2005) gave the TTCT to European American and Asian American middle school students (the latter being a mix of Chinese American, Korean

American, Japanese American, and Southeastern Asian Americans). There were no significant differences either between the European Americans and Asian Americans or between the different subgroups of Asian Americans.

What about the world beyond divergent thinking? J. C. Kaufman, Baer, and Gentile (2004) studied poems, stories, and personal narratives written by African American, Hispanic American, Asian American, and Caucasian eighth-grade students. There were no differences across ethnicity in the rated creativity. In a similar study, J. C. Kaufman, Niu, Sexton, and Cole (2010) found no ethnic differences among novice-rated creativity for poems or stories written by Caucasians, African Americans, Hispanic Americans, and Asian Americans. They did, however, find a curious result for rated stories. Both Caucasian and African American novice raters preferred stories written by Caucasians (as opposed to any other ethnicity), even though there were no differences overall (including ratings by Hispanic Americans and Asian Americans). Raters did not know the ethnicities of the writers.

On a related note, J. C. Kaufman, Baer, Agars, and Loomis (2010) asked laypeople to rate poems that were randomly assigned a stereotypically African American or Caucasian author's name for both genders or presented without authorship (actual data on the ethnicity of the writer were not available). When given the names, the raters showed a very slight preference for the work of Caucasian women. Although there was bias present, comparable work using résumés instead of creative products showed much larger discrepancies (Bertrand & Mullainathan, 2004; King, Madera, Hebl, Knight, & Mendoza, 2006). Lebuda and Karwowski (2013) examined how a creator's presumed name (typical or unusual) and gender impacted rating of creative work across four domains (art, music, poetry, and science). There was a general bias in favor of products bearing male names, and both music compositions and poems received higher scores if it was believed the creator had an unusual name (see also Proudfoot, Kay, & Koval, 2015).

However, regardless of this study on creativity and ethnicity, the issue is a complex one. People perceived to be part of the "in-group" are more likely to be considered more creative (Haslam, Adarves-Yorno, Postmes, & Jans, 2013). Adarves-Yorno, Haslam, and Postmes

232

(2008) found in two studies that people were more likely to rate a product as being creative if they thought it was produced by someone in their in-group (as opposed to an outgroup member). Going even further, if a person's social identity was made salient and the group norm was established as being conservative/nonprogressive, noncreative ideas were selected as being both preferred and as being more creative (Adarves-Yorno, Postmes, & Haslam, 2006).

Going back to the question of ethnicity, differences in creativity are less clear for Asian Americans. Most of the research is cross cultural and does not focus on Asian Americans but rather people from Asian countries (and is discussed in Chapter 10). There have been some studies, of course. Artwork produced by American college students, for example, was rated as more creative than art produced by Chinese students by both American and Chinese raters (Niu & Sternberg, 2001). Yet a similar study that compared American and Chinese drawings of geometric shapes found that the two groups were rated similarly for creativity by both American and Chinese raters (Chen et al., 2002). There were no differences in rated artwork between Chinese and British schoolchildren, except for the higher ratings earned by Chinese children who attended a weekend art school (Cox, Perara, & Fan, 1998). Another study found that Japanese children produced higher-rated drawings than British children (Cox, Koyasu, Hiranuma, & Perara, 2001).

Looking specifically at Asian Americans, Niu and Sternberg (2003) compared the creative performance of Asian Americans and non–Asian Americans, and found no difference between the two groups. Rostan, Pariser, and Gruber (2002) studied Chinese American and Caucasian students' artwork, with two groups in each culture: students with additional art training and classes and students with no such classes. Each group's artwork (one drawing from life and one drawing from imagination) was judged by both Chinese and American judges. There were no significant differences between cultures from either set of judges. The only differences found were that art students (regardless of ethnicity) received higher ratings for their artwork than did nonart students. Paletz and Peng (2009), as part of a larger study, looked at creativity on a rated problem-construction task and ethnicity. They found that Asian American and Caucasian college students did not differ significantly.

233

Cheng, Sanchez-Burks, and Lee (2008) examined the creativity of Asian Americans as it related to identity integration, the degree to which a person feels that his or her disparate social identities (such as being Asian and being American) are complementary. They used a cooking simulation in one part of their study in which participants were presented with Asian-only, American-only, or Asian and American possible ingredients. When presented with stimuli from multiple cultures, Asian Americans with high identity integration were more creative; this finding disappeared in the Asian-only or American-only settings. These findings can be seen as comparable to the findings discussed earlier about balanced bilinguals and acculturated Hispanic Americans demonstrating more creativity.

Pfeiffer and Jarosewich (2007) looked at teacher ratings of gifted children on the Gifted Rating Scales–School Form (GRS; Pfeiffer & Jarosewich, 2003); there were no differences by ethnicity (African American, Asian American, Caucasian, and Hispanic American) on either the Creativity or Artistic Talent scales. These findings echo an earlier study by Harty, Adkins, and Sherwood (1984), who studied ethnic differences (African American and Caucasian) across several measures of giftedness. Teacher ratings of creativity were one of the few measures to show no differences by ethnicity. In contrast, however, another study found that teachers rated Caucasian students as being more creative than Hispanic American students, with highly acculturated Hispanic Americans receiving higher marks than less acculturated Hispanic Americans (Masten, Plata, Wenglar, & Thedford, 1999).

I haven't discussed the research on self-assessments (I will), so take the following with a grain of salt. J. C. Kaufman (2006), in one of the many series of endless studies that looked at creativity across domains, asked over 3,500 people to rate themselves in 56 different domains across five factors (social-communications, visual-artistic, verbal-artistic, science-analytic, and sports). He found that African Americans tended to give the highest self-ratings in creativity, regardless of domain. Native Americans also rated themselves higher in the science-analytic domains, and Hispanic Americans rated themselves higher on the social-communications domains. Ivcevic and Kaufman (2013) compared self-ratings on intelligence and creativity in Caucasians, African Americans, and Hispanic Americans. They

234

found that Caucasians and more educated people tended to give themselves higher ratings on everything, but there was an interaction with socioeconomic status. The differences between middle- and working-class ratings were higher in minorities than in Caucasians, and the ethnic differences were notably higher for intelligence than for creativity. Among the middle-class sample, African Americans rated themselves higher for creativity than did Caucasians; the opposite effect was found for intelligence.

Remember that openness to experience is closely tied to creativity (and if I say it again I win $100 from the Repetitive Repetitive Awards Awards). There tend to be no meaningful differences on any personality factors across cultures (e.g., Goldberg, Sweeney, Merenda, & Hughes, 1998; McCrae & Costa, 1997). However, Heuchert, Parker, Stumpf, and Myburgh (2000) found that White South Africans scored higher on openness to experience than Black South Africans (much of this difference was in the subcomponent of openness to feelings). Allik and McCrae (2004) found that people from European and Western cultures tended to be more open to experience than people from Asian and African cultures. D. Schmitt, Allik, McCrae, and Benet-Martínez (2007), in a massive study of 17,837 people from 56 nations, found that people from South American and European countries were the most open to experience (Chile was the highest), with people from South Asian countries generally being less open to experience. African countries were in the middle. It is worth noting, though, that Saucier and Goldberg (2001) studied personality labels in 13 languages (including English). They found that openness to experience was the only one of the Big Five personality factors to *not* be comprised of similar words regardless of language. The factor can focus more on intellect, creativity, or unconventionality, for example, depending on the culture. Openness to experience, therefore, can be considered a concept more readily accepted in Anglo cultures (Benet-Martínez & Oishi, 2008).

There are fewer personality studies on ethnic differences with American populations. Asian Americans have been generally found to be less open to experience than Caucasians (e.g., Benet-Martínez & Karakitapoglu-Aygün, 2003), yet the same studies found similar differences between first-generation Asian Americans and later-generation Asian Americans. Eap et al. (2008) found similar results, with the added information that openness was significantly correlated with acculturation. Unfortunately, cultural or ethnic differences have not been studied in depth using personality facets.

Gender Differences in Creativity

No simple conclusions can be drawn from examining the many studies that report gender differences (or lack thereof) on creativity tests. Some studies show women do better; other studies show men do better; still other studies show no difference. Baer and Kaufman (2008) reviewed the extensive literature on gender differences and found that most studies found no differences or mixed results. A recent review suggested that most differences are due to gender-related differences in cognitive styles or strategies in solving problems (Abraham, 2015).

Generally, there is a trend showing women scoring higher on verbal measures and men scoring higher on figural/mathematical measures (mirroring the larger cognitive findings in achievement tests). In one study, for example, Hong, Peng, O'Neil, and Wu (2013) found no differences in domain-general divergent thinking, but women scored higher on fluency, flexibility, and elaboration on domain-specific (modern Chinese history) divergent thinking. It is also interesting to note that He and Wong (2011) tested nearly 1,000 schoolchildren and broadly found no gender differences in a measure of creative ability. However, they found much greater variability in males. In other words, the boys were more likely to get extreme scores (whether very good or very bad).

Interestingly, androgyny is linked with creativity. Several studies have shown that people with high masculine and feminine traits (for example, both ambitious and compassionate) tend to demonstrate more creativity (Keller, Lavish, & Brown, 2007; Norlander, Erixon, & Archer, 2000). A recent investigation suggests that androgyny is more creatively beneficial to women than to men (Stoltzfus, Nibbelink, Vredenburg, & Hyrum, 2011). Other studies have examined physical characteristics related to testosterone exposure. Karwowski and Lebuda (in press) examined the ratio of Nobel Prize–nominated writers' facial width to their upper facial height (from the upper lip to the eyebrow); a higher ratio is linked with more postpuberty

236

testosterone. Writers with higher ratios were nominated at younger ages. However, the winners with the higher ratio tended to have to wait longer for the award. Karwowski and Lebuda interpret this result as being due to higher testosterone being linked with being impulsive and dominant, which may bring early recognition but a lesser chance of actually being selected. In a study of actors, Karwowski and Lebuda (2014) examined the ratio of the length of the second and fourth fingers (pointer and ring fingers). In this case, the pattern associated with more femininity was related to creative accomplishments.

Most large-scale studies of personality do not show gender differences in openness to experience (Collins & Gleaves, 1998; Goldberg et al., 1998). There is a trend, already discussed, for rewards to impact men and women differently (with females being less creative when rewards are present). There is also an interaction with education; women with higher levels of education tend to be more creative than less-educated women—there is no such difference in men (Matud, Rodriguez, & Grande, 2007).

It is important to note that there is a large inconsistency between gender differences on creativity tests and actual creative accomplishment. Although gender differences on creativity tests are minor or nonexistent, differences in real-world creative accomplishment are large and significant (Simonton, 1994). Murray (2003), in a review of human accomplishment, notes that out of 4,002 people he categorized as "significant," only 88 (2%) were female. He further points out that women comprised only 4% of all Nobel Prize winners from 1901 to 1950—and then only 3% of all winners from 1951 to 2000. The question is not simply a matter of older sources or accounts being biased; current awards show just as much male dominance.

Why do women not reach the same creative peaks as men? Helson (1990) argued that cultural values, social roles, and sexist thinking are now recognized as key reasons for the comparative lack of creative accomplishment by women. Piirto (1991) notes that girls do not show less creative achievement until *after* high school and college, indicating that a key issue may be a conflict between personal versus professional demands. It is also important to note Baer's work, discussed earlier, that indicates that women's creativity may be more susceptible to the negative effects of evaluation (and subsequent loss of intrinsic motivation).

Of course, old-time psychologists had quite different opinions. In response to complaints that virtually no women were elected to high administrative positions at the American Psychological Association (APA), E. G. Boring (1951), in an article titled "The Woman Problem," wrote that:

> All along the question of marriage interferes with the woman's assured planning. Can a woman become a fanatic in her profession and still remain marriageable?
>
> Yes, she can, for I know some, but I think a woman must be abnormally bright to combine charm with concentration. These women make the synthesis by being charmingly enthusiastic. . . . Some women readers will undoubtedly think me callous to the frustration of others, but I am asking only for realism. (p. 681)

What's frightening is how many men (in academia, in institutions, in most places) still believe Boring's logic.

NOT JUST CREATIVITY

I do feel duty-bound to note that creativity is but one of many variables that has been suggested as a supplement to the traditional admissions package. Indeed, one of the strongest proponents of going beyond the SATs and GPA does not include creativity on his list. N. Schmitt (2012) focused on 12 different noncognitive constructs as being ripe for admissions use. These included the ability to acquire knowledge (which certainly seems cognitive), intellectual curiosity, artistic/cultural appreciation, and adaptability (which would all seem to be related to creativity), and eight other absolutely valid and important traits: multicultural appreciation, leadership, interpersonal skills, social responsibility, physical/psychological health, career orientation, perseverance, and ethics.

Much of Schmitt's work has used these variables, so it is relevant to creativity but certainly not exact. Working with his research team, he has found that these variables improve GPA prediction above and beyond standardized tests and further relate to additional possible outcome variables (Oswald, Schmitt, Kim, Ramsay, & Gillespie, 2004). Further, the use of these variables, he and his team argues, would reduce ethnic bias in admissions (Sinha, Oswald, Imus, & Schmitt, 2011).

LOOKING AHEAD

Are the patterns of creative abilities different across gender and ethnicity from patterns of intellectual achievement? Might creativity measures allow for a better-informed measure of cognitive capabilities for school admissions than the current SAT–GPA formulas typically used? Early results from Sternberg (2008) and the other studies I've highlighted indicate that everyone has some capacity for being creative, and I believe this concept is encouraging. But there's a lot more work to be done. As J. Alfred Prufrock might ask, is it worth it?

When I was discussing the lack of differences found by ethnicity on creativity measures with one colleague, he said that the discrepancies found between intellectual achievement and creativity were simply a matter of error. All IQ or achievement tests, he argued, were really measures of g, and if anyone found different results on tests of creativity, it was simply that these assessments were flawed measures of g, and the findings were therefore worthless.

I am reminded of my father's discussion (A. S. Kaufman, 1999) of maternal effects on intelligence, specifically the research on identical twins who either shared or didn't share a placenta (e.g., Rose, Uchida, & Christian, 1981). In brief, twins who shared a placenta were more alike on both verbal and nonverbal measures of intelligence, whereas twins that did not share a placenta were less similar on nonverbal intelligence (if you are interested in more information about this, see Chapter 2 in A. S. Kaufman & Lichtenberger, 2006). The findings were unique at the time, and they have been little explored since. Indeed, other scholars in the field have either explained them away or simply ignored them as an aberration. But it was less the specific details about the twins studies but rather my father's response that struck me. He wrote that "the findings are, however, sufficiently provocative to challenge all known heritability estimates pertaining to intelligence and personality"

239

(pp. 627–628). That's toned down, though; what he would say in his talks (e.g., A. S. Kaufman, 2004) was that if these findings *might* be true, then how *dare* we not consider their implications?

So let's return to the question of how creativity can play a role in admissions and hiring, and whether creativity might improve fairness and equity in these decisions. There is no one obvious, correct answer. I'm not arguing that all of the research supports this contention; it doesn't. The studies are scattered and sometimes sloppily conducted. It may seem like each study uses a different measure of creativity. The findings on gender differences may be encouraging, or they may be identical to the findings on cognitive achievement. The findings on special education may mean nothing at all.

However, I think there's something there. Too many studies indicate that creativity may be a real or perceived intellectual strength for people who may be underserved by achievement or placement tests. I'd like to see more research. I'd like to see more colleges consider creativity as a supplemental or optional admissions tool. But most of all, I'd like to see some outstanding students who might otherwise slip through the cracks be able to go to college or graduate school. If it is within our power to make this happen, then how dare we not explore these issues?

Let's say that we magically work out the admissions and hiring dilemma, and we can change how we work things. Imagine that creativity is now used as an important metric, and universities and organizations alike heed the call and bring in more creative folks. Fairness abounds. Now what? How can the environment—speaking broadly—enhance creativity? Whether we're talking about the environment of one's home life, the classroom, the organization, one's physical surroundings, or culture and geography, how can we best nurture creativity?

REFERENCES

Abraham, A. (2015). Gender and creativity: An overview of psychological and neuroscientific literature. *Brain Imaging and Behavior*. Advance online publication. doi:10.1007/s11682-015-9410-8

Acar, S., & Runco, M. A. (2014). Assessing associative distance among ideas elicited by tests of divergent thinking. *Creativity Research Journal, 26,* 229–238.

Acar, S., & Runco, M. A. (2015). Thinking in multiple directions: Hyperspace categories in divergent thinking. *Psychology of Aesthetics, Creativity, and the Arts, 9*, 41–53.

Ackerman, P. L., Kanfer, R., & Calderwood, C. (2013). High school advanced placement and student performance in college: STEM majors, non-STEM majors, and gender differences. *Teachers College Record, 115*, 1–43.

Adarves-Yorno, I., Haslam, S. A., & Postmes, T. (2008). And now for something completely different? The impact of group membership on perceptions of creativity. *Social Influence, 3*, 248–266.

Adarves-Yorno, I., Postmes, T., & Haslam, S. A. (2006). Social identity and the recognition of creativity in groups. *British Journal of Social Psychology, 45*, 479–497.

Allik, J., & McCrae, R. R. (2004). Toward a geography of personality traits patterns of profiles across 36 cultures. *Journal of Cross-Cultural Psychology, 35*, 13–28.

American Psychological Association, Coalition for Psychology in Schools and Education. (2015). *Top 20 principles from psychology for preK–12 teaching and learning.* Retrieved from http://www.apa.org/ed/schools/cpse/top-twenty-principles.pdf

Argulewicz, E. N., & Kush, J. C. (1984). Concurrent validity of the SRBCSS Creativity Scale for Anglo-American and Mexican-American gifted students. *Educational & Psychological Research, 4*, 81–89.

Baer, J., & Kaufman, J. C. (2008). Gender differences in creativity. *Journal of Creative Behavior, 42*, 75–106.

Baer, J., & McKool, S. (2009). Assessing creativity using the consensual assessment. In C. Schreiner (Ed.), *Handbook of assessment technologies, methods, and applications in higher education* (pp. 65–77). Hershey, PA: IGI Global.

Baldiga, K. (2014). Gender differences in willingness to guess. *Management Science, 60*, 434–448.

Baldwin, A. Y. (2001). Understanding the challenge of creativity among African Americans. *Journal of Secondary Gifted Education, 12*, 121–125.

Baldwin, A. Y. (2003). Understanding the challenge of creativity among African Americans. *Inquiry, 22*, 13–18.

Baldwin, A. Y. (2011). I'm Black but look at me, I am also gifted. In T. C. Grantham, D. Y. Ford, M. S. Henfield, M. T. Scott, D. A. Harmon, S. Porcher, & C. Price (Eds.), *Gifted & advanced Black students in school* (pp. 13–22). Waco, TX: Prufrock Press.

Basadur, M., & Gelade, G. A. (2005). Modelling applied creativity as a cognitive process: Theoretical foundations. *Korean Journal of Thinking and Problem Solving, 15*, 13–41.

Basadur, M., Gelade, G., & Basadur, T. (2014). Creative problem-solving process styles, cognitive work demands, and organizational adaptability. *Journal of Applied Behavioral Science, 50*, 80–115.

Benet-Martínez, V., & Karakitapoglu-Aygün, Z. (2003). The interplay of cultural syndromes and personality in predicting life satisfaction comparing Asian Americans and European Americans. *Journal of Cross-Cultural Psychology, 34*, 38–60.

Benet-Martínez, V., & Oishi, S. (2008). Culture and personality. In O. P. John, R. W. Robins, & L. A. Pervin (Eds.), *Handbook of personality: Theory and research* (pp. 542–567). New York, NY: Guilford Press.

Bennett, R. E., & Rock, D. A. (1995). Generalizability, validity, and examinee perceptions of a computer-delivered formulating-hypotheses test. *Journal of Educational Measurement, 32*, 19–36.

Bertrand, M., & Mullainathan, S. (2004). Are Emily and Brendan more employable than Latoya and Tyrone? Evidence on racial discrimination in the labor market from a large randomized experiment. *American Economic Review, 94*, 991–1013.

Bleske-Rechek, A., & Browne, K. (2014). Trends in GRE scores and graduate enrollments by gender and ethnicity. *Intelligence, 46*, 25–34.

Boring, E. G. (1951). The woman problem. *American Psychologist, 6*, 679–682.

Bridgeman, B., McCamley-Jenkins, L., & Ervin, N. (2000). *Predictions of freshman grade-point average from the revised and recentered SAT I: Reasoning Test* (College Board Research Report No. 2000–1). New York, NY: The College Board.

Briel, J., Bejar, I., Chandler, M., Powell, G., Manning, K., Robinson, D., et al. (2000). *GRE horizons planning initiative (Graduate Record Examination). A research project funded by the GRE Board Research Committee, the GRE Program, and the Educational Testing Service Research Division*. Princeton, NJ: Educational Testing Service.

Callahan, C. M., Hunsaker, S. L., Adams, C. M., Moore, S. D., & Bland, L. C. (1995). Instruments used in the identification of gifted and talented students. *American Educational Research Journal, 45*, 150–165.

Chamorro-Premuzic, T. (2006). Creativity versus conscientiousness: Which is a better predictor of student performance? *Applied Cognitive Psychology, 20*, 521–531.

Chen, C., Kasof, J., Himsel, A. J., Greenberger, E., Dong, Q., & Xue, G. (2002). Creativity in drawing of geometric shapes: A cross-cultural examination with the consensual assessment technique. *Journal of Cross-Cultural Psychology, 33*, 171–187.

Cheng, C. Y., Sanchez-Burks, J., & Lee, F. (2008). Connecting the dots within creative performance and identity integration. *Psychological Science, 19*, 1178–1184.

242

Clark, B. (1988). *Growing up gifted* (3rd ed.). Columbus, OH: Merrill.

Collins, J. M., & Gleaves, D. H. (1998). Race, job applicants, and the Five-Factor Model of Personality: Implications for Black psychology, industrial/organizational psychology, and the Five-Factor Theory. *Journal of Applied Psychology, 83,* 531–544.

Cox, M. V., Koyasu, M., Hiranuma, H., & Perara, J. (2001). Children's human figure drawings in the UK and Japan: The effects of age, sex, and culture. *British Education, 16,* 47–56.

Cox, M. V., Perara, J., & Fan, X. U. (1998). Children's drawing ability in the UK and China. *Psychologia, 41,* 171–182.

Crocker, J., & Major, B. (1989). Social stigma and self-esteem: The self-protective properties of stigma. *Psychological Review, 96,* 608–630.

Cropley, A. J., & Cropley, D. H. (2009). *Fostering creativity: A diagnostic approach for higher education and organizations.* Cresskill, NJ: Hampton Press.

Cropley, D. H. (2015). *Creativity in engineering: Novel solutions to complex problems.* San Diego, CA: Academic Press.

DeBono, E. (1992). *Serious creativity: Using the power of lateral thinking to create new ideas.* New York, NY: HarperCollins.

Devine, P. G. (1989). Stereotypes and prejudice: Their automatic and controlled components. *Journal of Personality and Social Psychology, 56,* 5–18.

Eap, S., DeGarmo, D. S., Kawakami, A., Shelley, N. H., Hall, G. C. N., & Teten, A. L. (2008). Culture and personality among European American and Asian American men. *Journal of Cross-Cultural Psychology, 39,* 630–643.

Edwards, O. W., & Oakland, T. D. (2006). Factorial invariance of Woodcock-Johnson III scores for Caucasian Americans and African Americans. *Journal of Psychoeducational Assessment, 24,* 358–366.

Fairweather, E. C., Cramond, B., & Landis, R. N. (2015). Are creativity tests susceptible to coaching? *Asia Pacific Education Review, 16,* 1–6.

Fiske, S. T., Cuddy, A. J., Glick, P., & Xu, J. (2002). A model of (often mixed) stereotype content: Competence and warmth respectively follow from perceived status and competition. *Journal of Personality and Social Psychology, 82,* 878–902.

Ford, D. Y. (2003). Desegregating gifted education: Seeking equity for culturally diverse students. In J. H. Borland (Ed.), *Rethinking gifted education* (pp. 143–158). New York, NY: Teachers College Press.

Frederiksen, N. O. (1959). *Development of the test "Formulating Hypotheses": A progress report* (Office of Naval Research Technical Report, Contract Nonr-2338[00]). Princeton, NJ: Educational Testing Service.

Frederiksen, N. O., & Evans, F. R. (1974). Effects of models of creative performance on ability to formulate hypotheses. *Journal of Educational Psychology, 66,* 67–82.

Frederiksen, N. O., Evans, F. R., & Ward, W. C. (1975). Development of provisional criteria for the study of scientific creativity. *Gifted Child Quarterly, 19*, 60–65.

Gaither, S. E. (2015). "Mixed" results multiracial research and identity explorations. *Current Directions in Psychological Science, 24*, 114–119.

Gaither, S. E., Remedios, J. D., Sanchez, D. T., & Sommers, S. R. (2015). Thinking outside the box: Multiple identity mind-sets affect creative problem solving. *Social Psychological and Personality Science, 6*, 596–603.

Gallagher, A. M., & DeLisi, R. (1994). Gender differences in Scholastic Aptitude Test—mathematics problem solving among high-ability students. *Journal of Educational Psychology, 86*, 204–211.

Ghonsooly, B., & Showqi, S. (2012). The effects of foreign language learning on creativity. *English Language Teaching, 5*, 161–167.

Gill, A., & Brajer, V. (2012). Wonderlic, race, and the NFL draft. *Journal of Sports Economics, 13*, 642–653.

Glover, J. A. (1976a). Comparative levels of creative ability in black and white college students. *Journal of Genetic Psychology, 128*, 95–99.

Glover, J. A. (1976b). Comparative levels of creative ability among elementary school children. *Journal of Genetic Psychology, 129*, 131–135.

Goldberg, L. R., Sweeney, D., Merenda, P. F., & Hughes, J. E., Jr. (1998). Demographic variables and personality: The effects of gender, age, education, and ethnic/racial status on self-descriptions of personality attributes. *Personality and Individual Differences, 24*, 393–403.

Grantham, T. (2013). Creativity and equity: The legacy of E. Paul Torrance as an upstander for gifted black males. *The Urban Review, 45*, 518–538.

Hamdani, M. R., Valcea, S., & Buckley, M. R. (2014). The relentless pursuit of construct validity in the design of employment interviews. *Human Resource Management Review, 24*, 160–176.

Harty, H., Adkins, D. M., & Sherwood, R. D. (1984). Predictability of giftedness identification indices for two recognized approaches to elementary school gifted education. *Journal of Educational Research, 77*, 337–342.

Haslam, S. A., Adarves-Yorno, I., Postmes, T., & Jans, L. (2013). The collective origins of valued originality: A social identity approach to creativity. *Personality and Social Psychology Review, 17*, 384–401.

He, W., & Wong, W. (2011). Gender differences in creative thinking revisited: Findings from analysis of variability. *Personality and Individual Differences, 51*, 807–811.

Heath, S. (1983). *Ways with words: Language, life, and work in communities and classrooms*. New York, NY: Cambridge University Press.

Hedges, L. V., & Nowell, A. (1995). Sex differences in mental test scores, variability, and numbers of high-scoring individuals. *Science, 269*, 41–45.

Helson, R. (1990). Creativity in women: Outer and inner views over time. In M. A. Runco & R. S. Albert (Eds.), *Theories of creativity* (pp. 46–58). Newbury Park, CA: Sage.

Herrnstein, R. J., & Murray, C. A. (1994). *The bell curve.* New York, NY: Free Press.

Heuchert, J. W. P., Parker, W. D., Stumpf, H., & Myburgh, C. P. H. (2000). The Five-Factor Model in South African college students. *American Behavioral Scientist, 44,* 112–125.

Hong, E., Peng, Y., O'Neil, H. F., & Wu, J. (2013). Domain-general and domain-specific creative-thinking tests: Effects of gender and item content on test performance. *Journal of Creative Behavior, 47,* 89–105.

Hough, L. M. (1992). The "Big Five" personality variable construct confusion: Description versus prediction. *Human Performance, 5,* 139–155.

Hough, L. M., & Dilchert, S. (2010). Personality: Its measurement and validity for employee selection. In J. L. Farr & N. T. Tippins (Eds.), *Handbook of employee selection* (pp. 299–319). London, England: Routledge.

Hunsaker, S. L., & Callahan, C. M. (1995). Creativity and giftedness: Published instrument uses and abuses. *Gifted Child Quarterly, 39,* 110–114.

Hunter, S. T., Cushenbery, L., & Freidrich, T. M. (2012). Hiring an innovative workforce: A necessary yet uniquely challenging endeavor. *Human Resource Management Review, 22,* 303–322.

Hyde, J. S., & Kling, K. C. (2001). Women, motivation, and achievement. *Psychology of Women Quarterly, 25,* 364–378.

Isaksen, S. G., & Treffinger, D. J. (2004). Celebrating 50 years of reflective practice: Versions of creative problem solving. *Journal of Creative Behavior, 38,* 75–101.

Iscoe, I., & Pierce-Jones, J. (1964). Divergent thinking, age, and intelligence in white and Negro children. *Child Development, 35,* 785–797.

Ivcevic, Z., & Kaufman, J. C. (2013). The can and cannot do attitude: How self estimates of ability vary across ethnic and socioeconomic groups. *Learning and Individual Differences, 27,* 144–148.

Jaquish, G. A., & Ripple, R. E. (1984). A life-span developmental cross-cultural study of divergent thinking abilities. *International Journal of Aging & Human Development, 20,* 1–11.

Jellen, H. G., & Urban, K. K. (1989). Assessing creative potential world-wide: The first cross-cultural application for the Test of Creative Thinking–Drawing Production. *Gifted Education International, 6,* 78–86.

Jenkins, A. H. (2005). Creativity and resilience in the African American experience. *The Humanistic Psychologist, 33,* 25–33.

Jensen, A. R. (1998). *The g factor: The science of mental ability.* Westport, CT: Praeger.

Jiang, J., Wang, S., & Zhao, S. (2012). Does HRM facilitate employee creativity and organizational innovation? A study of Chinese firms. *International Journal of Human Resource Management, 23,* 4025–4047.

Karwowski, M., & Lebuda, I. (2014). Digit ratio predicts eminence of Polish actors. *Personality and Individual Differences, 64,* 30–34.

Karwowski, M., & Lebuda, I. (in press). Written on the writer's face? Facial width-to-height ratio among nominees and laureates of the Nobel Prize in Literature. *Creativity Research Journal.*

Kaufman, A. S. (1999). Genetics of childhood disorders: Genetics and intelligence II. *Journal of the American Academy of Child and Adolescent Psychiatry, 38,* 626–628.

Kaufman, A. S. (2004, July). *Profile analysis, process deficits, and other provocative puzzles.* Invited Division 16 address presented at the meeting of the American Psychological Association, Honolulu, HI.

Kaufman, A. S., & Lichtenberger, E. O. (2006). *Assessing adult and adolescent intelligence* (3rd ed.). New York, NY: John Wiley.

Kaufman, J. C. (2006). Self-reported differences in creativity by gender and ethnicity. *Journal of Applied Cognitive Psychology, 20,* 1065–1082.

Kaufman, J. C. (2010). Using creativity to reduce ethnic bias in college admissions. *Review of General Psychology, 14,* 189–203.

Kaufman, J. C., & Agars, M. D. (2009). Being creative with the predictors *and* criteria for success. *American Psychologist, 64,* 280–281.

Kaufman, J. C., Baer, J., Agars, M. D., & Loomis, D. (2010). Creativity stereotypes and the Consensual Assessment Technique. *Creativity Research Journal, 22,* 200–205.

Kaufman, J. C., Baer, J., & Gentile, C. A. (2004). Differences in gender and ethnicity as measured by ratings of three writing tasks. *Journal of Creative Behavior, 38,* 56–69.

Kaufman, J. C., Niu, W., Sexton, J. D., & Cole, J. C. (2010). In the eye of the beholder: Differences across ethnicity and gender in evaluating creative work. *Journal of Applied Social Psychology, 40,* 496–511.

Kaufman, J. C., Plucker, J. A., & Baer, J. (2008). *Essentials of creativity assessment.* New York, NY: Wiley.

Kaufman, S. B. (2007). Sex differences in mental rotation and spatial visualization ability: Can they be accounted for by differences in working memory capacity? *Intelligence, 35,* 211–223.

Kaufman, S. B. (2013). *Ungifted: Intelligence redefined.* New York, NY: Basic Books.

Keith-Spiegel, P., Tabachnick, B. G., & Spiegel, G. B. (1994). When demand exceeds supply: Second-order criteria used by graduate school selection committees. *Teaching of Psychology, 21,* 79–81.

Keller, C. J., Lavish, L. A., & Brown, C. (2007). Creative styles and gender roles in undergraduate students. *Creativity Research Journal, 19,* 273–280.

Kharkurin, A. V. (2012). *Multilingualism and creativity.* Bristol, England: Multilingual Matters.

King, E. B., Madera, J. M., Hebl, M., Knight, J. L., & Mendoza, S. (2006). What's in a name? A multiracial investigation of the role of occupational stereotypes in selection decisions. *Journal of Applied Social Psychology, 36,* 1145–1159.

Kling, K., Noftle, E. E., & Robins, R. W. (2013). Why do standardized tests underpredict women's academic performance? The role of conscientiousness. *Social Psychological and Personality Science, 4,* 600–606.

Kuncel, N. R., & Hezlett, S. A. (2007). Standardized tests predict graduate students' success. *Science, 315,* 1080–1081.

Kuncel, N. R., Hezlett, S. A., & Ones, D. S. (2001). A comprehensive meta-analysis of the predictive validity of the Graduate Record Examinations. *Psychological Bulletin, 127,* 162–181.

Kuzmits, F., & Adams, A. (2008). The NFL Combine: Does it predict performance in the National Football League. *Journal of Strength and Conditioning Research, 22,* 1721–1727.

Kyllonen, P. C. (2008). *The research behind the ETS personal potential index (PPI).* Princeton, NJ: Educational Testing Service.

Kyllonen, P. C., Walters, A. M., & Kaufman, J. C. (2014). Noncognitive constructs in graduate education. In C. Wendler & B. Bridgeman (Eds.), *The research foundation for the GRE revised general test: A compendium of studies* (pp. 5.8.1–5.8.6). Princeton, NJ: Educational Testing Service.

Landrum, R. E., Jeglum, E. B., & Cashin, J. R. (1994). The decision-making processes of graduate admissions committees in psychology. *Journal of Social Behavior & Personality, 9,* 239–248.

Lebuda, I., & Karwowski, M. (2013). Tell me your name and I'll tell you how creative your work is: Author's name and gender as factors influencing assessment of product originality in four different domains. *Creativity Research Journal, 25,* 137–142.

Lee, H., & Kim, K. H. (2011). Can speaking more languages enhance your creativity? Relationship between bilingualism and creative potential among Korean American students with multicultural link. *Personality and Individual Differences, 50,* 1186–1190.

Leikin, M., & Tovli, E. (2014). Bilingualism and creativity in early childhood. *Creativity Research Journal, 26,* 411–417.

Lyons, B. D., Hoffman, B. J., & Michel, J. W. (2009). Not much more than g? An examination of the impact of intelligence on NFL performance. *Human Performance, 22,* 225–245.

Mackintosh, N. J. (2011). *IQ and human intelligence* (2nd ed.). New York, NY: Oxford University Press.

Manly, J. J., Miller, S. W., Heaton, R. K., Byrd, D., Reilly, J., Velasquez, R. J., . . . HIV Neurobehavioral Research Center (HNRC) Group. (1998). The effect of Black acculturation on neuropsychological test performance in normal and HIV positive individuals. *Journal of the International Neuropsychological Society, 4,* 291–302.

Marland, S. (1972). *Education of the gifted and talented. Report to the Congress of the United States by the U.S. Commissioner of Education.* Washington, DC: Department of Health, Education and Welfare.

Masten, W. G., Plata, M., Wenglar, K., & Thedford, J. (1999). Acculturation and teacher ratings of Hispanic and Anglo-American students. *Roeper Review, 22,* 64–65.

Mattern, K. D., Patterson, B. F., Shaw, E. J., Kobrin, J. L., & Barbuti, S. M. (2008). *Differential validity and prediction of the SAT®* (College Board Research Report No. 2008-4). New York, NY: The College Board.

Matud, M. P., Rodríguez, C., & Grande, J. (2007). Gender differences in creative thinking. *Personality and Individual Differences, 43,* 1137–1147.

McClain, M. C., & Pfeiffer, S. (2012). Identification of gifted students in the United States today: A look at state definitions, policies, and practices. *Journal of Applied School Psychology, 28,* 59–88.

McCrae, R. R., & Costa, P. T., Jr. (1997). Personality trait structure as a human universal. *American Psychologist, 52,* 509–516.

Montag, T., Maertz, C. P., & Baer, M. (2012). A critical analysis of the workplace creativity criterion space. *Journal of Management, 38,* 1362–1386.

Mount, M. K., & Barrick, M. R. (1995). The Big Five personality dimensions: Implications for research and practice in human resources management. *Research in Personnel and Human Resources Management, 13,* 153–200.

Moy, J. W., & Lam, K. F. (2004). Selection criteria and the impact of personality on getting hired. *Personnel Review, 33,* 521–535.

Muller, D. (2013). Reforming premedical education—out with the old, in with the new. *New England Journal of Medicine, 368,* 1567–1569.

Murphy, K. R., Cronin, B. E., & Tam, A. P. (2003). Controversy and consensus regarding the use of cognitive ability testing in organizations. *Journal of Applied Psychology, 88,* 660–671.

Murray, C. (2003). *Human accomplishment: The pursuit of excellence in the arts and sciences, 800 B.C. to 1950.* New York, NY: HarperCollins.

Niu, W., & Sternberg, R. J. (2001). Cultural influence of artistic creativity and its evaluation. *International Journal of Psychology, 36,* 225–241.

Niu, W., & Sternberg, R. J. (2003). Societal and school influences on student creativity: The case of China. *Psychology in the Schools, 40,* 103–114.

Noftle, E. E., & Robins, R. W. (2007). Personality predictors of academic outcomes: Big Five correlates of GPA and SAT scores. *Journal of Personality and Social Psychology, 93,* 116–130.

Norlander, T., Erixon, A., & Archer, T. (2000). Psychological androgyny and creativity: Dynamics of gender-role and personality trait. *Social Behavior and Personality, 28,* 423–435.

Oswald, F. L., Schmitt, N., Kim, B. H., Ramsay, L. J., & Gillespie, M. A. (2004). Developing a biodata measure and situational judgment inventory as predictors of college student performance. *Journal of Applied Psychology, 89,* 187–207.

Paletz, S. B. F., & Peng, K. (2009). Problem finding and contradiction: Examining the relationship between naive dialectical thinking, ethnicity, and creativity. *Creativity Research Journal, 21,* 139–151.

Paunonen, S. V., Rothstein, M. G., & Jackson, D. N. (1999). Narrow reasoning about the use of broad personality measures for personnel selection. *Journal of Organizational Behavior, 20,* 389–405.

Pfeiffer, S. I. (2008). *Handbook of giftedness in children.* New York, NY: Springer Science.

Pfeiffer, S. I. (2015). *Essentials of gifted assessment.* Hoboken, NJ: Wiley.

Pfeiffer, S. I., & Jarosewich, T. (2003). *Gifted rating scales.* San Antonio, TX: The Psychological Corporation.

Pfeiffer, S. I., & Jarosewich, T. (2007). The gifted rating scales-school form: An analysis of the standardization sample based on age, gender, race, and diagnostic efficiency. *Gifted Child Quarterly, 51,* 39–50.

Piirto, J. (1991). Why are there so few? (Creative women: Visual artists, mathematicians, musicians). *Roeper Review, 13,* 142–147.

Pretz, J. E., & Kaufman, J. C. (2015). Do traditional admissions criteria reflect applicant creativity? *Journal of Creative Behavior.* Advance online publication. doi:10.1002/jocb.120

Price-Williams, D. R., & Ramirez III, M. (1977). Divergent thinking, cultural differences, and bilingualism. *Journal of Social Psychology, 103,* 3–11.

Proudfoot, D., Kay, A. C., & Koval, C. Z. (2015). A gender bias in the attribution of creativity: Archival and experimental evidence for the perceived association between masculinity and creative thinking. *Psychological Science, 26,* 1751–1761.

Puccio, G. J., & Cabra, J. F. (2010). Organizational creativity. In J. C. Kaufman & R. J. Sternberg (Eds.), *The Cambridge handbook of creativity* (pp. 145–173). New York, NY: Cambridge University Press.

Ramist, L., Lewis, C., & McCamley-Jenkins, L. (1994). *Student group differences in predicting college grades: Sex, language, and ethnic groups* (College Board Research Report No. 93-1). New York, NY: The College Board.

Reis, S. M., & Renzulli, J. S. (2003). Research related to the schoolwide enrichment triad model. *Gifted Education International, 18*, 15–39.

Renzulli, J. S. (1977). *The Enrichment Triad Model: A guide for developing defensible programs for the gifted and talented.* Mansfield Center, CT: Creative Learning Press.

Renzulli, J. S. (1978). What makes giftedness? Reexamining a definition. *Phi Delta Kappan, 60*, 180–184, 261.

Renzulli, J. S. (1994). Teachers as talent scouts. *Educational Leadership, 52*, 75–81.

Renzulli, J. S. (2012). Reexamining the role of gifted education and talent development for the 21st century: A four-part theoretical approach. *Gifted Child Quarterly, 56*, 150–159.

Renzulli, J. S., Gentry, M., & Reis, S. M. (2014). *Enrichment clusters: A practical plan for real-world, student-driven learning* (2nd ed.). Waco, TX: Prufrock Press.

Renzulli, J. S., Smith, L. H., White, A. J., Callahan, C. M., Hartman, R. K., Westberg, K. L., et al. (2004). *Scales for rating the behavioral characteristics of superior students.* Mansfield Center, CT: Creative Learning Press.

Reynolds, C. R. (2000). Methods for detecting and evaluating cultural bias in neuropsychological tests. In F. Strickland & C. R. Reynolds (Eds.), *Handbook of cross-cultural neuropsychology* (pp. 249–285). New York, NY: Plenum.

Rose, R. J., Uchida, I. A., & Christian, J. C. (1981). Placentation effects on cognitive resemblance of adult monozygotes. *Progress in Clinical and Biological Research, 69*, 35–41.

Rostan, S. M., Pariser, D., & Gruber, H. E. (2002). A cross-cultural study of the development of artistic talent, creativity and giftedness. *High Ability Studies, 13*, 123–155.

Sackett, P. R., Borneman, M. J., & Connelly, B. S. (2008). High stakes testing in higher education and employment: Appraising the evidence for validity and fairness. *American Psychologist, 63*, 215–227.

Salgado, J. F., Moscoso, S., & Berges, A. (2013). Conscientiousness, its facets, and the prediction of job performance ratings: Evidence against the narrow measures. *International Journal of Selection and Assessment, 21*, 74–84.

Saucier, G., & Goldberg, L. R. (2001). Lexical studies of indigenous personality: Premises, products, and prospects. *Journal of Personality, 69*, 847–879.

Schmader, T., & Johns, M. (2003). Converging evidence that stereotype threat reduces working memory capacity. *Journal of Personality and Social Psychology, 85*, 440–452.

Schmidt, F. L., & Hunter, J. E. (1998). The validity and utility of selection methods in personnel psychology: Practical and theoretical implications of 85 years of research findings. *Psychological Bulletin, 124*, 262–274.

Schmitt, D. P., Allik, J., McCrae, R. R., & Benet-Martínez, V. (2007). The geographic distribution of Big Five personality traits: Patterns and profiles of human self-description across 56 nations. *Journal of Cross-Cultural Psychology, 38,* 173–212.

Schmitt, N. (2012). Development of rationale and measures of noncognitive college student potential. *Educational Psychologist, 47,* 18–29.

Shade, B. J. (1986). Is there an Afro-American cognitive style? An exploratory study. *Journal of Black Psychology, 13,* 13–16.

Silverman, L. K. (2009). *Giftedness 101.* New York, NY: Springer Publishing Company.

Simonton, D. K. (1994). *Greatness: Who makes history and why.* New York, NY: Guilford Press.

Sinha, R., Oswald, F., Imus, A., & Schmitt, N. (2011). Criterion-focused approach to reducing adverse impact in college admissions. *Applied Measurement in Education, 24,* 137–161.

Sloane, P. (1992). *Lateral thinking puzzles.* New York, NY: Sterling Publishing.

Smith, T. (2007). Quirky essays a window to future success? *National Public Radio.* Retrieved from http://www.npr.org/templates/story/story.php?storyId7384490

Soares, J. A. (2012). The future of college admissions: Discussion. *Educational Psychologist, 47,* 66–70.

Solomon, G. S., Haase, R. F., & Kuhn, A. (2013). The relationship among neurocognitive performances and biopsychosocial characteristics of elite National Football League draft picks: An exploratory investigation. *Archives of Clinical Neuropsychology, 28,* 9–20.

Steele, C. M. (1997). A threat in the air: How stereotypes shape intellectual identity and performance. *American Psychologist, 52,* 613–629.

Steele, C. M., & Aronson, J. (1995). Contending with a stereotype: African-American intellectual test performance and stereotype threat. *Journal of Personality and Social Psychology, 69,* 797–811.

Stemler, S. E., Grigorenko, E. L., Jarvin, L., & Sternberg, R. J. (2006). Using the theory of successful intelligence as a basis for augmenting AP exams in psychology and statistics. *Contemporary Educational Psychology, 31,* 344–376.

Stemler, S. E., Sternberg, R. J., Grigorenko, E. L., Jarvin, L., & Sharpes, K.(2009). Using the theory of successful intelligence as a framework for developing assessments in AP Physics. *Contemporary Educational Psychology, 34,* 195–209.

Sternberg, R. J. (1996). *Successful intelligence.* New York, NY: Simon & Schuster.

Sternberg, R. J. (2006). Creating a vision of creativity: The first 25 years. *Psychology of Aesthetics, Creativity, and the Arts, S,* 2–12.

Sternberg, R. J. (2008). Applying psychological theories to educational practice. *American Educational Research Journal, 45*, 150–165.

Sternberg, R. J. (2010). *College admissions for the 21st century*. Cambridge, MA: Harvard University Press.

Sternberg, R. J., Bonney, C. R., Gabora, L., & Merrifield, M. (2012). WICS: A model for college and university admissions. *Educational Psychologist, 47*, 30–41.

Sternberg, R. J., & Coffin, L. A. (2010). Admitting and developing "new leaders for a changing world." *New England Journal of Higher Education, 24*, 12–13.

Sternberg, R. J., Kaufman, J. C., & Grigorenko, E. L. (2008). *Applied intelligence*. New York, NY: Cambridge University Press.

Sternberg, R. J., & Lubart, T. I. (1995). *Defying the crowd*. New York, NY: Free Press.

Sternberg, R. J., & the Rainbow Project Collaborators (2006). The Rainbow Project: Enhancing the SAT through assessments of analytical, practical and creative skills. *Intelligence, 34*, 321–350.

Sternberg, R. J., & Williams, W. M. (1997). Does the Graduate Record Examination predict meaningful success in the graduate monitoring of psychologists? A case study. *American Psychologist, 52*, 630–641.

Stewart, N. (1953). *Creativity: A literature survey* (ETS Research Report Series: RM 53–08). Princeton, NJ: Educational Testing Service.

Stoltzfus, G., Nibbelink, B. L., Vredenburg, D., & Hyrum, E. (2011). Gender, gender role, and creativity. *Social Behavior and Personality, 39*, 425–432.

Tendayi Viki, G., & Williams, M. L. J. (2014). The role of identity integration in enhancing creativity among mixed-race individuals. *Journal of Creative Behavior, 48*, 198–208.

Torrance, E. P. (1971). Are the Torrance Tests of Creative Thinking biased against or in favour of disadvantaged groups? *Gifted Child Quarterly, 15*, 75–80.

Torrance, E. P. (1973). Non-test indicators of creative talent among disadvantaged children. *Gifted Child Quarterly, 17*, 3–9.

Van Iddekinge, C. H., Roth, P. L., Raymark, P. H., & Odle-Dusseau, H. N. (2012). The criterion-related validity of integrity tests: An updated meta-analysis. *Journal of Applied Psychology, 97*, 499–530.

Wallace, C. E., & Russ, S. W. (2015). Pretend play, divergent thinking, and math achievement in girls: A longitudinal study. *Psychology of Aesthetics, Creativity, and the Arts, 9*, 296–305.

Walpole, M. B., Burton, N. W., Kanyi, K., & Jackenthal, A. (2001). *Selecting successful graduate students: In-depth interviews with GRE users* (GRE Board RR No. 99–11R, ETS RR No. 02–8). Princeton, NJ: Educational Testing Service.

Walters, A. M., Plante, J. A., Kyllonen, P. C., Kaufman, J. C., & Gallagher, A. M. (2004). *System and method for evaluating applicants*. U.S. Patent No. US2004/0053203.

Wanek, J. E., Sackett, P. R., & Ones, D. S. (2003). Towards an understanding of integrity test similarities and differences: An item-level analysis of seven tests. *Personnel Psychology, 56,* 873–894.

Weiss, L. G., Chen, H., Harris, J. G., Holdnack, J. A., & Saklofske, D. H. (2010). WAIS-IV use in societal context. In L. G. Weiss, D. H. Saklofske, D. L. Coalson, & S. E. Raiford (Eds.), *WAIS-IV clinical use and interpretation: Scientist-practitioner perspectives* (pp. 97–140), San Diego, CA: Elsevier.

Wertheimer, L. K. (2008). College applicants get creative to a fault. *The Boston Globe.* Retrieved from http://www.boston.com/news/education/higher/articles /2008/01/15/college_hopefuls_get_ creative_to_a_fault

Yoon, S. N. (2005). *Comparing the intelligence and creativity scores of Asian American gifted students with Caucasian gifted students.* Unpublished doctoral dissertation, Purdue University, West Lafayette, IN.

Zha, P., Walczyk, J. J., Griffith-Ross, D. A., Tobacyk, J. J., & Walczyk, D. F. (2006). The impact of culture and Individualism-Collectivism on the creative potential and achievement of American and Chinese adults. *Creativity Research Journal, 18,* 355–366.

Zwick, R. (2013). *Disentangling the role of high school grades, SAT® Scores, and SES in predicting college achievement* (ETS RR No. 13-09). Princeton, NJ: Educational Testing Service.

Creative Environments: Life, Classrooms, Workplaces, and the World

n many ways, this chapter is the one I was dreading. Most layperson books on creativity are focused on Making! You! More! Creative! and perhaps as a result, I have found this topic a little less interesting. Any time a study comes out that suggests that simple, easy things can be done to make you more creative (Eat more cheese! Listen to jazz! Stare at a picture of Morgan Freeman!), the media jumps on it and the little factoids make the lists of "10 easy ways you can be more creative," as if creativity is a simple algebraic secret.

That said, there's legitimate research (and a lot of it) on the creative press (environment). Speaking broadly, the environment can mean many things—from your home life to your immediate surroundings to the classroom to the workplace to your culture/home country. This topic is a growing one within psychology (Davies et al., 2013; Glăveanu, 2010a, 2010b; Sawyer, 2012).

HOME ENVIRONMENTS

In the field of intelligence, the "nature–nurture" controversy is still a hot topic. Are people born with a certain amount of intelligence? Can we improve our intelligence? If we think that we're dumb, should we blame our parents for passing along "dumb" genes, or should we blame our parents for creating an environment where we were not properly encouraged? Note, incidentally, that *not* blaming parents is not an option.

Within intelligence, this is a heated topic with fierce opinions. Indeed, some of the first work on intelligence was conducted by Francis Galton because he wanted to show that genius was hereditary; I'm sure the fact that his cousin was Charles Darwin had nothing to do with it. Galton was mostly wrong about his approach, but I will leave the details to companion volumes in the series, such as *Intelligence 101* (Plucker & Esping, 2013), *Genius 101* (Simonton, 2009), and *IQ Testing 101* (A. S. Kaufman, 2009). Indeed, if you get a full set of all of the 101 books and read the seventh word on page 114 in each one, you will be able to scramble out a very special message.

This topic within creativity has produced less research and fewer fistfights. Several studies have looked at the genetics of creativity using a twin-study approach, in which identical twins are compared to fraternal twins to see how alike they are in creative ability (Grigorenko, LaBuda, & Carter, 1992; Reznikoff, Domino, Bridges, & Honeyman, 1973). These studies are inconsistent but have found low to moderate heritability of creativity, lower than what is typically found in intelligence studies (Barbot, Tan, & Grigorenko, 2013; A. B. Kaufman, Kornilov, Bristol, Tan, & Grigorenko, 2010). That said, these types of studies are more likely to use self-report or survey methodology, as opposed to creative performance, so there are a lot of unknowns. Indeed, genetic effects may vary based on the specific creativity task analyzed (Velázquez, Segal, & Horwitz, 2015). There have also been studies on specific genes associated with creativity (Kéri, 2009; Volf, Kulikov, Bortsov, & Popova, 2009); I will not go into detail about this work for fear of revealing my ignorance, but I would refer the interested reader to Barbot et al. (2013).

Genetics and questions of heredity aside, it is reasonable to argue that some environments are more conducive to creativity than others. One chunk of work has focused on birth order. Some studies show firstborns as being more likely to be accomplished (Roe, 1952; Simonton, 1987), but accomplished isn't necessarily the same as creative (although there is clearly some overlap). Indeed, Sulloway (1996) found that the firstborn child was more likely to achieve power and privilege, but later-born children were more likely to be open to experience and revolutionary. A firstborn child might end up running the family business, whereas a later-born child might strike out in a new field and buck tradition. This trend extends across many domains—if you examine how prominent scientists reacted when Darwin proposed his classic (and controversial) theory of natural selection, 83% of the people who supported the theory were later-born children, and only 17% were firstborn (Sulloway, 1996).

Another nuance is to look at sibling constellation—so not just birth order or number of siblings, but also how far apart in age the siblings are, as well as their gender. M. Baer, Oldham, Hollingshead, and Costa Jacobsohn (2005) found that any birth-order effects were greatly impacted by sibling constellation. Firstborns were most affected; with more age differences in their siblings, their creativity went down—which makes sense; it likely means there were more enforced child-care responsibilities. Having different-gender siblings, however, helped increase firstborn creativity. Szobiová (2008) found a gender effect; women who had siblings of both genders were the most creative.

Although being a firstborn or later-born child isn't totally about genetics, it's also not something that you have a whole lot of control over. Neither are familial loss and other personal tragedies. Simonton (1994, 2009) reviews many studies that show that losing a parent before age 10 is much more common in eminent people than in average Joes. Other disasters that are more likely to befall the well known include bouts of poverty, physical illness, and (depending on your take-away from Chapter 8), mental illness. Remember, though, that Big-C and little-c (or mini-c) can be quite different constructs. Dai et al. (2012), for example, found evidence of a "creativity gap," comparable to the achievement gap, among eighth-grade students, with students of higher socioeconomic status (SES) showing more creativity than lower-SES students.

CLASSROOM ENVIRONMENTS

I have published extensively about this topic (Beghetto, Kaufman, & Baer, 2014; Beghetto & Kaufman, in press), so if you are particularly interested in more than a quick run-through, I would refer interested readers to those books.

Much of the core work on classroom environments has grown out of Amabile and Hennessey's work on intrinsic motivation (Amabile, 1996; Hennessey, Amabile, & Martinage, 1989; Hennessey, 2010, 2015b). Based on what they found on intrinsic motivation and creativity (covered in Chapter 6), we can identify some potential creativity killers in the classroom. Things that trigger extrinsic motivation in a negative way can theoretically decrease student creativity. Time limits, social comparison and competition, obvious rewards tied to routine behaviors, public evaluations, even praise—all can potentially harm student creativity (Hennessey, 2010).

What we can look for are the potential for micromoments— those times when something unscripted and surprising happens in the classroom, and the teacher and student are both willing to take the plunge to see what happens next (Beghetto, 2013). What is more likely to happen, according to Beghetto, is that teachers may "kill ideas softly" through dismissal—even if that is not the intention. Teachers and students are used to games of intellectual hide-and-seek (Beghetto, 2010), in which the teacher knows the correct answer and the students guess what it is. Imagine I'm teaching a lesson on the Declaration of Independence and I ask, "Who were the five members of the committee tasked to write the declaration?" There are five correct answers (John Adams, Benjamin Franklin, Thomas Jefferson, Roger Sherman, and Robert Livingston). There are no opportunities for real discussion and no chance for creativity. At best, students can get a correct answer.

Even worse is the possibility of creative mortification (Beghetto, 2014), in which a teacher or mentor gives an overly sharp, negative evaluation of creative work that is holding the student to an unrealistic standard (i.e., Pro-c or Big-C). When a student feels this type of shame, it may well kill the creative spirit and desire to be creative (Beghetto, 2013). Beghetto and Kaufman (2007) thus propose the Goldilocks Principle of Feedback—ideally, feedback should be neither too hard nor too soft. Hard feedback is the harsh tones that can lead to creative mortification, and it is obviously damaging.

It is important to also realize that soft feedback, filled with undeserved praise and general compliments that ignore genuine flaws, can be equally negative. A student who develops overconfidence is not well served; these are the people we see on *American Idol* and comparable shows, convinced they are supremely talented because they have been told so for their entire lives. At some point, reality will hit and it will feel like the emperor's new clothes; they will wonder why no one was ever honest with them. Or, conversely, they may end up wondering why the world never appreciates their talents. Narcissists consider themselves to be more creative than other people, but no one agrees (Furnham, Hughes, & Marshall, 2013; Goncalo, Flynn, & Kim, 2010). The ultimate goal in feedback is to find the elusive balance that combines criticisms with praise in a constructive way.

Beghetto (2005) offers several specific recommendations. Teachers should set challenging goals for students. They should encourage them to find aspects of an assignment that hold personal relevance. They should minimize to whatever extent they can the external forces of assessment. Teachers should encourage students to learn from mistakes, not to avoid them. And they should try to nudge students to be performance focused and not task focused. Offering too many criticisms, even if well-intentioned, can lead to students offering fewer problem solutions (Gibson & Mumford, 2013).

Davies et al. (2013) reviewed studies on creative learning environments and identified several factors that could help support creativity. Some have already been discussed, but others include the chance for collaboration with peers, working outside of school, a game-based approach to learning, and partnering with local groups. Karwowski (2015) further found that students who have peers with higher creative self-concepts are more likely to have higher creative self-concepts themselves.

What are the side effects of schools that do not value creativity? Students can often show slumps in their creative development. Torrance (1968) found evidence for a fourth-grade slump; more recently, Yi, Hu, Plucker, and McWilliams (2013) noted a fourth-grade slump in Chinese students (as well the importance of the school's climate). Others have pointed to a different age for the slump, such as Lau and Cheung's (2010) study that found a slump in sixth grade.

WORK ENVIRONMENTS

Amabile and Gryskiewicz (1989) identify eight aspects of the work environment that stimulate creativity: adequate freedom, challenging work, appropriate resources, a supportive supervisor, diverse and communicative coworkers, recognition, a sense of cooperation, and an organization that supports creativity. Leader support is especially important to creativity among subordinates in the workplace (Amabile, Schatzel, Moneta, & Kramer, 2004). A good supervisor can inspire creativity through consulting with her workers, recognizing positive performance, and showing social and emotional support.

Amabile and Gryskiewicz (1989) also discuss four aspects that restrain creativity: time pressure, too much evaluation, an emphasis on keeping the status quo, and too much organizational politics. External events, such as downsizing, also can negatively impact creativity in the workplace (Amabile & Conti, 1999). During larger times of economic depression, industries that require innovation (such as those in technology) may suffer more globally (Amabile & Conti, 1997).

Basic affordances play an important role as well. A key factor in employee creativity (in addition to motivation and organizational encouragement) is being given enough time to complete a task (Unsworth & Clegg, 2010). Similarly, having enough workplace resources (such as funds, materials, and facilities) is strongly related to creativity (Amabile, Conti, Coon, Lazenby, & Herron, 1996).

One specific example of a work-related influence on creativity is how much conflict occurs with group performance. It is easy to confuse task and interpersonal cohesiveness—members of a group with high interpersonal but low task cohesiveness might love one another but not work particularly well together. Craig and Kelly (1999) found that an interaction between high levels of both task and interpersonal cohesiveness produced the most creative group work. Karwowski (2011; Karwowski & Lebuda, 2013) argues that there are three primary factors underlying the ideal creative climate; in addition to task and interpersonal cohesiveness, there is also a dynamic-energetic component. This third element represents the stability of the overall system—is there enough flexibility to allow for risk taking in the first place? If you speak Polish, I recommend Karwowski's (2009) book on this topic (if you don't, it will be a harder read).

Kurtzberg and Amabile (2000) propose that a moderate amount of conflict about the task itself will lead to more creative outcomes. However, other types of conflict, such as those that relate to personal relationships or to the actual process of working together, will lower creative performance (and, generally, not be a lot of fun). Consistently, De Dreu (2006) found evidence for a curvilinear relationship between task conflict and team innovation. Collaborative problem solving helped mediate the negative impact of the conflict. Harvey (2013) found that extremely diverse groups generated a larger number of ideas than less diverse groups, but when a final idea was selected, there were no differences.

Similarly, the idea of "psychological safety" has been proposed as a mutual feeling in a group that risk taking is okay (Edmondson, 1999). One way that psychological safety can be increased is by a leader meeting with team members and talking honestly and openly with them (Roussin, 2008); another is to enable employees to speak up and voice dissatisfaction (Detert & Burris, 2007). Ford and Sullivan (2004) argue that experiencing psychological safety can aid both innovative contributions and personal satisfaction.

This connection between psychological safety and creativity may explain why political correctness can help creativity, even if it may seem counterintuitive to some. One study looked at the impact of establishing a political correctness (PC) norm before having groups generate ideas. If the groups were of the same gender (whether all male or all female), then the PC instructions lowered creativity. But if the groups were mixed gender, those in the PC condition were more creative (Goncalo, Chatman, Duguid, & Kennedy, 2015). The authors suggest that PC norms can reduce uncertainty for both males and females, thereby allowing them to risk being creative.

Another line of research is to look at ethnic differences within the group composition. McLeod, Lobel, and Cox (1996) compared homogenous groups (all Caucasian) to ethnically diverse groups (including African Americans, Hispanic Americans, and Asian Americans) on a brainstorming task. The heterogeneous groups produced ideas rated as more effective and feasible. Milliken and Martins (1996) also found that ethnic diversity was linked with higher idea quality in group tasks. Cady and Valentine (1999) looked at both ethnic and gender diversity and how they related to quality of ideas generated during a brainstorming task. They found that increased ethnic diversity was associated with a higher quality of ideas, yet increased gender diversity was associated with a lower quality of ideas.

Paletz, Peng, Erez, and Maslach (2004) studied three-person heterogeneous teams that were either primarily Caucasian or primarily minority (most minority participants were Asian American). They asked the teams to create an ending to an ambiguous story; the endings were then rated by appropriate experts. The rated creativity did not significantly differ based on the dominant membership of the group (Caucasian, Asian American, or other ethnicity). Interestingly, groups predominantly comprised of minorities reported enjoying the task more. Chatman, Polzer, Barsade, and Neale (1998) found that demographic diversity in creative group work helped the most when organizational culture was more collectivistic than individualistic (which is consistent with the boost that balanced and acculturated bilinguals get in creativity). Other studies have also found that teams that have members from diverse backgrounds are more innovative (Choi, 2007; Yap, Chai, & Lemaire, 2005) and that groups consisting of members with more multicultural experience are more creative (Tadmor, Satterstrom, Jang, & Polzer, 2012).

Leaders also play an essential role in establishing the work environment (Mumford, Scott, Gaddis, & Strange, 2002). One way is that good leaders will model creative behavior, thereby reinforcing the idea that it's okay to be creative (Jaussi & Dionne, 2003). Indeed, supervisors with higher creative self-efficacy were more likely to encourage their employees to be creative, resulting in workers who were more engaged in being creative (Huang, Krasikova, & Liu, 2016). Leaders can also recognize creativity in others, much as an expert should be able to (West et al., 2003). They can help shape the climate so it is closer to the kind Amabile and Gryskiewicz (1989) describe (Amabile et al., 2004; Mumford & Hunter, 2005). Further, leaders can also make sure that their workers have access to enough resources to be creative, such as time and information about relevant projects (Reiter-Palmon & Illies, 2004) and access to resources (Mumford, Hunter, Eubanks, Bedell, & Murphy, 2007).

A particular type of leadership that is strongly associated with higher employee creativity is transformational leadership (Shin & Zhou, 2007). Transformational leaders motivate their employees to be creative and offer support for their creativity (Gong, Huang, & Farh, 2009). A transformational leader will ensure that the workplace offers psychological safety (Carmeli, Reiter-Palmon, & Ziv, 2010; Carmeli, Sheaffer, Binyamin, Reiter-Palmon, & Shimoni, 2014). In contrast, a poor leader can sap the meaning out of work, thereby stifling organizational creativity (Amabile & Kramer, 2012).

IMMEDIATE PHYSICAL ENVIRONMENT

The creative environment is often considered metaphorically—your work environment is a fancy way of including your boss, coworkers, and general office climate in a single expression. But the creative environment can also be quite literally your immediate physical surroundings (Dul, Ceylan, & Jaspers, 2011). Steidle and Werth (2013) examined how light versus dark can make people more or less creative. They conducted a series of studies in which people were first primed for the concepts of light and dark by describing a time when they were in a bright or dark situation. People who were mentally primed for darkness showed a preference for speed over accuracy (in other words, were more likely to take risks) and generated more creative ideas. Next, the authors did a series of studies where they physically manipulated the amount of light in the room. People in dim lighting did better on creativity tasks and poorer on analytic thinking tasks. Steidle and Werth (2013) argue that the visual message conveyed by a room changes when it is darker and people feel free from constraints.

A different set of results emerged when managers were asked to view photographs of offices that varied on many physical dimensions and then rate them on their creative potential. Their choices reflected a belief that offices that would inspire creativity would be brightly lit, with cool colors (blue, green, or violet) and low complexity. The presence of plants, a window, and a computer were also associated with higher creative potential (Ceylan, Dul, & Aytac, 2008). Stone and Irvine (1994) also found a mild positive effect for the presence of a window on creative performance. However, a study of college students found that cool colors were negatively associated with creativity (McCoy & Evans, 2002).

Ijzerman, Leung, and Ong (2014) explored the interaction between temperature and type of task. They rooted their work in a situated model of creative cognition, in which they proposed some creative tasks that emphasize identifying relationships and making connections between concepts (which they call relational creativity) and other tasks that require being flexible across categories and breaking away from what is currently known (which they call referential creativity). They argued that your physical surroundings, such as temperature, could help or hurt your performance, with their hypothesis that physical heat would help relational creativity and cold would help referential creativity. They conducted four experiments in which they manipulated the temperature to be either warm or cold (sometimes by actually changing the temperature and sometimes by having the participant hold something that was either warm or cold) and varied the creativity tests to be either relational (such as making drawings, thinking of gift ideas for friends, or categorizing objects) or referential (such as recognizing metaphors or thinking of product names). As theorized, heat led to better performance in relational creativity and cold was associated with higher scores on measures of referential creativity. My colleague Jessica Hoffman points out that a mediating factor in many of these studies may be mood; however, you may think twice before you decide what type of latte to order!

A pair of studies specifically examined plants and word association tasks (related to fluency and remote associations). Men scored notably better with a plant present, with no difference in women (Shibata & Suzuki, 2002), yet a subsequent study found that women performed better with a plant present as compared with a magazine stand or nothing, with no difference in men (Shibata & Suzuki, 2004). I'm not fully sure how to interpret these somewhat contradictory findings beyond remembering (another) quote from one of my favorite movies, *House of Games*: "Some people say one thing . . . some people say something else" (Mamet, 1987). Meanwhile, a different study indicates that people who eat plants may be more creative—or, rather, those who eat their fruits and vegetables report feeling more creative (Conner, Brookie, Richardson, & Polak, 2015).

Complete immersion in plants (and other outdoor accoutrement) may do quite more. Atchley, Strayer, and Atchley (2012) tested members of different Outward Bound groups who spent 4 days in nature, away from technology. They gave the Remote Associates Test (RAT) to half the group before the wilderness excursion and to the other half after the trip. People taking the test after their time in the woods did notably better. The RAT, as you may remember, is quite confounded with intellectual abilities, and the sample size (26 in each group) is small. But it's an interesting study.

Oppezzo and Schwartz (2014) looked at the impact of taking a walk in nature. Across four (small) experiments, they found that taking a walk outside boosted creativity (above and beyond simply being outside or taking an indoor walk). The key may be the walk, and not nature; Colzato, Szapora, Pannekoek, and Hommel (2013) found that acute exercise was associated with a slight increase in divergent thinking in athletes (nonathletes, however, did much worse). A different retrospective study found that organized athletic involvement in childhood (such as little league) was negatively correlated to divergent thinking scores, but unstructured sports (such as playing ball with friends) was positively correlated (Bowers, Green, Hemme, & Chalip, 2014).

A. Leung et al. (2012), playing with the idea of "thinking outside the box" and other metaphors, had participants physically reenact such metaphors in a series of experiments. So in one study they used both hands to represent "on one hand" and "on the other hand," and in others they actually solved problems inside and outside of a box. A. Leung et al. (2012) found that when the participants embodied the creativity phrase, they showed more cognitive flexibility and were more creative.

Meanwhile, Vohs, Redden, and Rahinel (2013) conducted a series of experiments that looked at whether the immediate surrounding environment was orderly or disorderly. Neatness was positively associated with some variables, such as choosing healthier food or being charitable, but people surrounded by mess were more creative. There have been some sharp criticisms of the paper, most notably the issue of many potential confounding differences between the "orderly" and "disorderly" rooms, such as the level of mess and the presence of objects such as a boom box or an oddly placed book (Zwaan, 2013).

Many of these recent studies were quite well publicized in the media, as have been the studies on background color and creativity. R. Mehta and Zhu (2009) found that the color red enhanced detail-oriented tasks, and blue was associated with an increase in creativity. But then Lichtenfeld, Elliot, Maier, and Pekrun (2012) found that green showed evidence of enhancing creativity.

Without disparaging any of the researchers behind these studies, there's a reason why the media jumps on these ones. They make creativity sound easy ("if only I'd taken a walk and then sat at a messy desk with green wallpaper!"), yet effortless creativity is a pipe dream (Cropley, 2006; J. C. Kaufman, 2015). Creativity is hard work. It may sound like I am criticizing all of these studies, and that is not my goal. Many are quite good and important. But I want to see them replicated. How many studies are left in the file drawer? I can imagine someone conducting a series of tests: Does chocolate increase creativity? No. Do strawberries increase creativity? No. Does cinnamon increase creativity? Aha! But, joking aside, when the best of these studies have been consistently reproduced and integrated into theory and applied in practice, they will represent very meaningful work. Until then, I hesitate to label any a cure-all.

Your environment can also extend to auditory as well as visual surroundings. Hillier, Alexander, and Beversdorf (2006) studied the impact of an auditory stressor (a small amount of white noise) on cognitive flexibility. What they found was that basic cognitive functioning (measured with verbal and figural tasks) was not affected— but scores on a remote associations test (which measures creativity to a degree) were affected. A level of white noise that did not impact intellectual performance made people slower and worse at a creativity-related task. R. Mehta, Zhu, and Cheema (2012) examined high, moderate, and low ambient noise. Unsurprisingly, high levels of ambient noise (comparable to loud traffic) reduced creative performance. However, being exposed to moderate levels of noise (akin to hearing a car pass by) was associated with higher creativity as compared with low levels (such as a normal conversation). People were also more likely to show a preference for buying a more creative product with moderate ambient noise. Sometimes the way people handle noise represents an interaction with cognition. One study of undergraduates found that having a wider breadth of attention was correlated with writing more creative poems, yet distracting loud noise disrupted creative performance more in those students with a wide breadth of attention (Kasof, 1997).

Physical environment can further extend to how well your body matches your environment. In a clever study, Abe (2010) made a physical version of the Unusual Uses Test with plastic plates. He used two sizes of plates, and found that when the size of your hands is a better match for the size of the object you are handling, you are more creative. Meanwhile, a pair of studies suggests that resting in a flotation tank (in the dark) may boost creativity (Forgays & Forgays, 1992; Suedfeld, Metcalfe, & Bluck, 1987). Vartanian and Suedfeld (2011) found that students who engaged in a 4-week program of time in a flotation tank showed increased technical ability in jazz performance. Norlander, Bergman, and Archer (1998) found that such flotation tanks increased originality but had a negative effect on creative problem solving.

INSTRUCTIONS AND OTHER WAYS TO PRIME FOR CREATIVITY

Giving instructions to be creative will typically increase performance on divergent thinking or related creativity tasks (Harrington, 1975). Katz and Poag (1979) found that telling college students to be creative led to an increase in fluency scores in males, but not in females. One possible explanation they suggested was that given that the task was verbal, males may have needed the boost more given their typical inclination toward figural and spatial tasks. Another possibility, consistent with the work of J. Baer (1997, 1998), is that female participants were more tuned into the expectation of evaluation implied by those instructions. So the instructions may have increased creativity in both males and females but the expectation of evaluation decreased female creativity, thereby canceling out the benefit.

Subsequent investigations have explored the specifics of how instructions can impact creativity. One study found that instructing people to be creative, practical, or analytical raises performance in these areas (comparable to the Sternberg interventions discussed in Chapter 9). If the instructions matched someone's preferred thinking style, a particular increase was noted. So someone who is told to be creative and who naturally has a creative thinking style will show the largest amount of increased creativity (O'Hara & Sternberg, 2001). The impact of simply telling people to be creative has been found across cultures (America and China) and domains (verbal, artistic, and mathematical; Chen et al., 2005). Runco, Illies, and Reiter-Palmon (2005) found that telling someone to be creative in a specific way (i.e., "think of things that will be thought of by no one else") resulted in higher divergent thinking (DT) scores than simply telling them to be more creative in a general way. Runco, Illies, and Eisenman (2005) found an interaction between the instructions (emphasizing originality, appropriateness, both, or neither) and the type of DT task (realistic or unrealistic). Realistic tasks with appropriateness-focused instructions drew more appropriate ideas, and unrealistic tasks with originality-focused instructions produced more original ideas.

Nusbaum, Silvia, and Beaty (2014) gave two types of instructions: "Be fluent" (come up with many different ideas) and "be creative." People told "be fluent" generated more responses than the "be creative" group, but this latter group came up with responses that were rated as being more creative. They also administered a measure of fluid intelligence; it correlated weakly under the "be fluent" condition but strongly under the "be creative" condition. Nusbaum et al. (2014) argue that this finding relates to the underlying mechanisms of divergent thinking, specifically supporting the idea that we use a top-down approach when we are creative. In other words, we have a certain amount of control over our creativity and how we choose to be creative. We may be better at regulating how we are creative than we might think, an idea I explore further in Chapter 11.

Another way to improve creativity can be to feel nostalgic. People who were primed to feel nostalgic were subsequently more creative than a control group (Ye, Ngan, & Hui, 2013). It is important to note that the state-versus-trait distinction applied here; the key was making someone actively feel nostalgic in the moment. Those who were prone to be nostalgic in general did not have any particular advantage or disadvantage. Why would the state of feeling nostalgic increase creativity? A subsequent study found that one connection was that openness to experience was a moderator (van Tilburg, Sedikides, & Wildschut, 2015). Remember from Chapter 5 that openness is highly related to creativity, and one component of openness is introspection (Connelly, Ones, Davies, & Birkland, 2014).

How else is it possible to change people's creativity? Certainly, some tools may help foster creativity. There has been a spate of recent research on how video games can be used for educational purposes, and creativity can be one of these end results (Fabricatore & López, 2013; Shute, Ventura, & Kim, 2013). If a video game (or any other type of technology, such as a smartphone app) can encourage people to behave in creativity-supportive ways (such as by being open to new experiences or helping monitoring progress), then this line of work could be an exciting development in the creativity world.

A final way that can't be ruled out is the role that some prescription drugs may play in increasing creativity. Some promising work in neuroscience suggests that taking a beta blocker, such as propranolol, facilitates creativity and cognitive flexibility better than other drugs, such as adrenergic and dopamine agonists and a peripheral nervous system beta blocker (nadolol) (Beversdorf, Hughes, Steinburg, Lewis, & Heilman, 1999; Beversdorf, White, Chever, Hughes, & Bornstein, 2002; S. Smyth & Beversdorf, 2007). However, propranolol did not raise performance better than a placebo on standard-level RAT items. Campbell, Tivarus, Hillier, and Beversdorf (2008) found that participants tested after taking propranolol demonstrated higher cognitive flexibility performance on harder items. Oxytocin has also been linked to higher cognitive flexibility and (slightly) higher creative performance (De Dreu, Baas, & Boot, 2015).

269

A recent fascinating study by Polner, Nagy, Takáts, and Kéri (2015) examined patients with Parkinson's disease undergoing dopaminergic drug therapy as treatment. They compared the patients, who were receiving dopamine agonist monotherapy, against controls; both groups were tested before any treatments. The side effects of the drugs included both increased impulsivity and unusual experiences, which could be mild hallucination, perceptual distortions, or superstitious beliefs. After 12 weeks of treatment, the patients showed higher levels of schizotypy than the controls—and higher scores on divergent thinking. This study offers a mechanism to understand many reports of increased artistic and verbal creativity in patients with Parkinson's disease (e.g., Canesi, Rusconi, Isaias, & Pezzoli, 2012).

Some drugs for attention deficit hyperactivity disorder (ADHD), such as Adderall and Ritalin, are often thought to have a positive impact on cognitive abilities (White, Becker-Blease, & Grace-Bishop, 2006). One study looked at young boys with ADHD when they were not taking their medicine (in this case, Ritalin). They were slightly less creative than a control group, but this difference disappeared when they resumed taking Ritalin. Adderall has a curious relationship with creativity (Farah, Haimm, Sankoorikal, & Chatterjee, 2008). People with naturally lower creativity showed stronger ability on the RAT while on the drug, whereas those with naturally higher creativity did poorly. A different drug, modafinil, has been shown to increase cognition; the effects for creativity were in the right direction but did not reach significance (Müller et al., 2013), thereby providing another reason to hate statistics.

We already know that drugs such as caffeine (Childs & de Wit, 2008) and Ritalin (M. Mehta et al., 2000) boost general alertness and cognition, and propranolol itself has been used to help alleviate test anxiety and improve SAT scores (Faigel, 1991). As with many drugs that have legitimate uses, people abuse them to improve performance. Although some of the drugs that improve cognitive ability may have a negative effect on creativity (Mohamed, 2014), there are undoubtedly drugs that will have a positive effect on creativity. Might the same writers who currently rail against steroid abuse in athletes someday take different drugs to boost their own creativity?

Recreational drug and alcohol use is a completely different topic, which I tackle in Chapter 11.

270

CULTURAL ENVIRONMENTS

An environment can be as broad as the culture you live in. There are many ways of comparing countries and cultures; for example, Karwowski and Lebuda (2013) examined how both monetary resources and the climate (literally, meaning an ideal temperature) can predict country-level creative production. Culture can mean many things. Most of the studies I will discuss consider culture as "Big-C" culture— your country's central ideas, foundations, and principles (e.g., Hennessey, 2015a). But culture, as Vlad Glăveanu emphasizes, can also mean the everyday objects and people we interact with all the time. There are many meanings of culture, and although I will focus more on what might be called Big-C culture, it does not mean that they are not all important.

The most studied cultural distinction is likely the split between East and West. The most common approach (although not necessarily the best) is to simply see how Eastern and Western cultures compare on creativity measures, which I discussed in Chapter 9. Most studies show Western cultures outperforming Eastern cultures on divergent thinking measures as well as rated products and self-assessments.

Why does this trend occur? Part of the answer is that the measures used for these comparisons are nearly always also Western. Yet Eastern definitions of creativity can differ. Early views of creativity in China tended to mirror Western views, in part because there is no direct way of translating "creativity" into Chinese (Lan & Kaufman, 2012). As China and other countries developed their own definitions and theories of creativity, the ideas of high moral standards and honors become prevalent (Niu, 2012). The Western need for novelty and individuality is less intense; Eastern cultures may focus more on collaboration within one's environment and adapting to the changing environment (Niu & Kaufman, 2013). Some have argued that Eastern cultures see creativity as a means to an end, with an emphasis on the appropriateness component of creativity (K. Leung & Morris, 2011). Others say that creativity is simply less encouraged in Chinese cultures as opposed to American culture (Niu & Sternberg, 2001).

Li (1997) proposed horizontal and vertical traditions of creativity. Horizontal traditions, which are favored by Western cultures, tend toward changing and modifying preexisting structures—think of an artist like Picasso, constantly challenging the limits of an art form. In vertical traditions, however, the nature of the work is much more constrained and consistent with past work. Therefore, Li (1997) argues, a piece's worth depends more on how well the artist is able to capture his or her subject matter. Similarly, Averill, Chon, and Hahn (2001) propose that both Eastern and Western cultures value the effectiveness of a creative piece, but the West values the novelty of a piece much more than the East. Of much more interest to the East is whether a piece is authentic, representing the creator's personal values and beliefs.

Why does this difference occur between East and West? One answer may lie in the theory of interdependence (collectivistic) versus independence (individualistic). This theory argues that North Americans and Western Europeans see themselves as independent. Their motivations and goals follow accordingly. In contrast, Asian cultures are more interdependent and have a higher sense of group responsibility. These cultures are motivated by different variables, such as group harmony (Markus & Kitayama, 1991). Indeed, Eastern conceptions of creativity often include ethics and morality (Lau, Hui, & Ng, 2004).

Ng (2001; see also Ng & Smith, 2004) has argued that it is this emphasis that is responsible for East–West differences in creativity. People who are focused on group cohesiveness and are "nice" (a term Ng uses without specific positive connotations) are less creative; people who are creative are less "nice." Goncalo and Staw (2006) primed groups to be either individualistic or collectivistic; individualistic groups generated both a higher number of ideas and more creative ideas than collectivistic groups. However, Bechtoldt, Choi, and Nijstad (2012) argued that there are many different ways that individualism–collectivism can manifest itself. You might think of yourself as being more collectivist (I'm like other people!) or individualist (I'm a special snowflake!), which is called self-construal. But your values might be different—you might think that you're like other people but wish you were unique. Bechtoldt et al. separately primed groups of people on both the self-construal and value aspects. They found that groups primed to value collectivism produced more ideas than groups primed to value individualism, but the most original ideas came from the interaction between being primed to

272

value collectivism and yet having an individualist self-construal (i.e., "I am myself, but it is good to work together").

Other studies have examined the question in more naturalistic settings. Walton and Kemmelmeier (2012) examined how an individualistic versus collectivistic organizational orientation would impact creativity using scenarios; they found that both gender and the presence of a perceived threat presented an interaction. With no threat present, men were more creative with an individualist organization and women were more creative with a collectivistic organization. However, when there was a perceived threat, both genders were more creative with the hypothetical collectivistic organization. Other studies have examined people living within individual or collectivistic cultures. Rinne, Steel, and Fairweather (2013) found a connection between nationwide creativity indices and individualism. G. Saad, Cleveland, and Ho (2015) studied people living in individualistic or collectivist cultures. They found that individualistic people generated more ideas, but collectivist responses were of higher quality.

Perhaps counterintuitively, Eastern views of creativity are more concerned with "status" than Western views. The Chinese connect creativity more with influential and important people (Yue, 2004); relatedly, they are also more likely to associate it with business and politics (Rudowicz & Hui, 1998). The idea of saving face may be a factor in lower Eastern creativity; believing in the idea of face logic was associated with lower creativity across three cultures, and when people's social image was increased, cultural differences in creativity were reduced (Miron-Spektor, Paletz, & Lin, 2015).

The Chinese have also been shown to endorse stereotypes that they are less creative than Westerners both at the mini-c and Pro-c levels (Wang & Greenwood, 2013). Interestingly, they will continue to support these beliefs even when shown evidence that there are no differences (Wong & Niu, 2013). Indeed, these stereotypes persist even as the Chinese government has placed creativity as a top priority in national educational plans (Pang & Plucker, 2012). Similar efforts are in place in Korea (Choe, 2006).

Yuan and Zhou (2015) offer a theory that incorporates issues of status and collectivism. They highlight the concept of power distance, which is the extent to which a culture accepts that status and power are distributed unequally (Hofstede, 2001). Eastern cultures

273

tend to have higher power distances than Western cultures. Yuan and Zhou argue that higher power distances lead to groups being less likely to share ideas and more likely to be dominated by the opinions of a few higher-status people. Further, a group may come to an agreement without synthesizing disparate opinions, meaning that the kind of problem solving that occurs with natural conflict will not take place. There are potential interventions that Yuan and Zhou suggest, such as a leader modeling creative behavior and having strategies in place that allow debate.

Yet another possibility is that the differences are overblown. Plucker, Runco, and Lim (2006) found no difference in creative potential between Korean students and American students; similarly, Lim and Plucker (2001) found that Koreans and Americans hold similar concepts about the nature of creativity. Many studies of how Western and Eastern cultures differ in their views of creativity look at implicit beliefs (which I discuss in some detail in Chapter 11). Consider what Lim, Plucker, and Im (2002) discovered when comparing Korean and American viewpoints on intelligence. When views on intelligence were measured in a traditional way, in which people were asked to rate how different behaviors were associated with intelligence, Koreans highly valued social harmony as a key component of intelligence. Yet with a change in measurement— asking them to rate profiles of fictional people who demonstrated these traits—Korean and American beliefs began to converge. Nuances in how these questions are assessed matter greatly.

Sundararajan and Raina (2014) argue that cross-cultural studies of creativity invariably overestimate social influences on creativity; creativity is a choice at the level of the individual. It is important to not let this point get lost; if you're studying two cultures, finding a difference becomes a (publishable) story. Finding that everyone is the same may be a happy, shiny discovery, but it's a lot harder to place it in a good journal. Such are the realities of scientific research.

Another note on cultural differences in creativity: having basic knowledge about other cultures may increase your own creativity. A. Leung, Maddux, Galinsky, and Chiu (2008) found that when students were given information about another culture (China), they subsequently wrote more creative stories set in a different culture (Turkey) as compared with students who had not been exposed.

A. Leung and Chiu (2010) studied Caucasian students who had not traveled abroad. First they replicated the findings of A. Leung et al. (2008) and added two new conditions: one in which students were exposed to both Chinese and American cultures and one in which they were exposed to a fusion of the two cultures. These two additional groups also outperformed the control and a group only exposed to American culture. Indeed, this increase in creativity was still found a week later. de Bloom, Ritter, Kühnel, Reinders, and Geurts (2014) looked at the potential beneficial impact of brief, fun travel; they found that people showed increased cognitive flexibility (but no difference on originality) after going on a vacation.

Other studies have examined actual multicultural experience. Exposure to other countries increased idea receptiveness (related to openness to experience) and idea generation (A. Leung & Chiu, 2010). In a different study, creativity was positively correlated with multicultural exposure in people who were high on openness to experience, but negatively correlated for less open people. It is possible that if particularly close-minded people travel abroad, they may actually become less creative.

Maddux and Galinsky (2009) conducted five experiments that examined living in a different country (not simply traveling). They found a connection between how long someone lived abroad and the individual's creativity; in addition, simply getting people who'd lived abroad to think about their experiences increased creativity (see also Lee, Therriault, & Linderholm, 2012). The amount that people were able to adapt to the other culture was also related to creativity. Maddux, Adam, and Galinsky (2010) further emphasized the importance of multicultural learning in helping people benefit creatively from having lived in a foreign culture.

Going beyond individual benefit, Godart, Maddux, Shipilov, and Galinsky (2015) studied how executives' foreign work experiences predicted company-wide innovation. They analyzed breadth (working in many different cultures), depth (time spent working in other cultures), and cultural distance (working in cultures that are very different from your own). Depth was most related to organizational creativity and was always a positive predictor. Breadth and cultural distance were most important when depth was lower; in addition, at very high levels they were negatively related to creativity.

275

Hempel and Sue-Chan (2010) proposed that expatriates are a valuable way to study cross-cultural creativity. They argue that when people assimilate into a new country, their host country will see them as less novel but more useful. In contrast, their home country will now see them as less useful but more novel. Consistent with this idea, Tadmor, Galinsky, and Maddux (2012) studied "biculturals"— people who lived abroad and were able to identify with both their home country and their host country (as opposed to people who completely assimilated or stayed fully separate). Such biculturals were not only more creative at divergent thinking tasks but also more creative at work (and more likely to receive promotions). C. S. Saad, Damian, Benet-Martínez, Moons, and Robins (2013) compared biculturals across the degree to which their cultural identity was blended. Those who were more blended showed higher domain-general creativity within a bicultural context; in a single-culture context, there was no difference.

With all of this talk about different cultures, how you interact within your own culture also matters. People with a larger primary social network—as in friends whom they actually know in real life— were found to be more creative. Unfortunately for Facebook folks, having a larger broad social network was not related to creativity (Kéri, 2011).

LOOKING AHEAD

Environments impact creativity in many ways. Perhaps they can help by giving people permission to be creative or think in a cognitively flexible way or else be more open to experiences. Another way is that any environment can shape our perceptions of creativity—whether it's our own creativity, someone else's creativity, or creativity as a general topic. A good teacher or boss can make us feel like we're creative, even if we didn't consider ourselves creative before. In the next chapter, I dig into the topic of creative perceptions. How do we perceive our own creativity? What do we think about creative people? How reliable are self-assessments, anyway?

REFERENCES

Abe, K. (2010). Interaction between body and environment in creative thinking. *Cognitive Studies: Bulletin of the Japanese Cognitive Science Society, 17,* 599–610.

Amabile, T. M. (1996). *Creativity in context: Update to "The social psychology of creativity."* Boulder, CO: Westview Press.

Amabile, T. M., & Conti, R. (1997). Environmental determinants of work motivation, creativity, and innovation: The case of R&D downsizing. In R. Garud, P. R. Nayyar, Z. B. Shapira, R. Garud, P. R. Nayyar, & Z. B. Shapira (Eds.), *Technological innovation: Oversights and foresights* (pp. 111–125). New York, NY: Cambridge University Press.

Amabile, T. M., & Conti, R. (1999). Changes in the work environment for creativity during downsizing. *Academy of Management Journal, 42,* 630–640.

Amabile, T. M., Conti, R., Coon, H., Lazenby, J., & Herron, M. (1996). Assessing the work environment for creativity. *Academy of Management Journal, 39,* 1154–1184.

Amabile, T. M., & Gryskiewicz, N. D. (1989). The creative environment scales: Work environment inventory. *Creativity Research Journal, 2,* 231–253.

Amabile, T. M., & Kramer, S. (2012). How leaders kill meaning at work. *McKinsey Quarterly, 1,* 124–131.

Amabile, T. M., Schatzel, E. A., Moneta, G. B., & Kramer, S. J. (2004). Leader behaviors and the work environment for creativity: Perceived leader support. *The Leadership Quarterly, 15,* 5–32.

Atchley, R. A., Strayer, D. L., & Atchley, P. (2012). Creativity in the wild: Improving creative reasoning through immersion in natural settings. *PLoS ONE, 7,* e51474.

Averill, J. R., Chon, K. K., & Hahn, D. (2001). Emotions and creativity, East and West. *Asian Journal of Social Psychology, 4,* 165–183.

Baer, J. (1997). Gender differences in the effects of anticipated evaluation on creativity. *Creativity Research Journal, 10,* 25–31.

Baer, J. (1998). The case for domain specificity in creativity. *Creativity Research Journal, 11,* 173–177.

Baer, M., Oldham, G. R., Hollingshead, A. B., & Costa Jacobsohn, G. (2005). Revisiting the birth order-creativity connection: The role of sibling constellation. *Creativity Research Journal, 17,* 67–77.

Barbot, B., Tan, M., & Grigorenko, E. (2013). The genetics of creativity: The generative and receptive sides of the creativity equation. In O. Vartanian, A. S. Bristol, & J. C. Kaufman (Eds.), *Neuroscience of creativity* (pp. 71–93). Cambridge, MA: MIT Press.

Bechtoldt, M. N., Choi, H. S., & Nijstad, B. A. (2012). Individuals in mind, mates by heart: Individualistic self-construal and collective value orientation as predictors of group creativity. *Journal of Experimental Social Psychology, 48*, 838–844.

Beghetto, R. A. (2005). Preservice teachers' self-judgments of test taking. *Journal of Educational Research, 98*, 376–380.

Beghetto, R. A. (2010). Intellectual hide-and-seek: Prospective teachers' prior experiences with creativity suppression. *International Journal of Creativity & Problem Solving, 20*, 29–36.

Beghetto, R. A. (2013). *Killing ideas softly? The promise and perils of creativity in the classroom.* Charlotte, NC: Information Age Publishing.

Beghetto, R. A. (2014). Creative mortification: An initial exploration. *Psychology of Aesthetics, Creativity, and the Arts, 8*, 266–276.

Beghetto, R. A., & Kaufman, J. C. (2007). Toward a broader conception of creativity: A case for "mini-c" creativity. *Psychology of Aesthetics, Creativity, and the Arts, 1*, 73–79.

Beghetto, R. A., & Kaufman, J. C. (in press). *Nurturing creativity in the classroom* (2nd ed.). New York, NY: Cambridge University Press.

Beversdorf, D. Q., Hughes, J. D., Steinburg, B. A., Lewis, L. D., & Heilman, K. M. (1999). Noradrenergic modulation of cognitive flexibility in problem solving. *NeuroReport, 10*, 2763–2767.

Bowers, M. T., Green, B. C., Hemme, F., & Chalip, L. (2014). Assessing the relationship between youth sport participation settings and creativity in adulthood. *Creativity Research Journal, 26*, 314–327.

Cady, S. H., & Valentine, J. (1999). Team innovation and perceptions of consideration: What difference does diversity make? *Small Group Research, 30*, 730–750.

Campbell, H. L., Tivarus, M. E., Hillier, A., & Beversdorf, D. Q. (2008). Increased task difficulty results in greater impact of noradrenergic modulation of cognitive flexibility. *Pharmacology, Biochemistry, and Behavior, 88*, 222–229.

Canesi, M., Rusconi, M. L., Isaias, I. U., & Pezzoli, G. (2012). Artistic productivity and creative thinking in Parkinson's disease. *European Journal of Neurology, 19*, 468–472.

Carmeli, A., Reiter-Palmon, R., & Ziv, E. (2010). Inclusive leadership and employee involvement in creative tasks in the workplace: The mediating role of psychological safety. *Creativity Research Journal, 22*, 250–260.

Carmeli, A., Sheaffer, Z., Binyamin, G., Reiter-Palmon, R., & Shimoni, T. (2014). Transformational leadership and creative problem-solving: The mediating role of psychological safety and reflexivity. *Journal of Creative Behavior, 48*, 115–135.

Ceylan, C., Dul, J., & Aytac, S. (2008). Can the office environment stimulate a manager's creativity? *Human Factors and Ergonomics in Manufacturing & Service Industries, 18*, 589–602.

Chatman, J. A., Polzer, J. T., Barsade, S. G., & Neale, M. A. (1998). Being different yet feeling similar: The influence of demographic composition and organizational culture on work processes and outcomes. *Administrative Science Quarterly, 43*, 749–780.

Chen, C., Kasof, J., Himsel, A., Dmitrieva, J., Dong, Q., & Xue, G. (2005). Effects of explicit instruction to "be creative" across domains and cultures. *Journal of Creative Behavior, 39*, 89–110.

Childs, E., & de Wit, H. (2008). Enhanced mood and psychomotor performance by a caffeine-containing energy capsule in fatigued individuals. *Clinical Psychopharmacology, 16*, 13–21.

Choe, I. (2006). Creativity—A sudden rising star in Korea. In J. C. Kaufman & R. J. Sternberg (Eds.), *The international handbook of creativity* (pp. 395–420). New York, NY: Cambridge University Press.

Choi, J. N. (2007). Group composition and employee creative behavior in a Korean electronics company: Distinct effects of relational demography and group diversity. *Journal of Occupational and Organizational Psychology, 80*, 213–234.

Colzato, L. S., Szapora, A., Pannekoek, J. N., & Hommel, B. (2013). The impact of physical exercise on convergent and divergent thinking. *Frontiers in Human Neuroscience, 7*. doi:10.3389/fnhum.2013.00824

Connelly, B. S., Ones, D. S., Davies, S. E., & Birkland, A. (2014). Opening up openness: A theoretical sort following critical incidents methodology and a meta-analytic investigation of the trait family measures. *Journal of Personality Assessment, 96*, 17–28.

Conner, T. S., Brookie, K. L., Richardson, A. C., & Polak, M. A. (2015). On carrots and curiosity: Eating fruit and vegetables is associated with greater flourishing in daily life. *British Journal of Health Psychology, 20*, 413–427.

Craig, T. Y., & Kelly, J. R. (1999). Group cohesiveness and creative performance. *Group Dynamics, 3*, 243–256.

Cropley, A. J. (2006). In praise of convergent thinking. *Creativity Research Journal, 18*, 391–404.

Dai, D. Y., Tan, X., Marathe, D., Valtcheva, A., Pruzek, R. M., & Shen, J. (2012). Influences of social and educational environments on creativity during adolescence: Does SES matter? *Creativity Research Journal, 24*, 191–199.

Davies, D., Jindal-Snape, D., Collier, C., Digby, R., Hay, P., & Howe, A. (2013). Creative learning environments in education: A systematic literature review. *Thinking Skills and Creativity, 8*, 80–91.

de Bloom, J., Ritter, S., Kühnel, J., Reinders, J., & Geurts, S. (2014). Vacation from work: A "ticket to creativity"? The effects of recreational travel on cognitive flexibility and originality. *Tourism Management, 44*, 164–171.

279

De Dreu, C. K. W. (2006). When too little or too much hurts: Evidence for a curvilinear relationship between task conflict and innovation in teams. *Journal of Management, 32,* 83–107.

De Dreu, C. K. W., Baas, M., & Boot, N. C. (2015). Oxytocin enables novelty seeking and creative performance through upregulated approach: Evidence and avenues for future research. *Wires Cognitive Science.* Advance online publication. doi:10.1002/wcs.1354

Detert, J. R., & Burris, E. R. (2007). Leadership behavior and employee voice: Is the door really open? *Academy of Management Journal, 50,* 869–884.

Dul, J., Ceylan, C., & Jaspers, F. (2011). Knowledge worker creativity and the role of the physical work environment. *Human Resource Management, 50,* 715–734.

Edmondson, A. C. (1999). Psychological safety and learning behavior in work teams. *Administrative Science Quarterly, 44,* 350–383.

Fabricatore, C., & López, X. (2013). Fostering creativity through educational video game development projects: A study of contextual and task characteristics. *Creativity Research Journal, 25,* 418–425.

Faigel, H. C. (1991). The effect of beta blockade on stress-induced cognitive dysfunction in adolescents. *Clinical Pediatrics, 30,* 441–445.

Farah, M. J., Haimm, C., Sankoorikal, G., Smith, M. E., & Chatterjee, A. (2008). When we enhance cognition with Adderall do we sacrifice creativity? A preliminary study. *Psychopharmacology, 202,* 541–547.

Ford, C., & Sullivan, D. M. (2004). A time for everything: How timing of novel contributions influences project team outcomes. *Journal of Organizational Behavior, 21,* 163–183.

Forgays, D. G., & Forgays, D. K. (1992). Creativity enhancement through flotation isolation. *Journal of Environmental Psychology, 12,* 329–335.

Furnham, A., Hughes, D. J., & Marshall, E. (2013). Creativity, OCD, narcissism and the Big Five. *Thinking Skills and Creativity, 10,* 91–98.

Gibson, C., & Mumford, M. D. (2013). Evaluation, criticism, and creativity: Criticism content and effects on creative problem solving. *Psychology of Aesthetics, Creativity, and the Arts, 7,* 314–331.

Glăveanu, V. P. (2010a). Paradigms in the study of creativity: Introducing the perspective of cultural psychology. *New Ideas in Psychology, 28,* 79–93.

Glăveanu, V. P. (2010b). Principles for a cultural psychology of creativity. *Culture and Psychology, 16,* 147–163.

Godart, F. C., Maddux, W. W., Shipilov, A. V., & Galinsky, A. D. (2015). Fashion with a foreign flair: Professional experiences abroad facilitate the creative innovations of organizations. *Academy of Management Journal, 58,* 195–220.

Goncalo, J. A., Chatman, J. A., Duguid, M. M., & Kennedy, J. A. (2015). Creativity from constraint? How the political correctness norm influences creativity in mixed-sex work groups. *Administrative Science Quarterly, 60,* 1–30.

Goncalo, J. A., Flynn, F. J., & Kim, S. H. (2010). Are two narcissists better than one? The link between narcissism, perceived creativity, and creative performance. *Personality and Social Psychology Bulletin, 36,* 1484–1495.

Goncalo, J. A., & Staw, B. M. (2006). Individualism-collectivism and group creativity. *Organizational Behavior and Human Decision Processes, 100,* 96–109.

Gong, Y., Huang, J. C., & Farh, J. L. (2009). Employee learning orientation, transformational leadership, and employee creativity: The mediating role of employee creative self-efficacy. *Academy of Management Journal, 52,* 765–778.

Grigorenko, E. L., LaBuda, M. L., & Carter, A. S. (1992). Similarity in general cognitive ability, creativity, and cognitive styles in a sample of adolescent Russian twins. *Acta Geneticae Medicae Gemellologiae, 41,* 65–72.

Harrington, D. M. (1975). Effects of the explicit instructions to "be creative" on the psychological meaning of divergent thinking test scores. *Journal of Personality, 43,* 434–454.

Harvey, S. (2013). A different perspective: The multiple effects of deep level diversity on group creativity. *Journal of Experimental Social Psychology, 49,* 822–832.

Hempel, P. S., & Sue-Chan, C. (2010). Culture and the assessment of creativity. *Management and Organization Review, 6,* 415–435.

Hennessey, B. A. (2010). Intrinsic motivation and creativity in the classroom: Have we come full circle? In R. A. Beghetto & J. C. Kaufman (Eds.), *Nurturing creativity in the classroom* (pp. 329–361). New York, NY: Cambridge University Press.

Hennessey, B. A. (2015a). Creative behavior, motivation, environment and culture: The building of a Systems Model. *Journal of Creative Behavior.* Advance online publication. doi:10.1002/jocb.97

Hennessey, B. A. (2015b). If I were Secretary of Education: A focus on intrinsic motivation and creativity in the classroom. *Psychology of Aesthetics, Creativity, and the Arts, 9,* 187–192.

Hennessey, B. A., Amabile, T. M., & Martinage, M. (1989). Immunizing children against the negative effects of reward. *Contemporary Educational Psychology, 14,* 212–227.

Hillier, A., Alexander, J. K., & Beversdorf, D. Q. (2006). The effect of auditory stressors on cognitive flexibility. *Neurocase, 12,* 228–231.

Hofstede, G. (2001). *Culture's consequences: Comparing values, behaviors, institutions and organizations across nations*. Thousand Oaks, CA: Sage.

Huang, L., Krasikova, D. V., & Liu, D. (2016). I can do it, so can you: The role of leader creative self-efficacy in facilitating follower creativity. *Organizational Behavior and Human Decision Processes, 132*, 49–62.

Ijzerman, H., Leung, A. K.-Y., & Ong, L. (2014). Perceptual symbols of creativity: Coldness elicits referential, warmth elicits relational creativity. *Acta Psychologica, 148*, 136–147.

Jaussi, K. S., & Dionne, S. D. (2003). Leading for creativity: The role of unconventional leader behavior. *The Leadership Quarterly, 14*, 475–498.

Karwowski, M. (2009). *Klimat dla kreatywności. Koncepcje, metody, badania*. Warsaw, Poland: Wydawnictwo DIFIN (in Polish).

Karwowski, M. (2011). Teachers' personality and perception of the climate for creativity in a school. *International Journal of Creativity & Problem Solving, 21*, 37–52.

Karwowski, M. (2015). Peer effect on students' creative self-concept. *Journal of Creative Behavior*. Advance online publication. doi:10.1002/jocb.102

Karwowski, M., & Lebuda, I. (2013). Extending climato-economic theory: When, how, and why it explains differences in nations' creativity. *Behavioral and Brain Sciences, 36*, 493–494.

Kasof, J. (1997). Creativity and breadth of attention. *Creativity Research Journal, 10*, 303–315.

Katz, A. N., & Poag, J. R. (1979). Sex differences in instructions to "be creative" on divergent and nondivergent test scores. *Journal of Personality, 47*, 518–530.

Kaufman, A. B., Kornilov, S. A., Bristol, A. S., Tan, M., & Grigorenko, E. L. (2010). The neurobiological foundation of creative cognition. In J. C. Kaufman & R. J. Sternberg (Eds.), *Cambridge handbook of creativity* (pp. 216–232). New York, NY: Cambridge University Press.

Kaufman, A. S. (2009). *IQ testing 101*. New York, NY: Springer Publishing Company.

Kaufman, J. C. (2015). Creativity is more than silly, more than art, more than good: The diverse career of Arthur Cropley. *Creativity Research Journal, 27*, 249–253.

Kéri, S. (2009). Genes for psychosis and creativity. *Psychological Science, 20*, 1070–1073.

Kéri, S. (2011). Solitary minds and social capital: Latent inhibition, general intellectual functions and social network size predict creative achievements. *Psychology of Aesthetics, Creativity, and the Arts, 5*, 215–221.

Kurtzberg, T. R., & Amabile, T. M. (2000). From Guilford to creative synergy: Opening the black box of team level creativity. *Creativity Research Journal, 13*, 285–294.

Lan, L., & Kaufman, J. C. (2012). American and Chinese similarities and differences in defining and valuing creative products. *Journal of Creative Behavior, 46*, 285–306.

Lau, S., & Cheung, P. C. (2010). Developmental trends of creativity: What twists of turn do boys and girls take at different grades? *Creativity Research Journal, 22*, 329–336.

Lau, S., Hui, A. N. N., & Ng, G. Y. C. (Ed.). (2004). *Creativity: When East meets West.* Singapore: World Scientific.

Lee, C. S., Therriault, D. J., & Linderholm, T. (2012). On the cognitive benefits of cultural experience: Exploring the relationship between studying abroad and creative thinking. *Applied Cognitive Psychology, 26*, 768–778.

Leung, A. K.-Y., & Chiu, C.-Y. (2010). Multicultural experiences, idea receptiveness, and creativity. *Journal of Cross-Cultural Psychology, 41*, 1–19.

Leung, A. K.-Y., Kim, S., Polman, E., Ong, L. S., Qiu, L., Goncalo, J., & Sanchez-Burks, J. (2012). Embodied metaphors and creative "acts." *Psychological Science, 23*, 502- 509.

Leung, A. K.-Y., Maddux, W. W., Galinsky, A. D., & Chiu, C. (2008). Multicultural experience enhances creativity: The when and how. *American Psychologist, 63*, 169–181.

Leung, K., & Morris, M. W. (2011). Culture and creativity: A social psychological analysis. In D. De Cremer, J. K. Murnighan, & R. van Dick (Eds.), *Social psychology and organizations* (pp. 371–395). New York, NY: Routledge.

Li, J. (1997). Creativity in horizontal and vertical domains. *Creativity Research Journal, 10*, 107–132.

Lichtenfeld, S., Elliot, A., Maier, M. A., & Pekrun, R. (2012). Fertile green: Green facilitates creative performance. *Personality and Social Psychology Bulletin, 38*, 784–797.

Lim, W., & Plucker, J. (2001). Creativity through a lens of social responsibility: Implicit theories of creativity with Korean samples. *Journal of Creative Behavior, 35*, 115–130.

Lim, W., Plucker, J., & Im, K. (2002). We are more alike than we think we are: Implicit theories of intelligence with a Korean sample. *Intelligence, 20*, 185–208.

Maddux, W. W., Adam, H., & Galinsky, A. D. (2010). When in Rome . . . Learn why the Romans do what they do: How multicultural learning experiences facilitate creativity. *Personality and Social Psychology Bulletin, 36*, 731–741.

Maddux, W. W., & Galinsky, A. D. (2009). Cultural borders and mental barriers: The relationship between living abroad and creativity. *Journal of Personality and Social Psychology, 96*, 1047–1061.

Mamet, D. (1987). *House of games: A screenplay.* New York, NY: Grove Press.

Markus, H. R., & Kitayama, S. (1991). Culture and the self: Implications for cognition, emotion, and motivation. *Psychological Review, 98*, 224–253.

McCoy, J. M., & Evans, G. W. (2002). The potential role of the physical environment in fostering creativity. *Creativity Research Journal, 14*, 409–426.

McLeod, P. L., Lobel, S. A., & Cox, T. H. (1996). Ethnic diversity and creativity in small groups. *Small Group Research, 27*, 248–264.

Mehta, M. A., Owen, A. M., Sahakian, B. J., Mavaddat, N., Pickard, J. D., & Robbins, T. W. (2000). Methylphenidate enhances working memory by modulating discrete frontal and parietal lobe regions in the human brain. *Journal of Neuroscience, 20*, RC65.

Mehta, R., & Zhu, R. J. (2009). Blue or red? Exploring the effect of color on cognitive task performances. *Science, 323*, 1226–1229.

Mehta, R., Zhu, R. J., & Cheema, A. (2012). Is noise always bad? Exploring the effects of ambient noise on creative cognition. *Journal of Consumer Research, 39*, 784–799.

Milliken, F. J., & Martins, L. L. (1996). Searching for common threads: Understanding the multiple effects of diversity in organizational groups. *Academy of Management Review, 21*, 402–433.

Miron-Spektor, E., Paletz, S. B. F., & Lin, C. C (2015). To create without losing face: The effects of face cultural logic and social-image affirmation on creativity. *Journal of Organizational Behavior, 36*, 919–943.

Mohamed, A. D. (2014). The effects of modafinil on convergent and divergent thinking of creativity: A randomized controlled trial. *Journal of Creative Behavior.* Advance online publication. doi:10.1002/jocb.73

Müller, U., Rowe, J. B., Rittman, T., Lewis, C., Robbins, T. W., & Sahakian, B. J. (2013). Effects of modafinil on non-verbal cognition, task enjoyment and creative thinking in healthy volunteers. *Neuropharmacology, 64*, 490–495.

Mumford, M. D., Hunter, S. T., Eubanks, D. L., Bedell, K. E., & Murphy, S. T. (2007). Developing leaders for creative efforts: A domain-based approach to leadership development. *Human Resource Management Review, 17*, 402–417.

Mumford, M. D., Scott, G. M., Gaddis, B., & Strange, J. M. (2002). Leading creative people: Orchestrating expertise and relationships. *Leadership Quarterly, 13*, 705–750.

Ng, A. K. (2001). *Why Asians are less creative than Westerners.* Singapore: Prentice-Hall.

Ng, A. K., & Smith, I. (2004). Why is there a paradox in promoting creativity in the Asian classroom? In L. Sing, A. Hui, & G. Ng (Eds.), *Creativity: When East meets West* (pp. 87–112). Singapore: World Scientific Publishing.

Niu, W. (2012). Confucian ideology and creativity. *Journal of Creative Behavior, 46,* 274–284.

Niu, W., & Kaufman, J. C. (2013). Creativity of Chinese and American cultures: A synthetic analysis. *Journal of Creative Behavior, 47,* 77–87.

Niu, W., & Sternberg, R. J. (2001). Cultural influence of artistic creativity and its evaluation. *International Journal of Psychology, 36,* 225–241.

Norlander, T., Bergman, H., & Archer, T. (1998). Effects of flotation REST on creative problem solving and originality. *Journal of Environmental Psychology, 18,* 399–408.

Nusbaum, E. C., Silvia, P. J., & Beaty, R. E. (2014). Ready, set, create: What instructing people to "be creative" reveals about the meaning and mechanisms of divergent thinking. *Psychology of Aesthetics, Creativity, and the Arts, 8,* 423–432.

O'Hara, L. A., & Sternberg, R. J. (2001). It doesn't hurt to ask: Effects of instructions to be creative, practical, or analytical on essay–writing performance and their interaction with students' thinking styles. *Creativity Research Journal, 13,* 197–210.

Oppezzo, M., & Schwartz, D. L. (2014). Give your ideas some legs: The positive effect of walking on creative thinking. *Journal of Experimental Psychology: Learning, Memory, and Cognition, 40,* 1142–1152.

Paletz, S. B. F., Peng, K., Erez, M., & Maslach, C. (2004). Ethnic composition and its differential impact on group processes in diverse teams. *Small Group Research, 35,* 128–157.

Pang, W., & Plucker, J. A. (2012). Recent transformations in China's economic, social, and education policies for promoting innovation and creativity. *Journal of Creative Behavior, 46,* 247–273.

Plucker, J. A., & Esping, A. (2014). *Intelligence 101.* New York, NY: Springer Publishing Company.

Plucker, J. A., Runco, M. A., & Lim, W. (2006). Predicting ideational behavior from divergent thinking and discretionary time on task. *Creativity Research Journal, 18,* 55–63.

Polner, B., Nagy, H., Takáts, A., & Kéri, S. (2015). Kiss of the muse for the chosen ones: De novo schizotypal traits and lifetime creative achievement are related to changes in divergent thinking during dopaminergic therapy in Parkinson's disease. *Psychology of Aesthetics, Creativity, and the Arts, 9,* 328–339.

Reiter-Palmon, R., & Illies, J. J. (2004). Leadership and creativity: Understanding leadership from a creative problem-solving perspective. *Leadership Quarterly, 15,* 55–77.

Reznikoff, M., Domino, G., Bridges, C., & Honeyman, M. (1973). Creative abilities in identical and fraternal twins. *Behavioral Genetics, 3,* 365–377.

Rinne, T., Steel, G. D., & Fairweather, J. (2013). The role of Hofstede's individualism in national-level creativity. *Creativity Research Journal, 25,* 129–136.

Roe, A. (1952). *The making of a scientist.* New York, NY: Dodd, Mead.

Roussin, C. J. (2008). Increasing trust, psychological safety, and team performance through dyadic leadership discovery. *Small Group Research, 39,* 224–248.

Rudowicz, E., & Hui, A. (1998). Hong Kong Chinese people's view of creativity. *Gifted Education International, 13,* 159–174.

Runco, M. A., Illies, J. J., & Eisenman, R. (2005). Creativity, originality, and appropriateness: What do explicit instructions tell us about their relationships? *Journal of Creative Behavior, 39,* 137–148.

Runco, M. A., Illies, J. J., & Reiter-Palmon, R. (2005). Explicit instructions to be creative and original: A comparison of strategies and criteria as targets with three types of divergent thinking tests. *Korean Journal of Thinking & Problem Solving, 15,* 5–15.

Saad, C. S., Damian, R. I., Benet-Martínez, V., Moons, W. G., & Robins, R. W. (2013). Multiculturalism and creativity: Effects of cultural context, bicultural identity, and ideational fluency. *Social Psychological and Personality Science, 4,* 369–375.

Saad, G., Cleveland, M., & Ho, L. (2015). Individualism–collectivism and the quantity versus quality dimensions of individual and group creative performance. *Journal of Business Research, 68,* 578–586.

Sawyer, R. K. (2012). *Explaining creativity: The science of human innovation* (2nd ed.). New York, NY: Oxford University Press.

Shibata, S., & Suzuki, N. (2002). Effects of the foliage plant on task performance and mood. *Journal of Environmental Psychology, 22,* 265–272.

Shibata, S., & Suzuki, N. (2004). Effects of an indoor plant on creative task performance and mood. *Scandinavian Journal of Psychology, 45,* 373–381.

Shin, S. J., & Zhou, J. (2007). When is educational specialization heterogeneity related to creativity in research and development teams? Transformational leadership as a moderator. *Journal of Applied Psychology, 92,* 1709–1721.

Shute, V. J., Ventura, M., & Kim, Y. J. (2013). Assessment and learning of informal physics in Newton's Playground. *Journal of Educational Research, 106,* 423–430.

Simonton, D. K. (1987). Developmental antecedents of achieved eminence. *Annual of Child Development, 5,* 131–169.

Simonton, D. K. (1994). *Greatness: Who makes history and why.* New York, NY: Guilford Press.

Simonton, D. K. (2009). *Genius 101.* New York, NY: Springer Publishing Company.

Steidle, A., & Werth, L. (2013). Freedom from constraints: Darkness and dim illumination promote creativity. *Journal of Environmental Psychology, 35,* 67–80.

Stone, N. J., & Irvine, J. M. (1994). Direct or indirect window access, task type, and performance. *Journal of Environmental Psychology, 14*, 57–63.

Suedfeld, P., Metcalfe, J. and Bluck, S. (1987). Enhancement of scientific creativity by flotation REST (restricted environmental stimulation technique). *Journal of Environmental Psychology, 7*, 219–231.

Sulloway, F. J. (1996). *Born to rebel*. New York, NY: Vintage.

Sundararajan, L., & Raina, M. K. (2014). Revolutionary creativity, East and West: A critique from indigenous psychology. *Journal of Theoretical and Philosophical Psychology, 35*, 3–19.

Szobiová, E. (2008). Birth order, sibling constellation, creativity and personality dimensions of adolescents. *Studia Psychologica, 50*, 371–381.

Tadmor, C. T., Galinsky, A. D., & Maddux, W. W. (2012). Getting the most out of living abroad: Biculturalism and integrative complexity as key drivers of creative and professional success. *Journal of Personality and Social Psychology, 103*, 520–542.

Tadmor, C. T., Satterstrom, P., Jang, S., & Polzer, J. T. (2012). Beyond individual creativity: The superadditive benefits of multicultural experience for collective creativity in culturally diverse teams. *Journal of Cross-Cultural Psychology, 43*, 384–392.

Torrance, E. P. (1968). A longitudinal examination of the fourth grade slump in creativity. *Gifted Child Quarterly, 12*, 195–199.

Unsworth, K. L., & Clegg, C. W. (2010). Why do employees undertake creative action? *Journal of Occupational and Organizational Psychology, 83*, 77–99.

Van Tilburg, W. A. P., Sedikides, C., & Wildschut, T. (2015). The mnemonic muse: Nostalgia fosters creativity through openness to experience. *Journal of Experimental Social Psychology, 59*, 1–7.

Vartanian, O., & Suedfeld, P. (2011). The effect of the flotation version of restricted environmental stimulation technique (REST) on jazz improvisation. *Music and Medicine, 3*, 234–238.

Velázquez, J. A., Segal, N. L., & Horwitz, B. N. (2015). Genetic and environmental influences on applied creativity: A reared-apart twin study. *Personality and Individual Differences, 75*, 141–146.

Vohs, K. D., Redden, J. P., & Rahinel, R. (2013). Physical order produces healthy choices, generosity, and conventionality, whereas disorder produces creativity. *Psychological Science, 24*, 1860–1867.

Volf, N. V., Kulikov, A. V., Bortsov, C. U., & Popova, N. K. (2009). Association of verbal and figural creative achievement with polymorphism in the human serotonin transporter gene. *Neuroscience Letters, 463*, 154–157.

Walton, A. P., & Kemmelmeier, M. (2012). Creativity in its social context: The interplay of organizational norms, situational threat, and gender. *Creativity Research Journal, 24*, 208–219.

Wang, B., & Greenwood, K. M. (2013). Chinese students' perceptions of their creativity and their perceptions of Western students' creativity. *Educational Psychology, 33,* 628–643.

West, M. A., Borrill, C. S., Dawson, J. F., Brodbeck, F., Shapiro, D. A., & Haward, B. (2003). Leadership clarity and team innovation in health care. *The Leadership Quarterly, 14,* 393–410.

White, B. P., Becker-Blease, K. A., & Grace-Bishop, K. (2006). Stimulant medication use, misuse, and abuse in an undergraduate and graduate student sample. *Journal of American College Health, 54,* 261–268.

Wong, R., & Niu, W. (2013). Cultural difference in stereotype perceptions and performances in nonverbal deductive reasoning and creativity. *Journal of Creative Behavior, 47,* 41–59.

Yap, C., Chai, K., & Lemaire, P. (2005). An empirical study on functional diversity and innovation in SMEs. *Creativity and Innovation Management, 14,* 176–190.

Ye, S., Ngan, R. L., & Hui, A. N. (2013). The state, not the trait, of nostalgia increases creativity. *Creativity Research Journal, 25,* 317–323.

Yi, X., Hu, X., Plucker, J., & McWilliams, J. (2013). Is there a developmental slump in creativity in China? The relationship between organizational climate and creativity development in Chinese adolescents. *Journal of Creative Behavior, 47,* 22–40.

Yuan, F., & Zhou, J. (2015). Effects of cultural power distance on group creativity and individual group member creativity. *Journal of Organizational Behavior.* Advance online publication. doi:10.1002/job.2022

Yue, X. D. (2004). Whoever is influential is creative: How Chinese undergraduates choose creative people in Chinese societies. *Psychological Reports, 94,* 1235–1249.

Zwaan, R. (2013). 50 questions about messy rooms and clean data. In *Zeistgeist: Psychological experimentation, cognition, language, and academia.* Retrieved from http://rolfzwaan.blogspot.com/2013/08/50-questions-about-messy-rooms-and.html

288

Creative Perceptions (of Self and Others)

What do we think about creative people? Do we like them? Hate them? Think they smell funny? It is important to first distinguish between implicit and explicit beliefs. Explicit beliefs are ones we can verbalize. I believe that people should be nice to dogs. Stephen Sondheim is a genius. Pop Tarts are tasty but too many calories for me to justify having them in the house. Scientists are very good at explicating their beliefs—if someone has a theory, he or she will likely not just state it once but repeat it and repeat it until people cite it. Implicit beliefs are those that are bubbling under the surface. They include unconscious thoughts and sometimes hidden biases. For example, maybe you know someone who is an architect whom you don't particularly like. You may have negative feelings about architects in general, even if you're not sure why. If someone were to ask you whether you particularly disliked architects, you would probably say "no" (Greenwald & Banaji, 1995).

IMPLICIT THEORIES OF CREATIVITY

This difference is very important when we talk about how people think about creativity. Mueller, Melwani, and Goncalo (2012) found that people did not have an explicit bias against creativity. However, their implicit beliefs were more complex. The researchers primed some participants to feel uncertain. In the first study, they offered additional payment based on a random lottery system (as opposed to a control group not offered anything extra); in the second study, they directed participants to write an essay that either praised or criticized the concept of uncertainty. In both studies, neither group of participants showed any explicit bias against creativity (indeed, most showed a slight positive association). However, both the "uncertainty" and "criticizing uncertainty" groups showed more implicit bias against creativity than did the control or "praising uncertainty" groups.

What's fascinating is that people dislike uncertainty, even though it can be a very positive thing at times. For example, if we know something good is coming (we've won a prize), not knowing the details can enhance our pleasure. In fact, we feel better and the good feelings last longer. This increase is particularly strong when we can use mental imagery to wonder about our prize (Lee & Qiu, 2009). This so-called pleasure paradox means that thinking too much about potentially good yet unknown outcomes can actually lower our pleasure (Wilson, Centerbar, Kermer, & Gilbert, 2005). Reading all of the spoilers about a television show finale in *Entertainment Weekly* may actually make us enjoy that episode less.

Yet we continue to dislike uncertainty and we gravitate toward the mainstream. Remember how much group norms can change our beliefs about creativity, even to the point of having people rate less creative work as being more creative (Adarves-Yorno, Postmes, & Haslam, 2006)? People tend to like the status quo (Eidelman & Crandall, 2012). We like something more if it simply exists (Eidelman, Crandall, & Pattershall, 2009). This principle is the driving force behind the mere exposure effect (Zajonc, 2001), which finds that repeated exposure to something makes us eventually prefer it. There, at last, is an answer to when someone asks you "Why does Coke bother to advertise?"

People tend to underestimate ideas that are particularly original (Licuanan, Dailey, & Mumford, 2007) and instead prefer ideas that are socially acceptable and safe. It is not surprising that most innovative products fail (Heidenreich & Spieth, 2013). Such creative products can encounter passive and active resistance from consumers (Ram & Sheth, 1989), particularly those who are older (Laukkanen, Sinkkonen, Kivijärvi, & Laukkanen, 2007). Consumers can postpone adopting new technology, reject it, or actively oppose it—with higher perceived risk (to self, society, or cultural norms), the more the potential active resistance (Kleijnen, Lee, & Wetzels, 2009). We must not, however, overlook the possibility that some new products are just not great ideas. A handless nose-hair trimmer may have seemed like a great idea in the boardroom, but most people don't need one.

The result of these somewhat depressing studies is, of course, reflected in our views toward those people who dare to break the social norm. A striking study by Mueller, Goncalo, and Kamdar (2011) showed that creative employees were not perceived as showing high leadership potential—even when these employees who were being rated were simply parroting prewritten creative responses as opposed to being spontaneously creative themselves.

Creative people are also often seen as being outsiders and eccentric. The extreme, of course, is how much people endorse the "mad genius" stereotype, regardless of truth (Kaufman, Bromley, & Cole, 2006). But it goes beyond just seeing creative people as being potentially crazy; people actually appreciate artwork more if they think the creator is more insane or eccentric (Van Tilburg & Igou, 2014). Such attitudes can be rooted in a desire to punish or ostracize people who are creative, perhaps out of simple jealousy (Schlesinger, 2002). One small positive note is that people who have a naturally independent self-concept may be able to take social rejection and use it to further their creativity (S. H. Kim, Vincent, & Goncalo, 2013).

Unfortunately, such generally negative perceptions of creative people can extend to the classroom. Westby and Dawson (1995) found that teachers claimed to like creative students—yet when asked to define creativity, they used words such as "well behaved" or "conforming." When the same teachers were asked to rate fake student profiles comprised of adjectives typically used to describe either creative or less creative people, they preferred the profiles of less creative students. Aljughaiman and Mowrer-Reynolds (2005) found a similar paradox—teachers said they like creativity, but often do not understand what it means. Other work has shown that teachers associate creativity mostly with the arts (Seo, Lee, & Kim, 2005) and do not see a connection between motivation and creativity (de Souza Fleith, 2000). Schacter, Thum, and Zifkin (2006) observed elementary teachers over multiple lessons and found that few used teaching techniques that supported creativity. A recent qualitative study of poetry teachers found that many were resistant to assess the creativity in student work, with some doubting that creativity could even be assessed (Myhill & Wilson, 2013).

There's a socioeconomic confound at work here, as well. Teachers in private schools gave higher creativity ratings for their students than did public school teachers (Eason, Giannangelo, & Franceschini, 2009). Of course, it could be that private school students are just more creative (the simplest explanations can be true). However, the authors interpreted the results as suggesting that private school teachers are more likely to value creativity. Such teachers were more likely to have enough resources than were public school teachers.

Hong, Hartzell, and Greene (2009) studied how teacher beliefs, specifically goal orientations (recall the discussion in Chapter 6), impacted the instructional practices. Teachers with learning goals used instructional techniques that facilitated student creativity. Yet outside pressures (school standards, standardized test scores) may force some teachers to gravitate toward performance goals and the values associated with them. Similarly, teachers with a more democratic teaching style saw the value in creative-but-undesirable behaviors, whereas teachers with a more autocratic style preferred desirable-but-uncreative student behavior (Kwang & Smith, 2004).

Why might teachers undervalue creative students? Part of the reason is that creativity is associated with nonconformity, impulsivity, and disruptive and disagreeable behavior. This finding was discussed by Torrance (1963) and has been repeatedly confirmed by other studies (e.g., A. J. Cropley, 1992; Karwowski, 2010). Bachtold (1974) surveyed teachers, parents, and students and found that creativity was not considered to be important; there was a high discrepancy between creative descriptors and traits that were highly valued. All groups preferred people with a good sense of humor, consideration for others, health, and self-confidence (which are perfectly fine attributes, of course).

This attitude was memorably spoofed by the show *Phineas and Ferb*, about two young boys with vivid imaginations. A running gag in every episode is that their older sister tries to bust them for misbehavior, but through various mechanisms their mother never sees any proof. In one show, they actually do get busted and get sent to a reform school (Gaylor, Olson, & Povenmire, 2009). The school is run by a sadistic headmaster (voiced by Clancy Brown, the sadistic warden from *The Shawshank Redemption*) whose goal is to drive any ounce of creativity out of his charges. He drills them to repeat that "Creative acts are imitable and dangerous," and later says, "Ah, Phineas and Ferb. Such curious and self-reliant children. So fun-loving, imaginative and creative. Fortunately, we got to them just in time" (Gaylor et al., 2009). What's scary is that this spoof is only slightly exaggerating what some people may quietly think.

This association doesn't come out of thin air. Creative students *can* be a pain in the ass (certainly, I know I was an annoying kid; I just hope I was also creative). Students rated by teachers as being hyperactive, impulsive, and disruptive scored higher on a test of creative fluency (Brandau et al., 2007). Similarly, K. H. Kim and Van-Tassel-Baska (2010) found that creativity was related to behavioral problems in underachieving high school students.

These findings have also been reproduced in Eastern cultures. Teachers and parents in America and India reported favorable views of creativity, but also linked several words associated with mental illness (emotional, impulsive) with creativity (Runco & Johnson, 2002). Tan (2003) found that student teachers in Singapore preferred students with pleasant dispositions (such as kind or friendly) to students who were more creative and risk-taking individuals. Chan and Chan (1999) found that Chinese teachers associated socially undesirable traits with student creativity; they argue that in Chinese culture, nonconforming or expressive behavior can be interpreted as arrogant or rebellious; similar findings have been found in Turkish teachers (Güncer & Oral, 1993). Similar to the studies that found that even people who like creativity may not understand exactly what it is, Lau and Li (1996) found that students who were the most popular were also the most likely to be rated as the most creative.

BEYOND LIKE OR DISLIKE

Beyond liking or disliking it, what are everyday people's implicit beliefs about creativity? Typically, these types of studies have examined what traits we associate with creativity. Some early work by Gough and colleagues (Gough, 1979; Gough & Heilbrun, 1965) used adjectives to measure personality, and this method was later applied to creativity. Welsh (1975) found two core beliefs within self-perceptions: "intellectence" (intellectual behavior and functioning) and "origence" (aesthetics and originality). Alas, these terms do not exactly roll off the tongue.

Sternberg's (1985) landmark study on layperson theories of creativity asked many different groups of people and outlined four dimensions: nonentrenchment, aesthetic taste/imagination, perspicacity, and inquisitiveness. Creativity was seen as distinct from intelligence, albeit with much overlap. Related descriptors included unconventionality, inquisitiveness, imagination, and freedom. There were domain differences within more professional groups; Sternberg also found that art professors believed that creativity entailed originality and taking risks, whereas professors in nonart areas (such as business, philosophy, and physics) emphasized traits such as problem solving and being insightful.

Lim and Plucker (2001) replicated Sternberg's work in a Korean population (it is interesting to note how many beliefs about creativity are universal, although obviously there are many studies that highlight cultural differences). Wickes and Ward (2006) looked at gifted adolescents and what they believed about both their own creativity and others' creativity using items from a creativity descriptor checklist. Student self-beliefs centered around four factors: risk taking, awkwardness, intellect, and impulsiveness. Those same students' beliefs about others resulted in four quite different factors: artistic

294

individualism, activity level, popularity, and questioning. Note that the gifted students used much more positive personality attributes when thinking of creativity in other people.

Another way of studying implicit theories is to specifically compare them to explicit theories. Sen and Sharma's (2011) examination of creativity beliefs in India tested beliefs about the Four P's and found that creativity was more likely to be described as a holistic essence of an individual (i.e., the person), and less likely to be focused on the product or process. A study of teachers in Serbia produced similar results (Pavlović, Maksić, & Bodroža, 2013).

A pair of studies tested people's perceptions of Kirton's (1976) adaptor–innovator distinction (see Chapter 2) and found that the innovative style was considered significantly more creative than the adaptor style (Puccio & Chimento, 2001; Ramos & Puccio, 2014). In an exploration of how laypeople distinguish levels of the Four-C Model, Kaufman and Beghetto (2013a) found that the basic ideas of not creative, mini-c, little-c, and Big-C are distinct concepts. However, it was more difficult for people to separate little-c and Pro-c contributions. Karwowski (2009) had earlier shown that laypeople could distinguish little-c and Big-C.

Other studies focus on artists. Both artists and nonartists held implicit beliefs that artists were imaginative and expressive, for example, but only artists considered them to be emotional (Runco & Bahleda, 1986). Romo and Alfonso (2003) studied Spanish painters and found that one of the implicit theories that the painters held about creativity involved the role of psychological disorders. This theory stated that isolation and personal conflicts were at the heart of art. Glück, Ernst, and Unger (2002) found that artists themselves can differ based on their format; "free" artists (such as painters and sculptors) embraced the idea of the "artistic personality" and believed strongly in the importance of originality, but "constrained" artists (such as designers and architects) focused more on the importance of functionality. Hass (2014) compared perceptions of a creative product across six domains (art, design, music, science, technology, and writing) and found that the products in the artistic domains (art, music, and writing) were rated higher on nonentrenchment and aesthetic taste than those products in the nonartistic domains.

Glăveanu (2014) asked people to rate 16 different professions on the amount of creativity required for success. Unsurprisingly, the four artistic professions (actor, musician, painter, and writer) received the highest scores. He also measured reaction time, and people were quickest to give their evaluations for these same professions. Yet when Glăveanu asked the same people to come up with questions to determine whether an unknown object was creative or not, their questions were more focused on whether the object was useful than whether it was original.

Hass and Burke (2015) studied the interaction of domain and perspective in implicit beliefs about creativity. They varied both the domain (music, art, and what they called gadgetry) and the perspective (first person, in which people imagined themselves creating something, or third person, in which people imagined an existing product), asking participants to rate descriptors and traits based on Sternberg (1985). Associated traits varied by domain; consistent with past work, creativity in art and music was rated higher than gadgetry on the dimensions of nonconforming, imaginative, and aesthetic. Yet perspective played an interactive and sometimes confusing role; first-person ratings were notably lower than third-person ratings for art and music on the aesthetic and imagination dimensions, but higher for gadgetry. Thus, the first-person ratings showed fewer domain-based differences on this dimension. I wonder if the average person may be better able to visualize making a gadget than music or art?

Baas, Koch, Nijstad, and De Dreu (2015) examined laypeople's beliefs about how their activities, thoughts, mood, and motivation influence their own creativity. Fascinatingly, most people are not only wrong (compared with what the research shows) about virtually everything connected to their creativity, but their beliefs are not even connected to their own experiences. As Baas et al. (2015) insightfully point out, there are real-world ramifications of this discrepancy. When I first started work at Educational Testing Service, there was a huge room filled with toys and fun things that they must have thought would stimulate creativity. Playing with wacky objects may seem to boost creativity, but without organization-level value and encouragement for new ideas, such a "creativity room" is a colossal waste of money. By the time I left 2 years later, it was long gone. The only remnant is that most of my early publicity pictures have me holding very bizarre and oversized objects. Parents and industries alike think the wrong things will help their children/workers be creative and throw money at expensive stopgaps instead of making subtle conceptual changes.

DRUG USE AND CREATIVITY: FACTS VERSUS PERCEPTIONS

I've discussed in great detail the stereotypes and implicit views of creativity as it relates to mental illness (compared with the actual muddled results). Related to this idea of perceiving creativity as a risky, potentially dark endeavor is its association with alcohol and recreational drug use. Do we feel the need to connect drug use and creativity because we like "punishing" people who are creative (and, by extension, more likely to be successful)? Plucker and Dana (1998a) argue that we want this relationship to exist for these types of reasons. Creativity becomes more mysterious, and therefore the burden some people may feel to be creative is removed. In adolescents, they also note, the creativity–drug connection may provide a convenient excuse for experimentation. Indeed, Novacek, Raskin, and Hogan (1991) studied adolescent explanations for using illicit drugs, and one of the five reasons was to enhance creativity (for those who need to know the other four reasons, they were belonging, coping, pleasure, and aggression).

What does the research say about creativity and drug use? Most studies have found little or no connection. Plucker and Dana (1998b) found that past histories of alcohol, marijuana, and tobacco usage were not correlated with creative achievements; familial drug and alcohol use also was not significantly associated with creative accomplishments (Plucker & Dana, 1998a) or creative personality attributes (Plucker, McNeely, & Morgan, 2009). Humphrey, McKay, Primi, and Kaufman (2015) did find that illegal drug use predicted self-reported creative behaviors even when openness to experience was controlled.

Bourassa and Vaugeois (2001) studied the effect of marijuana on creativity. They found that those who smoked marijuana before a divergent thinking task showed no beneficial effects if they were new users, and a negative effect if they were experienced users. They did find a placebo effect, however—people who thought they were taking marijuana were more creative than those who thought they were taking the placebo. Hicks, Pedersen, Friedman, and McCarthy (2011) examined this potential placebo effect by priming people to either think about alcohol or marijuana (as compared to control groups) and then take the Remote Associates Test. For both samples, participants who thought about marijuana or alcohol were then more creative. They also found this same effect with divergent thinking (but not with an analytic task).

A study of particularly potent cannabis showed that it impaired divergent thinking in regular users (Kowal et al., 2015). Conversely, though, a different study tested marijuana users when sober and when on the drug. People who were normally less creative did show an increase in verbal fluency when stoned (Schafer et al., 2012). The same study, incidentally, found higher levels of schizotypy and psychosis when participants were on the drug. Minor et al. (2014) studied divergent thinking, marijuana usage, and schizotypy, and although they found a significant correlation between marijuana use and higher divergent thinking (only in those without schizotypy), it was not particularly notable. A study of currently abstinent cannabis users, abstinent Ecstasy users, and controls showed that the cannabis users scored slightly higher on originality, and the Ecstasy users had very slightly higher self-reported creativity (Jones, Blagrove, & Parrott, 2009).

Fewer studies have been conducted on harder drug use, but both abstinent cocaine users (Colzato, Huizinga, & Hommel, 2009) and users of the stimulant Khat (Colzato, Ruiz, van den Wildenberg, & Hommel, 2011) showed signs of lower cognitive flexibility.

Norlander and Gustafson conducted a series of studies looking at alcohol consumption during various stages of the creative process, with half of the participants randomly assigned to drink alcohol and the other half serving as controls. First, they looked at three groups—alcohol, control, and a placebo group. Those given alcohol did poorer on creativity tasks (along with measures of persistence and deductive reasoning). They further studied alcohol consumption during the incubation stage of the creative process (see Chapter 2); the alcohol group showed higher originality on a scientific creativity task, but there were no other differences (Norlander & Gustafson, 1996). A later study found that the alcohol group scored higher on originality in a divergent thinking test, but lower on flexibility than the control group (Norlander & Gustafson, 1998). More recently, Jarosz, Colflesh, and Wiley (2012) found that intoxicated people (blood-alcohol content of .075) solved more items on the Remote Associates Tests (and did them faster) than their sober counterparts.

The actual link behind drug or alcohol use and creativity is inconsistent. For every study that shows any type of benefit, others show a negative impact or no results. Why does the drug–creativity connection persist? There is evidence that creators do use more drugs, regardless of whether it helps them. One study of writers, artists, musicians, and controls found that musicians used more cocaine and marijuana than the other groups, and artists used more caffeine. There were no differences for alcohol, narcotics, hallucinogens, and tranquilizers (Kerr, Shaffer, Chambers, & Hallowell, 1991). Could the reason for drug use be rooted in social expectancy? Lapp, Collins, and Izzo (1994) gave participants either tonic water or tonic water mixed with vodka, and then (randomly) told them that the drinks were either nonalcoholic or alcoholic. They found no pharmacological effects of alcohol on creativity—but they found a strong placebo effect, indicating that the social expectation of alcohol's effect on creativity is more important than the alcohol itself. Janiger and de Rios (1989), in a 7-year study of LSD and artistic creativity, found that artists believed that LSD had improved their perceptions and made them more creative, but little difference was detectable in their art.

Based on the available research, it seems that any connection between recreational drug and alcohol use and creativity (good or bad) is mostly in the mind. The actual creative work is likely not impacted. The supposed link between alcohol/drug use and creativity will likely continue, however, regardless of what the data say (much as in the mental illness–creativity debate). People who want an excuse to try recreational drugs will have to say, "I want to do this because it's fun," not for the noble purpose of creation.

SELF-ASSESSMENTS OF CREATIVITY

I have discussed at some length how laypeople view creativity as a general construct. But how do they see their own creativity? Is there a match between self-rated creativity and actual creativity? Certainly, in discussing creativity measurement (as in Chapter 4), the easiest thing in the world would be to use self-assessments. Could it work? Perhaps everyone would simply say, "Yes, I'm incredibly creative, oh naïve researcher"? But maybe they'd be accurate. Think of the time and money we could save!

Sometimes it's as easy as asking, "Rate your creativity on a scale from 1 to 10." Another format is to show a picture of a typical IQ bell curve and ask, "Using a scale with 100 being average, rate your own creativity." Other investigations have detailed surveys that walk people through the process of evaluating their own creativity, whether analyzing domains or types of action/thought.

So what's the scoop? Unsurprisingly, self-report measures tend to correlate highly with one another (e.g., Fleenor & Taylor, 1994; Kaufman & Baer, 2004; Reiter-Palmon, Robinson-Morral, Kaufman, & Santo, 2012). Unfortunately, this trend doesn't mean much; it would be weird if asking the same types of questions about the same topic in the same general manner did *not* correlate.

The big question is whether people are accurate about their own creativity. As with most topics, you can make a case both ways. Some studies show a connection between self-ratings and divergent thinking scores. Many of these studies come from the lab of Adrian Furnham and his colleagues (Batey, Chamorro-Premuzic, & Furnham, 2010; Furnham, 1999; Furnham, Batey, Anand, & Manfield, 2008; Furnham, Zhang, & Chamorro-Premuzic, 2006). Self-ratings of creativity often correspond to supervisor ratings (Ng & Feldman, 2012) and teacher ratings (Beghetto, Kaufman, & Baxter, 2011).

Another approach is to see if people can accurately identify their most creative ideas. Silvia (2008) gave participants a divergent thinking task and then asked them to pick which responses they thought were their most creative. Most people were able to choose the same responses that external raters identified as being more creative. More creative people tended to be better at this task (see also Grohman, Wodniecka, & Klusak, 2006).

Other studies have looked at rated creative performance across different domains and self-assessments (Denson & Buelin-Biesecker, 2015; Karwowski, 2011; Kaufman, Evans, & Baer, 2010; Priest, 2006). There tends to be much less of a connection (if any) when more real-life creativity tasks are used. Why might this be?

It does make sense at a gut level that people might not always be in touch with their own abilities or qualities. Shows like *American Idol* reveal just how many people think they are talented or creative or special—and are not. Indeed, the Kaufman et al. (2010) study, which found little relationship between creative self-beliefs and creative performance, suggested an *American Idol Effect*.

At a broader level, people often are simply unaware of how bad or incompetent or untalented they actually are (Dunning, Johnson, Ehrlinger, & Kruger, 2003; Kruger & Dunning, 1999), particularly in more general, subjective, or complex tasks (Zell & Krizan, 2014). If you spend some time on YouTube or blogs and see or read people's creative output, you already know that for every truly interesting or different video or post, there are dozens of other unfunny, painful, and navel-gazing material right alongside the good stuff.

There is a theoretical basis for self-reported creativity being a meaningful concept at higher levels of creativity and less important information at lower levels. Part of the reason is the idea of metacognition, the ability to monitor one's own learning, perform self-evaluation, and then make plans accordingly (Everson & Tobias, 1998; Flavell, 1979). Someone who was high in metacognitive abilities would know his or her limitations, be able to seek help, and estimate success with reasonably high accuracy. Metacognition is not necessarily directly connected to higher creativity (Hong, Peng, & Wu, 2010), although it can be a moderating factor between having creative ideas and seeing them to fruition (Puryear, 2015).

Kaufman and Beghetto (2013b) offer the specific concept of creative metacognition, which has two components. One is how accurate you are at assessing your own creativity; the other is whether you know when to be creative. Just as there are good times to juggle (a parade) and bad times to juggle (a funeral), so are there good and bad times to be creative. It is incredibly important to recognize when conformity is the better choice than creativity.

Yet what goes up usually goes down—and whereas high metacognition will lead to better creative performance, low metacognition may lead to lower creative performance. Indeed, Kruger and Dunning (1999) argue that people who do poorly in intellectual (and social) realms may suffer from a "double whammy"—they are not only underperformers, but they also have lower metacognitive abilities and therefore are unable to recognize their poor perfor-mance (you can mock them silently, if you would like).

A key point is that general self-ratings ("I'm creative!") are differ-ent from specific self-ratings about a product ("That's a really creative painting I did!"). The studies I've discussed have looked at general self-ratings. Pretz and McCollum (2014) looked at both general and specific ratings using divergent thinking, an essay task, and a caption. Global self-assessments of creativity were not particularly related to creative performance (consistent with some of the past findings discussed earlier), but specific task assessments did predict rated cre-ativity on that task. Kaufman, Beghetto, and Watson (2015) studied elementary schoolchildren across three domains (writing, art, and sci-ence). They used specific ratings that aligned with the mini-c/little-c distinction—in other words, they asked both whether the product was personally creative and if someone else would consider the product to be creative. Their mini-c art ratings predicted expert ratings of their art, and their mini-c and little-c writing ratings predicted the expert rat-ings of their creative writing (the results weren't so good for science).

Creative metacognition can intersect with personality and the ability to give accurate ratings of other people's creativity. Birney, Beckmann, and Seah (2015) had people rate their own work and other people's work. Structured conditions (which gave more specific criteria, akin to D. H. Cropley & Kaufman, 2012) generally produced more accurate ratings. Under unstructured conditions, people who evaluated their own work first were less accurate when subsequently rating other work (i.e., corresponding to a different group's ratings). People high on conscientiousness were less severely impacted by the lack of structure; those who were more open to experience were more accurate at rating other people's work—but not necessarily their own.

A final point to ponder is the relationship between self-efficacy ("I think I can, I think I can") and creativity. Higher self-efficacy is associated with higher creativity (Bandura, 1997; Karwowski, 2011; Prabhu, Sutton, & Sauser, 2008). Tierney and Farmer (2002) proposed the concept of creative self-efficacy (CSE) as representing a person's beliefs about how creative he or she can be. These beliefs are often rooted in a situational context (Jaussi, Randel, & Dionne, 2007), so you might have high cre-ative self-efficacy for one context but not another. In the classroom, teacher support predicted student creative self-efficacy (Beghetto, 2006).

A broader view of creative self-efficacy also includes creative personal identity, which reflects how much someone values creativity (e.g., Randel & Jaussi, 2003). In other words, believing that you are creative may be important as a factor by itself, regardless of whether you actually are creative.

Creative self-beliefs and self-assessments are usually not sufficient to use as the sole measure of creativity. However, as more studies are done on this topic, there is strong support for the idea that creative self-beliefs may better predict creative performance or creative achievement than personality (Karwowski & Lebuda, in press).

LOOKING AHEAD

I've talked about how people perceive creativity, such as whether it is a good or a bad thing. And throughout the book I've gone into tremendous (some might say obsessive) detail about how we define, measure, theorize, and categorize creativity. But—what's the truth? Cutting to the WGASA question (i.e., who cares), should we care about creativity? Is it good to be creative?

REFERENCES

Adarves-Yorno, I., Postmes, T., & Haslam, S. A. (2006). Social identity and the recognition of creativity in groups. *British Journal of Social Psychology, 45,* 479–497.

Aljughaiman, A., & Mowrer-Reynolds, E. (2005). Teachers' conceptions of creativity and creative students. *Journal of Creative Behavior, 39,* 17–34.

Baas, M., Koch, S., Nijstad, B. A., & De Dreu, C. W. (2015). Conceiving creativity: The nature and consequences of laypeople's beliefs about the realization of creativity. *Psychology of Aesthetics, Creativity, and the Arts, 9,* 340–354.

Bachtold, L. M. (1974). The creative personality and the ideal pupil revisited. *Journal of Creative Behavior, 8,* 47–54.

Bandura, A. (1997). *Self-efficacy: The exercise of control.* New York, NY: Macmillan.

Batey, M., Chamorro-Premuzic, T., & Furnham, A. (2010). Individual differences in ideational behavior: Can the Big Five and psychometric intelligence predict creativity scores? *Creativity Research Journal, 22,* 90–97.

Beghetto, R. A. (2006). Creative self-efficacy: Correlates in middle and secondary students. *Creativity Research Journal, 18,* 447–457.

Beghetto, R. A., Kaufman, J. C., & Baxter, J. (2011). Answering the unexpected questions: Exploring the relationship between students' creative self-efficacy and teacher ratings of creativity. *Psychology of Aesthetics, Creativity, and the Arts, 5,* 342–349.

Birney, D. P., Beckmann, J. F., & Seah, Y. Z. (2015). More than the eye of the beholder: The interplay of person, task, and situation factors in evaluative judgements of creativity. *Learning and Individual Differences.* Advance online publication. doi:10.1016/j.lindif.2015.07.007

Bourassa, M., & Vaugeois, P. (2001). Effects of marijuana use on divergent thinking. *Creativity Research Journal, 13,* 411–416.

Brandau, H., Daghofer, F., Hollerer, L., Kaschnitz, W., Kellner, K., Kitchmair, G., . . . Schlagbauer, A. (2007). The relationship between creativity, teacher ratings on behavior, age, and gender in pupils from seven to ten years. *Journal of Creative Behavior, 41,* 91–113.

Chan, D. W., & Chan, L. K. (1999). Implicit theories of creativity: Teachers' perception of student characteristics in Hong Kong. *Creativity Research Journal, 12,* 185–195.

Colzato, L. S., Huizinga, M., & Hommel, B. (2009). Recreational cocaine polydrug use impairs cognitive flexibility but not working memory. *Psychopharmacology, 207,* 225–234.

Colzato, L. S., Ruiz, M. J., van den Wildenberg, W. P., & Hommel, B. (2011). Khat use is associated with impaired working memory and cognitive flexibility. *PloS One, 6,* e20602.

Cropley, A. J. (1992). *More ways than one: Fostering creativity.* Westport, CT: Ablex Publishing.

Cropley, D. H., & Kaufman, J. C. (2012). Measuring functional creativity: Empirical validation of the Creative Solution Diagnosis Scale (CSDS). *Journal of Creative Behavior, 46,* 119–137.

Denson, C., & Buelin-Biesecker, J. (2015, June). *Investigating the relationship between students' creative self-efficacy and their creative outcomes.* Paper presented at American Society for Engineering Education, Seattle, WA.

de Souza Fleith, D. (2000). Teacher and student perceptions of creativity in the classroom environment. *Roeper Review, 22,* 148–153.

Dunning, D., Johnson, K., Ehrlinger, J., & Kruger, J. (2003). Why people fail to recognize their own incompetence. *Current Directions in Psychological Science, 12,* 83–86.

Eason, R., Giannangelo, D. M., & Franceschini, L. A. (2009). A look at creativity in public and private schools. *Thinking Skills and Creativity, 4,* 130–137.

Eidelman, S., & Crandall, C. S. (2012). Bias in favor of the status quo. *Social and Personality Psychology Compass, 6*, 270–281.

Eidelman, S., Crandall, C. S., & Pattershall, J. (2009). The existence bias. *Journal of Personality and Social Psychology, 97*, 765–775.

Everson, H. T., & Tobias, S. (1998). The ability to estimate knowledge and performance in college: A metacognitive analysis. *Instructional Science, 26*, 65–79.

Flavell, J. H. (1979). Metacognition and cognitive monitoring: A new area of cognitive developmental inquiry. *American Psychologist, 34*, 906–911.

Fleenor, J. W., & Taylor, S. (1994). Construct validity of three self-report measures of creativity. *Educational and Psychological Measurement, 54*, 464–470.

Furnham, A. (1999). Personality and creativity. *Perceptual and Motor Skills, 88*, 407–408.

Furnham, A., Batey, M., Anand, K., & Manfield, J. (2008). Personality, hypomania, intelligence and creativity. *Personality and Individual Differences, 44*, 1060–1069.

Furnham, A., Zhang, J., & Chamorro-Premuzic, T. (2006). The relationship between psychometric and self-estimated intelligence, creativity, personality, and academic achievement. *Cognition and Personality, 25*, 119–145.

Gaylor, B., Olson, M. (Writers), & Povenmire, D. (Director). (2009, February 16). Phineas and Ferb get busted! In J. S. Marsh & D. Povenmire, *Phineas and Ferb* [Television program]. Disney-ABC Domestic Television.

Gläveanu, V. P. (2014). *Distributed creativity: Thinking outside of the creative individual.* London, England: Springer.

Gluck, J., Ernst, R., & Unger, F. (2002). How creatives define creativity: Definitions reflect different types of creativity. *Creativity Research Journal, 14*, 55–67.

Gough, H. G. (1979). A creative personality scale for the adjective check list. *Journal of Personality and Social Psychology, 37*, 1398–1405.

Gough, H. G., & Heilbrun, A. B., Jr. (1965). *The adjective check list manual.* Palo Alto, CA: Consulting Psychologists Press.

Greenwald, A. G., & Banaji, M. R. (1995). Implicit social cognition: Attitudes, self-esteem, and stereotypes. *Psychological Review, 102*, 4–27.

Grohman, M., Wodniecka, Z., & Klusak, M. (2006). Divergent thinking and evaluation skills: Do they always go together? *Journal of Creative Behavior, 40*, 125–145.

Güncer, B., & Oral, G. (1993). Relationship between creativity and nonconformity to school discipline as perceived by teachers of Turkish elementary school children, by controlling for their grade and sex. *Journal of Instructional Psychology, 20*, 208–214.

Hass, R. W. (2014). Domain-specific exemplars affect implicit theories of creativity. *Psychology of Aesthetics, Creativity, and the Arts, 8*, 44–52.

305

Hass, R. W., & Burke, S. (2015). Implicit theories of creativity are differentially categorized by perspective and exemplar domain. *Thinking Skills and Creativity*. Advance online publication. doi:10.1016/j.tsc.2015.10.001

Heidenreich, S., & Spieth, P. (2013). Why innovations fail—The case of passive and active innovation resistance. *International Journal of Innovation Management, 17*, 1–42.

Hicks, J. A., Pedersen, S. L., Friedman, R. S., & McCarthy, D. M. (2011). Expecting innovation: Psychoactive drug primes and the generation of creative solutions. *Experimental and Clinical Psychopharmacology, 19*, 314–320.

Hong, E., Hartzell, S. A., & Greene, M. T. (2009). Fostering creativity in the classroom: Effects of teachers' epistemological beliefs, motivation, and goal orientation. *Journal of Creative Behavior, 43*, 192–208.

Hong, E., Peng, Y., & Wu, J. (2010, August). *Effects of explicit instruction, metacognition, and motivation on creative performance.* Paper presented at the American Psychological Association, San Diego, CA.

Humphrey, D. E., McKay, A. S., Primi, R., & Kaufman, J. C. (2015). Self-reported drug use and creativity: (Re)establishing layperson myths. *Imagination, Cognition, and Personality, 34*, 181–203.

Janiger, O., & de Rios, M. D. (1989). LSD and creativity. *Journal of Psychoactive Drugs, 21*, 129–134.

Jarosz, A. F., Colflesh, G. J. H., & Wiley, J. (2012). Uncorking the muse: Alcohol intoxication facilitates creative problem solving. *Consciousness & Cognition, 21*, 487–493.

Jaussi, K. S., Randel, A. E., & Dionne, S. D. (2007). I am, I think I can, and I do: The role of personal identity, self-efficacy, and cross-application of experiences in creativity at work. *Creativity Research Journal, 19*, 247–258.

Jones, K. A., Blagrove, M., &Parrott, A. C. (2009). Cannabis and Ecstasy/MDMA: Empirical measures of creativity in recreational users. *Journal of Psychoactive Drugs, 41*, 323–329.

Karwowski, M. (2009). I'm creative, but am I creative? Similarities and differences between self-evaluated small and big-C creativity in Poland. *International Journal of Creativity & Problem Solving, 19*, 7–26.

Karwowski, M. (2010). Are creative students really welcome in the classroom? Implicit theories of "good" and "creative" student' personality among Polish teachers. *Procedia Social and Behavioural Sciences Journal, 2*, 1233–1237.

Karwowski, M. (2011). It doesn't hurt to ask...But sometimes it hurts to believe. Predictors of Polish students' creative self-efficacy. *Psychology of Aesthetics, Creativity, and the Arts, 5*, 154–164.

Karwowski, M., & Lebuda, I. (in press). Creative self-concept: A surface characteristic of creative personality. In G. J. Feist, R. Reiter-Palmon, & J. C. Kaufman (Eds.), *Cambridge handbook of creativity and personality research.* New York, NY: Cambridge University Press.

Kaufman, J. C., & Baer, J. (2004). Sure, I'm creative—but not in mathematics!: Self-reported creativity in diverse domains. *Empirical Studies of the Arts, 22,* 143–155.

Kaufman, J. C., & Beghetto, R. A. (2013a). Do people recognize the Four Cs? Examining layperson conceptions of creativity. *Psychology of Aesthetics, Creativity, and the Arts, 7,* 229–236.

Kaufman, J. C., & Beghetto, R. A. (2013b). In praise of Clark Kent: Creative metacognition and the importance of teaching kids when (not) to be creative. *Roeper Review, 35,* 155–165.

Kaufman, J. C., Beghetto, R. A., & Watson, C. (2015). Creative metacognition and self-ratings of creative performance: A 4-C perspective. *Learning and Individual Differences.* Advance online publication. doi:10.1016/j.lindif.2015.05.004

Kaufman, J. C., Bromley, M. L., & Cole, J. C. (2006). Insane, poetic, lovable: Creativity and endorsement of the "mad genius" stereotype. *Imagination, Cognition, and Personality, 26,* 149–161.

Kaufman, J. C., Evans, M. L., & Baer, J. (2010). The American Idol Effect: Are students good judges of their creativity across domains? *Empirical Studies of the Arts, 28,* 3–17.

Kerr, B., Shaffer, J., Chambers, C., & Hallowell, K. (1991). Substance use of creatively talented adults. *Journal of Creative Behavior, 25,* 145–153.

Kim, K. H., & VanTassel-Baska, J. (2010). The relationship between creativity and behavior problems among underachievers. *Creativity Research Journal, 22,* 185–193.

Kim, S. H., Vincent, L. C., & Goncalo, J. A. (2013). Outside advantage: Can social rejection fuel creative thought? *Journal of Experimental Psychology: General, 142,* 605–611.

Kirton, M. (1976). Adaptors and innovators: A description and measure. *Journal of Applied Psychology, 61,* 622–629.

Kleijnen, M. H. P., Lee, N., & Wetzels, M. G. M. (2009). An exploration of consumer resistance to innovations and its antecedents. *Journal of Economic Psychology, 30,* 344–357.

Kowal, M., Hazekamp, A., Colzato, L., van Steenbergen, H., van der Wee, N. J., . . . Hommel, B. (2015). Cannabis and creativity: Highly potent cannabis impairs divergent thinking in regular cannabis users. *Psychopharmacology, 232,* 1123–1134.

Kruger, J., & Dunning, D. (1999). Unskilled and unaware of it: How difficulties in recognizing one's own incompetence lead to inflated self-assessments. *Journal of Personality and Social Psychology, 77,* 1121–1134.

Kwang, N. A., & Smith, I. (2004). The paradox of promoting creativity in the Asian classroom: An empirical investigation. *Genetic, Social and General Psychology Monographs, 130,* 307–330.

Lapp, W. M., Collins, R. L., & Izzo, C. V. (1994). On the enhancement of creativity by alcohol: Pharmacology or expectation? *American Journal of Psychology, 107*, 173–206.

Lau, S., & Li, W. L. (1996). Peer status and perceived creativity: Are popular children viewed by peers and teachers as creative? *Creativity Research Journal, 9*, 347–352.

Laukkanen, T., Sinkkonen, S., Kivijärvi, M., & Laukkanen, P. (2007). Innovation resistance among mature consumers. *Journal of Consumer Marketing, 24*, 419–427.

Lee, Y. H., & Qiu, C. (2009). When uncertainty brings pleasure: The role of prospect image ability and mental imagery. *Journal of Consumer Research, 36*, 624–633.

Licuanan, B. F., Dailey, L. R., & Mumford, M. D. (2007). Idea evaluation: Error in evaluating highly original ideas. *Journal of Creative Behavior, 41*, 1–27.

Lim, W., & Plucker, J. (2001). Creativity through a lens of social responsibility: Implicit theories of creativity with Korean samples. *Journal of Creative Behavior, 35*, 115–130.

Minor, K. S., Firmin, R. L., Bonfils, K. A., Chun, C. A., Buckner, J. D., & Cohen, A. S. (2014). Predicting creativity: The role of psychometric schizotypy and cannabis use in divergent thinking. *Psychiatry Research, 220*, 205–210.

Mueller, J. S., Goncalo, J. A., & Kamdar, D. (2011). Recognizing creative leadership: Can creative idea expression negatively relate to perceptions of leadership potential? *Journal of Experimental Social Psychology, 47*, 494–498.

Mueller, J. S., Melwani, S., & Goncalo, J. A. (2012). The bias against creativity: Why people desire but reject creative ideas. *Psychological Science, 23*, 13–17.

Myhill, D., & Wilson, A. (2013). Playing it safe: Teachers' views of creativity in poetry writing. *Thinking Skills and Creativity, 10*, 101–111.

Ng, T. W., & Feldman, D. C. (2012). Employee voice behavior: A meta-analytic test of the conservation of resources framework. *Journal of Organizational Behavior, 33*, 216–234.

Norlander, T., & Gustafson, R. (1996). Effects of alcohol on scientific thought during the incubation phase of the creative process. *Journal of Creative Behavior, 30*, 231–248.

Norlander, T., & Gustafson, R. (1998). Effects of alcohol on a divergent figural fluency test during the illumination phase of the creative process. *Creativity Research Journal, 11*, 265–274.

Novacek, J., Raskin, R., & Hogan, R. (1991). Why do adolescents use drugs? Age, sex, and user differences. *Journal of Youth and Adolescence, 20*, 475–492.

Pavlović, J., Maksić, S., & Bodroža, B. (2013). Implicit individualism in teachers' theories of creativity: Through the "Four P's" looking glass. *International Journal of Creativity & Problem Solving, 23*, 39–57.

Plucker, J. A., & Dana, R. Q. (1998a). Alcohol, tobacco, and marijuana use: Relationships to undergraduate students' creative achievement. *Journal of College Student Development, 39*, 472–481.

Plucker, J. A., & Dana, R. Q. (1998b). Creativity of undergraduates with and without family history of alcohol and other drug problems. *Addictive Behaviors, 23*, 711–714.

Plucker, J. A., McNeely, A., & Morgan, C. (2009). Controlled substance-related beliefs and use: Relationships to undergraduates' creative personality traits. *Journal of Creative Behavior, 43*, 94–101.

Prabhu, V., Sutton, C., & Sauser, W. (2008). Creativity and certain personality traits: Understanding the mediating effect of intrinsic motivation. *Creativity Research Journal, 20*, 53–66.

Pretz, J. E., & McCollum, V. A. (2014). Self-perceptions of creativity do not always reflect actual creative performance. *Psychology of Aesthetics, Creativity, and the Arts, 8*, 227–236.

Priest, T. (2006). Self-evaluation, creativity, and musical achievement. *Psychology of Music, 34*, 47–61.

Puccio, G. J., & Chimento, M. D. (2001). Implicit theories of creativity: Laypersons' perceptions of the creativity of adaptors and innovators. *Perceptual and Motor Skills, 92*, 675–681.

Puryear, J. S. (2015). Metacognition as a moderator of creative ideation and creative production. *Creativity Research Journal, 27*, 334–341.

Ram, S., & Sheth, J. N. (1989). Consumer resistance to innovations: The marketing problem and its solutions. *Journal of Consumer Marketing, 6*, 5–14.

Ramos, S. J., & Puccio, G. J. (2014). Cross-cultural studies of implicit theories of creativity: A comparative analysis between the United States and the main ethnic groups in Singapore. *Creativity Research Journal, 26*, 223–228.

Randel, A. E., & Jaussi, K. S. (2003). Functional background identity, diversity, and individual performance in cross-functional teams. *Academy of Management Journal, 46*, 763–774.

Reiter-Palmon, R., Robinson-Morral, E. J., Kaufman, J. C., & Santo, J. B. (2012). Evaluation of self-perceptions of creativity: Is it a useful criterion? *Creativity Research Journal, 24*, 107–114.

Romo, M., & Alfonso, V. (2003). Implicit theories of Spanish painters. *Creativity Research Journal, 15*, 409–415.

Runco, M. A., & Bahleda, M. D. (1986). Implicit theories of artistic, scientific and everyday creativity. *Journal of Creative Behavior, 20*, 93–98.

Runco, M. A., & Johnson, D. J. (2002). Parents' and teachers' implicit theories of children's creativity: A cross-cultural perspective. *Creativity Research Journal, 14*, 427–438.

Schacter, J., Thum, Y. M., & Zifkin, D. (2006). How much does creative teaching enhance elementary school students' achievement? *Journal of Creative Behavior, 40,* 47–72.

Schafer, G., Feilding, A., Morgan, C. J. A., Agathangelou, M., Freeman, T. P., & Curran, H. V. (2012). Investigating the interaction between schizotypy, divergent thinking and cannabis use. *Consciousness and Cognition, 21,* 292–298.

Schlesinger, J. (2002). Issues in creativity and madness, part two: Eternal flames. *Ethical Human Sciences & Services, 4,* 139–142.

Sen, R. S., & Sharma, N. (2011). Through multiple lenses: Implicit theories of creativity among Indian children and adults. *Journal of Creative Behavior, 45,* 273–302.

Seo, H., Lee, E., & Kim, K. (2005). Korean science teachers' understanding of creativity in gifted education. *Journal of Advanced Academics, 16,* 98–105.

Silvia, P. J. (2008). Discernment and creativity: How well can people identify their most creative ideas? *Psychology of Aesthetics, Creativity, and the Arts, 2,* 139–146.

Sternberg, R. J. (1985). Implicit theories of intelligence, creativity, and wisdom. *Journal of Personality and Social Psychology, 49,* 607–627.

Tan, A. G. (2003). Student teachers' perceptions of teacher behaviors for fostering creativity: A perspective on the academically low achievers. *Korean Journal of Thinking and Problem Solving, 13,* 59–71.

Tierney, P., & Farmer, S. M. (2002). Creative self-efficacy: Its potential antecedents and relationship to creative performance. *Academy of Management Journal, 45,* 1137–1148.

Torrance, E. P. (1963). *Education and the creative potential.* Minneapolis, MN: University of Minnesota Press.

Van Tilburg, W. A. P., & Igou, E. R. (2014). From Van Gogh to Lady Gaga: Artist eccentricity increases perceived artistic skill and art appreciation. *European Journal of Social Psychology, 44,* 93–103.

Welsh, G. S. (1975). *Creativity and intelligence: A personality approach.* Chapel Hill, NC: University of North Carolina Press.

Westby, E. L., & Dawson, V. L. (1995). Creativity: Asset or burden in the classroom? *Creativity Research Journal, 8,* 1–10.

Wickes, K. N. S., & Ward, T. B. (2006). Measuring gifted adolescents' implicit theories of creativity. *Roeper Review, 28,* 131–139.

Wilson, T. D., Centerbar, D. B., Kermer, D. A., & Gilbert, D. T. (2005). The pleasures of uncertainty: Prolonging positive moods in ways people do not anticipate. *Journal of Personality and Social Psychology, 88,* 5–21.

Zajonc, R. B. (2001). Mere exposure: A gateway to the subliminal. *Current Directions in Psychological Science, 10,* 224–228.

Zell, E., & Krizan, Z. (2014). Do people have insight into their abilities? A metasynthesis. *Perspectives on Psychological Science, 9,* 111–125.

12

Is Creativity A Good Thing or A Bad Thing?

t's easy—and it may be part of our painfully optimistic human nature—to assume that abilities will be used for good. Think of the construct of emotional intelligence (Mayer & Salovey, 1997), which I discussed in Chapter 8. Is Dr. Hannibal Lecter from *The Silence of the Lambs* emotionally intelligent? It is hard to answer no when you examine the definition of emotional intelligence, which entails four abilities: (1) perceiving, appraising, and expressing emotions; (2) accessing and producing feelings in aid of cognition; (3) comprehending information on affect and using emotional knowledge; and (4) regulating emotions for growth and contentment (Mayer, Salovey, & Caruso, 2000). Hannibal Lecter has all four; he is terrific at understanding other people's feelings (and exploiting this knowledge), he uses his own feelings to help him think (such as his ability to concentrate and listen to music to prepare for killing the two guards), he understands quite a bit about emotion and affect (as is clear from his "reading" of

311

Clarice), and he can certainly regulate his emotions toward outcomes that are useful to him (such as escaping from jail).

Is Hannibal Lecter creative? Was Adolf Hitler creative? How about Ted Bundy, Voldemort, Charles Manson, Vito Corleone, Jesse James, Lizzie Borden, or that guy who used to pick on you in the sixth grade? Creativity is often seen as having an inherent moral component to it (e.g., Gardner, 1993, and many Eastern approaches, such as Niu, 2012). If morality and ethics are part of what it means to be creative, then these people cannot be creative. If to be a creative person is to be a good person, then it's hard to argue that Josef Stalin or John Wilkes Booth were particularly creative. Indeed, Sternberg (2010) discussed how both Stalin and Hitler still have followers today, showing that their ideas have "lived on" and stood the test of time—one hallmark for determining if someone is "Big C." It is the lack of morality needed for lasting creativity that has led Sternberg (2003, 2010) to argue for the equal importance of wisdom. Indeed, Kampylis and Valtanen (2010) consider there to be three main factors of creativity: the creator's intentions, creator-specific effects, and societal-level consequences. They see creativity as a benevolent, ethical act.

Yet doesn't the possible dark side of creativity make you a little curious to hear more?

MALEVOLENT CREATIVITY

Creativity's potential for bad deeds has been an idea floating around since Aristotle (Becker, 2014). My friend Vlad Glăveanu notes that it may go back even further; consider the story of Prometheus, whose creative works were so risky and boundary-breaking (such as stealing fire and giving it to man) that he was chained to a rock, forever to have his liver eaten by a big eagle. Today, looking back, he seems heroic—but Zeus certainly would have disagreed.

Throughout history, creators have used their skills in ways that have led to tremendous negative impact. One obvious example is how Robert Oppenheimer and other scientists involved with the Manhattan Project channeled their creative energies into building a bomb that killed hundreds of thousands and loomed as a possible apocalyptic end of days (Hecht, 2015). Before we dive in too far, there is an important nuance between whether a creative act is intended to be bad or if bad things end up happening. Clark and James (1999) describe "negative creativity" as something that ends with a bad outcome even without a bad intention. A worker might think of creative ways to steal from a company without wanting the company to go out of business. The actual goal might simply be selfish ("I want that stapler!"), without thinking of the overarching context.

In contrast, malevolent creativity is defined as creativity that is deliberately planned to damage others (Cropley, Kaufman & Cropley, 2008; Cropley, Cropley, Kaufman, & Runco, 2010). If negative creativity is someone taking office supplies without wanting to hurt the company, then malevolent creativity is someone stealing essential company secrets to sell to its competitors with the specific desire to do harm. Malevolent creativity can be seen in terrorism (Gill, Horgan, Hunter, & Cushenbery, 2013; Gill, Horgan, & Lovelace, 2011) and criminal behavior (Cropley & Cropley, 2013b).

The typical study on malevolent creativity looks at various negative attributes associated with people who are creative. And there are quite a few. Creative folks are more likely to manipulate test results (Gino & Ariely, 2012), tell more types of creative lies (Walczyk, Runco, Tripp, & Smith, 2008), be deceptive during conflict negotiation (De Dreu & Nijstad, 2008), and show less integrity (Beaussart, Andrews, & Kaufman, 2013). Other work has looked at how people can think of ways to be creative in malevolent ways. Such people are more likely to be physically aggressive (S. Lee & Dow, 2011) and have lower emotional intelligence (Harris, Reiter-Palmon, & Kaufman, 2013). It is important to emphasize that there is not necessarily any causality implied; indeed, one study found that a person's creativity did not predict the person's ethical behavior (in any way) at a later point in time (Niepel, Mustafić, Greiff, & Roberts, 2015).

Another approach to studying the underbelly of creativity is to see how negative contextual or individual variables might enhance creativity. For example, when people are primed to be distrustful, creative cognitive ability increased if the person was being creative in private (Mayer & Mussweiler, 2011). Riley and Gabora (2012) found that threatening stimuli provoked more creative responses than did nonthreatening stimuli. They argue that such threats can invoke disequilibrium, and creativity can help reduce such cognitive disso-nance (e.g., Akinola & Mendes, 2008). Mai, Ellis, and Welsh (2015) point out that creative people may be more likely to make unethical justifications, thus leading to poor ethical behavior. Further, Vincent and Kouchaki (2015) found that workers who felt that their level of creativity was unusually high compared to that of others in the or-ganization were more likely to feel entitled and behave unethically.

One problem with studying malevolent creativity is that it's nearly impossible to study at the Pro-c or Big-C level. Consider evil to be a domain, just like creative writing. It's hard to study profes-sional writers, but it's possible. Might professional criminals who are notably creative be the exact ones who are never caught (and thus couldn't be forced to take our tests)? If we wanted to study the creative process in malevolence, wouldn't this quest make us observe people doing bad things? Even the most liberal institutional review board might object.

As a result, most research has focused on mini-c or little-c levels with hypothetical situations. Yet the original conception of malevo-lent creativity was more rooted in Pro-c or Big-C (Cropley et al., 2008). One of the key examples is the terrorist events of September 11, 2001. Cropley, Kaufman, White, and Chiera (2014) use hypothetical scenar-ios of little-c and Pro-c malevolent creativity to see how people rated both the creativity and malevolence of different actions (for example, a student who needed more time on an essay might ask the professor or call in a bomb threat). In general, actions that were morally am-biguous or complex were considered to be more creative.

ANNOYANCES AND OBNOXIA

Not all bad attributes of creativity are necessarily evil. They can just be inconvenient, costly, or annoying. I've already discussed in the last chapter how there might be some basis for the creativity bias in school; creative kids can be disruptive. The same basic tenet holds in the workplace as well. Creative people are not necessarily "company" people. For one, they are more likely to show poor attention to de-tail and lower performance quality (Miron, Erez, & Naveh, 2004);

conformists demonstrated higher performance quality. Further, Madjar, Greenberg, and Chen (2011) found that more radically creative people (as rated by supervisors) were more personally focused on their careers—in other words, they cared more about their individual accomplishments. People who were rated as more routine were more devoted to the company. Creative team members are more likely to increase task conflict and reduce how well the team follows standards (Miron-Spektor, Erez, & Naveh, 2011).

Remember from the discussion of the creative personality (Chapter 5) that some creative people, especially scientists, are more likely to be disagreeable. And, of course, even with many of the creativity–mental illness findings being disputed or controversial, there are still a number of studies that link creative behavior with subclinical illnesses (such as hypomania or schizotypy, as discussed in Chapter 8).

Creative people can be a hassle. Life is easier with conformity. I remember that the first time my wife and I went to New Orleans, we went to the Café Du Monde for the restaurant's famous beignets. There was a line around the block, and we were about to unhappily give up when a kind waitress met our eye. She told us to just sit down at the next table that emptied out. We pointed at the line, and she shrugged. "That line's for take-out. If you sit down at a table, we'll take your order and bring out whatever you want." My wife and I looked at each other for a moment—could this be true? Why were so many people waiting on line, then? Did they not know this trick? The waitress overheard and shrugged. "Some people just like waiting in line."

I can't put it any simpler than our waitress did. Some people like order. Some people like to know that everything will come in its turn; if that means waiting an hour for delicious beignets instead of taking a risk, so be it. In every university, there are two types of people who join committees. There are the people who want to get stuff done and cut through all the paperwork, and there are the people who rejoice in the minutiae of triplicate forms and cringe at the threat of an external audit. Both types have their place and purpose, even though each type likely dislikes the other. Without some desire for rules or protocol or conformity, we swim in chaos. Without some risk taking and originality, we sink in our own muck.

Creativity is a tool that can be used for good or bad purposes. The world would not necessarily be a better place if everyone was more creative—a more *interesting* place, perhaps, but not a better one. Creative people have their flaws and foibles. They may not always be the gung-ho team players who get their paperwork handed in on time. But, unsurprisingly, I see creativity as a good thing. I'd like to end the chapter by highlighting all of the good that creativity can do.

THE HEALING POWER OF CREATIVITY

I've discussed in some depth the literature surrounding mental illness and creativity in Chapter 8. The flip side of the coin is that there are arrays of studies that show the healing powers of expressive forms of creativity. The arts can be used as a coping mechanism or as a distraction against physical pain (Zausner, 2007). Indeed, if there is a genuine connection between creative genius and mental illness, it could easily be the creativity in their lives that kept some of the geniuses afloat and as healthy as possible.

The research on expressive writing and mental and physical health, often measured by doctor visits, self-assessments, risk taking, and life success, has been propelled by the work of James Pennebaker and colleagues (Pennebaker, 1997; Pennebaker & Beall, 1986; Pennebaker, Mayne, & Francis, 1997). Expressive writing, in which people are randomly assigned to write for 15 to 20 minutes a day on an emotional topic, can help people cope more effectively with traumas (Frisina, Borod, & Lepore, 2004). Studies have found positive (if sometimes small) benefits when expressive writing is done over both short and long intervals of time (Pennebaker, 1997; Travagin, Margola, & Revenson, 2015).

One of the central components to expressive writing having a positive effect is the need for a narrative (Pennebaker & Seagal, 1999). When people retell stories of traumatic events, they organize them in their minds. This act enables them to manage and store away the event, thereby reducing excessive rumination (which is often linked to depression; Nolen-Hoeksema, Larson, & Grayson, 1999). The narrative acts as part of the healing process. Writing in a more fragmented fashion helps people much less (Smyth, True, & Souto, 2001).

Another finding is that writers who shift their use of the first-person singular (e.g., *I, me, my*) to third person (e.g., *he, she, they*) are better off than those who continue to use the first-person singular (Stirman & Pennebaker, 2001). This suggests that a shift in perspective is an important element, and is consistent with the idea of storytelling. This concept is similar to the belief that one of the critical ingredients in psychotherapy is to tell a coherent story or narrative about important life events that one can embrace and accept as one's own (Mahoney, 1995). Story-making has long been thought to contribute to good mental health, not only in times of trauma, but also throughout the life span (McAdams, 1999; Sexton & Pennebaker, 2004).

J. C. Kaufman and Sexton (2006) argue that it is the healing power of the narrative that may be responsible for the Sylvia Plath Effect. The formation of a story has been identified as a key component in the health effects of writing. Yet poems do not carry the same narrative structure that stories do. Poems are less likely than other types of writing to tell a story with a beginning, middle, and end. Many poems do not have narratives; most stories and plays do. It is not evident that writing poetry would have the same benefits as other kinds of writing. Therefore, they argue, it is *not* that writing poetry may cause mental illness, but rather that poets may not reap the same mental health benefits from writing that other writers experience. Stephenson and Rosen (2015) contrasted writing a haiku (either about nature, a negative life event, or a neutral topic) versus writing a narrative (on a neutral topic) multiple times. Their narrative group showed decreases in anxiety and depression (consistent with the expressive writing work). The people who wrote haikus about nature or a negative life event showed increased creativity (but with no difference in depression or anxiety).

It is not only writing that can help. There has been extensive work on art therapy, although it has been less empirically validated than the benefits of expressive writing (Forgeard Mecklenburg, Lacasse, & Jayawickreme, 2014). De Petrillo and Winner (2005) tested whether art could help catharsis. They had participants look at images and videos of tragedy (such as 9/11 and the Holocaust), and then asked them to either draw a picture or simply copy shapes. The people who were actually producing visual art then showed an improved mood—regardless of whether their art was happy or sad. A second experiment used a word puzzle as a control condition and found the same results. Drake, Coleman, and Winner (2011) also induced a sad mood, and then had participants either write or draw. The people assigned to draw showed more improved moods than the people who wrote. Consistent with other studies (Pizarro, 2004), this finding suggests that the short-term benefits of expressive writing may be less notable than the long-term benefits.

The reason behind the art-making matters, however. Dalebroux, Goldstein, and Winner (2008) distinguished between whether people drew to vent or to distract themselves with a positive emotion. They found that distraction led to better mood than venting (and distraction through art worked better than being distracted by a symbol search task). Similarly, Drake et al. (2011) asked their participants if they were using the task (regardless of whether it was writing or drawing) to vent or to distract themselves. Again, the ones who were trying to distract themselves showed improved mood. Drake and Winner (2012) found that drawing-as-distraction was better for mood than both drawing-as-venting and simply sitting and letting time pass. Finally, Drake and Winner (2013) demonstrated this same pattern with children; drawing improved mood when it was being used to distract, but not when used to vent (or when they simply copied a drawing). Do note that these studies looked only at short-term mood; you can't use this finding as a reason to sit and watch *Airplane!* over and over again instead of talking about your feelings.

Creativity can heal more than the unpleasantness of a psychologist showing you sad pictures. It can help build resiliency to major trauma. Indeed, being able to grow from trauma is associated with creativity (Forgeard, 2013). Among survivors of Hurricane Katrina, people who demonstrated creative thinking were more likely to be resilient and show higher positive well-being than those who did not (Metzl, 2009). Not all people who overcome trauma will be able to utilize their creativity to cope, of course. In a study of survivors of the Rwandan massacre, approximately 25% believed they had become more creative; the majority, however, believed there had been no change (Forgeard et al., 2014).

The arts in general can have a beneficial effect for all people. Some propose that art is viewed as a puzzle to be interpreted and solved (Leder, Belke, Oeberst, & Augustin, 2004) and others that the key is our aesthetic appreciation of the artwork (Locher, Overbeeke, &

318

Wensveen, 2010). Reading fiction, particularly literary fiction, can also bring many positive benefits (Djikic & Oatley, 2014; Mar, Oatley, Djikic, & Mullin, 2011). For example, studies have shown that reading fiction (as opposed to nonfiction) can increase cognitive empathy (Djikic, Oatley, & Moldoveanu, 2013b) and open-mindedness (Djikic, Oatley, & Moldoveanu, 2013a). Further, reading fiction can lead to a better affective and cognitive theory of mind (Kidd & Castano, 2013); in other words, people who read have a deeper understanding of other people's emotions and beliefs. Black and Barnes (2015) extended this work to also include watching high-quality television, such as *The West Wing* or *Lost* (alas, my countless hours spent on *The Simpsons* have been to no avail).

Acting has its own benefits. Goldstein and Winner (2012) studied elementary and high school students who were trained in either acting or the visual arts. Both age groups who took acting showed increased empathy as compared with the visual arts group, and the older kids also showed increased theory of mind. Another study found that students taking acting classes were better able to express their emotions than were students who took other types of art classes (Goldstein, Tamir, & Winner, 2013).

The arts can also help you hold on to your brains; Roberts et al. (2015) examined older adults (85 years and up) and found that engaging in the arts (or crafts) held off cognitive impairment. In another study of adults with dementia, active singing—show tunes, no less, much to my joy—led to improved cognition (Maguire, Wanschura, Battaglia, Howell, & Flinn, 2015).

There are underlying neuropsychological explanations for this phenomenon. Speer, Reynolds, Swallow, and Zacks (2009) conducted a neuroimaging study that observed people while they were reading. When their participants read about a character performing an activity, the region of the brain associated with that specific activity would often light up. We understand the stories we read by simulating the action in our minds, which can thus increase our identification with fictional characters and thereby increase our empathy for them.

Curiously, one study examined the interaction of genre and found that increased interpersonal sensitivity was strongest in those who read romances or suspense thrillers (Fong, Mullin, & Mar, 2013). I admit I would've predicted otherwise, and am glad I can now feel morally superior as I devour my daily dose of Coben, Deaver, Lippman, Lehane, Gerritsen, or other thriller writers.

Smith (2014a, 2014b) has analyzed how people perceive the world as they enter a museum, midway through their visit, and as they leave. What he has found across several investigations is that it is midway through touring a museum that people peak on how they relate to others—from the immediate people around them to the world in general. There is a slight decline as they leave, but the take-home point is that museums—and, likely, many other cultural institutions—actually make us better people.

MORE GENERAL BENEFITS

Even beyond the curative powers of creativity, it's a good talent to have. Creativity researchers are not always the best at coming up with studies specifically showing why it's an important construct to study (or possess), but there is nonetheless a solid stream of research and theory supporting creativity's place in the world. Florida (2002) called creativity the most important economic resource of the 21st century; there's a reason why business continues to invest in creativity and innovation. Even with our love of the status quo, creative products are still seen as more desirable (Horn & Salvendy, 2009). Having a general "pro-creativity" approach can often lead to a breakthrough in the marketplace (e.g., K. Lee, Rho, Kim, & Jun, 2007). It's not uncommon for companies to hire chief innovation officers (CIOs; Rosa, Qualls, & Fuentes, 2008). Business tends to simply assume that creativity/innovation is a good thing; with some exceptions (Staw, 1995), there are surprisingly few papers that question the basic conceit of whether creativity is necessarily a good investment for companies.

For the person operating at the Pro-c level, creativity leads to more promotions, higher salaries, and better career satisfaction (Seibert, Kraimer, & Crant, 2001). Creativity measured in college for engineering students predicted patent submissions and general creative work 15 years later (Clapham, Cowdery, King, & Montang, 2005). Entrepreneurs who are more creative also tend to reach higher peaks of success (Ames & Runco, 2005).

320

At the little-c or mini-c level, creativity helps our daily lives. Creative folks tend to be in better physical health (Stuckey & Nobel, 2010) and have a higher state of general well-being (Plucker, Beghetto, & Dow, 2004; Richards, 2007). In addition to its healing benefits, creativity can increase social harmony (King & Pope, 1999) and resiliency (Metzl, 2009), relieve burdens (Goncalo, Vincent, & Krause, 2015), and reduce personal stress (Nicol & Long, 1996) and exhaustion/depletion from work (Eschleman, Madsen, Alarcon, & Barelka, 2014).

Creativity is also sexy. People want their future mate to be creative (Geher & Kaufman, 2013). Both men and women find artistic creativity specifically attractive in a mate (S. B. Kaufman et al., 2015), and creative people report more sexual activity than do less creative folks (Beaussart, Kaufman, & Kaufman, 2012; Clegg, Nettle, & Miell, 2011). Seeing images of people we're attracted to may make us more creative (Griskevicius, Cialdini, & Kenrick, 2006). On a longer-term level, people with higher everyday creativity also enjoyed better romantic relationships (Campbell & Kaufman, 2015), although artistic creativity was a negative predictor (perhaps because everyday creativity is to be shared, whereas art is often done alone).

I would like to see more research not simply showing that creativity is associated with good things but also showing that creativity is *more* connected with positive outcomes than are other traits. There's a limited amount of hours in the day, workplace resources, school budget allocations; it's not enough to show that creativity is important. Is creativity *more* important than critical thinking or chess club or motivational training or brushing your teeth? In most cases, we don't know. Forgeard and Kaufman (2015) found that most papers treat creativity as the dependent variable (something to be predicted), not the independent variable (as a predictor of something). Less than 10% of papers discuss in detail why creativity matters in the first place. If we ever want to be taken seriously, I believe that this gap needs to be rectified.

That said, and as a softer point on which to end this chapter, I see creativity as its own source of joy. I'm not a clinical psychologist, but I've always loved the principle behind logotherapy (Frankl, 2006)—that the key to a happy life is to find your meaning. Frankl argued that there are three ways of finding meaning. One is by creating a work or doing an action, another by experiencing a thing or interacting with someone, and the third is how people face unavoid-able suffering. Most of us are privileged enough to not have to deal with continued anguish and thus have the luxury of finding our own meaning. It could be family and friends or work and altruistic deeds; creativity is another source of meaning. When we create, when we are engaged in Flow, when we share our creative work . . . these moments can be as good as the world gets.

LOOKING AHEAD

You've stuck with me pretty far, and I appreciate it. At this point, there's not much else to see or do here—just a brief epilogue.

REFERENCES

Akinola, M., & Mendes, W. B. (2008). The dark side of creativity: Biological vulnerability and negative emotions lead to greater artistic creativity. *Personality & Social Psychology Bulletin, 34,* 1677–1686.

Ames, M., & Runco, M. A. (2005). Predicting entrepreneurship from ideation and divergent thinking. *Creativity and Innovation Management, 14,* 311–315.

Beaussart, M. L., Andrews, C. J., & Kaufman, J. C. (2013). Creative liars: The relationship between creativity and integrity. *Thinking Skills and Creativity, 9,* 129–134.

Beaussart, M. L., Kaufman, S. B., & Kaufman, J. C. (2012). Creative activity, personality, mental illness, and short-term mating success. *Journal of Creative Behavior, 46,* 151–167.

Becker, G. (2014). A socio-historical overview of the creativity-pathology connection: From antiquity to contemporary times. In J. C. Kaufman (Ed.), *Creativity and mental illness* (pp. 3–24). New York, NY: Cambridge University Press.

Black, J., & Barnes, J. L. (2015). Fiction and social cognition: The effect of viewing award-winning television dramas on theory of mind. *Psychology of Aesthetics, Creativity, and the Arts, 9,* 423–429.

Campbell, K., & Kaufman, J. C. (2015). Do you pursue your heart or your art?: Creativity, personality, and love. *Journal of Family Issues, 36,* 1–24.

Clapham, M. M., Cowdery, E. M., King, K. E., & Montang, M. A. (2005). Predicting work activities with divergent thinking tests: A longitudinal study. *Journal of Creative Behavior, 39,* 149–166.

Clark, K., & James, K. (1999). Justice and positive and negative creativity. *Creativity Research Journal, 12,* 311–320.

Clegg, H., Nettle, D., & Miell, D. (2011). Status and mating success amongst visual artists. *Frontiers in Psychology, 2.*

Cropley, D. H., & Cropley, A. J. (2013). *Creativity and crime: A psychological analysis.* New York, NY: Cambridge University Press.

Cropley, D. H., Cropley, A. J., Kaufman, J. C., & Runco, M. A. (Eds.). (2010). *The dark side of creativity.* New York, NY: Cambridge University Press.

Cropley, D. H., Kaufman, J. C., & Cropley, A. J. (2008). Malevolent creativity: A functional model of creativity in terrorism and crime. *Creativity Research Journal, 20,* 105–115.

Cropley, D. H., Kaufman, J. C., White, A. E., & Chiera, B. A. (2014). Layperson perceptions of malevolent creativity: The good, the bad, and the ambiguous. *Psychology of Aesthetics, Creativity, and the Arts, 8,* 400–412.

Dalebroux, A., Goldstein, T. R., & Winner, E. (2008). Short-term mood repair through artmaking: Attention redeployment is more effective than venting. *Motivation and Emotion, 32,* 288–295.

De Dreu, C. K. W., & Nijstad, B. A. (2008). Mental set and creative thought in social conflict: Threat rigidity versus motivated focus. *Journal of Personality and Social Psychology, 95,* 648–661.

De Petrillo, L., & Winner, E. (2005). Does art improve mood? A test of a key assumption underlying art therapy. *Art Therapy: Journal of the American Art Therapy Association, 22,* 205–212.

Djikic, M., & Oatley, K. (2014). The art in fiction: From indirect communication to changes of the self. *Psychology of Aesthetics, Creativity, and the Arts, 8,* 498–505.

Djikic, M., Oatley, K., & Moldoveanu, M. C. (2013a). Opening the closed mind: The effect of exposure to literature on the need for closure. *Creativity Research Journal, 25,* 149–154.

Djikic, M., Oatley, K., & Moldoveanu, M. C. (2013b). Reading other minds: Effects of literature on empathy. *Scientific Study of Literature, 3,* 28–47.

Drake, J. E., & Winner, E. (2012). Confronting sadness through art-making: Distraction is more beneficial than venting. *Psychology of Aesthetics, Creativity, and the Arts, 6,* 251–266.

Drake, J. E., & Winner, E. (2013). How children use drawing to regulate their emotions. *Cognition and Emotion, 27,* 512–520.

Drake, J. E., Coleman, K., & Winner, E. (2011). Short-term mood repair through art: Effects of medium and strategy. *Art Therapy: Journal of the American Art Therapy Association, 28,* 26–30.

Eschleman, K. J., Madsen, J., Alarcon, G. M., & Barelka, A. (2014). Benefiting from creative activity: The positive relationships between creative activity, recovery experiences, and performance-related outcomes. *Journal of Occupational and Organizational Psychology, 87*, 579–598.

Florida, R. (2002). *The rise of the creative class and how it's transforming work, life, community and everyday life.* New York, NY: Basic Books.

Fong, K., Mullin, J. B., & Mar, R. A. (2013). What you read matters: The role of fiction genre in predicting interpersonal sensitivity. *Psychology of Aesthetics, Creativity, and the Arts, 7*, 370–376.

Forgeard, M. J. (2013). Perceiving benefits after adversity: The relationship between self-reported posttraumatic growth and creativity. *Psychology of Aesthetics, Creativity, and the Arts, 7*, 245–264.

Forgeard, M. J. C., & Kaufman, J. C. (2015). Who cares about imagination, creativity, and innovation, and why? A review. *Psychology of Aesthetics, Creativity, and the Arts.* Advance online publication. doi:10.1037/aca0000042

Forgeard M. J. C., Mecklenburg A. C., Lacasse J. J., & Jayawickreme E. (2014). Bringing the whole universe to order: Creativity, healing, and posttraumatic growth. In J. C. Kaufman (Ed.), *Creativity and mental illness* (pp. 321–342). New York, NY: Cambridge University Press.

Frankl, V. E. (2006). *Man's search for meaning.* Boston, MA: Beacon Press.

Frisina, P. G., Borod, J. C., & Lepore, S. J. (2004). A meta-analysis of the effects of written emotional disclosure on the health outcomes of clinical populations. *Journal of Nervous and Mental Disease, 192*, 629–634.

Gardner, H. (1993). *Creating minds.* New York, NY: Basic Books.

Geher, G., & Kaufman, S. B. (2013). *Mating intelligence unleashed.* New York, NY: Oxford University Press.

Gill, P., Horgan, J., Hunter, S. T., & Cushenbery, L. D. (2013). Malevolent creativity in terrorist organizations. *Journal of Creative Behavior, 47*, 125–151.

Gill, P., Horgan, J., & Lovelace, J. (2011). Improvised explosive device: The problem of definition. *Studies in Conflict & Terrorism, 34*, 732–748.

Gino, F., & Ariely, D. (2012). The dark side of creativity: Original thinkers can be more dishonest. *Journal of Personality and Social Psychology, 102*, 445–459.

Goldstein, T. R., Tamir, M., & Winner, E. (2013). Expressive suppression and acting classes. *Psychology of Aesthetics, Creativity, and the Arts, 7*, 191–196.

Goldstein, T. R., & Winner, E. (2012). Enhancing empathy and theory of mind. *Journal of Cognition and Development, 13*, 19–37.

Goncalo, J. A., Vincent, L. C., & Krause, V. (2015). The liberating consequences of creative work: How a creative outlet lifts the physical burden of secrecy. *Journal of Experimental Social Psychology, 59*, 32–39.

Griskevicius, V., Cialdini, R. B., & Kenrick, D. T. (2006). Peacocks, Picasso, and parental investment: The effects of romantic motives on creativity. *Journal of Personality and Social Psychology, 91*, 63–76.

Harris, D. J., Reiter-Palmon, R., & Kaufman, J. C. (2013). The effect of emotional intelligence and task type on malevolent creativity. *Psychology of Aesthetics, Creativity, and the Arts, 7*, 237–244.

Hecht, D. K. (2015). *Storytelling and science: Rewriting Oppenheimer in the nuclear age*. Amherst, MA: University of Massachusetts Press.

Horn, D., & Salvendy, G. (2009). Measuring consumer perception of product creativity: Impact on satisfaction and purchasability. *Human Factors and Ergonomics in Manufacturing, 19*, 223–240.

Kampylis, P., & Valtanen, J. (2010). Redefining creativity—Analyzing and definitions, collocations, and consequences. *Journal of Creative Behavior, 4*, 191–214.

Kaufman, J. C., & Sexton, J. D. (2006). Why doesn't the writing cure help poets? *Review of General Psychology, 10*, 268–282.

Kaufman, S. B., Kozbelt, A., Silvia, P., Kaufman, J. C., Ramesh, S., & Feist, G. J. (2015). Who finds Bill Gates sexy? Creative mate preferences as a function of cognitive ability, personality, and creative achievement. *Journal of Creative Behavior.* Advance online publication. doi:10.1002/jocb.78

Kidd, D. C., & Castano, E. (2013). Reading literary fiction improves theory of mind. *Science, 342*, 377–380.

King, B. J., & Pope, B. (1999). Creativity as a factor in psychological assessment and healthy psychological functioning. *Journal of Personality Assessment, 72*, 200–207.

Leder, H., Belke, B., Oeberst, A., & Augustin, D. (2004). A model of aesthetic appreciation and aesthetic judgements. *British Journal of Psychology, 95*, 489–508.

Lee, K., Rho, S., Kim, S., & Jun, G. J. (2007). Creativity-innovation cycle for organizational exploration and exploitation: Lessons from Neowiz—A Korean Internet company. *Long Range Planning: International Journal of Strategic Management, 40*, 505–523.

Lee, S., & Dow, G. T. (2011). Malevolent creativity: Does personality influence malicious divergent thinking? *Creativity Research Journal, 23*, 73–82.

Locher, P. J., Overbeeke, C. J., & Wensveen, S. A. G. (2010). Aesthetic interaction: A framework. *Design Issues, 26*, 70–79.

Madjar, N., Greenberg, E., & Chen, Z. (2011). Factors for radical creativity, incremental creativity, and routine, noncreative performance. *Journal of Applied Psychology, 96*, 730–743.

Maguire, L. E., Wanschura, P. B., Battaglia, M. M., Howell, S. N., & Flinn, J. M. (2015). Participation in active singing leads to cognitive improvements in individuals with dementia. *Journal of the American Geriatrics Society, 63,* 815–816.

Mahoney, M. J. (1995). *Cognitive and constructive psychotherapies: Theory, research, and practice.* New York, NY: Springer Publishing Company.

Mai, K. M., Ellis, A. P., & Welsh, D. T. (2015). The gray side of creativity: Exploring the role of activation in the link between creative personality and unethical behavior. *Journal of Experimental Social Psychology, 60,* 76–85.

Mar, R. A., Oatley, K., Djikic, M., & Mullin, J. (2011). Emotion and narrative fiction: Interactive influences before, during, and after reading. *Cognition and Emotion, 25,* 818–833.

Mayer, J., & Mussweiler, T. (2011). Suspicious spirits, flexible minds: When distrust enhances creativity. *Journal of Personality and Social Psychology, 101,* 1262–1277.

Mayer, J. D., & Salovey, P. (1997). What is emotional intelligence? In P. Salovey & D. J. Sluyter (Eds.), *Emotional development and emotional intelligence: Educational implications* (pp. 3–34). New York, NY: HarperCollins.

Mayer, J. D., Salovey, P., & Caruso, D. R. (2000). Models of emotional intelligence. In R. J. Sternberg (Ed.), *Handbook of intelligence* (pp. 396–420). New York, NY: Cambridge University Press

McAdams, D. P. (1999). Personal narratives and the life story. In L. A. Pervin, O. P. John, et al. (Eds.), *Handbook of personality: Theory and research* (Vol. 2, pp. 478–500). New York, NY: Guilford Press.

Metzl, E. S. (2009). The role of creative thinking in resilience after hurricane Katrina. *Psychology of Aesthetics, Creativity, and the Arts, 3,* 112–123.

Miron, E., Erez, M., & Naveh, E. (2004). Do personal characteristics and cultural values that promote innovation, quality, and efficiency compete or complement each other? *Journal of Organizational Behavior, 25,* 175–199.

Miron-Spektor, E., Erez, M., & Naveh, E. (2011). The effect of conformist and attentive-to-detail members on team innovation: Reconciling the innovation paradox. *Academy of Management Journal, 54,* 740–760.

Nicol, J. J., & Long, B. C. (1996). Creativity and perceived stress of female music therapists and hobbyists. *Creativity Research Journal, 9,* 1–10.

Niepel, C., Mustafić, M., Greiff, S., & Roberts, R. D. (2015). The dark side of creativity revisited: Is students' creativity associated with subsequent decreases in their ethical decision making? *Thinking Skills and Creativity.* Advance online publication. doi:10.1016/j.tsc.2015.04.005

Niu, W. (2012). Confucian ideology and creativity. *Journal of Creative Behavior, 46,* 274–284.

Nolen-Hoeksema, S., Larson, J., & Grayson, C. (1999). Explaining the gender difference in depressive symptoms. *Journal of Personality and Social Psychology, 77,* 1061–1072.

Pennebaker, J. W. (1997). Writing about emotional experiences as a therapeutic process. *Psychological Science, 8,* 162–166.

Pennebaker, J. W., & Beall, S. (1986). Confronting a traumatic event: Toward an understanding of inhibition and disease. *Journal of Abnormal Psychology, 95,* 274–281.

Pennebaker, J. W., Mayne, T. J., & Francis, M. E. (1997). Linguistic predictors of adaptive bereavement. *Journal of Personality and Social Psychology, 72,* 166–83.

Pennebaker, J. W., & Seagal, J. D. (1999). Forming a story: The health benefits of narrative. *Journal of Clinical Psychology, 55,* 1243–1254.

Pizarro, J. (2004). The efficacy of art and writing therapy: Increasing positive mental health outcomes and participant retention after exposure to traumatic experience. *Art Therapy, 21,* 5–12.

Plucker, J. A., Beghetto, R. A., & Dow, G. (2004). Why isn't creativity more important to educational psychologists? Potential, pitfalls, and future directions in creativity research. *Educational Psychologist, 39,* 83–96.

Richards, R. L. (2007). Everyday creativity: Our hidden potential. In R. Richards (Ed.), *Everyday creativity and new views of human nature* (pp. 25–54). Washington, DC: American Psychological Association.

Riley, S., & Gabora, L. (2012). Evidence that threatening situations enhance creativity. In *Proceedings of the 34th Annual Meeting of the Cognitive Science Society* (pp. 2234–2239). Houston TX: Cognitive Science Society.

Roberts, R. O., Cha, R. H., Mielke, M. M., Geda, Y. E., Boeve, B. F., Machulda, M. M., . . . Petersen, R. C. (2015). Risk and protective factors for cognitive impairment in persons aged 85 years and older. *Neurology, 84,* 1854–1861.

Rosa, J. A., Qualls, W. J., & Fuentes, C. (2008). Involving mind, body, and friends: Management that engenders creativity. *Journal of Business Research, 61,* 631–639.

Seibert, S. E., Kraimer, M. L., & Crant, J. M. (2001). What do proactive people do? A longitudinal model linking proactive personality and career success. *Personnel Psychology, 54,* 845–874.

Sexton, J. D., & Pennebaker, J. W. (2004). Non-expression of emotion and self among members of socially stigmatized groups: Implications for physical and mental health. In I. Nyklicek, L. Temoshok, & A. Vingerhoets (Eds.), *Emotional expression and health* (pp. 321–333). New York, NY: Brunner-Routledge.

Smith, J. K. (2014a). Art as mirror: Creativity and communication in aesthetics. *Psychology of Aesthetics, Creativity, and the Arts, 8,* 110–118.

Smith, J. K. (2014b). *The museum effect: How museums, libraries, and cultural institutions educate and civilize society.* Lanham, MD: Rowman & Littlefield.

Smyth, J., True, N., & Souto, J. (2001). Effects of writing about traumatic experiences: The necessity for narrative structure. *Journal of Social & Clinical Psychology, 20,* 161–172.

Speer, N. K., Reynolds, J. R., Swallow, K. M., & Zacks, J. M. (2009). Reading stories activates neural representations of visual and motor experiences. *Psychological Science, 20,* 989–999.

Staw, B. (1995). Why no one really wants creativity. In C. Ford & D. Giola (Eds.), *Creative action in organizations* (pp. 161–166). Thousand Oaks, CA: Sage.

Stephenson, K., & Rosen, D. H. (2015). Haiku and healing: An empirical study of poetry writing as therapeutic and creative intervention. *Empirical Studies of the Arts, 33,* 36–60.

Sternberg, R. J. (2003). *WICS: Wisdom, intelligence, and creativity, synthesized.* Cambridge, England: Cambridge University Press.

Sternberg, R. J. (2010). *College admissions for the 21st century.* Cambridge, MA: Harvard University Press.

Stirman, S. W., & Pennebaker, J. W. (2001). Word use in the poetry of suicidal and non-suicidal poets. *Psychosomatic Medicine, 63,* 517–523.

Stuckey, H. L., & Nobel, J. (2010). The connection between art, healing, and public health: A review of current literature. *American Journal of Public Health, 100,* 254–263.

Travagin, G., Margola, D., & Revenson, T. A. (2015). How effective are expressive writing interventions for adolescents? A meta-analytic review. *Clinical Psychology Review, 36,* 42–55.

Vincent, L., & Kouchaki, M. (2015). Creative, rare, entitled, and dishonest: How commonality of creativity in one's group decreases an individual's entitlement and dishonesty. *Academy of Management Journal.* Advance online publication. doi:10.5465/amj.2014.1109

Walczyk, J. J., Runco, M. A., Tripp, S. M., & Smith, C. E. (2008). The creativity of lying: Divergent thinking and ideational correlates of the resolution of social dilemmas. *Creativity Research Journal, 20,* 328–342.

Zausner, T. (2007). Artist and audience: Everyday creativity and visual art. In R. L. Richards (Ed.), *Everyday creativity and new views of human nature: Psychological, social, and spiritual perspectives* (pp. 75–89). Washington, DC: American Psychological Association.

Epilogue: The Future of Creativity

've been studying creativity my entire professional career, and I've had a blast. I love creativity. I love discovering new ways that people can be creative. Whether I'm discovering a new favorite film or book or getting hooked on a new television show or video game or being briefly entertained by a viral video or photo, I love seeing the depth of our creativity. I'm excited to see how technology makes it so much easier to share our work, not to mention how it makes it possible to be creative in new ways (such as Photoshop) or makes things that were once very expensive (such as a video camera) instantly accessible.

I think technology will continue to impact creativity research, as well. As it currently stands, it is now easy to collect data online (instead of with paper and pencil), with only mild differences between new and traditional methods (Hass, 2015). Such technology allows researchers to recruit participants from around the world. I think that the future of creativity testing likely lies with computers and the capacity to develop programs that can use textual analysis or similar developments to automatically score creative work in a way that corresponds to expert opinion (Kaufman, 2015). It is already possible to use video games as a stealth assessment for creativity (Kim & Shute, 2015; Shute & Ventura, 2013). Some researchers have developed mobile phone apps to help people self-assess creativity (Reisman, in press), and as discussed earlier, other ongoing work is refining the automatic scoring of divergent tests (Acar & Runco, 2014, 2015).

Meanwhile, computers themselves are becoming creative. IBM's Watson, not resting on its laurels after winning on *Jeopardy!*, can now suggest original and complex recipes (Sydell, 2014). Programmed on both the chemistry of the ingredients and on human taste preferences, Watson can write recipes that have never been cooked before and that should taste delicious when prepared. The computer can even take into account food allergies. Meanwhile, Google has arranged for its information neural network to enter a feedback loop when analyzing pictures. Such a process eventually results in a wide array of astounding pictures that seem to come from the computer's "brain" and are surreal and haunting (Hern, 2015). You can argue that Watson and the Google networks aren't themselves creative but are rather a testament to the brilliance of human programmers, but that only depends on how large of a role intent plays in your conception of creativity. Airplanes and cars can take us farther and faster than walking ever could, all rooted in human ingenuity. Computers may well someday make creative genius an everyday occurrence. The field of computational creativity is largely devoted to designing and programming computer systems that can produce creative work (Colton, Pease, Corneli, Cook, & Llano, 2014), and I believe that a better dialogue between our fields would be mutually beneficial. Dexter and Kozbelt (2013) are already taking a step in this direction, proposing that free and open-source software represents a way of answering key questions about creativity.

I hope that as the field progresses, communication between disciplines increases. After all these years, it still strikes me as weird when I find an article about creativity that doesn't cite anything from creativity journals. Many of the papers I've cited in this book from social or industrial psychology are guilty of this practice. It is so easy to end up rediscovering fire or building a square wheel if you don't learn what's already been done. But seeing such omissions makes me further appreciate the people who make the effort to understand multiple aspects of the topic they study. I love the researchers whom I've called "scholarly bilingual" (Kaufman, 2014)—people who speak the language of creativity but also speak the languages of other disciplines, such as engineering or neuroscience. Through their work and through more collaborations and through increased efforts to communicate our work to other fields and the outside world, almost anything is possible.

It's become a cliché to start a creativity book or article by quoting Guilford's (1950) presidential address. It may be just as much of a cliché to bring him in near the end, but note how he began: "I discuss the subject of creativity with considerable hesitation, for it represents an area in which psychologists generally...have feared to tread" (p. 444). Indeed, it has been and is still such an area. So bless the researcher who dares to study creativity—and by doing so risks the National Science Foundation (NSF) grant, or tenure, or getting a job in the first place. A big thanks to those who are working with me to answer those people who ask if creativity researchers are trying to dissect the golden goose, or if creativity has a place in education or psychology or business, or if it's even a science at all. I love you all, and I love what I do.

I think it's the best job in the world.

REFERENCES

Acar, S., & Runco, M. A. (2014). Assessing associative distance among ideas elicited by tests of divergent thinking. *Creativity Research Journal, 26,* 229–238.

Acar, S., & Runco, M. A. (2015). Thinking in multiple directions: Hyperspace categories in divergent thinking. *Psychology of Aesthetics, Creativity, and the Arts, 9,* 41–53.

Colton, S., Pease, A., Corneli, J., Cook, M., & Llano, T. (2014). Assessing progress in building autonomously creative systems. In *Proceedings of the Fifth International Conference on Computational Creativity.* Retrieved from http://computationalcreativity.net/iccc2014/wp-content/uploads/2014/06//8.4_Colton.pdf

Dexter, S., & Kozbelt, A. (2013). Free and open source software (FOSS) as a model domain for answering big questions about creativity. *Mind & Society, 12,* 113–123.

Guilford, J. P. (1950). Creativity. *American Psychologist, 5,* 444–454.

Hass, R. W. (2015). Feasibility of online divergent thinking assessment. *Computers in Human Behavior, 46,* 85–93.

Hern, A. (2015, June 18). Yes, androids do dream of electric sheep. *The Guardian.* Retrieved from http://www.theguardian.com/technology/2015/jun/18/google-image-recognition-neural-network-androids-dream-electric-sheep

Kaufman, J. C. (2014). Joining the conversation: A commentary on Glăveanu's critical reading. *Creativity: Theories—Research—Applications, 1,* 220–222.

Kaufman, J. C. (2015). Why creativity isn't in IQ tests, why it matters, and why it won't change anytime soon . . . probably. *Journal of Intelligence*, 3, 59–72.

Kim, Y. J., & Shute, V. J. (2015). Opportunities and challenges in assessing and supporting creativity in video games. In G. P. Green & J. C. Kaufman (Eds.), *Videogames and creativity* (pp. 101–123). San Diego, CA: Academic Press.

Reisman, F. K. (in press). Please teacher, don't kill my kid's creativity: Creativity embedded into K-12 teacher preparation and beyond. In R. A. Beghetto & J. C. Kaufman (Eds.), *Nurturing creativity in the classroom* (2nd ed.). New York, NY: Cambridge University Press.

Shute, V. J., & Ventura, M. (2013). *Measuring and supporting learning in games: Stealth assessment.* Cambridge, MA: MIT Press.

Sydell, L. (2014, October 27). I've got the ingredients. What should I cook? Ask IBM's Watson. *National Public Radio.* Retrieved from http://www.npr.org/sections/alltechconsidered/2014/10/27/359302540/ive-got-the-ingredients-what-should-i-cook-ask-ibms-watson

Index

ability tests, 151–152
abstract thinking, 155
academic achievement, 96,
    152–156, 238–239
academic majors, 52
accidental plagiarism, 154
ACT. *See* American College Testing
action, 16, 98
actor, 16
Adams, John, 259
adaptability, 238
adaptors versus innovators, 23,
    35, 295
ADHD. *See* attention deficit
    hyperactivity disorder
Advanced Placement (AP) Test for
    Psychology, Statistics, and
    Physics, 218, 225
advance forward incrementation,
    32–33, 34
aesthetic creativity, 35–36
aesthetic engagement, 101, 102
aesthetics, 6, 11, 102, 294
affect, 311
  negative, 194
  positive, 192, 193, 194
affective engagement, 101, 102
affordances, 16, 260
aggression, 96, 189, 297
agreeableness, 95, 96, 107

Allen, Woody, 187
American College Testing
    (ACT), 152
American Idol (show), 259, 301
American Idol Effect (Kaufman,
    Evans, & Baer), 301
American Psychological
    Association, 9, 238
  Coalition for Psychology in
    Schools and Education,
    220–221
Amusement Park Theoretical (APT)
    model of creativity, 48–61
  domains, 57–58
  general thematic areas, 50–56
  initial requirements, 49–50
  microdomains, 58–60
  strange bedfellows, 60–61
androgyny, 236
Angelou, Maya, 17
"Angry Berts," 10
annoyances, 314–316
Anouilh, Jean, 43
anthropology
  biological, 51
  cultural, 51
anxiety
  and creativity, 181, 184, 185,
    188, 317
  social, 54

Made in United States
North Haven, CT
11 September 2022

23995749R00202